From Coal Oil Lights to Satellites

Memoirs of a Haliburton County Redneck

Ray Y.C. Miller

Note for Librarians: a cataloguing record for this book that includes Dewey Decimal
Classification and US Library of Congress numbers is available from the Library and
Archives of Canada. The complete cataloguing record can be obtained from their online
database at:
www.collectionscanada.ca/amicus/index-e.html
ISBN 1-4120-4894-x
Printed in Victoria, BC, Canada

TRAFFORD

Offices in Canada, USA, Ireland, UK and Spain

This book was published *on-demand* in cooperation with Trafford Publishing. On-demand
publishing is a unique process and service of making a book available for retail sale to the
public taking advantage of on-demand manufacturing and Internet marketing. On-demand
publishing includes promotions, retail sales, manufacturing, order fulfilment, accounting and
collecting royalties on behalf of the author.

Book sales for North America and international:
Trafford Publishing, 6E–2333 Government St.,
Victoria, BC V8T 4P4 CANADA
phone 250 383 6864 (toll-free 1 888 232 4444)
fax 250 383 6804; email to orders@trafford.com

Book sales in Europe:
Trafford Publishing (UK) Ltd., Enterprise House, Wistaston Road Business Centre,
Wistaston Road, Crewe, Cheshire CW2 7RP UNITED KINGDOM
phone 01270 251 396 (local rate 0845 230 9601)
facsimile 01270 254 983; orders.uk@trafford.com

Order online at:
www.trafford.com/robots/04-2702 .html

10 9 8 7 6 5 4 3 2 1

From Coal Oil Lights to Satellites

This engrossing book is an autobiography of a man living in a time of unprecedented change. Following thousands of years of slow scientific advancement and comparatively minor inventions, we live in a time when change is evident daily.

Born in the Highlands of Haliburton County, Ontario, Canada, in a house on a dirt road, with no electricity or indoor plumbing, Ray Miller takes the reader through the many phases of his life filled with financial, medical, and emotional challenges.

Read how the rapid pace of modern innovation took him from transportation by horse and buggy to supersonic air travel and from word of mouth to cell phones. Follow his experiences; sometimes moving, often humorous, as relationships and hard work take him through his fascinating life.

Dedication

This book is lovingly dedicated
to my grandchildren,
Kayla, James, Jason, Kevin, Erik, and Sakura
in the fond hope that they may read it
and come to know where their Grandpa is "coming from."

About the cover

Renowned artist David Alexander Risk
has skilfully depicted the house where I was born.
It shows the coal oil lamp that lit our front room
in the early days of my childhood,
and the bright star in the upper corner is a satellite.

Acknowledgements

I must acknowledge the people that have supplied me with information and facts to verify the happenings that I have written from memory.

Jack Brezina – Editing, and guidance.
David Alexander Risk- Front Cover.
David Dollo: Carl Dugan: Carolyn Emmerson::
Michael W. Gilbert: Ruby Gilbert: Mabel Hewitt:
Hazel Johnson: Floyd Miller: Scott Miller:
Yvonne Newell: Bill Prentice: Laurie-Lee Steels:

Special mention to my wife Caryl for proofreading and her loving guidance and understanding.

Introduction

I believe there has been greater technical and environmental change during my lifetime than in any other time in known history.

I will attempt to take you through these changes by relating interesting experiences during my life. You will notice the changes taking place as you read. It will become evident that there is gradually more money, fantastic inventions, and more travel as vehicles and roadways improve.

Every chapter is an event that actually occurred, based entirely on memory, verified by entries in my Father's, Mother's and my own diaries. I have vivid recollection of things as they happened.

About Me

I was born on May 25, 1937 in a house on a dirt (not gravel) road between Minden and Kinmount, Ontario, Canada, to a couple struggling through the Depression, with rumours of another war on the horizon. I was the youngest of four children. Hazel was then 16, Floyd 9, and Mabel 5.

We were not sheltered from the real things in life as children. My parents often said, "If they're old enough to ask the question, they are old enough to know the answer." We were not told that storks delivered babies. We were present when animals produced their young, and often were called upon to assist at a very early age. I helped turn a calf in the birth canal when I was seven, and the procedure was explained as we went. We were not sheltered from the breeding process either.

Slaughter was a way of life. We raised animals so we would have meat.

War was not kept a mystery. Our soldiers went to war, where they would be shot at and could be killed. If I didn't understand what was happening when news came of the war, my parents would take time to explain it. There is no need to lie to children. Lies only have to be explained later, and they cause a child to distrust everyone.

During my pre-school years, we had to make use of all sources of food or income in order to survive. My parents sometimes spoke of a time before my birth when they went to town to do the weekly shopping with ten dozen eggs, which they hoped to trade to the local grocer, and fifty-eight cents. This was all the money they had to their name at that time.

We lived on two hundred acres of which only thirty was workable for agricultural purposes. The remainder was woodland or pasture, and like most of Haliburton County, consisted of a thin layer of sod clinging to rock. Indeed, as I look back now, the land that we cultivated was only a few inches of soil with rocks showing above ground in several places. We would work the fields for crops, and many stones appeared. We would pick those by hand and pile them where the land was not workable. Although the fields are grown up now with trees, these stone piles are still evident.

Everyone in the neighbourhood was the same. No one had much, but friends and neighbours worked together for a united cause. That cause was survival. There was no jealousy or envy. Neighbours admired each other and were happy to help each other get ahead in any way possible.

Times were tough, but thanks to hard work, which the family shared, we never went to bed hungry, and there was always a trace of humour to cheer us through rough times.

Things are better now; people have many more material things. Nevertheless, I sometimes look back and cherish the simpler life of my childhood.

Ray Y.C. Miller, Author.

Index

Index

Our House

The house was on the west side of the road, five miles from Minden toward Kinmount. The Hillier brothers built it sometime before the turn of the century. They also built No. 5 School two miles north from there, and the house that Mrs Fred Barry lives in now.

Grandma Miller's maiden name was Carolyn Schroter. She married Bill Scheffee and moved into the house. Scheffee died of cancer.

In the 1890's she married my Grandfather Ernest Miller who was fresh from Germany at the time. Grandpa left Germany as a stow-away because he didn't believe in what was happening there. His name was Mullar. Grandma gave birth to eight children in that house, (including my father).

Therefore, the house was built well before 1890.

The foundation was built from flat stone gathered from fields on the property, with lime mortar to hold them in place.

The main frame was constructed of large timbers hewn by hand from softwood logs cut from the nearby woods. Men would chip the logs on one side with a broad axe until it was flat, then turn it over, and do the same on the other side. The corner posts and plate beams were hewn on all four sides to make a square timber. Studs for the walls were hewn on two sides. Marks from the broad axe were evident any time the frame was laid bare for renovations or upgrades.

The post and beams were mortised by hand using a mallet and chisel. One timber would have a square hole mortised into it, and the adjoining piece would have a tenon exactly the same size and depth in the proper location to make a smooth fit. The tenon would then be fitted into the mortise and a round hole bored through the whole thing by a hand powered boring machine. A round peg was whittled to fit the hole and driven through. The pin was cut off on both sides. This peg would swell and shrink with humidity changes, so sometimes the whole structure was prone to sway a little in the wind. The house would creak and groan during high winds.

After the main frame was erected, rough sawn boards were nailed to it. The nails were square and made of iron, not like the wire nails that became available later. A board was nailed at

the bottom then one part way up. The studding was nailed wherever the builders thought it necessary. Studding did not stand end to end or maintain any form of constant spacing side to side.

The outside was sided with boards placed horizontally. These shrunk leaving spaces between them. Some knots fell out so this didn't turn much wind or cold. In the photo on the left, you can see how the siding is warped and separating. You can imagine how the wind whistled right through the cracks and into the walls causing ghostly moans.

Paint and varnish was not available locally, and any that could be found was expensive and not of good quality, so the wood was left to age and blacken.

It is believed this photo was taken around 1918, the same year as Mother and Dad were married. Mother and Dad are standing behind, and Grandma Dugan is centre front. Although I am

1

not sure, I believe that the lady on the extreme right is Mother's sister Maggie Wruth. The other lady is unknown to me at this time, but may be Aunt Ida Lindop.

The builders walled the inside with horizontal boards, and covered them with a wallboard made of paper fibre. This wallboard was about an eighth of an inch thick and was corrugated, like shipping boxes are today but thinner. Decorative wallpaper was glued to the wallboard.

Dad and I removed the inner lining in an upstairs bedroom to feed an electric wire through the wall. We found a board that was an inch and a quarter thick by eighteen inches wide. It was virgin pine without a knot in it for sixteen feet. It smelled of turpentine. Imagine how that would burn. This board would cost a pretty penny today, but it was used for sheathing then.

Windows were single pane. Sometimes the putty would fall away allowing the glass to shake and rattle in the wind. I remember storm sashes being fitted sometime during my very young life and the difference that made in the heat of the house was phenomenal.

No insulation was available so the walls were hollow.

Sometime between the 1918 and 1930, Dad covered the house on the outside with rolled roofing, carefully tarring the edges of each strip to make it wind proof. The result was a much warmer house with less drafts. You will also notice that the windows have been painted. The people in this picture are Mother, Hazel, and Floyd.

The hollow walls made every wall a chimney that would create a draft when the air in the cavities became heated. When I was old enough to realize that I was sleeping in a firetrap, I became very nervous about fire.

On February 20, 1984, the house caught fire. It was reduced to ashes in fifteen minutes. Luckily, no one was hurt.

At the time of the fire I was in intensive care in St Joseph's hospital in Peterborough for treatment of chest pains. The nurse came in carrying one of the Minden papers and said, "As you were once a native of Minden I thought I would bring you some local reading."

On the front page was a picture of our house in flames. She didn't know that it was my homestead as the name of the current owner was Butler, not Miller.

That evening, Floyd, Hazel, and Mabel came to visit me. As they were about to leave I said, "Do you guys have something to tell me before you go?"

They said, "No," looking puzzled.

I pulled the paper out from under the covers and put it on my chest.

They said that they were afraid to tell me, as they didn't know if my heart could take the news.

The house as it was when Mother arrived as a bride May 1st 1918

Mother with Dad's drivers Bell and Nell in 1918

2

Grandma Miller's children were all born in the house.
From left to right:
Aunt Mabel married Albert Noess and lived in Vantage Saskatchewan.
Dad married Lillian Dugan and lived in Minden.
Aunt Clara married Arnold McElwain and lived in Gelert and later moved to Lindsay.
Uncle Herb married Leona Sipe and then married Teresa Blair after Aunt Leona died and lived in Haliburton.
Aunt Frances, married Allan Hagen, and then Al Smith after Allan died and lived in Haliburton.
Aunt Violet married Bert Blair and lived in Oshawa.
Aunt Lena married Ross Blair and lived in Oshawa.
Uncle Stewart, married Gertie Blair and lived in Whitby.
Picture taken at a family reunion in Lindsay on July 13th, 1952.

How we Prepared for Winter

In the days of the Depression, during what is often referred to as the 'Dirty Thirties,' there was a yearly ritual that worked and everyone used it.

There were no refrigerators, no freezers, and no 'picking it up at the store' as roads were plugged with snow or axle deep in mud from early November until mid May. Trips to town were often two weeks or more apart and were usually to get the mail.

Receiving mail daily wasn't important. There was no credit, so there were no bills that required immediate attention. The mail usually consisted of 'The Family Herald', the monthly version of 'The Free Press Weekly', 'The Farmer's Advocate', and sometimes a letter from one of Mother's siblings in Lochlin nine miles away, (a twenty-minute drive today) or from Dad's sister in Vantage, Saskatchewan.

Everyone lived on a small farm. Yes, we called the little collection of out buildings, a house, and a couple of hundred or so acres of sod over rock, a farm. Nevertheless, as modest as our farm was, they kept us alive, and thanks to a lot of common sense, we were never hungry. Most of all, we were happy and comparatively more content then we are today.

A wood-fired cook stove in the kitchen, a wood-fired box stove in the front room, heated our house and another box stove in the parlour. Everyone cut wood in his spare time and maintained around 100 face cord in the yard in various stages of drying at all times.

We tried to maintain a herd of eight milk cows. That was about all the farm would support. If we had a good crop of hay and didn't need the money from the sale of calves in the fall we would have room to 'winter over' the seven calves. This would be a bumper year as the following fall, when the cattle came in from pasture, we had seven new calves plus seven yearlings to sell. We might even be able to afford turkey for Christmas that year and I may look forward to an orange in my Christmas stocking.

We needed milk for 'the table' in winter To achieve that we selected one cow the summer before, and much as she roared and leaped on the other cows every three weeks, to tell us she needed courtship, she didn't get it!. Instead she spent the day in the stable so she wouldn't upset the other cows causing them to hold their milk up at milk time.

Having not been bred, this cow, called a 'stripper', would give a little milk twice a day all winter, providing fresh milk for drinking and cream for baking.

This was also good planning, as each cow needs a year off from reproducing every few years to give her organs a rest. The calves remained healthier this way. A strong calf meant everything to us. Many dairy herds are now bred each year for milking purposes only, and the calves are not important.

We had a fertile area for a vegetable garden. It was located near the house to deter predators. The family dog was on guard against them.

By spring, there would be a great pile of manure in front of the cow and horse stable doors. This was spread on the fields to help the crops, but a selected load of fine, fertile stuff was spread thickly on the garden.

After the manure was spread, Dad would 'run the plough through it' even though the soil was likely still very soft from the year before. This was to loosen it more and mix in the manure.

By the twenty fourth of May, when the earth would be nice and warm and the risk of frost was less likely, the whole family would converge on this piece of ground with rakes and hoes in hand to plant our garden. The soil was raked out flat and turnip, tomato, carrots, corn, lettuce, radish, cucumbers, cabbage, lots of cooking onions, green onions, and lots and lots of beans of

4

different varieties were carefully spaced and planted about three widths of the seed deep. Then long rows of corn were planted along the west side by the fence. The rows ran north and south, so the sun coming up in the east would hit each row evenly, shine up the rows, end to end, as it passed to the south, and hit the other side as it set in the west. The garden would supply us with fresh vegetables all summer. The taste of the first new potatoes, corn on the cob, string beans, radish, cucumbers and green onions from the garden is unequalled by store bought produce.

We didn't have running water so watering our crops was strictly up to nature. If we had a spell of very dry weather we would have to carry water from the well, or the spring if the well was dry. The watering was for the tender plants only. Because of the effort involved we didn't over water, just enough to keep them alive until the next rain.

Potatoes were always planted in the field across the road because they took up a lot of space. Besides predators don't bother potatoes. That field was completely covered by Highway 121 when they straightened the curve in the 1970s.

Around September 15, we would dig the potatoes. If we had more than we needed we would let it be known in town, and sell them for seventy-five cents or a dollar per seventy-five pound bag. If we didn't have enough we would go looking to buy. Mother's brother, Will Dugan, at Lochlin, grew potatoes for sale each year. We would make the trip there in our Model A and Dad's trusty trailer bouncing along behind.

We pulled up the unpicked beans, with full dry pods hanging on dry stalks, and spread them on an old canvas on the barn floor.

There was a wonderful tool called a flail. A handle with a short stick fastened to the end of it by some means that would allow it to swing in every direction. By swinging this thing over your head just right, you could hit the floor with the end piece landing flat on the floor. It would flail things with great intensity. If you didn't do this just right you could hit yourself on the back of the head. The little knobs on the back of my head are not all knowledge bumps!

After the beans were flailed sufficiently we would take a hayfork and remove the stalks leaving a heap of beans on the canvas. By lifting the sides of the canvas to the middle, we would have a pile of beans and chaff. This was scooped up with a grain shovel and put through the fanning mill to remove the chaff. The beans were caught in a clean flour bag, and stored in the pantry for use that winter.

Cooking onions were pulled, put into six-quart baskets, and stored in the cellar.

The corncobs that hadn't been used for relish or fresh corn on the cob, were now dry and hard. They were removed from the stalks, taken to the garage, and using our hands, we would wrench the dry kernels off the cobs into bushel baskets. The dry kernels were then poured into flour sacks and stored.

Turnips and carrots were pulled and topped. There was a special bin in the cellar for them.

Tomatoes were canned and stored in jars on shelves in the cellar.

Cucumbers were made into various kinds of pickles, and some corn was made into corn relish.

Each fall we would make a trip to apple country, on the shore of Lake Ontario, for our winter supply of apples.

In the spring, we would purchase two little pigs from neighbours, Fred Barry, George Kellett or Uncle Will Dugan, for anywhere from five to fifteen dollars each.

It was fun to go and select our tiny pigs from a pen. We had to avoid the tusks of the sow as we reached in and caught them, one by one, by a hind leg, slip it head first into a jute bag, and tie it. We had to use a jute bag, as a cotton bag would suffocate the pig on the way home. When placed in the pen, these tiny creatures would disappear into the warmth of a pile of fresh straw in the corner. However, they would always come out when we came around with a pail of warm milk mixed with pig starter, or just plain chop, if starter wasn't available.

Feeding lots of chop would change these adorable playful little fellows to big old pigs by fall. When we were reasonably sure that the weather was cold enough for the meat to keep, we would slaughter them.

Our meat was quartered, and then hung in the drive shed where it would freeze. Burying it in snow wasn't an option as wildlife would surely find it.

Should a freak thaw occur during the winter Dad would watch the meat carefully. If there were danger of it spoiling, he would cut it up and pack it into a salt barrel kept for this purpose. Whatever was left over by the time spring thaws started was also packed in salt. This made the meat a little salty, but no one ever complained.

Beef was a little different. When it was not feasible to slaughter one of our own cattle, we would buy half a cow from a neighbour.

Most springs we would order one hundred day old chicks by mail from Henderson Chick Hatchery in Port Hope. We would receive a reply advising of the shipping date, and they would arrive in Kinmount by train. Hewitt Transport would get a whole truckload, and work late into the night delivering chicks. The chicks had to be delivered that day or they would die. The transport would drop ours off, and Mother would have to pay a dime for cartage from Kinmount.

It was an exciting time when our chicks arrived. These balls of fur with feet and a bill were fun to watch. Mother or Dad would remove any that hadn't survived the trip, and then feed the rest some oatmeal and water. They were kept in the woodshed in the box they came in for a day or two before releasing them into a fenced off area in the henhouse. This protected area assured that the older hens wouldn't tramp on them.

We could order all hens, all roosters or half-and-half. Most people ordered half-and-half so the roosters could be killed in the fall for meat along with some hens too old to lay eggs anymore. The carcasses were hung by the feet in the drive shed.

A successful partridge and deer hunt would add variety to our winter meat.

In the fall, Dad would order flour, salt, sugar, and sometimes a keg of molasses, from the local merchants. It would arrive weeks later in Kinmount by train. The order would be brought home, and put in a special pantry upstairs, that had been made as mouse proof as possible. If signs of mice appeared during the winter, bags being chewed, or the appearance of droppings, the point of entry was found, and covered with the lid from a tin can.

This is a sample order.

.

    1 cwt Keystone Flour
    1 cwt Keystone Pastry Flour
    1 cwt xxxx Special Flour
    10 cwt xxxx General Purpose Flour
    50 lbs Table Salt
    50 lbs. Brown Sugar
    50 lbs Keg Black Molasses
    1 cwt Bran

This would insure a healthy menu for the winter, but much care had to prevail. These larders of food had to be checked almost every day. If food was destroyed or spoiled, it meant 'doing without' until a replacement was available. It never happened to us, as Mother and Dad were very particular.

It was very comforting to see all this food. It meant that we would survive nicely until spring without the aid of outsiders.

Dad's tobacco was sold in sealed tins to keep it moist. A package of 'tailor made' cigarettes received from anyone at Christmas, (or a couple of cigars), brought a big smile, and the aroma of cigar smoke would fill the house later on Christmas day. If his tobacco ran low, any one of us would happily walk the five miles to Minden, through deep snow, to get a new supply. Without it, he quickly became hard to please. He never hit any of us in his entire life, but life was much nicer if he had smokes!

My parents were good providers. We were never hungry, but they also believed strongly in the adage "Waste not, want not." If I was caught throwing away a partly eaten apple, I would be told, "You may chase crows for less than that before you die."

During the war, many things were rationed in order to feed the troops overseas. We received ration coupons for things like sugar, tea, and salt. We were issued ration coupons that could be used during a set period of time. Dad could use six months of coupons to order winter supplies. Special licenses were available, but hard to obtain. Beekeepers, for example, could order extra sugar when it was available.

Controlling Predators

Our attitude toward wild animals would totally enrage the animal rights activist of to-day. If wild animals were coddled, as they are now, our livelihood would have been in grave jeopardy.

We did not abuse wildlife. We would follow any injured beast for miles and days to finish it off, so it would not suffer. Kills had to be clean and complete. That is why every male in every family learned at an early age how to safely and accurately handle a gun.

My dad's 44-40 was always hanging above the kitchen door along with a 22, and a 25-calibre rifle, with at least one box of shells for each, on a shelf inside the back door.

When we worked in the fields, there was usually a gun nearby, loaded with shells.

It is my opinion, and the opinion of many older people, that the gun laws today are idiotic. Individuals with criminal intent will always find a way to acquire weapons, and when they do, they are sure they will be the only one at the crime site with firearms. The victim is unarmed. Their gun is under lock and key, and the ammunition in another room locked up.

Those living in the country, where wild animals are now abundant, are helpless if a child or cherished pet is attacked. A person has to find two keys before he can defend his possessions, one to unlock the gun and another to unlock the ammunition. By this time, it would be far too late.

All species on earth must live together. Predators kill to survive. So did we It is as simple as that.

This was our attitude toward wild animals and why.

Bears

Every bear that was ever seen anywhere, at anytime, was shot, without exception. Bears kill and eat people, pets, and cattle. There were upwards of fifty head of cattle in woodland pastures in the five miles between our place and Minden any given summer. Every beast we had was an important part of our food supply, so the family felt the loss of a cow for months.

When cows would give birth in the pasture, bears would smell the birth and help themselves to the tender tasty helpless calf while the cow could only watch and bawl.

Children, women, and dogs often searched for cattle in the woods, to bring them home in the evening. They were at high risk of getting between a sow bear and her little ones. Anyone or anything that wanders into that locality is dead.

There was a choice: between the safety of our food supply and family, or the bear; the bear always lost.

Wolves

Wolves kill sheep, cattle, pets, deer, and people.

They are merciless killers of deer in winter. When a crust forms on the snow, they are in their glory. They can run easily on the crust while the deer's tiny hoofs pierce through to the ground. With the deer's legs sticking through the crust it is helpless. When I come on to the site of one of these kills, I want to kill every wolf I see.

Anyone forced to stand helplessly by and watch through a window as a pack of wolves tore a dog apart on the veranda, as my parents did, would shoot them too.

A pack of howling wolves once followed me in the dark of night. It certainly confirmed my attitude about wolves, as I think it would anyone.

Weasels Kill every weasel you see. Weasels kill chickens. They creep into a hen house at night through the tiniest crack, and kill the entire flock by biting their throats, and drinking the blood. They will also kill your cat the same way.

7

When we depended on our flock for eggs and winter meat, the loss of even one chicken was serious stuff.

Think about it. The weasel eats, or you do. Kill the weasel.

Skunks

This is getting repetitive.

Kill every skunk you see.

They spray your dog and make its life unbearable; they also make a horrible mess of a vegetable garden.

Raccoons

Now here is a real pest on the farm. Kill every one you see.

Coons destroy everything in their path. They make an absolute mess of a garden, rendering it useless in one night. Just when we thought our corn was ready to eat, they move in and have a corn party all their own. Our corn patch would be useless after one attack.

They tore grain sacks apart, and destroyed the contents.

They got into sheds and attics creating havoc.

They annoyed our dog keeping the whole family awake at night.

Although they are very cute, it is us or them. The raccoon has to go.

Groundhogs

These are dangerous on a farm. They dig holes all through the fields. The farmer can be seriously injured when a wheel hits one of these. Horses break legs when they step into a groundhog hole. A horse with a broken leg is useless.

Horses were the only way to work the fields and the main source of transportation. A team of horses was a necessity. The loss of a horse was second only to the death of a member of the family. That was why the penalty for stealing a horse was very severe just before my time.

Kill every groundhog you see. I spent many leisure hours as a lad strolling through our fields with the 22 under my arm hunting groundhogs.

Hawks

Seeing a chicken hawk circle high in the sky above our barnyard would bring the rifle off the wall every time. Hawks will pick out a hen, then, swoop from high in the air, pounce on her with powerful claws, and carry her away screeching. We lost a chicken; and the rest of the flock would not lay eggs for several days after witnessing a hawk attack.

Moose

Moose were part of our food supply. Therefore, even though having a moose in our pasture was food, it was also a pest in a different way. If our pastureland was barely providing enough to grass to feed our herd, the addition of a moose often stretched it to the limit.

A moose never jumps over anything; it just goes through it, including our fences. To find our fence destroyed by a moose and our cattle out on the road was frustrating. Luckily, when this would take place it usually meant that the animal was moving to another area, and would not be back.

Moose were tolerated, but only until we could do something about it. Because of this, very few moose were near farms.

We did not believe in killing anything just for the fun of it, and those who did were considered idiots. We killed for food, and to keep our families safe.

Many animals were a source of food. Their existence was a vital part of our survival, so killing unnecessarily would be foolish.

Learning How

Working on the Kinmount Road in 1933   **Road Camps near our place. 1930s**

We were proud people a lifetime ago. We learned how to do things properly, so we could look back at the end of each day and be proud of our accomplishment. There is no sense in achieving a lot in a day if it has to be redone tomorrow.

Work was physical. Hay was forked by hand, and ditches were dug with pick and shovel. Major excavations, like basements, were dug with horse and scraper, and earth was moved in wheelbarrows. Holes in rocks were drilled by hand. A person slept well after a ten or fourteen hour day doing these things.

Because work was hard, we learned how to achieve the best result with the least effort. This is something that is not taught in schools. Experienced workers and your own experience right on the job teach it. I had three superiors, Dad, Floyd, and Doward, and because they each had different ways of achieving their goals, I was able to sort out what I thought was the best from each and come up with one of my own.

The two things that bother me the most about workers of today, are sloppy workmanship, and poor planning.

Not long ago, I gave a delivery driver a hard time when he drove his truck into my driveway with a load of building products. The material had to come off the back of the truck, and that was pointing toward the road. He also had the additional length of the truck to carry it. The smart thing would have been to back in. Then the load simply comes straight off the truck to the pile.

I am not alone in my feelings. Last summer we hired Paul Brohm to install some drywall and insulation in the storage area above our garage. When the truck arrived with the material, the driver drove in. I overheard the following conversation.

Getting out of the truck, the driver chirped, "Good morning, how are you this morning."

Paul said, "I'm fine thank you, but what in hell is the matter with you?"

Looking puzzled, the driver questioned "Why?"

"What the ____ are you doing in here head first. Now you have to back out and turn around!"

"But I didn't want to hold traffic up while I backed in off the road" the driver explained.

"Good thinking fellow, now you have to hold it up twice, while you both back out AND back in. Turn the damned thing around then call me. I have work to do" Paul said as he disappeared back up the stairs to work while he waited.

This is a good example of not practising good work procedures. The driver had been here before, and knew there wasn't room for him to turn in our driveway. He should have known to back in!

Many times, I see workers do idiotic things. Like piling lumber off a truck right where they are going to build the building. Then it has to be moved before the building can be erected. Pile it close but to the side, out of the way.

I watched workers shingle a roof across the street from where I lived in Peterborough.

It appeared that the youngest worker had been elected to carry the shingles up onto the roof. He did this well, except he placed every bundle right where the workmen would be laying shingles. As a result, they had to move them twice to get the job done. The proper procedure would have been to place the shingles on the roof near where the bundle would be exhausted just as the layer reached that area. Then a full, opened bundle should have been within reach. If the carrier had known how to work, the whole crew would have achieved much more that day, with much less effort.

I watched a pool installer dig a shallow trench in our back yard last summer. He spread each shovel full of dirt across the grass as if he was broadcasting fertilizer or spreading sand on ice. Then, when he was ready to fill the trench, he had no soil to fill it with. He had to bring some in a wheelbarrow from fifteen feet away to fill the trench. He knew he had to refill the trench, so why not pile his soil right next to the trench in a little row. Then, all he would have to do was slide it back in to the ditch. Same work accomplished with half the time and a quarter the effort.

Many years ago, when I was eight or ten, Floyd and I were hauling wood out of the woods with the team and wagon. When the wagon was full, Floyd said, "I think that is about enough." I had a block of wood in my hands, and when he said that, I dropped it back onto the woodpile.

Without saying a word, he walked all the way around the wagon to where I was standing, and while planting the hardest kick on my ass I have ever experienced he said "Don't ever let me catch you doing that again."

I said "What?" rubbing my ass.

"Throw anything that you have in your hands back on the pile like that. Throw it on the wagon and be done with it. Now pick it up and put it on the wagon and we'll go." Sometimes one end has to hurt a little to make the other end pay attention. Point taken and lesson learned.

Once when I was driving for Hewitt Transport, I was sent to a private dwelling in Toronto to pick up a used refrigerator that I was to bring to a cottage in Haliburton. It was buried in the garage. When the shipper heard that I would be there in a few minutes, he said that he would have it dug out to speed things up.

He did, but he piled a table saw, a lawn mower, a couple of garbage cans, some rakes and everything that was in front of the refrigerator, all over the driveway.

This prevented me from backing up his driveway to the garage where the refrigerator could have been loaded directly onto the truck. Instead, he and a neighbour carried it through the assortment of obstructions to the street, and then loaded it there.

It would have been much less work and so much faster if he had simply piled those items at the side of the driveway. Same work accomplished with much less effort. The first implement on any job should be your brain.

Map of area prior to Muskoka Cut off.

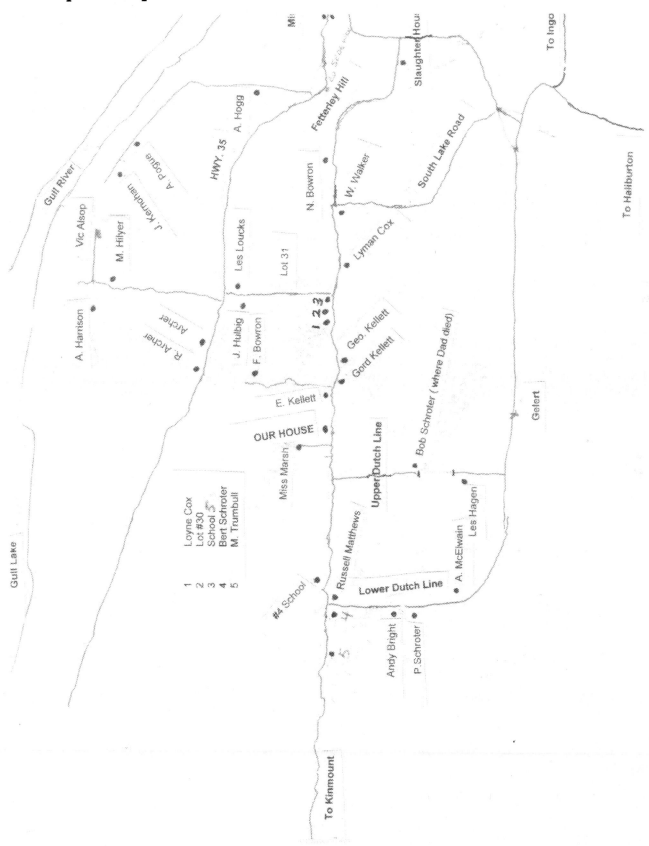

Dad's Wood Machine

In the early 1900s, all homes in this area were heated with wood. Men would go to the bush with crosscut saws, select cull trees to cut into wood logs, and drag them to the house with horses. They would also cut the limbs from the tops, load them onto sleighs, and haul them in for wood. They lifted these onto sawhorses and cut them into firewood stove lengths with a bucksaw. This was long hard work but it was the only method available at the time.

Sometime in the early part of 1920s, Dad got the idea that he could come up with a better way. He knew there were Gilson gasoline engines available, so he started looking for a dealer. Where he found one, I don't know, but he acquired a one cylinder eight horsepower model, and began to create a plan around it. His plan was to invent a machine that he could haul around with horses and use to cut the piles of limbs and logs in people's yards into firewood. The machine he designed did the job easier, faster. It was nothing short of genius for the day.

In his book 'Whispering Pines' John Hulbig called it a 'hit and miss' engine and that wasn't a bad description at all. It only fired its one cylinder when it was needed to keep it going. This made a very unstable sound when it was idling. The motor sounded like 'BANG, flop, flop, flop, flop, flop, BANG, flop, flop, flop, giving the impression that it was about to stop before it fired again. Each time the two large flywheels would slow to a certain speed, the governors would close the valves and switch the ignition on, and it would fire. When a load would come on it, the governors would close until the load was satisfied and it would return to its odd rhythm. A load would cause it to fire constantly and it would sound BANG, bang, bang, bang, bang, BANG, flop, flop, flop, BANG.

He searched and found a circular saw, about three feet across, a mandrel shaft for it to spin on, a couple of pulleys, some large springs, some chain, a whole bunch of scrap metal, some bolts, a wide flat belt and some hardwood timbers.

He put on his felt hat, sat on the pile of timbers, lit his pipe, took his axe across his knee, he was READY.

He set to work with his tools, his blacksmith forge, some chisels, an axe, a bright idea, and a hell of a lot of determination. He measured, cut, sawed, fitted, aligned, swore, pried, heated, bent, lifted, chopped, swore some more, cut the belt to length and laced it, invented a way to tighten it, built a tool box, found a place to mount the gas tank, and built a wood machine. He painted the whole thing dark green and then stepped back to admire his invention.

This is what many people referred to as Milt's buzz saw machine. This picture was taken just after he had tried it out on a pile of wood in our yard and before he headed out on his first paying job.

This is Mother filling engine's cooling tank with water.

Dad and his machine became very popular. He travelled in circuits up and down roads, that took him to Lochlin, Ingoldsby, south of Kinmount, Norland, and north of Minden. When he was too far from home to return for the night, he would stay and they would board him, and feed and stable his horses for an adjustment in the cutting charge.

It took at least two men to bring logs to the machine, one to keep the saw fed, Dad on the saw, and one to throw blocks after it had been cut. Neighbours would follow along the same as they would for threshing, and share the work with each other.

Our family held this machine in high regard. It took us right through the Depression with the last entry in his journal being a job for Morgan Trumbull in September of 1943.

The machine was retired then, as far as doing work for hire, but it still cut many piles of wood for ourselves and remained in our family until it was sold at auction, after he died in 1989. I don't know who bought it at the sale but I do hope it has been maintained and not destroyed. I would like to know where it is now.

Entries in Our Diaries
From February 18th 1936 to May 15th 1942

There are a number of chapters in this book entitled 'Entries in our Diaries'. These are direct quotes taken from the diaries of Dad, Mother and my own. I have added my comments which appear in italics after each entry.

Dad kept records, journals, and diaries from the time he purchased the house from his mother in 1914 until he died in 1959. Mother kept diaries off an on, and continued for a few years after Dad died. I kept a diary sporadically until early sixties.

I have written in a short explanation in italics for some that do not quite warrant a chapter in order to take you through the phases of my life as I journey From Coal Oil Lights to Satellites.

1936, February 18: Train Snowbound at Gelert. *An example how deep the snow often was in those days.*

1937, May 25: Baby Boy born Ray. *Here I was, brand new, still had the stickers and tags attached. It was nine-o-clock in the morning. They sent Floyd outside to sit on the woodpile. Hazel milked three cows because Mother was busy. I have no idea where Mabel was but you can bet she was up to no good somewhere!*

November 17: Hydro Surveyors Surveyed Line past Home. *Not even hydro lines on that road yet.*

November 23: Worked Six Hours for HEPC with the team for $5.40 $13.00 for two poles in field. *Dad skidded some hydro poles, and pulled wire with the horses. This was big money in 1937.*

December 31: Started Wiring House. *Dad strung wire through house, and Lawrence Pritchard made the critical connections. There were two circuits in the whole house. Seven drop cord lights, (a bulb on the end of a cord from the ceiling with a pull chain to turn it on and off), and three base plugs, one in the kitchen, one in the front room, and one in an upstairs bedroom. All were two prongs, with no ground.*

1938, March 26: Electric Radio at Railway Station in Kinmount. *Dad ordered a radio from a catalogue. It arrived in Kinmount by train, but he did not have enough money to pay the freight. He picked it up a few days later.*

1939, January 1: Roads Blocked. *This meant that not even a horse could travel until horses could break a road with men shovelling them out when they were stuck*

January 26: Hewitt's Plowed Road. *Hewitt Transport had the contract to meet the train each day in Kinmount and transport any freight to stores in Minden as well as mail to Minden Post Office. At this time, they were trying to do it all year by truck so a snowplough was rigged on the front of the truck and with many men shovelling each time it was stuck, they plowed the road.*

February 6: Hewitt's Plowed Road Again. *Simply more snow.*

February 11: Walked to Minden Snow Deep Very Hard Walking. *I assume that Hewitt's had given up on trucks for the year and changed to horse drawn sleighs. This was referred to as 'the stage'. a left over name from the stagecoach of the Wild West I suppose.*

February 13: Ray Pritchard and Jim Trumbull Shovelling Roads. *They would be shovelling the deep drifts so the stage could get through.*

February 25: Floyd Walked To Minden for Mail. *This was a common mode of travel in winter.*

1940, January 28:   Cars Still Running but Roads are Tough Going. *The cars are doing well* this winter.

   September 25:   Got ready for wedding & dance Hazel & Doward J. *My sister Hazel married Doward Johnson. This is all that Dad recorded for this date. The dance was held upstairs in the old Minden town hall, which stood where the county buildings stand now. There was a long set of steps to this pavilion, with a landing half way up. The building was tall and draughty, with an iron fire escape leading down from a window.*

   October 16:   Jim Dugan Sr Died. *He was my Mother's father. I was three and a half years old. I vaguely remember him holding my hand, as he and I, and my cousin Yvonne walked in the orchard at his place in Lochlin.*

   December 6:   Took Team to Kinmount to Get Flour. *There was already too much snow for cars. Annual flour order was late.*

1941, February 24:   Snow Plowed Road from Lower Line to Minden. *There was a community horse drawn snowplough. Who ever had some spare time would hook on, plough to wherever another neighbour would come out and take over. This time he took it from Bert Schroter's house at the lower Dutch Line, all the way to Minden.*

   April 7:   Hazel Moved to Garage Lot 30. *Dad had purchased Lot 30 and 31, which was two miles from our place. He built a garage on it about 12 by 20 feet, Hazel and Doward moved into it. We always referred to as 'the other place' from then on. Garage pictured right.*

   May 3:   Started to Build House on Lot 30. *As soon as the garage was finished, he and Doward began to build a house. I recall seeing them on the roof of this building. I was four years old. The house still stands just south of John Hulbig's place.*

   Spring: Russell Brohm Bought 5 Yearlings for $150.00. *Russell Brohm was a cattle buyer from Norland. These yearlings were full grown and sold for $30.00 each.*

   September 2:   Floyd Bought Colts from Faulkner Dan and Dot. *Faulkners were horse breeders and dealers south of Kinmount. Dan was breachy (liked to jump fences) at first. Nevertheless, a few tumbles from carrying a Polk soon changed that and he became a good horse. Dot couldn't be broke to harness. She would kick when anyone tried to hitch her to anything and just missed Floyd's head once, knocking his hat flying. He sold her to the Kents who were famous for breaking horses to pull. She became a good horse but sadly, she died as the result of a mishap in the woods.*

   December 23:   Sold Two Hind Quarters of Beef 266 lbs at .15 cents $39.90. *This was a lot of money at that time. This was likely to Harry Easton of Easton's Meat Market, Cub Coneybeare's Grandfather.*

1942, January 22:   John H. Hulbig died. *John was a trusted man and friend of the family for years.*

   February 6:   Floyd Cut Foot 10:A.M. *He was working across the road. The cut was on top of his foot and severed an artery. Blood gushed with every beat of his heart. Mother bandaged it tight. He nearly bled out before they got him to Doctor Jamieson in Minden.*

   April 14:   Went To Lot 30 with Cutter. *Horse and cutter was the main mode of transportation when snow blocked the roads for automobiles. Horse and cutter pictured on the right.*

   April 17:   Moved Cook Stove Back into Summer Kitchen for Last Time. *Up until then, we always moved the cook stove into the front room and closed the kitchen up for winter. Dad had installed rolled roofing on the outside of the kitchen to stop drafts. From this day on the stove was not moved, and the kitchen was used all year.*

   April 20:   Wired Garage for Hydro. *This was a big move. It meant we could use power tools in the garage, and Dad could work late in the evening on long winter nights.*

   April 28:   Kinmount Burnt Down. *See chapter 'Minden and Kinmount Fires'.*

   April 30:   Lilly Collected $36.00 for Kinmount Fire.

May 15:   <u>East Side of Minden Burnt</u>. See chapter 'Minden and Kinmount Fires'

Minden and Kinmount Fires

The war was really heating up. News on the radio reported heavy allied casualties daily. On May 24 1941, the mighty German ship, The Bismarck, destroyed the British battleship The Hood. On December 11, 1941, Japan bombed Pearl Harbour, The same day Hitler lifted the ban on U-boats in US territorial waters and declared war on the USA. In January 1942, German U-Boats sank the 9000-ton British steamer, Cyclops, 300 miles east of Cape Cod. Supply convoys were encountering U-Boats in the West Atlantic. Allied warships had given chase to German submarines in Halifax Harbour. Dad heard on the news that blackouts were in effect nightly along the eastern seaboard of the United States in response to recent U-Boat activity along the coast.

Here at home it seemed the war was getting closer each day. Some unfriendly foreign people appeared in town. They spoke to no one, they picked up their groceries and left. They did not even get mail to anyone's knowledge.

A large white 'X' mysteriously appeared on a rock near the Orillia Water Light and Power dam north of Minden. Local people believed the dam had been marked for destruction. An explosion there would wipe Minden off the map, cause all the downstream control dams to overflow or be wiped out, and plunge Minden and nearby Orillia into darkness. People were worried that there were plans for 'softening up' tactics by the enemy. Dad worried.

It was Tuesday, April 28th 1942. Floyd spread five loads of manure on the fields. Dad, Mother, and I had been at Uncle Will Dugan's and picked up part of our order of fertilizer for the spring seeding. Mother, Mabel, and Floyd were cleaning sucker fish in the yard. Dad was in the shop working on something, I was being a five-year-old pain in the ass to everybody!

Faintly at first, we could hear the constant sound of a vehicle horn. It was coming from the north and progressively getting louder. It seemed to stop at Elmer's gate. We heard voices yelling.

Mother said, "What is going on?"

The sound of the horn started up again. We soon saw one of Hewitt Transport's trucks at the top of the hill. It was changing gears as it chugged through axle deep mud. There was no tarp on it and men's heads were visible above the open racks. The horn stopped for a minute as Dad came out of the shop. Lawrence Pritchard was standing on the running board yelling, "Kinmount is on fire." then seeing Dad he continued, "come on Milt, Kinmount is burning."

The truck stopped at our gate and I could see most of the men from our neighbourhood were already onboard. Dad and Floyd ran down the hill and hands reached down to help them up. The truck ground on over the hill to the south. Mother worried.

The truck let Floyd and Dad out at the road as we were getting out of bed the next morning. They were both dirty and very tired. Dad came into the kitchen, turned laughing and said, "Look Lil I lost the ass out of my pants." Sure enough the whole seat of his overalls was gone, as well as his underwear.

Mother said, "Good God Milt, you're burned too."

"You don't have to tell me that," he laughed. "I can feel that, but not bad though."

"Well come and get washed up and we'll see what I can do to help."

Mabel and I were anxious to know about the fire so we attacked Floyd about that.

He told us that the whole town had burned. It seemed to start at the water tower at the station, apparently from a spark from the train. The wind carried sparks right across town. Many roofs were made of cedar shingles and ignited easily. A fire truck also burned. Dad had been carrying a piece of furniture down a stairway when a crack opened in the wall and flames shot out burning him. Floyd said that the men on the truck teased him all the way home about it.

18

After the men had a rest, we all travelled to Kinmount to see the ruins with Dad sitting a little crooked in the seat. Then we went to Uncle Will's for the rest of the fertilizer.

Mother went from door to door, up and down our road the day after the fire and collected $36.00 for the victims.

In the early morning hours of Friday, May 15th 1942, fire started at the back of Percy Brintnell's Bakeshop. It burned every building on the east side of Minden's main street to the ground.

Arson was highly suspected in the Minden fire and many thought the Kinmount fire was also suspect.

The foreigners disappeared.

Entries in our Diaries
From June 19th 1942 to March 20th 1943

1942, June 19: School Gathering at Stouffer's. *There was an annual singing festival held at School Inspector Archie Stouffer's home on the north side of the river in Minden where Wild Swan Bed and Breakfast is now located. Singing groups from all the schools inspected by Mr. Stouffer would come and compete. There would be a May pole and sing-alongs and a great afternoon. I was in the singing group from SS # 5 after 1944 and Dad was there as the trustee representing that section.*

July 4: Hazel sick. Son. *Dad had a strange way of recording things sometimes. This baby was Morley.*

July 21: Horses Ran Away. *This was a rare occurrence with well-trained horses, but it did happen whenever something would spook the team. Whatever they were hitched to when they began to run, would start making an unusual noise as they ran uncontrollably around the yard. I remember, we were leaving the barn to gather hay when a hen flew out from under a patch of rhubarb. This spooked the horses and they ran back through the fields and over stone piles. They ran all through the fields ending up back at the barn with only the front axle of the wagon left. The damage was a major setback in the haying operation but no one was hurt badly, not even the horses. Luckily, Dad and Floyd were thrown from the wagon right at the start.*

August 7: Bought 1929 Ford from Russell Kellett for Parts. *Dad did a lot of mechanical work for others. He purchased this car and completely gutted it. There was nothing left but the body.*

August 10: Tore Down 1929 Ford for Parts. *Three days later, he stripped it and pulled the stripped body down by the woods below the barn with the horses. I used to stand where the steering wheel would be and pretend I was driving. The body may still be where he left it.*

August 25: Tore Down Veranda and Started to Build *Washroom. *I remember this quite vividly. He tore the veranda from the end of the kitchen and excavated it for a cistern with a horse and a man held scraper.*

August 29: Bought Washer $25.00. *My parents purchased this washer from Lawrence Pritchard in a showroom beside the Pritchard House. The building still stands and is a famous heritage house in Minden. The washing machine was the first white one Mother owned and was a wonderful appliance. It even had a wringer.*

October 30: Norman Bowron Died. *This was during the war. His son Ken was overseas at the time. One of the worst things about mail call when kin were in the army must have been to receive this kind of news.*

November 14: Made Hand Sleigh for Wood. *This old sleigh was a big part of my childhood. Dad made it to pull wood from the various piles in the yard right into the house, where it we transferred it into a wood box beside each stove. However, I took it over almost immediately as my bulldozer. It had two upright sticks at the rear to hold the wood from falling off, .but to me though they were steering clutch levers of my bulldozer. When Dad saw how engrossed I was with it, he made a plough for the front and I pushed it many a mile, ploughing paths around the yard and to the barn. I did not give this up until I was well in my teens.*

December 2: Snowed Twenty-Seven Inches with high winds. Roads Blocked for Cars. *Roads were blocked for cars early that year. Horses and walking would be the only mode of transportation until the roads dried up in the spring.*

December 22:   Robert Archer Died. *Robert lived on Highway 35 on what we still referred to as Archer's Flats. He was Nelson Archer's father.*

December 31:   Plowed, Road to Wallace Walker's with team. *There was still so much snow that vehicles could not use the road. This just made the sleighing easier for horses and the walking a whole lot better.*

1943, February 17:   William Cox Died. *He succumbed following a very unfortunate accident in the woods. He had a large family.*

March 20:   Clifford Schroter Here from War. *See chapter 'On Leave from the War'.*

*Washroom, The washroom was the building that Dad built when he tore the veranda off the house. He installed a cistern, with a room over it where Mother would wash laundry. There was a cistern pump at a sink that we used to washed our hands and face. Therefore, we always referred to this part of the house as "the washroom."

On Leave from the War

Nipper and I in Fall 1942

It was March 20th 1943. War was raging in Europe. Dad listened to every newscast he possibly could, hearing reports of troop movements 'over there'. Our allies had made some progress but the advance was slow and at the cost of many lives. Thousands of Canadians had already died in the pursuit of freedom. News filtered slowly to the home front then, and wives and mothers worried endlessly.

Floyd had been to Minden that day and heard that Andy Stevens had cut his foot badly working in the woods. Andy was a good neighbour and we had been troubled about the accident, but what was to happen next would cause us to forget this for a few hours anyway.

It was about 7:30 P.M. The weather had been colder than normal, with windy blustery days. There was a lot of snow left for this late date. We had gathered icicles from the eaves earlier to
make ice cream and saved them outside the door in a pail. Mother and Mabel were mixing the ingredients and Dad was putting the ice cream machine together on the table, when Nipper started to bark fiercely.

"Nipper hears something he doesn't like," Mother said as she went to look out of the North kitchen window. There was still an eerie glow, as darkness took charge of the late winter evening. She peered through the window then said, "It's a soldier Milt; I can see the shape of his hat." Nipper's bark turned friendly as he rushed down the driveway.

Mother went into the front room and watched as the figure turned up our driveway. "Oh good he is coming in here. It is so good to see them safe, at least for a little while."

She went to the back door with the rest of us trailing behind her as he arrived around the corner of the washroom*. She opened the door and grabbed someone in a long emotional embrace. She stepped back and there stood Clifford Schroter with a large smile on his face. He was in full uniform right from his regimental cap to his puttees and boots. Nipper was running around his heels, as happy as he could ever be.

He stepped inside, took off his knapsack and put it on the floor, removed his hat and slipped it under the epaulet on his shoulder. Then removed his gloves and put them on his other shoulder. With a loud, deep, "Ha," that belonged to Clifford alone he took Dad by the hand, pulled him toward him and his deep voice bellowed, "God Milt it is so good to see you."

He put his arm around Floyd's shoulders and said, "You're taking good care of them I see." Then he gave Mabel a hug I am sure she can feel yet.

He walked over to me. I looked up that six-foot soldier, and you will not believe the pride I had for him right then. He knelt down and I looked into those deep kind eyes. It was hard for me, a five-year-old boy, to understand why anyone would want to do him harm. Because my parents had told me about war, I knew that just days before the enemy had been shooting at him, and that he would return to the battlefield as soon as his furlough was over and he may never return.

He reached into his pack and as he handed me a chocolate bar he said, "This is just for you."

"Come on in for goodness sake and sit down. How long do you have? You'll have some ice cream with us won't you?" Mother babbled.

"You want to believe I am going to have some ice cream. Here let me help", he answered as he strolled in and sat at the kitchen table. We all just stood around looking at him until Dad broke the spell with, "You haven't been home yet have you Cliff."

"No I'm just on my way."

"How long do you have?"

"Seventy-two hours," he said as he pulled the ice cream machine closer. He turned to Mother, "Where's the stuff you to put into this?"

"Its right here," she answered, as she filled the inside container and brought it to him.

He put the container inside the bucket, installed the crank and giving it a whirl he said "Where's the ice Milt?"

"Oh God Cliff, I'm so stunned to see you I am not thinking."

Floyd went to the door and got the ice. I can still see Cliff sitting there cranking the little handle.

He asked how things were on the home front and talked about the fires in Minden and Kinmount, while we enjoyed the ice cream and some of Mother's cookies.

Then he went to his knapsack, retrieved a balaclava from it and put it over his head. He took his wedge cap from his shoulder and pulled it down snugly. He shook Dad's hand, then put on his gloves and patted me on the head.

"You'll walk around the road tonight in the dark won't you Clifford?" Mother asked as he reached for the door.

"No! It's shorter through the meadows."

"But its pretty dark out, and there's three feet of snow yet in the woods", Floyd said.

"It's not so dark once you get away from the lights, and your eyes get used to the dark, and there is a good crust on the snow now," he said.

"Watch for the beaver meadow creek," Mabel said. "It might not be frozen now."

"Some people have heard wolves over there in Snowdon," Dad said.

"As long as they don't have fixed bayonets I'll be fine" he joked.

We all went outside and watched as he climbed over the two fences across the road and disappeared over the hill toward the beaver meadow in the moonlight.

"Bob and Levigna will be so glad to see him," Mother said as she turned to go into the house.

The next day we had another surprise. John Hulbig and Ken Bowron arrived. Ken was also home on leave, and had come to get the motorcycle he had left in our implement shed when he went to war the year before. Ken was one of Floyd's best friends (and still is to this day). He spent a lot of time around our place as he grew up so he was like family. It was so good to see him so tall and slender in his uniform. He came into the house and it was like old times.

When he was ready to go he got his motorcycle from the shed. After a bit of trouble, he got it going and headed out the driveway. When he reached the top of the hill, he hit the brakes. The rear tire was on a bit of ice and it went sideways throwing him off. The motorcycle continued all the way to the bottom of the hill with Kenny running after it. Mabel stood there at the top, laughing at him. He recovered the bike, and after having a good laugh himself, he started it again and drove up the muddy road with mud flying.

It was brief but it was wonderful to have these guys around again.

On June 6th 1944, England invaded France, in an attempt to liberate the country from German occupation. Our thoughts were with the brave young men that carried out that mission.

On May 8th 1945, the war ended. Hitler had been defeated thanks to the bravery of these and thousands of others.

They did not have guided missiles, or fight from armoured vehicles, as we have today. It must be hell to have the enemy shot at them from every direction with only a helmet for protection.

There are only a few of those brave soldiers left now as age has succeeded where the enemy failed.

There were nearly 40,000 Canadians killed in World War Two and 55,000 wounded. Canada was a major source of supplies to the allied forces. Our automobile factories built jeeps and other wartime vehicles and the arsenal in Lindsay supplied ammunition. Clothing factories made uniforms and parachutes, while the Prairie Provinces shipped grain and agricultural products.

With all the capable young men overseas the elderly went to work in ammunition factories. In addition to helping the war effort, these older ammunitions worker inadvertently helped in the discovery of a treatment for those with heart conditions. It was noticed that chest pain was often more evident to those suffering from angina on weekends than during the week. Those people working with gunpowder and explosives seemed to enjoy relief from the condition while at work. They found that nitro glycerine was being absorbed through the skin and this chemical was widening the passage through partially blocked arteries giving blessed relief. The little white pill, nitro patch and spray was accidentally invented. It is used throughout the world to this day.

Clifford Schroter returned safely when the war was over. He was later killed while releasing the binding chains from a load of logs. The load tumbled from the truck crushing him. He left a wife Mary and a daughter Candy.

Ken Bowron also returned. He has spent his life in Minden working at Bagshaw Lumber, and later as a building inspector, and builder. He and his wife Jean live in the house where he was born, at the end of what is now known as Rice Road. They have two children, Heather and Kevin.

<u>Hay Devil</u>

They are often referred to as a "dust devil" or a tiny whirlwind but we called them "hay devils".* Whatever they are called, they can sometimes be quite entertaining and often annoying.

I am referring to those little tornadoes that form up on a hot still day in the summer. They usually last about five minutes and can get to be fairly large before they blow themselves out.

When I was about five or six years old I liked to play or just sit on the big rock beside the horse stable in the barnyard, and watch the hens or my Dad working. I was not strong enough yet to be of much use to anybody and I was too young to go to school, so I spent quite a lot of time there.

On this day, my Dad had cut hay in the centre field in the morning and raked the field behind the barn. He had removed the harness from the horses, Queen and Stella, and turned them out into the barnyard to rest. He then went into the field behind the barn to coil* the hay he had raked so it would sweat* for a time before he brought it into the barn.

I was watching a hen dust herself* under a rhubarb patch near the rail fence. The horses were standing side by side near the fence with their heads toward the barn. It was shady there.

I saw a hay devil form down by the swamp to the south of the barn. It was small at first, but grew tall quite quickly, then larger at the base. It started to move slowly toward the barnyard, climbed up the hill, and literally attacked that patch of rhubarb with the hen under it.

Stalks of rhubarb flew ten feet into the air as it moved about four feet out into the barnyard. It left a pile of rhubarb stalks there with the hen upside down under it. She looked quite puzzled: I guess she thought the sky had fallen!

The little devil then moved over to the barn doors, scrubbed the ramp clean, and piled all of that chaff and stuff into a neat little cone shaped heap.

The horses were next. Their tails and manes flew out as they leaned into the force of it, and nearly fell over when it moved on. Stella then kicked Queen, snorted, farted, and ran down over the hill toward the swamp. Queen just turned and watched her go, no doubt puzzled by Stella's behaviour.

It got into the fence and made it rattle like crazy. A top rail flew off and disappeared behind the barn.

Dad was working on the side hill and by now, he had noticed it. He watched as it sort of scrambled around in the field, and then headed straight for him.

He had a coil of hay all rounded up nicely with a good even top on it. This damned thing seemed to have eyes, as it made a perfect bee line for the coil. Dad saw it coming and put his fork over the coil to save it. It missed him entirely but just as he removed his fork; it headed for the coil again. Dad held the fork over the hay as it zeroed into the target. Hay flew. Dad backed away, and it proceeded to spread the hay over a five-foot circle. It moved to the south, swirled there for a bit and Dad took a swing at it with the fork. He then looked around to see if anyone was watching him as if he was embarrassed to be seen attacking the wind!

It then headed straight back along the road to the backfield, and got hung up in a big tree. The tree was too much for it and it was gone.

All this happened in about two minutes.

The only damage was a confused hen, (that doesn't take much), a perfectly good patch of rhubarb wrecked, (there was lots of that around anyway). Queen got kicked for no fault of her own, a very well shaped coil of hay ruined, and made Dad to look silly.

Hay Devils, I assume that some people have never seen these silly little things. They can become quite strong, but I have never heard of one doing a lot of damage. They can be seen very clearly as there seems to always be dust in the cone shaped swirl of air. Hence, the name 'dust or dirt devil', We always called them "hay devils" on the farm as they appeared at haying time and sometimes were full of hay instead of dust.

Hay sweating. **S**weating time was very important when hay was to be stored in bulk. Damp hay will form a rotting ball in the middle of the mow, which, which will crust over and create a tremendous amount of heat. Then the crust will break in a few months resulting in a fire caused by spontaneous combustion and burn the barn down. Today baled hay allows air to circulate between the bales that prevents this from happening.

Hen dusting herself- Free ranging hens will find a patch of dust, sit down, and then will throw dust up all over themselves with their feet. They will spread their wings and throw dust under them. I don't really know why they do this unless it is to control lice and mites. They seem to enjoy it, and do it often.

* *A coil of hay* is a very small haystack.

Coils of hay in the field

Entries in Our Diaries
From March 20th 1943 to February 7th 1945

1943, April 1: Floyd and Lilly went to Minden with Cutter. *Roads still impassable for cars and no bare spots or they would not have been able the use the cutter. They would likely go to get a few staples but usually these trips were for the mail, and Dad's tobacco.*

April 2: Floyd Walked to Kinmount. *I am guessing by the following entry that the mail had contained a notification that there was a parcel at the railroad station in Kinmount.*

April 3: Floyd got Grass Seed from Kinmount Station with Cutter. *Oops, it was grass seed, and he could not carry it, so had to return the next day with the horse and cutter.*

April 8: Lilly and Floyd went to Minden with Cutter. Very Hard Sleighing. *Snow is melting on the roads enough that Floyd would have to pick his way through the muddy areas in order to find snow or ice for the runners.*

April 10: Stage* is on Wheels to-day. *We called the regular daily trip that Hewitt Transport made from Minden to meet the train at Kinmount the stage. I assume this was short for the Wild West stagecoach. This stage was a little house with a chimney and stove. This thing had been on a light set of sleighs all winter, but there was not enough snow now so Hewitt Transport had transferred it to a light wagon.*

April 17: Floyd and Lilly went to Minden with Cutter. *There must have been a snowstorm during the last week.*

April 20: Heavy Snow fell. *Now we were back into winter.*

April 22: Went To Kinmount with Team for Grass Seed. *Obviously, all of it had not arrived on April third.*

April 24: Lilly and Floyd to Minden with Buggy First Car on Road since December 2 1942. *They have changed to the horse and buggy now. Roads would be very muddy. Mud, and ruts, would be two feet deep in places.*

April 29: Got Car Out and Went to Minden. First Time Car has been out Since November 28, 1942. *This would involve getting the battery from the basement, replacing the entire wheels, as it would be up on blocks since last fall. Water would have to be added to the radiator, since would have been drained last fall. (There was no such thing as anti-freeze yet). The motor would be cranked by hand as the battery was likely dead.*

June 19: Held school meeting at Number 4 School re closing it. Not Carried. *Number four school was near the corner of what is now County Road 1 and Highway 121. The motion to close it, because of lack of attendance, was defeated, but it was closed later, and the children were bussed to our school. John Hulbig was one of the bus drivers.*

August 25: Worked on Threshing Machine for Jim Minaker. *Jim Minaker was threshing this circuit at the time with a steam engine that wasn't self propelled. It was drawn by horses. The customers had to supply the wood, as well as feed and lodging for his two teams. I recall vividly having a pile of wood which would be situated near the engine for threshing. This time the engine developed a difficulty of some kind. I don't remember what the trouble was, but I remember it was parked in our yard. It rained hard several times while the men were working on it, holding up progress for several days. I wasn't very brave around this thing, as Jim had a habit of blowing the whistle and scaring me to death. I was glad to see this outfit leave.*

August 27: <u>Started to build Trailer House on Garage</u>. *I remember helping Dad tear a hole in the back of the garage so he could build a lean-to building there to house his trailer. It seemed funny to be able to walk right through the garage and out into the field.*

Fall: <u>Miss Thompson Teacher</u> *She boarded with Loyne and Evelyn Cox. There she met and married Loyne's brother Denzil.*

October 4: <u>Hazel son born. Keith.</u>

December 2: <u>Bought Sultan Stove $38.50</u>. *This was a new cook stove for the kitchen. It had a reservoir for heating water (this went well with the new cistern just built the previous year) and a warming closet. Mother honestly thought that there could be no more improvements in stoves.*

1944, January 17: <u>Mrs Jack Kellett Died</u> *Mother was probably there at the time as she attended the sick a lot. She also helped with most births in the area.*

February 23: <u>Went to Bobcaygeon to See Veterinarian McKinnon about Black Cow.</u> *She was very sick, and getting weaker by the day. She was just inside the stable door to the right.*

February 24: <u>Black Cow Died took Tumour to McKinnon</u>. *Dad and Mother had checked on her through the night but she was dead in the morning. They pulled her out into the barnyard with a horse and Dad opened her up. The tumour he found looked, for the entire world, like a pan of buns. Dr. McKinnon had a name for it but I don't remember it now.*

April 3: <u>Floyd Bought 8-Year-Old Tony Horse from Roy Barrett</u>. *I don't recall this horse at all, but I included it here to show how valuable horses were in those days. Horses were the most reliable power that drove every family at that time.*

April 16: <u>Hazel's Cow Died</u>. *Hazel and Doward had two children under the age of two. Milk was very important to the health of this family. The cow died giving birth. The womb came with the calf. This was not entirely rare. It happened at night and the birth was not due for several days, so Doward was not there to put it back. Oh, yes we did things like that then. I have often assisted in putting the 'calf bed', as we called it, back in place.*

April 25:. <u>Floyd's Team Ran Away</u>. *Dad and Floyd were trying to break the colts to a wagon beside the garage. Dot kicked, Dad yelled and spooked the horses. They didn't run far, as the gate was closed at the barn.*

May 1: <u>Doward Got Cow from Milburn</u>. *As I said before, milk was important so Doward wasted no time finding another cow.*

Summer: <u>Worked for Annie Cox 9-hour days for $4.00</u>. *After her husband died, Annie Cox built a store in Minden. It is the building you can still see up on the hill behind the store that now houses Riverview Furniture. It was originally a grocery store run by the Cox Brothers and their wives. He was proud to be paid 44 cents an hour.*

June 6:. <u>England Invaded France</u>. *D-day. We all listened intensely to the radio and thought of the young men from the community who were over there.*

July 2: <u>Dan Horse Cut Leg on Barb Wire Fence</u>. *This was a nasty cut to a hind leg. You could see the bone. Dr. McKinnon put 'bluestone' on it. It seemed to hurt each time, but Dan stood bravely still to have it applied, as though he knew it would help. It eventually healed fine. (Bluestone was an almost clear, rock-like substance which was ground to powder and rubbed on wounds).*

October 2: <u>Sold Dot horse to Kent's</u>. *As mentioned before.*

1945, January 19: <u>Hazel Girl born. Phyllis</u>

February 7: <u>Skiing Party</u>. *See chapter 'The Ski Party'.*

The Ski Party

One Monday afternoon in February, in 1945, as I arrived home from school, my mother greeted me with a concerned look and said, "I am very worried about your father. He put his snowshoes on this morning and has been walking up and down the ski hill all day. When I ask him why he just gets the same foolish grin on his face he has when he thinks he has outfoxed me about something." Looking out the west window of the kitchen, where we could barely see him in the near dark light of the winter evening, she said, "It is not like him to put so much effort into something that will never be of any advantage to anyone. Go call him for supper."

When I went to the fence beside the woodshed, I looked across the valley to the hill, we referred to as the ski hill because it was perfect for skiing and sledding in winter. It had a very steep part at the top, which levelled out some about a quarter of the way down, then went into a valley and, if you had enough momentum, you could glide on up a small hill to the back of the woodshed. You could then turn and sled back into the valley and a little way back up the big hill. The only disadvantage was a cow path that was created every winter as the livestock had to cross the face of the hill, just about half way down, to get to a spring the other side. This path would become hard packed and, when you hit it with skis, sled or toboggan, it could be disastrous if you were not ready for it.

A lot of snow had fallen that winter without a thaw of any kind to cause a crust. The roads had been completely plugged several times and were only passable on foot or horse drawn sled. I could see that Dad had shovelled snow against the cow path on both sides, and had tramped it, and practically the entire hill, with the snowshoes.

I called to him and when he came up to me, I asked him what he was doing. He said, "This is going to be great if it works out." The excitement on his face caused my childish fantasies to soar, but I really couldn't imagine what he was up to.

The same effort was quite evident when I got home Tuesday afternoon.

As I left the house on Wednesday morning he slipped a large brown envelope into my school bag and said, "Give that to the teacher and ask her to read it in class this morning. She will know what to do. Don't tell your Mother, as she will just fuss and worry."

I gave it to our teacher, who was a very pretty, young, unmarried lady whom we addressed as Miss Thompson. She came from nearby Gelert, but due to the difficulty in travelling much distance in winter, the teacher always boarded with Loyne and Evelyn Cox. She opened it, read the letter inside, took out the small envelopes, and looking very pleased, she patted the desk and said, "What a wonderful thing this is. Well done Mr Miller."

The day wore on slowly. I could hardly wait to find out what Dad was up to. It was tradition then to say a little evening prayer at the end of the school day just before class was dismissed at four o clock sharp. Miss Thompson had us put our books away five minutes early, we said the prayer, and then she announced that she had something really wonderful to tell the class. She picked up the paper and read it aloud.

Dear Miss Thompson;

Will you please read this letter out in class, and be sure to tell them that they are not to tell my wife.

This coming Saturday night, I plan a ski party on the hill beside my barn. The winter has been especially hard, the snow is now too deep for winter work in the woods, and I am sure the February blues plague every family in this community. I think it will help greatly to have something to get us all together for an evening. I have prepared letters in separate envelopes for the parents of each family in school. I think I have one for each, but if not, you can tell every child to tell their parents anyway.

I am really looking forward to meeting you again at the party, as I haven't had that pleasure since the evening of the Christmas Concert in December.

Sincerely,

Milton E Miller

School Trustee S S # 5 Lutterworth.

The weather had been clear night and day for almost a week. Every night it fell to thirty below and not warming much during the day. The part of the hill that Dad had tramped was now frozen hard. The snow he had shovelled against the upper side of the cow path made a nice long ramp making it still interesting but no one could get hurt. He was now just adding the finishing touches.

Saturday dawned clear and very cold. I was very excited. The hill was wonderful. I wanted so badly to try it with my skis but Dad thought it might tip mother off. I was quite sure that Mother had assumed it had something to do with skiing but I was sure she had no idea the magnitude of his plan.

He told Mother that he wanted to listen to a program on the radio that night so it would be better to do the barn chores before supper. Her only comment was, "The moon is going to be full tonight. I am going to enjoy the trip to the barn to do the late chores."

After the chores were done and supper was cleared away, Mother went into the front room. She was standing in the dark, looking out the window to the south where she could see everything outside clear as day, under the brilliant winter moon. She noticed a horse and cutter appear on top of the hill on the road. She called out to Dad, who was sitting with his ear to the radio in the kitchen., "Milt, there are some silly people out in this cold going somewhere. I hope they are bundled up warm and have lots of hot bricks under their blankets." By the time I had gone to her, we could hear the sleigh bells. She commented how the bells always sounded so nice. She pulled the chain that turned on the only light in the room, a bare bulb swinging on a supply cord.

She turned to go to the kitchen, then turned back as she noticed the bells were too close to be just passing on the road. She looked out the east window toward the road and called, "They are coming in here Milt, who can this be?"

She went to the kitchen where Dad had already lit the coal oil lantern and was approaching the door. It was Aunt Clara and Uncle Arnold McElwain. Mother was busy greeting them, telling them how glad she was they had come and was asking why, when she noticed another horse and cutter climbing the hill from the road. This was Aunt Gladys and Uncle Jim Dugan. My cousins, Yvonne and Erma, were crowded into the seat with them.

Everyone began unloading baskets of fresh baking, large pots, and pans, packages of tea and cocoa. The whole scene began to look like there would be a threshing gang to be fed. Mother looked at Dad, and the bewilderment could be seen even in the semi darkness. He said, "It's a ski party Lil. I didn't want you to know as I knew you would just rush about preparing." She smiled at him, and then started rushing about!

In the next hour or so, people arrived via every mode of transportation available at the time. They actually came out of the woods, as the Pratt family came cross-country from South Lake. The Perc Schroter family came. The Trumbulls, The Archers, The Walkers, Frank, and Winnie Bowron were soon to arrive. The fence was lined with horses, tied to it from the house all the way to the barn. People soon covered the ski hill, sliding on everything from pieces of cardboard to sleighs, toboggans, and skis. The men first gathered along the fence by the horses, but as time went on, they also joined in the fun, rushing back only when there was any kind of trouble among the horses.

Then Loyne and Evelyn arrived with the teacher. The men suddenly stood tall, sucked in their stomachs, and introduced themselves to her one by one. Women didn't wear slacks of any kind when outside then, but rather a dress going to just below the knee, long bloomers that reached to the top of long woollen stockings, and boots. Miss Thompson was dressed this way also, but in the moonlight even I, as a young child, noticed that she was prettier than I had noticed at school.

Of course Dad made his way to her, and greeted her, saying how glad he was that she had come. Then he went to the centre of the hill and, after clapping his hands and yelling loudly, he finally had everyone's attention. He introduced the teacher to anyone who hadn't met her. He then announced that no one was to leave the part of the hill that was tramped, as the snow was deep. The north side cow path had not been packed and there was glare ice there that could be very slippery. Also there was a danger of going into the tag alder swamp.

He proudly but quietly told Doward, Elmer, and some other men nearby as he picked up his toboggan and headed up the hill, that the teacher was going to be on his toboggan before the night was over.

Our trusted dog Nipper was having a time of his life. He always joined us any time we were on the hill, running about yapping, jumping on any sled or toboggan that had an inch of room at the back, hitching a ride down the hill. With all these opportunities, he was soon in full swing.

It wasn't long before Dad appeared at the very top of the hill, where it was really quite steep. Somehow he had persuaded the teacher to join him there for, "The ride of her life." The toboggan was a long one. He would stand kneel and hold the curled part at the front. He usually was quite clever at steering the thing as he sped down the hill.

This time would be different.

He positioned the toboggan between his feet standing as he instructed the teacher to "Just sit and hold the ropes at the sides, and, when I get on, just put your feet on each side of me." He had just lit his pipe and it was sparking in the moonlight. Miss Thompson said that she was ready, he gave the men who had gathered to assist the teacher and see him off, a smile that clearly said, and "I told you I would."

He dropped on his knees on the toboggan and they were off. A shower of sparks flowed from his pipe. The teacher's scarf starting to float behind her; a memorable sight in the moonlight that I have remembered all through the years.

They were nicely gaining speed, when they met Nipper on his way up the hill. He saw a nice piece of toboggan sticking out behind the teacher and decided to jump on board. He did this very well and without any difficulty for him, but it threw Dad a little out of control. He headed straight for the forbidden snow on the north side. The hill became even steeper over there, they were moving fast by the time they entered the deep snow. Soon there was a big cloud of snow surrounding them. They were heading for the raw cow path that, at that point, would be like a hard-packed wall of snow about two feet high buried in the loose snow. I could only hope he would know enough to lean back, which would raise the front of the toboggan, and there would be a chance they would not hit the path dead on. He managed to get the nose up and hit the path quite nicely, but this is where he unloaded the teacher, the dog, and a two foot long slat from the toboggan. Miss Thompson reappeared in a cloud of snow, trying to get her skirts back in order, and the dog was barking frantically around her. Dad became airborne and landed on the section of glare ice. He drifted across it at a slight angle, and seemed to gain speed as he approached the three feet high snow bank on the far side. Once more, he leaned back and climbed the bank and was once again airborne. This time he was high in the air and heading for the willows beside the swamp. He cleared the willows by two feet, then ploughed into the tag alders with a horrible thud. The tag alders bent over, then straightened behind him, and he was gone.

All was quiet for a moment. Then I heard Elmer Kellett say, "Milt went into to swamp." The men all ran toward where he was last seen.

There was a rustle deep in the tag alders. Then we could see the top of the alders begin to sway. Some of the men began to wade into the deep snow then stopped, as he appeared on the edge of the thicket. The dome fastener on top of the peak of his hat had come undone. His hat was down over his left eye with the peak pointing up above his right ear. His jacket was unbuttoned half way down, and his pipe was upside down. He was carrying the toboggan with his mitt through a great gap in the bottom where the slat had broken out. Elmer had waded through the deep snow and was the first to reach him. As he took the toboggan from Dad he said, trying not to laugh, "The teacher is waiting for another ride Milt," but he burst out in the middle of it, as did the whole crowd.

Some of the women joined us a few at a time, as the evening went by. I went to the house at one point to get warm. The kitchen stove was covered with pots and pans, and there was even some simmering on the box stove in the front room. There were buns, bread, and cookies of every kind imaginable. Women were slicing freshly cooked pork, and beef. A large pot of chicken soup and another of vegetable soup simmered at the back of the stove. Tea and coffee was brewing, and the wonderful aroma of fresh bread wafted throughout the house. Babies lay on the beds, some awake, others sleeping. Mother rushed about, lining up great piles of plates, cutlery, cups, and mugs, even though she was told several times by the other ladies, to sit down and relax.

Finding a new can of raw cocoa on the kitchen table Mother said, "What are we going to do with this?"

Edna Trumbull said, "I brought it to make hot chocolate, Lilly, I will make a paste from white sugar, milk and the chocolate now, and stir hot water into that later. They can add milk to their taste."

Mother replied, "Really Edna I never made it like that. I always just made what the kids call Cocoa mess with cold milk."

Edna, "I make that all the time, Morg and the kids love it."

At one time during the evening, the hill appeared to be crawling with children, young people, and many adults. Screams were heard, as some silly girl would fall off her sled, or skis. There were a few serious spills, like when Elwood Walker ran into Mabel with his toboggan and broke one of her teeth*, but there was always a responsible person on hand to soothe the ego and get the injured back into the fun.

At about 11'oclock, a voice broke through the din of the crowd. We looked toward the house and could see Gladys Kellett standing at the fence by the woodshed. She was screaming at the top of her voice that lunch was ready.

Those who were at the top of the hill came speeding down, and those who were part way up just turned and slid down from there. Women gathered small children and began to herd them toward the house. Nipper hopped a ride on the nearest passing sled, and then he joined the crowd as we raced toward the house. Some ran through the opening in the fence at the well and up the lane to the house, others climbed over and through the fence by the woodshed. The men checked on the horses as they passed them, adjusting their feed and making sure the horse blankets were covering them completely.

When I arrived at the house, the kitchen, washroom, and front room were all full of people dining heartily on meat sandwiches, drinks, and cookies. Men stood outside with handfuls of food and hot drinks. Some tried to use the top of nearby woodpiles for tables but the hot cups melted into the snow. I went in and pushed my way through to the goodies.

A few people returned to the hill for a last run or two, but most started for home after eating. Everyone expressed his or her gratitude for a great evening.

Elmer put his arm across Dad's shoulder and thanked Dad for a great evening. "I was a little disappointed that you didn't take the teacher for another run though." Dad just laughed.

"You are going to stay the night aren't you Arnold?" Dad said to Uncle Arnold.

"Oh yes, sure, if you have room Milt". Raymond Geeza looked in on our livestock and fired the stoves this evening for me, and will do the chores in the morning. "We will go first thing in the morning so that will be OK, but Jim and Gladys will be staying also, do you have room in the stable for the horse?"

"Oh sure, there is room in the stable for four and we only have two here right now." Dad said as he got down the coal oil lantern and picked up the water pail. "We'll go and tie them in now."

The moon was low in the early February sky as we left for the barn. Nipper, full of scraps from the party, joined us as Dad, Uncle Arnold, Uncle Jim and I walked to where the horses were tied. They untied them from the fence and we went to the well where they pumped water into the pails and held them up to the horses. I wrestled with Nipper in the snow.

Dad lit the lantern as he opened the horse stable door and spoke to our horses.

Uncle Arnold led his horse into the stable and then over next to the wall of the double stall. Uncle Jim kicked the pole* over, and led his horse into the stall. Uncle Arnold raised the pole and hung it on the chain. There already was hay in the mangers and a few oats in the oat box for each horse.

We all went around to the cow stable and checked the cattle. All was well, so we started toward the house. We could hear the frost snap in the trees as Nipper came running from where he had been playing with the foxes down by the swamp. We filled a pail of water at the well and went to the house.

Life was good.

***Pole;** *Where two horses were stabled in the same double stall, a pole was usually fastened to the manger in the middle. After a horse was tied in the furthest position, the pole was raised and hung on a chain. This prevented either horse from turning crosswise in the stall.*

__Broke one of her teeth:__ Incidents like this were laughed off then, but to-day it would be grounds for some kind of legal action. This is why parties like this cannot be enjoyed as they were on those precious times.

Note, *Hazel wasn't at this party because Phyllis was only weeks old.*

Entries in Our Diaries
From March 7th 1945 to March 12th 1947

1945, February 10: <u>Snowed and Drifted for Days Roads Plugged</u>. *It was usual to have a three-day storm in winter. However, when it happened it would blow snow over fences and cause drifting around the buildings. The wind would whip away snow right to the ground from one side of a building and cause a drift four or five feet high curving around the corners of the building. High winds would howl around the house and rattle the windows. Roads would be impassable, even for horses, as drifts would form six to eight feet high.*

February 13: <u>Erastus Robertson and I Started Work at Church in Kinmount</u>. *(From Dad's diary). This was the start of a very pleasant month in the middle of the winter for me.*

Protestants and Catholics did not mix much then. The Catholic church in Kinmount needed carpentry work done. Dad was a good carpenter, so they gave him, (a member of the Orange Lodge), the work. He needed a helper, so he contacted a good carpenter from Horseshoe Lake Road, above Minden, where Wes Sisson now lives. This was the day after the three-day blizzard ended so I have to assume that Erastus Robertson had been contacted before. I remember him arriving at our place on foot one afternoon to stay with us while the work was being done. The next morning they left for Kinmount with the car. Erastus was prepared to shovel through the drifts ahead of the car. Mother worried.

While he was there, I fondly recall many evenings being spent playing cards, often by coal oil lamp as hydro was not very reliable, and listening to he and Dad tell of their days work. Dad had plans to construct built-in cupboards in the kitchen.. One Saturday when they had nothing much to do, he and Erastus decided to make a door for a spice closet that was already in place. They built it out of lumber and a piece of a brand new material called masonite. They made the door, but when they attempted to hang it, that was another story. They spent hours adjusting hinges, but it just would not hang properly. Finally, Mother said, "For goodness sake, I thought you guys were carpenters." She looked at it and said, "Take off the bottom hinge." She cut some pieces from a Christie's soda biscuit box, the shape and size of the hinge, and put them under it, and said, "There, screw it back on." It fit perfectly!

March 6: <u>Worked for Maggie Hillier</u>. *When they had finished the work at the church in Kinmount, Dad and Erastus went to do a day's work for Maggie Hillier. Maggie was a kind spinster, who lived alone in a little house at the end of Hunter's Creek Road near Gull River. When she answered the door in her night attire, a stiff March wind blew her gowns far above her head revealing all. According to the story, Dad pulled Erastus back and tried to close the door. Erastus then pulled Dad back and tried to do the same thing. Mother's interpretation was that they pulled each other back so the door would remain open to lengthen the show. Maggie eventually closed the door herself.*

April 12: <u>Roosevelt Died</u>. *This was a sad day for the world. He had helped lead the political front during the war, and died just before he could realize victory.*

April 17: <u>Left Lilly on South Lake Road in Rain</u>. *Dad was a long time living this one down. They had gone to Lochlin station to get fertilizer that Uncle Will had ordered for him. They took the trailer and spent the day visiting. It was dark when they began their journey home with the loaded trailer. Somewhere near where South Lake Trailer Camp is now on the South Lake road, (which was only two ruts through the grass, and is now called Hospitality Road), it began to rain. Dad got out of the car to put a tarp over the fertilizer. He didn't realize that Mother got out to relieve*

34

herself. He got back into the car and drove on without her. He went a little way, talking to her with no answer. He said that he reached over and said, "What is the matter Lilly, you are not talking to me." The seat was empty. Here he was, in the dark with a trailer behind and nowhere to turn around so he just got out and waited. He could hear her splashing through the mud and water as she approached. I do not imagine life was very pleasant for him the rest of the way home.

May 8: <u>World War Two Ended</u>. *We were in school when someone came to the door and told the teacher that the war was over. We went on a picnic in Loyne Cox's field. Ruth Schroter suffered stomach pains that proved to be appendicitis. The students planned a victory garden. We dug up an area beside the well, and planted marigolds.*

August 28: <u>Floyd Worked for Dave Stamp</u>. *I included this entry to pinpoint an incident that happened sometime during Floyd's work with Dave. Floyd went to work for Dave on this date to help with a logging operation that Dave was going to do that winter, and to help with the chores. He stayed at Dave's, as roads were not good enough to commute. He came home some weekends, but mostly he stayed over. One time, when Dave was bringing him home, they stopped in Minden. Floyd was going to have a beer or two at one of the hotels before he walked home. Dave went to Jimmy Smith's to get his haircut. Floyd saw someone in Dave's car and, thinking it was Dave leaving to go home, he called out, "Hey Dave wait until I get my things." When he reached the car, he saw that it wasn't Dave in the car, but rather two guys that were stealing it. He reached in past one of them and grabbed the keys. A fight started and Dave came out of the barbershop to assist. There was no OPP here yet, so with the help of some friends, Floyd and Dave were able to subdue the thieves and helped town Police Lawrence Pritchard put them in the town jail until OPP officers picked them up. Floyd came home with skinned knuckles, as a result of taking a swing at a man, missing and hitting the brick on the barbershop wall instead.*

September 24: <u>Started Cupboards in Kitchen</u>. *Dad started to build the first set of built-in cupboards in the kitchen. Mother had been storing cooking utensils and baking ingredients in a sideboard*.*

November 5: <u>Fred McMullen Shot</u>. *A good friend of Mother and Dad's was accidentally shot dead in the woods during deer season. The bright orange hunting clothes were not available, so red handkerchiefs were sewn on the back of hunter's jackets and hats. This was not very visible at a distance, and Fred was mistaken for a deer. I don't recall any charges being laid.*

November 19: <u>Nipper Dog Died</u>. *Nipper was a good hunting dog as well as a perfect cattle dog and family pet. He came in with the hunters from a deer run and fell off the couch, dead. We suspected another hunter had poisoned him.*

December 7: <u>Broke Trail to School Ahead of Children</u>. *Snow was deep enough in early December to make it too difficult for children to break a trail. Dad would go as far as Elmer Kellett's, ahead of us, and then Elmer would go from there, and so on, until we got to school.*

1946,

May 19: <u>Minden Bank Robbed</u>. *A roomer at the Rockcliffe Hotel thought he saw someone on the roof of the bank in the middle of the night but was not sure enough to get help and didn't see anyone again. The next morning it was discovered thieves had cut a hole in the roof, to gain access to the vault. The walls of the vault had been fortified, but not its ceiling. The thieves seemed to be aware of that. I do not recall any arrest.*

May 25: <u>Received Pup for Birthday (Sooty)</u>. *Miss Marsh, (who spent summers in a house on a private lake two lots south of us), gave me a registered Golden Retriever for my birthday. It was light brown with a very black nose right up to her eyes. I thought she looked as though she had stuck her nose into a pail of soot, so I called her Sooty. The following December 18[t.h] the day of our annual Christmas concert, I was in the play so stayed at school to help make preparations. Sooty always met me at the gate, when I came home from school. When I did not come home, she started out toward the school to meet me. A drunk driver struck and killed her. Mother and Dad did not tell me about it until the concert was over so it would not affect my performance on stage.*

Spring: <u>TB X-rays Held At Haliburton</u>. *Tuberculosis was a threat. Doctors sent infected people from this area to Gravenhurst for treatment. All cattle were tested and everyone had to be X-rayed. A bus picked up schoolchildren at the school and took us to Haliburton Town Hall. I was amazed that the driver got that long bus around some of the corners and into our schoolyard. I really enjoyed my first bus ride and said that day I was going to become a bus driver*

Summer: <u>Put Hay Fork in Barn</u>. *This was quite a large operation.. This hayfork was a rope and pulley contraption that would lift hay from the wagon on the barn floor and then* move a trolley along a track over the mows where someone would trip it, allowing the hay to fall into the mow. This was a great work saver.

Summer: <u>Road Improved Between Upper and Lower Dutch Lines</u>. *Before this improvement the mile and one tenth of road between these two concession roads was very narrow and terribly twisted. The new road had two lanes.*

Summer: <u>Motorcycle Crash in Front of House Killed Driver</u>. *I do not have a date for this as it was written in a book that mother kept about things like this. I do remember it and that everyone thought it was because of the long straight stretch. The driver just got going too fast on the straight-away before he came to the curve in front of our house.*

August 12: <u>Floyd went to pick tobacco</u>. *With very little employment in the area, many young men would go to Windsor, Ontario to pick tobacco at this time of year. It was hard work, but it put money in their pockets.*

Fall: <u>Got Contract for School Wood</u>. *All schools burned wood then. Dad was a school trustee, so he could not tender until time to open tenders. If there were no other tenders, he would then put the year's supply of wood into the woodshed. This was extra money.*

December 21: <u>Albert Hewitt Died. Snow was very deep</u>. *They plowed the roads with horses, but it was too deep for them, so men shovelled the deep snow to enable his funeral to take place. He lived on Scotch Line Road. He was Gladys Kellett's father. I spent many Sundays visiting there with Gareth and his parents. I was very fond of this man as were most. He was a clever and hard working pillar of the community. He and his wife Sarah raised their three granddaughters Wanda, (Mrs. Garnet Davis), Wahneta, (Mrs. Lawrence Hogg) , and Carla, (Mrs Keith Fountain),after their daughter Margaret and her husband Carl Stamp died at a young age. Carl died at a wood bee in 1933 as a result of a heart problem and Margaret, in 1935, of burst appendix.. My sister, Mabel, married his son Murray in 1951. Albert was thrifty and always kept a supply of wood in the woodshed. That way he and his boys would have something to do on rainy day, splitting and piling it. Murray felt somewhat cheated when his young friends would go to town on rainy days and he had to stay home and split wood. He complained of this until his dying day.*

1947, January 27: <u>Widened Sleighs for Hector Bain</u>. *Horse drawn sleighs were quite narrow making it hard for a team to follow the track without crowding. It was also very easy to tip narrow sleighs on their side. Widening them was a great advantage, eliminating both these problems. Dad started to do the work. It took about a week. It involved a lot of sound, hardwood timber. He would shape the new bolsters, rollers, and beams with a drawknife. Holes were bored by hand, and then sheared with hot rods to heal the wood around them. I recall helping him and painting the finished sleighs red.*

March 4: <u>Snow Plough Stuck at Elmer's</u>. *See next chapter.*

*Sideboard; this was a dresser with special shelves and drawers for cups and saucers, and a compartment at the bottom for pots and pans. They had a high back and sometimes would have a mirror.

Snow Plow Stuck at Elmer's

The entries in Dad's Diary read:

March 2 1947   Sunday, Snowed all night. Hazel and Doward here. Mild

March 3 1947   Shovelled Boyd's roof off. 3'5" snow on level. Painted some racks on truck. Snowed and blowed all day.

March 4 1947   Snowplow in drift all last night . Road blocked from Elmer's to Kinmount .
   Walked to Minden and paid hydro bill. Has blowed for two days and nights

March 5 1947   Shovelled snow to road etc. Elmer Kellett hooked on hydro.

March 6 1947   Snowplow got through to here. Blocked still to Kinmount. Worked in shop, mild, 32 above.

It was late Saturday afternoon. Dad and I came out of the garage where we had spent the afternoon doing some painting on the truck and headed to the house for supper. Thinking it was too dark for this early in the day he looked back over his left shoulder at the sky and said, "Looks like a bad storm coming in Ray." The sky to the north west was very black. There was already a strong wind from the north west and large flakes of snow were falling. A strong gust of wind almost took my breath away and, for a few seconds, Dad disappeared into a cloud of blowing snow. I said, "I think it's already here."

Mother and Mabel were in the kitchen, working between the stove and the table. The table was partly set and they were busily cooking supper at the stove. I said, "It's getting wild out there."

Mabel said, "I'll say."

Mother looked out the west window toward the barn and said, "It has been clouding in for a while now, I don't like the wind'. The wind whistled around the corner of the house, snow flew, and the barn completely disappeared. It began to snow hard now.

After dinner, Dad and I got ready to go to the barn to do the early chores. It was dark now so we lit the coal oil lantern. As we were putting on our coats, Mabel joined us saying, "I'll go too so we can get back in before it gets too deep."

The glow from the bare, one hundred watt bulb in the outside light did little to light the yard. The wind swirled around the house, causing a drift about two feet high out from the house. The little lantern flickered in the wind and died almost immediately. Dad said, "Just a minute I will get the other lantern." The other lantern had a wind guard on one side. This one would withstand more wind, but only showed light in mostly one direction. We went back in and he got down the other lantern from the shelf and lit it. He handed the unlit lantern to Mabel and said, "We will take this one too so we can have light in both stables when we get there." He handed an empty water pail to me and said, "Here, take this. We might as well bring it back full."

Looking past us as we went out the door, mother appeared worried, "Be careful won't you."

The snow was deep in some places. We left the water pail in the pump house, as we passed the well. Snow blew in our faces and down our necks. We rolled up our collars, and plodded on.

When we got to the barn, Dad lit the stable lantern then, taking the other one, he went around to the horse stable to clean down the stalls, check for bedding and feed the horses oats from a bin in the corner. I cleaned the stalls down in the cow stable while Mabel fed the hens and gathered the eggs. Dad came back around, fed the cattle, and pushed hay through the opening in the cow stable, which led to the horse mangers. We checked for bedding around each cow, blew out the stable lantern, and headed back to the house. The storm raged on. At the well, I went inside the well house and pumped the pail full of water while the others waited in the storm. Dad carried the water back to the house and put it on the water pail table inside the washroom door.

We settled in for the evening. We turned on the radio and while we listened to The Grand Ole Opry from WSM Nashville, Tennessee and mother darned socks, the wind howled outside.

About ten o'clock while Dad went back to the barn to check the livestock before bed, mother got a lunch. Dad returned, covered with snow. Mother brushed him off and we ate, while WSM signed off the air. We all went to bed.

The next day the storm showed no sign of letting up. There was lots of drifting and the wind was high as we went to the barn to do the morning chores. It did not take the livestock long to go to the spring for water and return to the stable door. I barely had time to clean the stable before they were there pushing past me.

Doward and Hazel came just before noon, with Morley, Keith, and Phyllis. Doward, a veteran of bad roads, had chains on the back wheels. There was snow half way up the radiator, and he could not get up the hill to the house.

When she heard the car in the driveway, mother looked out and said, "What in the world are those kids doing out in this storm. The man should have his head examined."

They all climbed out of the car at the road and scrambled up the hill to the house. Mother, not being one to think one thing and say another, continued her barrage at Doward. "Why in God's green earth would you bring Hazel out on a day like this, let alone three little kids. You need someone to look at your head man."

Doward just smiled and said, "They wanted to come and I didn't think it was this bad. You can't hear the wind in our house as much as you do here and the snow is all blown off the hill by our house."

Hazel said, "Don't blame Doward, mom, he really didn't want to come but I kind of insisted and the kids hounded him to death."

Mother retorted, "Well the next time listen to the man."

Doward turned to dad "I was stuck twice on the way down Milt, there is a drift building out from the rocks just this side of Elmer and Gladys's, over four feet high. I barely got around it, and I was stuck this side of George and Lena's. Good thing I had a shovel."

Dad replied, "Well, you had better get back, as it is not getting any better out there."

"Oh, let the kids have a little play. Then we will go," said Doward

They stayed for about an hour, then left. We had no way of knowing if they got home, so Mother worried. Dad said "They are not out in the middle of nowhere, Lil. If they get stuck they will go to someone's house and it is only two miles." Mother worried anyway.

We did the chores again that night and then listened to Fibber McGee and Molly on radio.

Monday dawned with the storm still blowing. Dad, Mother and Mabel was getting ready to go to the barn as I left for school. Mother wrapped a scarf around my mouth and I headed out. The drift in front of the door was now over five feet high. They waded into it, while I walked around the corner close to the house where the wind had scoured the ground bare. I picked my way around drifts that had built up from the fences and snow piles. They would be very deep next the fence, rocks or snow plow cone, and taper off to near nothing on the other side of the road. Sometimes they would be a foot or two deep all the way and I would have to plunge through them. Just this side of Elmer's gate there was a flat area. The road was bare and the snow from there was building straight out in the middle of the road over the crest of a drop in the road. It ended with a wall five feet or more high. I tried the ditch, but it had drifted full. The wind took my breath away, as I kicked footsteps into the hard packed snow on the face of the drift. I was then able to climb up using these footholds. The top of the drift was hard enough to walk on, but the north wind almost blew me back off the drift.

There were not many at school so the teacher let us go early. It had snowed all day, but the wind was not as strong as we headed home.

The drift at Elmer's had now extended another eight or ten feet down the road toward our place and was seven feet or more high on the face. I jumped off it into the snow below. The wind was dying as darkness fell and the clouds were beginning to break up.

I was excited when I got home. As I removed my coat and hat I said, "Wow you should see the drift up there at Gareth's place - its seven feet high."

Mother said, "Your dad went over to Boyd's to shovel off the roof. He said that there is a lot of snow in the woods and there is three to four feet of new snow in the swamps where it hasn't drifted."

Mabel appeared from the front room. "How high did you say that huge drift was, fifteen feet?"

I knew she was just trying to get me going so I took a swing at her and said, "Bugger off asshole"

"Here now, watch the language," said Mother sharply.

Dad was coming in from the garage. "I got the racks on the left side painted today Ray."

I said, "Good I'll take a look after supper."

"Looks like the storm is breaking Lil," remarked Dad.

When we went to the barn that night, it was getting quite nice. The wind had almost stopped and the snow had ended. The moon showed through from time to time.

We all went to bed early that night. At about ten o'clock, I was asleep when the sound of an engine woke me. There had been no vehicles on the road since Doward made his trip on Sunday, so I jumped out of bed and headed into the hallway just on time to see Mabel go out the hall window dressed only in her nightdress. The window led out onto the kitchen roof where there was a roof ladder. I stuck my head out the window and, in the moonlight; I could see her going over the eave onto the roof of the main house. There was another roof ladder that led to the peak of the house.

Dad passed me in the hall as I pulled my head in.

"Where the hell did she go?" he said.

"Up unto the peak of the roof."

"She has no nerve that girl"

I went into my room and grabbed my pants. Dad already had his on. We pulled on our coats in the washroom and went outside.

Mabel was sitting on the very peak of the roof, the wind blowing her hair lightly, as she looked to the north. "I think it's the snow plow stuck in Ray's drift," she yelled."

Mother joined us. "What's going on?" she said.

"Mabel says the snow plow is stuck in that drift," said Dad.

"Where's Mabel?" replied Mother

I looked up on the roof "Up there."

Mother looked up at Mabel, "She will never live to be a woman Milt. She'll kill herself first. Mabel, get down out of there Get some clothes on. You'll freeze up there."

Mabel called down, "I'm fine; it's not that cold now."

The next day was nice and quite warm as I trundled off to school. When I cleared the hill, I could see the plow sitting on top of the drift. When I got up to it, I could see what had happened. It had a V plow on the front and a wing on one side. Instead of the plow going under the drift as the driver had expected, it planed right up on top. The truck followed it, but the wheels broke through the hard snow and spun themselves down until the whole thing was resting on the snow with wheels running free. The wing was hanging out over the side like the broken wing of a duck.

Dad walked past it on his way to Minden later that day. It had opened the road as far as it had come, so there was car traffic past the school at times.

It looked like someone had tried to free the plow sometime during the day as it had moved some between morning and the time when I passed it on the way home. The hydro truck had come as far as Elmer's, and had hooked their house up to the lines.

The plow was still there on my way to school and back the next day. Dad had shovelled our driveway and cleared all the doors when I got home.

The next day, on my way to school, it still had not moved, but I heard it go past the school toward Minden during the afternoon, and it was gone that afternoon. They told me that it turned at our gate and went back, but it had not plowed as it went I assumed it was broken. I do not recall how long it was before the road was opened to Kinmount.

We Have New Neighbours

Entries in Dad's diary read.

1947, March 20: Bought Cement Mixer. *This was a big deal as Dad did a lot of concrete work. Before that, he would mix the cement in a long tray by pulling it from end to end with a hoe while adding ingredients. He ordered it from the Eaton's Catalogue. I remember the day it arrived. He immediately rigged an electric motor to it and made provisions to attach a Johnson gasoline motor to it, if necessary. I shovelled a hell of a lot of ingredients into that old mixer.*

April 10: Roads Completely Impassable With Mud. *Roads were built with mud and very little gravel. As soon as the frost began to melt, wheels would sink right to the rock, sometimes two feet deep. Even high axle vehicles would bottom out and be stuck tight.*

August 21: Dunc Prentice Dug Foundation for New Implement Shed.

Summer: Muskoka Construction built cut off to Highway 35.

The war was now history and the boys were all home. Surveyors had been evident everywhere through the last two years. Dad had been surprised to learn from them that the Kinmount road was to receive a complete overhaul. Land was purchased from Dad and George Kellett for a road allowance that would change the road, making a cut-off to Highway 35 from just north of the school, to an area on the highway known then as Little Lake. The local people had always thought that the new road would continue over the hill from Fetterly Hill, which was near the slaughterhouse, to connect with the highway at Ed Sedgwick's house, where the bypass and main street now meet. Since Muskoka Construction had, the tender to build the cut-off, all the locals dubbed it 'Muskoka Cut-off' immediately.

During the fall and winter of 1946-47, trees and brush had been cleared and burned to make way for the cut-off. An area across from the school was also cleared.

One morning in late spring, the sound of heavy equipment could be heard getting louder outside the school. The screech of tracks soon joined the steady rumble of a diesel engine. We stretched our necks trying to see out the windows and were chastised by the teacher. I was terribly interested in what was going on.

Noon hour came and we went outside to investigate. Bulldozer tracks passed the school entrance and I could see a bulldozer parked beside a tree, in front of the driveway to the house on lot 30. A house trailer was also parked alongside the road a little farther along.

There had always been an elm tree beside a big rock in the middle of the road. A man was sitting on the rock, eating his lunch.

I asked the teacher if I could go over to our house. She knew darn well that I just wanted to see what was going on but she said "Yes" anyway.

When I got closer, I recognized the man on the rock as Dunc Prentice. He had already levelled a lot of ground around the gate and had uncovered the roots around the big elm tree that stood beside the rock.

"Good day young fellow," he said, as I got closer.

"Hello Mr Prentice," I said shyly.

"Just call me Dunc son, You're Milt Miller's boy... Ray isn't it?"

"Yeah ,I'm Ray. Is that your bulldozer?"

"Yeah, it's mine."

"Boy, it's strong. Is that your trailer too?"

"Yeah, I guess we are going to be neighbours lad."

"That will be great, but ...?"

"Moss Kellett told me that I can park our trailer in the old camp grounds across from your place."

"Wow," was all I said.

The school bell rang, so I said goodbye, and ran back to the school. A little later, I saw the top of the tree lean and then disappear over the knoll where John Hulbig's house now stands. The sound of the bulldozer faded some, as he worked on toward home.

On the way home, we saw that the tree and rock had both been pushed into the ditch . The hole that was left had been filled, allowing traffic to pass over it. The first bend in the road had been straightened. Wow!

There had always been another tree and rock half way between our place, at lot 30 and Loyne Cox's. The tree was gone. We could see where he had tried to move the rock, but it was too big for his machine.

When I got to the place, where the road workers camps had been during the Depression, he was busily setting his trailer up under a large spruce tree. A grey Studebaker pickup was nearby with an outhouse lying on its side in the back. His wife Millie came out of the trailer. She smiled and went back in.

"What's going on up at the camp grounds?," mother asked as I went through the kitchen door.

"Dunc Prentice is setting up a house trailer under that tree. Boy you should see what he done up at the other place to-day" I said excitedly.

"Mr. Prentice, Ray, call him Mr. Prentice," she corrected me.

"But he said to call him Dunc," I said.

"When did he tell you that?"

"I was talking to him at noon in front of the other place. You have to see. He moved that big rock and took away the tree in front of the gate up there."

"I hope it didn't make a big hole for someone to drive into," she worried.

"No! He levelled the road right out and made it straight. You can drive right through where the rock was."

"Well, wash up for supper. Your dad will soon be home."

After supper, Dad, Mother, and I went up to the trailer. As we turned in from the road, we could smell fresh cooking, and Dunc and Millie and their six-year-old son Tom were sitting out under the tree finishing their supper.

"Hello Milt," he said, as he stood up to greet Mother. There were greetings all around.

"Listen Dunc, what are you doing for water?"

"We brought some with us, but we were hoping we could get some from your well."

"There's a spring right down over the hill there. It's good water and, if you clean it out a bit, you will be able to dip a pail there."

"Oh great. Show me where it is," he said standing up again.

Tom and I followed them down through the underbrush and back to the trailer. We talked some, but we were both shy, so we just kind of followed.

"That is going to be just great," Dunc said to Millie as we returned. "I just need to clean it out with the shovel and we will be fine."

"I see you have a toilet to set up there you will need to do that tonight," Dad said looking toward the truck.

"Yes, right away. I guess back there, behind the trailer somewhere. I think it is fairly soft here for digging,"

"It's just sand Dunc. Do you have a round mouth shovel with you?" Dad questioned.

"There's one in the truck."

"I'll go and get another and give you a hand with this," Dad said, heading toward the road.

"No Milt, there is one there on the dozer."

They dug a hole. Dunc backed the truck up to it, and they tipped the toilet off over it and levelled it up.

Meanwhile, Tom and I listened to the conversation between Millie and Mother.

"If you need to wash anything, just come over and we will do it at our place," Mother offered.

"I plan to take most things to town to wash," said Millie.

41

"Well, Milt built me a nice washroom four or five years ago, and the cistern is full. The electric washer is right there, all we need to do is heat up some water on the stove you know."

"Thanks Lilly, I may need to rinse some things out once in a while."

"Well just bring them along anytime."

The men returned from setting up the toilet. "Well, thanks Milt that made short work of that."

"Glad to help Dunc. You have no hydro here. You should have set up in our yard and used our hydro."

"Good God no Milt, we wouldn't think of it. We have a good Coleman lamp, and a Coleman stove. I am going to put a canvas up on this side of the trailer so we can cook and eat out here, even when it rains. We will be finished on the road before the cold weather comes, so we will be fine. It will be fun camping here and it will save the trip home every day."

"Well the garden will be coming along soon, so we will bring you some fresh vegetables when they are ready."

"That would be great. We will pay you for them."

"You will like hell! And Ray can bring you fresh eggs and milk too."

We went home and started to milk the cows.

On August 21, Dunc used his bulldozer to level out the area where Dad and I built a new implement shed. He didn't charge us a cent. Instead, he lamented that that wasn't enough to pay for all my parents had done for them. We thought we were well paid.

Here is a picture of me standing on the implement shed as it was framed.

I remember having the Prentices there that summer as one of my most pleasant memories. We became real close neighbours, and our families were together many times. We had them for supper once, and had many short visits.

Because I was four years older than Tom our parents felt I was old enough to stay with him in the trailer, from time to time, while his parents went into town to have a beer with Millie's brother and sister- in- law, Jack and Doris Redner. Dunc would give me twenty five or fifty cents each time.

Tom became a successful businessman. He now operates the Construction Company known as 'Tom Prentice and Sons'. He has the same honest ethics his forefathers had and rightly boasts 'four generations of service to the area'. Now, nearly sixty years later, I am proud to say, "I have known him all my life."

He threatens me with great bodily harm every time I remind him that I once babysat him!

The Work Continues

I watched many things happen to our road during the early summer months of 1947. The snow plow had been stuck in March, leaving it completely plugged with snow, and it had been totally impassable for cars with mud in April. Now it was being straightened and widened. Dunc had removed the rock and tree from the front of the other place and the tree from the straight stretch between the school and Loyne Cox's. Dynamite had removed the rock that he couldn't handle there. The little hill just south of Loyne's gate had been dynamited, and the hill south of that had been blown away, causing us to truck our hay around a detour, through the field and out Gordon Ruttle's gate.

I remember the job foreman's first name being Eli and I think his last name was Jenkins but I am open to contradiction on that.

Local truckers included S.G.Nesbitt, Lorne Gartshore, and Don Lee, Roy Little, Tom Cunningham, Norman Silver, Mervin Teel, and Ken Bowron driving his uncle Frank's new Ford. It was a favourite pastime of mine to catch a ride with these guys and ride around to the pit and back around to home. I liked to watch the drivers change gears on the steep hills, the swing shovels load the trucks, and the bulldozers level it down when they dumped it.

I guess my attraction to trucks started here at this point and has lasted the rest of my life.

Two truckers and their wives came from the Parry Sound area and rented the house at the other place. One time I was riding with one of these guys when his wife was waiting at the gate to give him his lunch. She was a beautiful blonde who filled out her red top very nicely. As I admired her, I felt an unfamiliar pleasurable feeling. I was suddenly interested in what was filling out that top so very well.

I guess my attraction to well filled tops started at that driveway and has lasted the rest of my life.

Drinking while driving was not against the law, so many empty beer bottles were thrown from car windows and would accumulate along the ditches. I could get two cents a bottle for them. So hunting bottles was a worthwhile way to spend a Sunday afternoon. I went on one of these expeditions on summer Sunday and rode my bicycle along to the school and on to where the Muskoka cut-off left the existing road and headed west toward Highway 35. I wanted to see what was going on with the construction so I parked my bicycle against a fence and walked through the cut-off to the line fence, and crossed over into George Kellett's property.

Most of the blasting had been done and the rubble from the rock cuts had been moved into the valleys. There was a rough road winding through the road allowance where rock trucks and machinery could travel.

I was just approaching a rock cut when I heard the sound of one of the Euclids approaching from the direction of the Muskoka Construction camp on Highway 35. I had been taught as a child not to trespass on other people's property. So I ran up on the top of the rock and lay down behind the trunk of a fallen tree to hide while the truck passed. I could see through under the tree trunk.

I could see the smoke from the Euclid* along the top of the next hill, and then it crested the hill and went down into the valley. It snored up the hill toward where I was laying. Black smoke belched from the machine as it came up and stopped just past me. To my initial horror, it backed in and stopped with the box bed tight against my rock, almost touching the tree trunk hiding me. I was level with the bed of the truck, and only the length of the rock box from the occupants.

There was no cab on these things. And a young local lady from town was sitting on the engine cowl. A well-tanned young man was driving.

43

She was wearing a purple dress, with white polka dots, buttoned down the front, saddle shoes, and bobby socks. He was not wearing a shirt just jeans and no footwear. As he climbed from the driver's seat to the truck bed, I noticed a mattress on the floor.

His muscles rippled under his tanned skin as he helped her down from the head rack. As she looked up at him and giggled, she reached back, withdrew a hairpin from the back of her head, and shook her long brown hair loose. It fell down her back as she began to unbutton her dress. She pushed the dress off her shoulders and it fell to the truck bed about the same time as his jeans. She unfastened her bra and hunched her shoulders allowing it to fall to the floor. There, no more then ten feet in front of me, were the things that cause those tops to be so attractive. Her nipples swelled in the warm sun, and her chest heaved in anxious anticipation. She removed the rest of her clothing. She was stunning.

In order to keep this family reading I can't describe in detail what I saw that afternoon. Probably in another book, that will be designated as being adult reading.

He was a construction worker away from home; she was a young woman living life to the fullest. I was an inquisitive ten-year-old boy who learned much about life and love that day.

I lay there as still as I could in deep fear of being discovered. When they had left, I got on my bike and rode home.

I knew her well, and have often met her on the street. Each time, I remembered her as I saw her that day. I also remember that afternoon every time I drive through the rock cut on the Muskoka cut-off.

*A **Euclid** is a large truck designed to haul boulders. That particular machine weighed 22-tons empty, would haul a 22-ton payload, and its top speed was 22 miles per hour.

The Kinmount road, as it was known then, was straightened that year so much that it shortened the distance from Minden to Kinmount by more than half a mile. It was not brought to any kind of standard. Most of the earth used to widen and level was just plain fill from Morgan Trumbull and John Hulbig's fields. Although it was paved, it heaved with the frost and was soon very bumpy with broken pavement.

The curve in front of our house was straightened last in the early 70's when I still owned that property. I received $110.00 for the land. Unfortunately, when the lawyers searched the title, they discovered that a certain paper hadn't been properly filed when the land was deeded to me, and it had to be tended to before I got my money. To have this done cost $25.00. There wasn't much profit in that transaction, was there?

Entries in Our Diaries
From August 15th 1947 to October 25th 1948

1947, August 27: <u>Harry Welch Killed</u>. *It was Minden fair day and there was a dance on the main street. Harry Welch was directing traffic around the town with a lantern. Evelyn (Ez) Wruth was driving from Haliburton with Tom Sawyer's car, and did not see him. He hit Harry, killing him. There was a trial, and although many people were of the opinion that it was not entirely Ez's fault, the courts awarded the Welch family a sum of money. They garnisheed both Ez and Tom's wages until the entire sum was paid. Automobile insurance was not compulsory, and most car owners carried no insurance. Those who could afford it purchased insurance right away following the trial.*

1948, February 12: <u>Jack Kellett Died</u>. *Jack lived a half mile north of us, on the opposite side of the road. He spent his spare time sitting on the veranda on the south side of the house. I remember him saying to his grandson, "Donald, quit that God damned swearing. It sounds like hell. Where in hell do you hear that kind of language anyway?"*

March 24: <u>Calves Stuck in Burn.</u> *There was still patchy snow in the fields. The cattle decided to take a walk back through the fields for the first time this spring. When we went to put them in the stable for the night, there were two of last years calves missing. Dad went looking, and found them on the other side of the creek on the Crown land. Forest fires had burned this land a few years before, so we called it 'the burn'. The creek was raging with the spring run off. Dad decided that they would have to stay over there for the night, as it was getting dark. The next day we went and investigated. The only way they could have got over the creek, without being carried away by the current, was to have slid down a fallen tree from the cliff above. We looked the tree over, and sure enough, there were bits of fur, and a little hide on the trunk. Dad went down stream, where the creek was narrower, and walked across a log to the other side. The calves were hungry, scared, noisy and happy to see us. He then had me throw the end of a rope to him. He tied the rope around one of the calves' necks, and told me to wrap the rope once around a tree. He told me to take in the slack by sliding the rope around the tree whenever there was loose rope. He pushed the calf into the creek. It began to swim, but went downstream with the current. I kept taking up slack, and the calf arrived beside me on the bank. We did the same with the other calf. This was the first time I had experienced the power of a half hitch around something. It is amazing the strength of this arrangement. By simply wrapping the rope around a solid object, and then keep the rope tight by taking up the slack, the object the rope is around takes the force, not you.*

March 26: <u>School Caught on Fire</u>. *I was sitting in my seat. I remember Miss Thompson was standing behind her desk right under where the smoke pipe went through the ceiling. A crackling sound was heard and sparks fell right into her hair. She stepped aside and said, "Someone go for help the school is on fire." I could see fire above the thimble. We all went outside. An older boy ran to Loyne Cox's for help yelling, "Fire! Fire! The school is on fire!" Men soon arrived and carried water in buckets from the well pump, up the long ladder at the back of the school and into the attic. Other men put the fire out in the stove, and removed the pipes by standing on a chair on the teacher's desk. Soot had collected in the thimble, (which was an old washbasin with the bottom cut out), and caught fire from the heat of the pipes. They replaced the ceiling and built a new chimney. The new chimney came right down into the room, eliminating the pipes in the attic.*

Summer: <u>Ray and I Tore Bagshaw Camps Down and Rebuilt Them on Archer's Flat.</u>

July 3:   Started to Build New Woodshed. *Dad and I tore down the string of old buildings consisting of a toilet, open woodshed, log implement house, another shed and a lean-to and began to build a modern building there in it's place. If you were to visit our homestead on the Kinmount road, you would see that it is one of the two buildings still standing there.*

Fall: Mrs. Shaver Was Teacher. *We started this school year in September with a new teacher from Burnt River by the name of Mrs. Rettie. She had a problem right from the start with some of the troublesome kids, and soon the whole school was behaving very badly. She finally broke down, went home in the middle of the day, and never came back. The trustees hired Mrs. Victor Shaver from Miners Bay. She rang the bell the first morning. As we settled into our desks she brought out the strap. This was a piece of hard webbing, cut from a tug of horse harness, about a quarter of an inch thick, and an inch and a half wide. Straps were legal then. Her face became scarlet red. She looked out over the classroom, and brought the strap down hard on the corner of her desk. "My name is Mrs. Shaver. I am the teacher. I intend to finish this term. Is there anyone here that wants to discuss that with me?" She had no problems.*

October 8:   Floyd, Doward and Taylor Hogg Bought 2 Man Mall Chainsaw. *This was one of the first chainsaws in the area. Prior to this time, timber was cut with a two man crosscut saw. Floyd, Doward, and Taylor were going into the woods to fell and buck timber around Redstone or Kennises Lake. This huge machine took two men to operate. It had a three-foot blade and a powerful motor. Some of the Lumber Barons at the time were, Bill Curry, Bert Curry, Percy Lymburner, Hay And Company, Bruce L. Bagshaw, and Palm of Veneer. I do not remember which they were going to cut for that winter.*

October 25:   Trip to Orono for Apples

Going for Apples

The week of October 18th 1948 was busy at our place.

On Monday, Dad cleaned the chimneys, stove pipes and put the storm windows on.. Mother cleaned up the soot that escaped from the stovepipes and then cleaned the outside of the windows and helped Dad with the storms. Then he ploughed the south four acres of the field behind the barn and made a chimney tile*.

It snowed hard on Tuesday. Dad went to Minden to see where the threshers were, made another tile and put the cement mixer away for winter he bagged 5 bags of oats to be taken to Fenelon Falls to be ground into chop.

Wednesday, he threshed at Fred Barry's, and then at our place for an hour and 35 minutes. The yield was only 150 bushel of grain and cost $9.00.

Thursday, he threshed for Dick Hillier for one and three quarter hours, then ploughed half of the spring hill field in the afternoon.

Friday, he finished ploughing the spring hill, put some new boards in the platform of our 1931 Rugby Durant truck, and greased it.

It had frozen very hard overnight.

Saturday, he sharpened plough coulters* and put new bushings in a Ford starter.

Sunday, was really busy. Neighbours came and went all day, bringing empty bushel baskets and giving Dad money. Tomorrow was the day that he would go to Orono for apples. Aunt Maggie Wruth, (Mother's sister from Lochlin), came that day to stay with us a while. She had her grandson Bryce Gilbert, with her, as she was keeping him over the winter while his parents, Mervin and Ruby Gilbert cooked and chored* in the log camp for Bill Curry.

We loaded the empty baskets onto the truck, then went to the barn and loaded the five bags of oats. Dad looked at them on the truck then said," I think we should take another bagful, here hold that bag," as he opened the granary door. I held the bag as he filled it with oats shovelled from the bin in a scoop. As we put the tarp on the truck, I asked Dad if I could go.

"You have school tomorrow Ray."

"I know, but I am doing well this year and I haven't missed a day yet."

"You can't go because we already have your Mother and Maggie and the baby in the cab There is not room."

"I'll ride in the back." I pleaded.

"It might be cold in the morning; it will be cold back there."

"I'll wear lots of clothes and get under the tarp. I'll be okay until it warms up."

"Okay, you can go."

The thought of a day off school, and the adventure of going where I hadn't been before, was quite exciting. I had never been beyond Lindsay.

When we got to the house, Elmer, Gladys and Gareth Kellett were there. When I told Gareth that I was going, he asked his parents if he could go too. After a bit of debate, they agreed. Gareth stayed over that night.

It was still dark the next morning when Mother called Gareth and I out of bed. After much yawning, scratching and moaning, we struggled into some clothes and went down to breakfast. Mother, Dad, and Aunt Maggie were already eating.

"Come on you guys, get a move on. You we have chores to do," Mother said, as we came into the kitchen.

We each had a bowl of corn flakes and a piece of toast with jam.

It was cold and frost glistened on the grass in the light of the moon, as Gareth and I headed for the pasture to gather the cows. We brought them up to the barn. The fall moon shone through the door as we tied them in the stable. Mother came with a coal oil lantern and we each milked one of the three cows.

We carried the milk to the house, separated it, and put the cream into a cream can. It was breaking daylight as we took the skimmed milk to the barn, mixed it with chop, and fed the pigs. They were big now and soon would be slaughtered for winter meat.

Dad came around the barn.

"I have checked the horses and young cattle, they are okay. Don't forget to feed the hens," he said, as he headed for the house. "Don't feed the hens the new oats," he called over his shoulder. "Use the ones from the old bin." The hens were beginning to move around and the rooster crowed, as I opened the henhouse door and scattered a half gallon of oats around on the floor.

It was daylight now and a gentle breeze blew down from the north. My teeth chattered a little, as we ran along the road to the house.

I said, "I'm going to put on my winter underwear."

"Chicken...." Gareth teased.

"I don't care, I'm putting it on. You can go to hell."

We washed up with some warm water from the reservoir on the stove, and then changed into clean clothes. Gareth put on clothes that Elmer had returned with the night before. He teased as I put on my long underwear, so I smacked him and then ran. He was two years older than I and bigger.

Mother and Aunt Maggie were busy preparing food and diapers for the baby when we arrived in the kitchen. "One of you guys take that box of food to the truck with you," Mother said nodding her head toward a pasteboard box on the kitchen table.

"I'll get it", Gareth said as he strode toward it.

"Looks like some good stuff in here," he said looking into the box. "Gee there's pie and everything."

"Get your nose out of there, that stuff is for lunch," Mother said, as she picked up a box full of things for the baby.

We went outside to where Dad was checking the oil and tires on the truck.

"Get another gallon of oil from the garage there Ray. I have part of a can behind the seat but we may need more than that," he said, as he crawled under the rear of the truck to check the spare tire.

As I ran to the garage I heard Gareth say," Are the lights okay Milt?"

"I checked them yesterday Garof*." Dad answered. The sun was only half above the horizon as we turned onto the road from our driveway. Mother, Dad, Aunt Maggie, and the baby were squeezed into the narrow cab. Sixteen empty bushel baskets were nestled inside each other in the front corner of the truck rack. A box of food and six bags of oats were lined across the head rack.

I was headed for an adventure with my very best friend.

Life was good.

We sped along the newly improved road toward Kinmount. The old Rugby would get up to 45 or 50 miles an hour if it was coaxed enough. We had a long way to go. The wind whipped around the cab and under the tarp. We huddled together against the bags of oats.

"Damned cold isn't it?" Gareth chattered.

"I'm fine, I have my winter underwear on," I lied. I was cold too.

We had passed Morgan and Edna Trumbull's place when Dad pulled over and stopped. I scrambled over and looked out around the corner of the cab. Glen Trumbull was standing with one foot on the running board talking to Dad through the open window.

"Where are you going Glenn?" Dad said.

"Just to the railroad station. Thanks for stopping Milt, I'm damned near frozen."

"Well, climb into the back there, I don't think it is much warmer there, but at least we will get you out of the cold sooner."

He climbed over the head rack and joined us under the tarp.

"Where are you going?" He asked.

"Orono," I said.

"What?... In this thing ... you'll be lucky to get to Kinmount."

Ever the cocky one, and always defending me and my family, Gareth responded quickly, "It's better than anything you have, and you were damned glad to climb in, so shut up. Milt takes good care of this old truck. It'll get there."

We stopped at the bridge in Kinmount , Glenn climbed down and started walking toward the station where he was training to be a railroad station agent.

The sun was warmer when we stopped to get gasoline in Fenelon Falls. Gareth and I got out and walked around some to get warm.

"I think it will be warmer now," I said.

"I sure as hell hope so," Gareth replied. "It has been goddamned cold so far."

"Watch your language Gareth," Mother said through the open cab window.

"Sorry Lilly!"

We crossed the bridge and pulled into the gristmill on the east side of the street, near the railway track. Dad backed the truck up to a dock, which had been built low enough for horse-drawn wagons. The truck platform was a little higher. Gareth and I went to the back of the truck and removed one of the tailgate racks. Previously we had brought a lot of grain to have it ground and the operator knew us well.

"G'day young man," he said, as we started to drag the bags toward the platform. "How many bags today?"

"Just six," I replied tugging away.

"Hello Milt," he said tipping, the first bag onto a two wheeled hand truck. Dad climbed up onto the dock and helped us pull the rest of the bags to the back of the truck. The operator returned. "Want these ground into pig chop Milt?"

"No, grind this batch a little finer. I will be feeding it to the cows this winter."

"Have you killed your pigs yet?"

"No, we will be though, as soon as it gets cold enough to keep the meat."

"Well it won't be long now will it? Pretty well ready for winter are you Milt?"

"Oh yeah. We're going for apples now, then there will just be killing the pigs and we are ready."

"Yeah ,I see the baskets there in the truck. You can get a lot more with the truck than you did with the trailer behind the car." He went into the mill with two bags on the hand truck and returned.

"You will be picking your chop up on the way back tonight then?"

"Yes. I had better pay you now as you might be closed when we return."

"Oh no, that's alright Milt. I'll leave them on the dock and you can pay me the next time you're in."

"Like hell, I'll pay you now," Dad reached for his wallet, as he followed him into the office.

Gareth and I replaced the tailgate racks. The sun was starting to warm things up, so we decided to fold the tarp up and sit on it. Mother and Aunt Maggie were standing in front of the truck stretching their legs, when Dad returned. As soon as they were all settled back into the truck, we pulled out onto the street and turned south toward Lindsay.

Highway 35 went right through Fenelon Falls then. It was only paved in various places at that time.

We stopped at a little service station before we went into Lindsay. Dad topped up the oil in the engine and looked the truck over. Everyone used the washroom and Dad got each of us a chocolate bar and a bottle of pop. He told us to save the bottles as he had paid two cents deposit for them and we could get a refund when we took them back in Minden later. Soft drinks were five cents with a two cent deposit on the bottle.

Dad asked me to remove one of the tail racks from the truck and Aunt Maggie used the truck platform as a table to change the baby.

Highway 35 took a wide sweeping curve to the left where the road to the thunder bridge road went to the right. It was just a narrow gravel road then.

A mile or so further along, it took a sweeping turn to the right. At the edge of the town, it became Angeline Street. At the fair grounds, it turned left onto Colborne Street, and then right at William. At Kent street, Highway number 7 appeared as we turned left, then right onto Lindsay Street at the Academy Theatre. Number 7 went to the left, as we went straight onto a gravel road. This was still Highway 35, but it was scarcely wide enough to pass on, and there was grass growing right out to the gravel on the shoulders.

Neither Gareth nor I had ever been here before. The day had warmed up nicely, so we stood up and hung onto the front rack so we could see everything. We pointed out things to each other like the level fields and the big barns with silos as they appeared.

Highway 7A came in from Nestleton and Manchester to the right, and then, at the top of a steep hill, it veered away to the left toward Peterborough. This was also a narrow gravel road.

We went through Pontypool and it wasn't long before the road got narrower. We noticed that the soil was sandy and we were starting to climb a hill. There were pine trees on both sides as we topped the hill and began to wind around sandy cliffs and clumps of trees. We went past a school house* and through a valley, then up another hill. The truck groaned as Dad shifted and steered around sharp curves. The countryside levelled out again and there were apple orchards on both sides of the road. We went down grade for a while then turned left.

We turned at several side road corners, and then entered a lane where a sign read 'W.H.Gilson Orchards'. We were there.

We drove up a long lane to a brick house located on the left. To the right was a large shed where some workers were sitting around a work bench, eating lunch from lunch pails. A man came out of the shed. We removed one of the tail racks and climbed down from the back of the truck.

"Well, hello Milt. I was just wondering, the other day, when you would be coming. Good to see you again guy. How are you?"

Just then, there was a pop under the hood of the Rugby and steam poured out all around the hood.

Dad was standing beside the front wheel. He jumped as he turned toward it. "Damn," he said, I was afraid of that."

"What was that Milt? Not the rad, I hope," the man said.

"No, I suspect it is the top rad hose," Dad said, as he raised the side of the hood. "Yes, that's what it is," as he looked into the engine compartment.

"I knew it was getting bad, so I have a piece of a new hose with me," he continued. "The boys can change it after we eat. It will give them something to do. This is my wife Lilly, and my sister-in-law Maggie, Mr Gilson, and this is my son Ray," He laid his hand on my shoulder. "The bigger lad there is a neighbour's son, Garof."

"Well... good to meet you all," he said shaking Mother and Aunt Maggie's hands.

"There's an outhouse over there under the trees," Dad said to Mother, pointing toward a building.

"No, No, for goodness sake. Those ladies are not going to use that place! Go over to the house and knock on that door there My wife will show you to our bathroom."

"May we use that table over there to eat at?" Mother said, looking toward a table under an apple tree. She started toward the house carrying the baby.

"Most certainly, Mrs. Miller. By all means! Please do! And that tap by the shed is good drinking water if you need it."

"Thank you Mr. Gilson."

Mother and Aunt Maggie were greeted at the door by a lady and disappeared amidst a flurry of "hello and how are you".

"I'll be with you after you have had a lunch and settled a bit," Mr Gilson said walking toward the shed. We men all went to use the outhouse.

Gareth and I were looking at the broken hose under the hood when Dad came along.

"Don't touch it until it cools some," Dad said, as he got a screw driver and a pair of pliers from a custom built tool box under the side of the truck, and laid them on the fender.

Mother soon returned from the house and said, "Take that box of food over to the table Ray and spread the table cloth on the table." After I had done that, she and Aunt Maggie laid out the food. There were loaves of home-made bread, butter, pepper and salt, a large piece of cheese, five or six hard boiled eggs, a can of sardines, a large onion, a jar of corn relish, a jar of home-made jam, a home-made pumpkin pie, plates, cups and knives and forks. There were no seats, so we stood around the table and ate.

Mr Gilson came along when we had finished and said, "Well Milt what do you need this year?"

"What are your prices going to be? Any change from last year?"

"No... Not much. The Macs may be a little higher; we have been able to sell them quite easily, so the demand is a little greater."

Getting a list from his pocket Dad said, "Lets get started. We have a long way back." He turned to me, "You guys get started on that hose. There is a piece of hose in the toolbox. Measure it, mark it and bring it to me I will cut it for you." (Dad always had a really sharp pocket knife. The hoses weren't very thick in those days).

He and Mr Gilson went into the shed to pick out the apples.

I went over to the truck and picked up the screwdriver. Gareth joined me as I loosened the lower clamp and slid it off the end of the hose onto the collar of the rad. I tried the other clamp but it wouldn't loosen. I tried with all my might, but it wouldn't budge.

Gareth said, "Here... you damned weakling, give it to a man," as he reached past me.

"Never mind... jerk." I tried again to no avail.

"Oh, okay, asshole," I handed it to him. "You can't do it either."

He loosened it easily and pried the broken hose off the collars. I handed him the new hose, he held it in place and marked it with a pencil Dad had given me.

Dad and Mr Gilson had gone down a laneway between rows of trees and were picking out some apples. As we approached, I heard him say, "I have russets down at the other orchard Milt, and I will give you a slip of paper telling the chap there that you have paid me and you can go pick them up."

"How will I know where to go?"

"I'll draw you a map. It's not far."

Dad put the hose against a tree and cut it with his knife.

I had a little trouble getting the hose over the collars, but, with a little effort, it went into place. I then slipped the clamp over the end of the hose and tightened it as much as I could. I looked for the other clamp. It wasn't on the collar. I turned to Gareth, "Where is the clamp you took off, idiot."

"Right there, on the fender."

"Well, you were supposed to leave it on the collar, like I did, so it would be there for the new hose." I looked and could see that it wouldn't come apart at the adjustment easily. "Now we have to take the hose off again and put the clamp in place. Big help fellow."

"How the hell was I supposed to know that? I don't work with your Dad like you do. Here give me the damned screwdriver and I'll fix it."

Mother called from that table, "You fellows had better stop your arguing. One of you can come and get this box now and put it on the truck.."

When I come back, Gareth had removed the hose, put the clamp on, and was tightening the clamps. "I seen a pail over by that water tap," he said as he turned from the truck, "Get a pail of water and we'll fill it up." He climbed onto the front bumper and removed the rad cap.

"Oh sure, I carry the water and you pour it in. That's not fair."

"Just get the water and shut up."

"It's still not fair." I mumbled as I trod off toward the tap.

We filled the rad. I started the truck engine, and let it run for a few minutes, to work out any air pockets, and topped it up again.

Dad came and said, "Do you have those clamps really tight Ray?"

"As tight as I can get them Milt," Gareth spoke up. Dad took the screwdriver and tried them again.

"Okay Ray... you can back the truck into the shed. We have some apples to load there. Garof you can hand them up to me and I will place them." I get to drive the truck and Gareth has to lift apples. I stuck my tongue out at him. He shook his fist at me.

They loaded the apples, then Dad said, "Follow me through the orchard and we will get the rest.." Gareth stepped onto the running board.

Mother and Aunt Maggie were sitting on the table, with the baby playing between them, as we returned to the yard.

"Can we load up and get in now Milt?" Mother asked.

"Yeah, I just have to pay and we have to go over to another place to get the russets."

"What do I owe you?" He said turning to Mr Gilson, who had returned from the house.

"Okay," looking at a bill in his hand, "You have 14 bushel here and the other two at the other place makes it 16. It looks like $16.75."

"Okay," he reached into his pocket. "Oh...Juice, and cider. You said that the juice is twenty-five cents a gallon, and the cider is thirty-five. Is that right?"

"Yes."

"Give me four gallons of juice and two of cider."

"Someone bring out a case of juice in gallons, and a half a case of cider please." He yelled toward the shed. Gareth and I climbed into the back of the truck. A couple of workers brought two boxes over and put them on the back of the truck platform I moved them ahead and Gareth replaced the racks.

It was getting late. Mother worried.

We drove along gravel side roads to another orchard. As we drove up to the house, a man came out of a shed. "Can I help you?" He asked. Dad gave him the paper, and he turned to a fellow that had joined him.

"Get two russets." The fellow grabbed the handle of a nearby wagon and went into the shed. We removed one of the tail racks. He returned and handed two bushel up to us. We piled them up, put the tail rack back in place, and sat down on the folded tarp on top of the apples.

"What time is it Milt," Gareth asked as Dad climbed up on the side of the truck to get some apples for the passengers in the cab.

"A quarter after two."

"It took us over five hours to come here. You're going to have to tramp on it to get us home by midnight. And we have that Christly chop to pick up in Fenelon Falls."

"Watch your language, Gareth," Mother yelled from the cab.

"Sorry, Lilly."

"We do have that Christly chop to get on the way home you know Lil," Dad teased as he climbed behind the wheel and handed Mother the apples.

The trip home was quite uneventful. Sometimes it bordered on boring. We ate apples. We watched traffic. We stopped once to buy fuel and use the restrooms. It was getting very dark when we picked up the chop in Fenelon Falls.

After we had passed through Kinmount, I stood up and looked out over the cab. The wind was getting warmer now. The headlights cast a dim glow on the road ahead. (The truck system was only six volts then, but that was adequate for the times).

It was seven-thirty when we turned into the driveway at home.

We could hear the cows mooing at the stable where they were waiting to be milked.

We were all tired and hungry. Mother got out of the cab and took charge.

"I'll unlock the door. Milton can light the fire and the coal oil lantern, Maggie will get supper. Ray and Gareth, go change your clothes, take the lantern and hang it in the stable, gather the cows and tie them in. You two milk the same cows you milked this morning. I'll milk the other one. Gareth and I will bring the milk to the house and separate it while you, Ray, count the chickens, to make sure they are all in, and then shut them in for the night. Gareth will take the milk back to the barn and feed the pigs. Then, we can all eat supper and relax."

"Whoa, Lilly. You sound like a four star general," Aunt Maggie laughed as they reached the door. The baby was asleep in the cab.

"Jeez, I've never seen Lilly so wound up," Gareth said as he followed me up the stairs to change our clothes.

"She's tired. She just wants to get it done." I answered, as I started to undress.

While we were milking, Dad drove into the barnyard and backed up to the barn door. He unloaded the chop. He checked the horses and young cattle, then went back to the house where he put the truck into the woodshed, so the apples wouldn't freeze over night.

Everything went as Mother had planned except for a tiny hitch. When I counted the chickens on the roost there was one missing. I took the lantern and looked all through the cow stable, the barn floor, the horse stable, but there was no hen. I was reluctant to go behind the barn in the dark alone with only the lantern, but I knew if she were left out she would likely be eaten by a fox or a weasel before morning. I went around the barn and there she was, on the top rail of the fence. She was sound asleep. I pried her claws from the rail and carried her around and into the henhouse. I put her on the roost and she clamped her claws around the rail. She never even woke up.

Aunt Maggie had fried some side pork, warmed up some potatoes, and turnip that had been left over from yesterday. We finished off the onion and bread, and anything left from our lunch. We had rhubarb pie with fresh cream. Then we all listened to 'The Great Gildersleeve" on radio while Aunt Maggie rocked the baby to sleep.

Dad filled and lit his pipe.

Life was good.

It warmed up after that. It snowed a little on November 27th, but there was no more frost until November 28th. It went to 10 above 'F' on December 2nd, but warmed up again for nearly a week. Dad helped Doward kill his pigs on December 8th and they killed ours on December 11th. The weather was a big factor about keeping meat. Pigs weren't killed until it was cold enough to ensure the meat wouldn't go bad.

The Fall of 1948 was very open. I remember Dad complaining bitterly that there was not enough snow for sleighing with the horses in November.

__Chimney Tile;__ Dad had a form for making chimney tiles from concrete. Before he got the mixer, the concrete was mixed by hand, then pored into moulds to harden. There was a mould for a base, and one for a trim top, as well as a special form to provide a smoke pipe hole. They were in great demand, and were a significant source of income. He always kept a large stock on hand so orders could be filled as quickly as possible.

__Cooking and Choring;__ Ruby and Mervin Gilbert went into the logging camp to cook and chore for Bill Curry during the winter of 1948. They crossed the lake by boat in the fall before it froze over, and came out for Christmas, across the ice. They would go back after Christmas and not likely return until the cut was out in the spring. Ruby would cook and Mervin would fire the stove and prepare vegetables etc. They would be up in the morning, on time to prepare breakfast early enough for the cutting and skidding crews to be in the woods by daybreak, using coal oil lanterns to find their way. The 'chore boy', as the helper was called, would likely clean the horse stables and place fresh hay in the mangers for the horses. He would also keep the wood fires going in the bunkhouses during the day.

Aunt Maggie and Uncle Jim Wruth took care of the baby all winter so Ruby and Mervin could work in the logging camp to earn money.

__Garof;__ Dad always called Gareth "Garof", Even in his entry in his diary says 'Ray and Garof went too'.

__Plough Coulter;__ Fields were ploughed with a single furrow, walking plough, behind horses. It turned a little better than a foot of soil each pass. A plough coulter is the sharp knife that slices the sod slightly ahead of the plough's mouldboard. The mouldboard is the part of the plough that flips the furrow over.

__School;__ The school house mentioned is the one that can still be seen to the right of 35 and 115 highways approaching Enterprise Hill from the south. You can also see the road on which we travelled. Enterprise Hill is the area where highway 35 leaves 115 and turns north.

A Story of War

September 9th 1951. It was now over five years since the war ended in Europe. The returning soldiers very seldom spoke of any of their experiences over there. Many people including myself often wondered why.

I was helping a war vet, who had been in the Stormont, Dundas, & Glengarry Highlanders, build a combination henhouse and pigpen on his farm, when we stopped in mid-morning to have a break. I had noticed that he had a package of cigarettes in his shirt pocket, but he never lit one during the morning, and didn't light one now, during the break. Thinking this unusual, I asked why. This was his answer.

"I landed in England on my way to the front for the first time in 1942 with a very high fever. I was in hospital for a long period. My hair fell out and I have never been so sick in my life. Before that, I smoked regularly, but when I came out of hospital, I found that I could take smoking or leave it. I only smoke now when I want, and I can quit anytime I choose. I am not addicted. This was a great advantage to me during the time I spent on the front lines. There were times when we were away from the camp long enough to run out of smokes, which bothered those who at were addicted. Those lads suffered badly from their habit."

"I have often wondered how the war was fought. How did you fight? Where did you eat, and what was the routine for sleeping and that?" I asked.

"We would set up a camp consisting of sleeping tents, first aid, cookery, and a mess tent wherever we were ordered to go. Personnel carriers would then take us to the battle and return us when another platoon was brought up to replace those of us that who still alive. Of course we always carried canteens and enough rations for a few hours, if we were cut off from the camp, or fell behind enemy lines."

"Were you ever behind enemy lines?" I asked.

"Yes, I was once, during the liberation of Holland."

"How did that happen and what was it like?"

"I really don't think you want to hear that."

"Yes I do. I really do."

He looked away, and then looked directly at me. His demeanour changed. He looked at the ground, hesitated, and then began.

"We were fighting a serious pocket of resistance near Leeuwarden. It was near dark and the skies were heavy with rain clouds. The Germans were in retreat, but had dug in at a tree line up a slight hill from us. There was a large open field between us with a deep trench running at an angle across it. There were also a few foxholes dotting the open area. Holland was very flat, so we knew that there would be water in a trench that deep, but our superiors felt that it would be to great advantage if we could get a small contingent into that ditch where the soldiers could run along it and arrive right under the Jerry's machine gun nest and take them out with grenades. Five men were chosen for the trench, of which I was one. Two others were to try to get into the foxholes to give us rifle cover when we arrived. A barrage of gunfire kept the Germans busy while we ran several yards across the open field to the near end of the trench. We ran with heads down and heavy gear on our backs, and all made it, although bullets stirred the soil all around us. At one point, a bullet landed so close to my foot that I felt the jar right through the heavy sole of my boot. There was about a foot of water in the trench at the six-foot deep end. Just as we were running through the ditch, a couple of German planes came over. They strafed the field, then dropped bombs on our lines behind us. They circled and strafed again. This time the Jerries broke their lines and charged us, right behind the line of gunfire from the planes. Germans were leaping over our heads, running toward our lines. Suddenly we realized we were trapped behind the charging enemy and our lines were in full retreat. We pressed against the side of the trench from which the enemy was advancing, so they wouldn't see us and kill us. An enemy soldier noticed one of the lads in the foxhole, stopped, and pointed his gun into the hole. I drilled him, and he fell onto the guy in the hole. I watched as the dead German was pushed back out and rolled onto the ground. I knew my friend was all right for now.

"A halftrack sped across the trench, right where one of my comrades was standing. The front wheels jumped the ditch, but the bank gave way under the weight of the rear tracks at the rear. The Germans ran forward from their disabled vehicle, without noticing us, but dropped a grenade into the trench on the other side of the vehicle. The soil completely covered our guy, except for his head, which was right under one of the tracks. The engine was still running and the track was turning." He paused for a moment. "I watched as the track settled into the mud and slowly took his head off . The machine dropped and the tracks caught solid earth, stalling the engine. The trench was now divided in two, with two of us on each side.

"Training had taught us not to reveal our position by firing at any more enemy soldiers. They crossed the ditch with every means of transportation they had. We leaned hard against the wall. We also knew that the enemy would kill us or take us prisoner, as soon as they began mop up tactics of the area after the fighting ended. We heard the screams of dying men in the area where we had left our lines. We heard our heavy guns fade as they retreated into the darkness and night fell. Realizing the predicament we were in, the other fellow whispered, 'They are not going to capture and torture me.' Before I realized what he was doing, he placed his rifle under his chin and pulled the trigger. His head and helmet flew off and his body slid down the bank and into the water. I retrieved his dog tag and put it inside his blood soaked shirt so he would be identified when he was found. I was now alone.

"Darkness brought the coldness of the early spring night. Rain began to fall and became heavier and heavier. Little rivers of water began to run into my ditch. Activity on the surface began to diminish and the roar of artillery, in the direction of the front lines, began to die down. Water was rising but I could not scramble onto the surface, as there were Germans there who would capture me. I could still hear artillery fire in the distance; I knew they were fighting by the light of gunpowder explosions.

"It was dark. It was cold. I was standing in water up to my waist, and it was rising. I dug my feet into the sides of the trench but it was soft from the rain and I fell back each time. I could smell fuel. The tank of the disabled halftrack had ruptured. I was now in a lonely trench in Holland. Cold water, fuel, and mud were up to my armpits. I braced myself against the wall, put my rifle across my shoulders, closed my eyes, and thought of home. I remembered my childhood, only a few years before. I drifted on the edge of consciousness as my mind gave up. I was barely twenty-five years old. I hadn't lived. All I knew was childhood and three years of war.

"Daylight broke under clear skies. I looked around and saw that I was standing in a sea of mud, blood, and fuel. It was quiet. Then I heard the rustle of feet in the mud on the surface. A German soldier dropped down on the track of the halftrack. He was preparing to shoot in the direction of our lines. I drew a bead on his ear, said 'Boo' quietly. I will not soon forget the look on his face as he turned and saw I was enemy. He moved to turn his rifle on me. I pulled the trigger. A third eye appeared between his as the bullet entered his brain. He fell into the muddy water.

"I climbed up the vehicle and peered across the field. An allied soldier drew a bead on me. I raised my hands and began to repeat my name rank and serial number, loudly and clearly several times. He lowered his gun and said, "It's over soldier. We wiped the Germans out last night. Those who are not dead are prisoners. Breakfast is ready back at the camp, and you had better clean yourself up before your mother sees you." It was Clifford Schroter. His company had joined ours during the night.

"I learned the two fellows on the other side of the cave-in were gone. The Germans had seen them. The grenade they dropped into the pit as they charged on had done the trick. The fellow that I had saved before was now lying in the mud in his hole. I hadn't been able to save him this time. No one knew where the fellow from the other foxhole was at first, but he was found later by the mop up crew lying where he had fallen as he was gunned down." He stopped and in a few minutes, he seemed to return to present day.

In a moment he continued. "It was all worth it, as a few weeks later, on April 16th, 1945 we marched into Leeuwarden, where we were greeted with open arms. The Dutch had been under German control since surrendering to the Nazis on May 15th 1940. After five years of occupation they were all but starved. They have affectionately tended Canadian graves in their country and send tulips for our Tulip Festival in Ottawa ever since."

"Why is it that you guys don't tell about these things?" I asked.

"When we start to tell, we find that people don't want to hear. They either stop us, because they can't stand the horror, or they block us out, and we can tell they don't believe it. However, most of the time, memories of the horror are more than I can stand, and I have to blank them out. You wanted to hear, you listened Ray ... so you heard it."

"That was a horrible night for you. Did it bother you to kill guys?"

"Oh sure, it bothered us. I often thought about the German guys that fell around us. I would think about their parents who would never see their son again, because I was instrumental in ending his life. I would think sometimes about the life that soldier would have lived and never would, but it was them or us. We were there to stop the tyranny of Hitler's regime. Those soldiers didn't want to fight and die any more than we did, but the torture and genocide had to be stopped. We had to remember that Hitler was killing off his own elderly, mentally ill, and disabled. He was killing Jews by the millions just because they were Jews. He had U-boats in Halifax harbour. Buzz bombs were landing on England every day. He would have ruled the world if we hadn't stopped him. That was why we killed. Sometimes we would hesitate, only to see that same soldier kill one of ours. Then we would kill without either conscience or mercy."

"What would you say was the worst thing you had to do during the war, the one thing that will bother you for the longest?"

"I was on what they called clean-up detail, behind the front lines in Holland. Our job was to flush out any enemy who may be behind our advancing lines. We were dashing from building to building in a city that had been ravaged many times, as we had taken it once or twice only to be driven back. Little pockets of enemy soldiers would be flushed out from time to time and taken prisoner. We would sometimes know there was someone in basements of war-ravaged buildings and homes. We would identify ourselves, and call down three times for them to come out. If they didn't, we would drop a grenade down and carry on. It bothered me that some of those may have been women and children merely hiding from the horror of war. They wouldn't even know our language. However, we couldn't take the chance of being flanked once more by Germans who had hidden from our front lines. That will bother me until I die." He looked down for a minute then raised his head again. He brushed tears from his eyes.

"Was there a lot of depression in camps when you were not fighting or was morale kept up by training and other activities?" I asked stupidly.

"Mail call brought many mixed feelings. Some would receive good news while others would get bad. Parents died while we were there, and that kind of news would break them up badly. The worst were the 'Dear John' letters that some received. These lads left sweethearts at home who promised to wait for their return. They were over there being shot at; fighting hard for their country and a life that they had planned together with a girl, they loved enough to carry her picture into battle. The picture that had inspired them to carry on when everything had being blown apart all around them. The picture of a girl who now forgot them and married another. That was hard."

"You were a long time getting home after the war ended."

"Yes. The war ended on May 8th, but I didn't get home until New Year's Eve. I was on board the Queen Mary for Christmas. There were thousands of us over there. They were loading the boats with as many as possible. They would overload them by having men sleep and eat in shifts, to get them home as soon as possible.

There was mopping up to be done in some regions. We helped the country recover as much as possible. When there was nothing to do, we would sometimes form up drills and parade through the towns and cities we had liberated. We had drums and bugles, we already knew how to march, so all we needed was a drill formation, and we would entertain. The people who had been under strict German rule, were now free and enjoyed that a lot. "

He lit a cigarette, turned back to the cement block wall we were building, and began to work.

Allied forces suffered 5,304 casualties during the liberation of Holland. Many of those were Canadian.

The Germans blew holes in dykes as they withdrew, leaving Holland flooded.

The people of Holland still send tulips to Canada to this day.

Drum and Bugle Corps throughout the free western world copied the drills that he spoke of. I became an active part of those Corps in later years.

The soldier I had spoken to married and raised two children. He died in 2003 at the age of 83, as the result of a fall.

Entries in Our Diaries
From October 25th 1948 to October 8th 1951

1948, October: Bill Dugan's Dance in New House *Mother's two brothers both built new homes at this time. It was customary to have a house warming party in a new home.*

December 20: Bagshaw Brought Sleighs for Dad to widen. *Dad widened a lot of sleighs. It was a large and tedious job but he did it well.*

1949,

March 12: Curry Motors Opened new garage in Haliburton. *This was important stuff. Uncle Herb had been talking about Curry's big, new garage being built for weeks. The roads were getting muddy, so we left early in the morning to take advantage of the frost. There was a big celebration and a large, (or we considered it large then), display of new cars. Wow! They raffled off a new car. There were balloons, hot chocolate, and candy. The dealership is still there. They will move it to a new building and location in 2005.*

March 26: Formica Transport Stuck in Mud. *Eugene Formica owned one of the very first tractor-trailers in Haliburton County. He was under contract to haul barrelheads etc. for the International Cooperage in Eagle Lake. It was late afternoon when Dad and I heard the sound of a heavy vehicle over the hill to the south of us. It sounded like it was stuck in the deep mud, so he said, "Let's go, and see who it is." As we topped the hill, we could see Eugene's truck axle deep in mud. He was leaning against the front of the truck with his arms crossed. There was a machine of some kind on-board. "I don't think the horses will do you much good." Dad said, as we got nearer. "No Milt, it is right on the housing," he answered grimly. As we were standing looking it over, a Hydro Electric Power Commission truck approached from the south. It and was towing a pole trailer. As it tried to go around the transport, it too bogged down. All the workers jumped off and began to push. It crept ahead, spinning all the way. They all jumped back onto the truck, only to bog down again. Off they all climbed and pushed again. After several more pushes, they finally cleared the hill. Eugene crossed his arms and legs and leaned against the truck again saying, "No use me try," in his Italian accent. I can't remember how he got from there to Minden, but I expect he hitch-hiked and walked most of the way, as there was not much traffic that night. I do remember a grader passing the next day and seeing him in the cab. His truck went past shortly after that.*

April 23: Dad Dealt 1930 Ford on 1938 Plymouth. *It was the first car deal in my memory, and I was eleven years old. Dad and Mother went to Lindsay. Floyd and I were standing in the yard when this strange car turned into our driveway. We stood and watched as it climbed up the hill. The passenger door flew open and Mother stepped out. She left the door open so we could hear the radio. They had dealt at Manley Motors. Dad was very proud of this car, but his pride soon ebbed. It was to prove to be a large headache for him. There was no warranty or certification on used cars and he knew it needed a couple of replacement tires. It also needed a brake job and work on the steering. It was very hard to start in cool weather, and we eventually discovered it had a cracked block.*

Summer: Dad and I Built Cottages at Sandy Bay for Bruce Bagshaw. *We built two small cottages.*

Summer: Phyllis Got Polio. *There was a real threat of polio that year. Phyllis was treated at Thistletown Hospital.*

Aug 18:   Doward Started to Raise House *Doward raised the house and put a foundation under it. This house is now part of the go cart track just off Highway 35, two and a half miles south of Minden.*

Fall: First I Remember Putting Anti-freeze (alcohol) in Car. *Before this time, it was a practice to drain the radiator after every time you used a car in winter. Some people had tried coal oil, and kerosene in the radiators, but that wasn't very successful, as the oil didn't mix well with water. Alcohol worked better but it was expensive. Then came an alcohol-based anti-freeze for cars. This mixed well, but would boil away quickly and leave the mix freezable, if more wasn't added at the right time. There were a few cracked blocks as a result of this arrangement. It was not long though before the ethylene glycol anti-freeze we are familiar with to-day was used widely, ending all the draining of radiators.*

1950, April 5:   Started to Build House for Roy Hopkins. *Roy came into the county to work for Bagshaw Lumber at the mill. He decided to stay in the area and bought a piece of land from Dad on lot 31. Dad and I built a little one-room 26 by 20 foot cabin and an outhouse. Floyd was passing by the house a few years later and thought things seemed unusually quiet at Roy's. He turned back to investigate and found him dead in his rocking chair. His hand had fallen to the floor clutching his bible. Mother thought that was a wonderful way for Roy to meet his maker.*

April 19:   Sold Land For School Ground Extension. *More students were enrolling each year, as new families began to move to the area. There were now 21 students. There were classes from one grades to eight in one room. The play ground needed to be larger, so the school board purchased a piece of land from Dad. John Hulbig's House now stands on that extension.*

April 29:   Car Sale West of Lindsay. *Doward's 1929 (not quite sure of year) Pontiac was becoming unreliable. Someone heard of a car auction at a place on Highway 7, west of Lindsay, between Oakwood and Manila. Dad, Doward, and I went to see if there would be a suitable one to replace Doward's car. There were a few there and he picked out a green Chrysler. A fellow was moving vehicles about before the sale started and backed into Dad as he was looking at a car. He was thrown several feet, got up and dusted himself off. The driver was very concerned, but Dad was not injured. Doward bought the car. We were following him home when it suddenly began to smoke and quit running. The engine had seized up. This was very bad, as he had spent all his spare money on the car, and warranty was unheard of then. Doward and Dad returned the next day and towed it home using a home-made draw bar. Doward rebuilt the motor and painted the car a two tone brown. This proved to be a wonderful vehicle in the long run and provided reliable service for a long time.*

July 5:   Mother took sick with Pernicious Anemia. *Mother had not been well for a while. She seemed to have trouble standing sometimes and would lose her balance often and stagger until she would finally fall to the floor. We were quite concerned about this. On this day, she went into a coma of sorts several times. We took her to Dr Agnes Jamieson. The doctor ran some tests and sent them away, but things were slow then and it took many days for results to return. It was pernicious Anemia, as well as a liver condition. Dr. Jamieson put her on a regimen of vitamin shots. She had to have the shots repeated every two days, and take a very vile smelling drink called Ancabile. Mabel came home from the restaurant, Aunt Myrtle came for a while, and Gladys Kellett came most days, for a while, to help. Either Floyd or Dad had to take Mother to the doctor for shots. There was a time when she was in a semi-coma for hours. We thought we were going to lose her.*

August 21:   Started to Build New Blacksmith Shop. *That shop is under the roof behind the main building in the photo. It has a dark "diamond" design on it.. Dad didn't order quite enough shingles and he knew we would we run out, but he had a few bundles of another color. By putting in that diamond we had just enough.*

September 25:   Dad Bought Fordson Tractor. *This tractor was an ignorant damned thing. Only a determined mechanical genius could ever hope to keep it running. It arrived with steel-cleated wheels that would be wonderful on soil but when they struck a rock the steel had no traction, and it sat there and chattered. Dad had rubber treads bolted to the wheels to stop this. There is a tractor at the Minden Hills museum just like it.*

October 29: Moss Kellett Died. *I believe Moss owned the Dominion Hotel for a while. He died suddenly at his home.*

1951, January: I milked three cows night and morning and walked two miles to school. *Because of mother's illness, and the fact that there were three cows milking at the time, I would milk every morning. Dad would feed the cows and do the other chores but he never learned to milk and never milked a cow in his life.*

February 9: Fifty-Eight Below Zero at 7:00 AM This Morning Walked to School. *Cold and clear, very still, no wind at all.*

February 24: Dad and Uncle Herb Wired House at Lot 30 for Hydro. *Floyd and Marg were planning to get married and live there, so Dad and Uncle Herb wired the house for hydro.*

March 21: Mabel Married Murray Hewitt. *They went to Lindsay and were married. Floyd and Marg stood up for them. This marriage lasted fifty-two years and ended with Murray's death in August 2003.*

April 20: Minden Flooded. *Control dams were not in place and Minden flooded quite often in the spring. The main street was completely under water. The river nearly reached the bottom of the iron bridge that was there at the time. Dr. Jamieson's office was on the river's edge, at the corner, past where Keaney Chrysler is now. They had built a board-walk to the office, so patients could get there. I vividly recall watching Floyd carry Mother across that narrow walkway so she could get her shots.*

June 12: I Bought a Little Pig from George Kellett. *I decided that I would raise a pig and sell it in the fall, so I went to George Kellett's and looked them over. I bought one for five dollars and brought it home in a bran sack, in the carrier of my bicycle. When it came time to market the pig that fall, the bottom had fallen out of the pork market. I had to sell the bags the feed came in to break even. Story of my life!*

June 28: Finished School. *In spite of having the whooping cough all winter and missing a lot of school days, I passed into grade nine with 98% honours. I did not go to high school.*

July 9: Cut Lumber at Les Hagen's. *Les had a little sawmill. We often hauled logs there to be cut into lumber. He lived on what was recently renamed 'Vick Road' off County Road 1.*

August 7: Dad and I Started to Raise SS No 6 School. *SS No 6 School was at Miner's bay. The highway now bypasses it completely. It was sorely in need of a new foundation. The tender went out for the contract, but as so often happened, no one in the area was prepared to do the work. We were deep into our grain harvest, but the board asked Dad to consider doing it. He was a trustee, so they waived any possibility of conflict of interest and told him to go ahead. We borrowed some building jacks and gathered up every jack we could find. Then we went to Bagshaw Lumber and borrowed many old railroad ties to build cribs. It was a difficult job. There were two pail-a-day toilets attached to the building as well as a porch. Someone had added these and they were liable to separate from the main building. We had it jacked up close to the required height, and were nearly ready to begin laying the forms for the footings. I was under the building when Dad yelled, "Ray! Get the hell out from there, the damned thing is heading for the woods." I scrambled out from under the building and we stood and watched as the south east corner shifted nearly a foot to the south. The ties that we had it sitting on had checked, and had humped in the centre. When these rolled until the edges were flat against each other, the building stopped moving. We simply moved the footings to the buildings' new location and built the wall under it there. The owners of that property now can tell everyone that their building was nearly a foot farther north.. Pictured on the right is Mother standing to the south of the school just before we let it down on its new foundation.*

September 18: Floyd married Margaret Coulter. *They were married in the United Church in Minden. Taylor Hogg and Marg's sister Francis stood up for them. They had a dance upstairs in the Minden*

Arena, which was downtown. There was no such thing as amplification. Music was usually played for dances by a bunch of local people making up a band. I don't recall who all played for the dance, but I do remember Maurice Cooper singing "Show me the way to go home" in the parking lot as we were leaving. Marg and Floyd went west to see Aunt Mabel for their honeymoon.

September 25:   Grandma Dugan Died. *Mother's Mother. She lived at Lochlin. She was a kind and loving soul. I missed her.*

October 6:   Rode Disc Plough. *A regular plough would not work very well behind a tractor on our farm because the rocks were too close to the surface. A disc plough would, as the discs would lift the plough out of the ground and swing it aside, away from the obstacle. Dad purchased a two-furrow disc plough. He also installed a breakaway hitch that would disconnect the plough from the tractor should a solid obstacle be encountered. He tried to plough with no one on the seat of the plough but found that the disc needed to be lifted too often for this to work, so there had to be someone on the seat to work the levers. Guess who that was? When the discs would encounter a stone, the seat I was on would be hoisted two feet straight up in the air. As the disc rolled around the rock, it would go straight sideways for two feet. Then, as the implement realigned itself behind the tractor, it would drop and swing back the other way. There was only one lever to hang on to and nothing else. I spent a great deal of time picking myself up from freshly turned soil and running to catch up with the plough.. Dad was watching where he was going and often did not even know I had been pitched off. I would see a stone coming, and sometimes I was successful in clearing it. Other times, the hitch would disconnect as I was at the highest point and I would drop back with a pile-driving thud. I think I might have been six inches taller, if it had not been for this plough.*

October 8:   Threshed at John Hulbig's, and Fred Barry's.

***Pail-a-Day Toilet.** This was not a pleasant thing to look at, but it worked very well. It consisted of a regular toilet bowl connected to a 10" copper pipe. This pipe dropped directly into a buried septic tank. From the other end of the tank protruded a 4" weeping tile which ran out under the ground about 10' from the tank.*

Once a day a pail of water was poured down the toilet and a small block of yeast cake once a week.

A Tight Squeeze

Dad had me take his place with the neighbours threshing, so he could work elsewhere. We had found the day before that the threshers would finish at John and Andy Harrison's before noon.

I walked the three miles and waited on a rock by the gate at John Hulbig's farm for them to arrive. John's threshing was small, so we were soon finished there. When we left for Fred Barry's, I climbed onto the back of the separator to hitch a ride. When we arrived at Fred's, the gate was closed, so I jumped off to open it. I hadn't realized how fast the machine was moving and nearly fell as I ran full out to regain my balance. By the time, I had regained my balance I had run through the ditch and into the gate ahead of the tractor. Gordon Sharpless, who owned the threshing machine, was a quiet man. No one ever heard him raise his voice. He got off that tractor, asked me if I was all right, then he gave me the worst scolding I had ever received.

We moved to our place that evening and put Gord's mill in the barn for the night.

Gord looked at the mows*. We had a bumper crop that year. Dad had sown oats in two eight acre fields at the other place, and our barn was full with both mows packed with hay to three or four feet above the beams. Then we put the oats all the way to the rafters in the west mow and filled the scaffold to the peak. The only space that was left for straw was about six feet in the middle of the east mow.

"You have a fairly long set* this year Milt," Gord said as he stood looking up.

"I figure about four and a half to five hours," Dad said.

"Looks like you will have to put some straw in a stack outside."

"I sure hope not. It's a pain in the ass digging straw out of the snow in the winter every time you need a little bedding."

He parked the WD9 International tractor beside the ramp to the barn floor. He had a new tractor that was the envy of all farmers north of Lindsay. It was large. It had the same chassis and engine as a TD9 bulldozer, but with wheels and no blade. It was also the same as the stationary SD9 diesel engine that drove Bagshaw's mill.

It was dark when we got to the house. John Hulbig had arrived and John Harrison came driving Gord's car. They were about to leave, when Dad called out, "Just a minute John. Will you pick Nelson Archer up in the morning and bring him here with you?"

"I'll be glad to Milt." John replied.

"Okay John. Thanks."

Gord got in his car and went home to Gelert.

The next morning around six-thirty, Gord arrived. just as John Hulbig drove into the yard with Nelson Archer and Fred Barry in his car. Floyd drove in, they all got out, got their pitchforks from the car, and headed for the barn. Dawn was just beginning to break.

Elmer and George Kellett hadn't grown much grain that year and had cut theirs green for feed, so they were not threshing. This meant that they wouldn't be changing hands with Dad, so he had hired Nelson to help.

We started to erect the table where Fred would stand to feed the machine. Gord blocked the wheels of the mill and wound the big belt off the reel. He backed the tractor to the end of the belt and lined it up. He yelled, "All clear, all clear from the machine," He gave it a whirl, to check it for belt alignment. He had done this many times before and had it dead on the first time. He shut it off and went into the barn to set up the grain blower.

Fred climbed up onto the table and looked up into the mows. All he could see was grain.

"Where to hell are you going to put the straw Milt?" he asked?

62

"There's a bit of room in the east mow."

"You'll be putting some outside first then, until we get space on the scaffold."

"No, I'll put my boys in the straw mow. They will tramp it all in there if anybody can."

"It looks like it is going to be damned tight. How in hell are they going to get up there, I can't see the east mow at all from here?"

"They'll scramble up the blower when it is in place."

John and Nelson had climbed onto the mill and had taken the pin out of the straw blower, so it could be spun around into place. They raised it to the proper angle, pushed the nozzle through the scaffold toward the east mow, straightened it out and replaced the pin. Then they wound the telescopic extension right to its full length. It barely reached the mow.

Floyd and I straddled the blower, and using the control ropes for grip, we squeezed through the opening and into the straw mow. Dad had taken two boards from the end of the barn to give us some air. There was hardly enough height for us to stand at the peak.

I took a look out from one of these openings. The dawn showed signs of a bright day. The autumn sun was just beginning to break the horizon. Frost covered the roof of the horse stable directly below, and the cool fall breeze danced leaves around the well house. A rooster crowed in the henhouse and I could hear the cattle in the pasture behind the barn. I knew that the next few hours would be dirty, draughty, and hard, but I was surrounded by family, friends and neighbours. I knew all these men well and knew they could be trusted. Life was good.

In those days, all threshers wore handkerchiefs around their necks to stop chaff and dirt from going down their shirts, and another around their faces to cover their noses and mouths. Long sleeves, with tight cuffs, were a must. Threshing was dirty in all areas, but the straw mow was the worst. That damned blower threw everything at you, from thistles and straw to ragweed, and lots of dust. I have seen dust pour from the cracks in a barn until you could hardly see the barn. However, the worst was smut. Smut forms on the stocks of grain when it has been put in the mow a bit damp. It is a type of mould. The blue grey dust from it is very hard on the lungs. There were times when those working in the straw mow could barely see for all the dust and smut. This stuff itches like mad.

The hay had settled quite a lot since it had been put in there nearly three months before, so there was about two feet of space between the top of the hay and the rafters all the way down to the walls.

Floyd said, "I will throw the straw to you and you tramp as much as you can down between the rafters."

We could hear Nels and John take their place on the scaffold, ready to feed sheaves of grain to Fred on the table, where he would feed them into the mill.

The engine started. The blower swayed in the opening as the mill began to shake, and then everything settled down as it gained speed. We tightened our handkerchiefs, and pulled down our hats. Floyd went to the blower and pulled the hood back, allowing the first straw to be blown as far back into the mow as possible. It first hit the hayfork track and fell into the middle. He adjusted it so it went down into the space between the rafters. I waited until he had filled that space and had swung it toward the next space. Then I stuck my fingers between the roof straps and the shingles and swung myself on my back, using my feet to push the straw all the way to the wall. I scrambled back up and did it again. Then I went to the next space where he had already filled it and did the same. I could hardly see Floyd for dust now, as the engine roared and the mill chomped on a steady flow of grain. We continued to fill the rafters until the spaces were tramped solid with straw. Then we filled the peak starting at the back and tramped it with all our might.

Just as the mow was filled to the front, we could see a glimmer of light from where Nels and John were working. Then some sheaves fell away and I could see the men through the dust. Nels had been systematically taking grain from an area that would allow us to move onto the scaffold and fill it up as they emptied it into the mill. I could now see John throwing grain down through the scaffold and Fred's head and shoulders as he fed the mill. I slid on my back down the edge of the hay and wound up on my ass on the scaffold where it was now bare.

"G'Day," Nels said as he rhythmically forked sheaves to John.

Floyd turned the blower toward where I was. There was no room now to manoeuvre the hood, so he just moved it to the position where it did the most good, then we started forking the straw into every space available and tramping it. We were tight to the sheaves now. Nels took sheaves clearing scaffold floor and we would have to move right in and fill it. Sometimes the straw would roll down and cover a few sheaves. He would carefully pull them out and pitch them to John.

We worked our way across the scaffold from east to west, carefully maintaining as steep a slant as would stay, down to the feed table, by packing the straw as tight as possible and shaping it with our forks.

When the sheaves were completely removed from the blower hole on the west side of the scaffold that we had covered with a board, when the sheaves were put there in August, we removed the board and Floyd yelled, "Blower change."

Nels stopped pitching to John, who looked up at him inquisitively when the sheaves stopped coming.

"He wants to change the blower over to the other hole now," he told John.

"Oh," John turned to Fred, who was now looking up at him, wondering what had happened to stop the regular supply of sheaves. "We have to change the blower." he explained.

Fred turned to try to get Gord's attention.

The engine soon slowed and the mill chugged to a stop. Floyd had removed the board from the west hole and passed it over to me, standing on loose straw to my waist at the blower. It was soon removed, and I used the board to cover the east hole in the scaffold. While they were taking the blower down, and putting it back up through the other hole, with Floyd's help, I tramped some of the loose straw into the space where the blower had been. I then tramped a passage from the blower's new location to the empty space.

While all this was going on, Nels and John forked some sheaves away from the straw and piled them near the feedhole. The engine started, and the mill shook as it gained speed once more.

Floyd directed the blower toward where it had been before, and we tramped that cavity full to the rafters.

As we left the scaffold area and began to remove the sheaves from the west mow, it became increasingly difficult for Nels to pitch the sheaves far enough for John to reach them comfortably. Floyd started to pitch sheaves and I worked harder, as I attempted to keep the straw packed to the roof alone. I was away up near the rafters when I heard Nels say, "Yay," loudly. He moved over closer to the pile of sheaves. I then noticed that John had moved closer to Nels and Fred was now up on the scaffold feeding the table. Then I saw what had happened. Doward was now on the feed table feeding the mill. He and Hazel had dropped the kids off at school and had come to help. Hazel would be helping Mother with preparations to feed this bunch.

A little way into the west mow Nels suddenly yelled, "Smut!"

A white haze rose around his feet, as we all tightened the handkerchiefs around our mouths and noses and breathed solely through our noses. The blower belched out a blue haze, as we worked through a patch where the grain had not been absolutely dry when it was put there. The damp stalks had and formed a mould-like growth on them, but the grain would be okay.

The west sheaf mow was emptied slowly, maintaining an angle toward the feedhole and allowing us to tramp straw right up to within feet of the edge of the sheaves. Finally, all the sheaves were gone, except for a few at the feedhole. Nels and John then turned to help us, as they were not needed in the sheaves. Fred kept feeding Doward, until they were all gone.

I was away up at the peak of the barn, still tramping like everything, as Floyd and the others kept pushing straw up to me. I didn't know that the sheaf mow was now empty. I heard Floyd call my name and looked out over the straw. There was a slope down to the feedhole. Floyd was a little way down from me on the slope.

John and Fred had climbed down onto the floor of the barn, and had removed the feed table from the mill. They were shovelling the chaff from the floor, below where the table had been, into the mill, so the oats that had fallen from the sheaves during the whole operation, would be fanned out and go into the granary.

Nels said to Floyd, "You had better slide down here so I can catch you if you can't get stopped here." He put his hand up on a rafter and braced his feet against the beam.

Floyd slid down and was able to catch his feet on the beam. He stood up, and just as he was turning to me, I saw Dad look up past them as the mill slowed to a stop.

"Where is Ray?" he asked.

"I haven't seen him in hours," Nels answered, jokingly.

Seeing me away up at the peak, Dad started to laugh. "All I can see are his eyes," he said. I didn't know that my face was completely covered with dust.

Dad put a ladder up through the feed hole, and Floyd climbed down.

Nels looked up at me and said, "Are you coming or are you going to stay there for the winter?"

"It's a hell of a long way down from here Nels." I said

"Come on I'll catch you."

I started to climb down, but the straw gave way below my feet. I fell on my back and slid down the straw. I seemed to gain speed as I approached Nels. A bunch of straw went ahead of me right through the hole and down onto the floor. Nels reached out and caught my arm, as I passed him, heading for the floor about fifteen or twenty feet below. He stood me on my feet and said, "Here now wait for me."

I said, "Thanks Nels."

He climbed down over the beam and onto the ladder. I followed him onto the floor, where Dad was waiting.

"You got it all in guys. Good for you," Dad said looking at both Floyd and I.

"Not quite," I said, looking at the pile of straw that had preceded me down the slope and out of the mow, "We had that much left over."

Floyd had removed the handkerchief from his face. The part of his face which was covered was fairly white but the rest of his face was black.

"You look funny," I said as I removed mine.

"You too," he said as he turned toward the granary.

The table had been stowed in its place, on the side of the mill. The blower had been retrieved from the scaffold hole, and was now lying in its cradle on top of the machine. The belt had been re-rolled onto its reel. I held the pole up as Gord backed the tractor up to it, and dropped the draw pin into place. I placed the safety pin into it, and stepped out of the way.

"Thanks Ray," Gord said. Then he yelled "All clear." He eased the mill out of the barn and stopped in the yard.

He and I walked through the thresh floor to the granary, where the men had gathered. The granary was full to the door. Dad had placed some old doors across the opening as the grain filled the room, and it was full right to the ceiling. There were several full bags sitting beside the door. He had bagged the last few bushels. Fred scooped up a handful from the bin and let it sift through his hand.

"God Milt, it is really filled out too," referring to the fullness of the grains of oats.

"It's a good crop, Fred," Dad replied as he headed for the door.

As we went outside, the sun was shining brightly, but a cool October breeze came out of the north west. A flock of geese flew southward, far overhead. "Go you cowardly bastards," Fred said looking up.

"I don't blame them," Nels added, "I would go too, if I had wings."

When we got to the well, pitch forks were leaning against the well house, as the rest of the men had removed the handkerchiefs from their necks. They were dipping them into the water trough, using them to remove as much of the chaff and dust from their face and necks as they could and washing their hands. Gord passed us with the mill and stopped in the house yard. I looked at my watch. It was twenty to twelve.

Gord was checking the mill over and joined us as we passed him.

Dad was at the door of the house, as we approached it. He reached in his pocket and pulled out his wallet.

"How much do I owe you, Gord," he said as Gord approached him.

"The setting is seven dollars, and three and a half hours at two dollars and a half so that comes to fifteen dollars and seventy five cents." Dad paid him.

"What about you Nels."

"Is a couple of dollars okay Milt?" Dad paid him.

"How about you and John, Fred?"

"No Milt, we changed hands," they both said almost in unison.

"But you only got the lad. I couldn't be there. That is not the same."

"It is as far as I'm concerned, the lad is as good as any man," Fred said.

"That goes for me too," said John. Hearing this, I smiled proudly to myself.

We went into the kitchen.

"How did the grain turn out?" Mother asked Dad.

"Great. The granary is full and some in bags. It is good quality, too."

"That's good. The straw must have all gone into the barn as I didn't' see any being blown into the yard."

"All except what Ray brought out with him when he left," John laughed as he sat down.

"I noticed a blue haze once. There must have been some smut," Mother said.

"Just a little at the edge of the west mow. Not bad though," Nels answered as he walked past her to the table.

The table was laid out with huge plates of meat, bowls of gravy and mashed potatoes. A large bowl of carrots, and one of mashed turnip. On the cupboard behind us were several pumpkin, raisin, and apple pies. A pot of tea was simmering on the stove, and pitchers of water were placed in the middle of the table. Mother, Hazel, and Mabel waited to serve whatever was needed. Men heaped their plates more then once, and then had at least one piece of pie. At fourteen years of age, I had taken the place of a man in the barn, and also at the table.

We went outside and Gord headed for his machine.

"Floyd and Doward will take your car to Bert Schroter's for you," Dad said. He looked to where it had been parked in the morning, and seeing it was gone, he asked, "Where to hell did it go?"

Gord laughed, as he climbed onto the tractor. "Bert came this morning to see what time we would likely be finished here. Roy was with him. He took it back with him. Thanks Milt."

Gord started the WD9, reached down and released the brake, and drove out of the yard. He turned south and went over the hill toward his next job.

"That's one hell of a tractor," Doward exclaimed. "Did you hear how that thing runs, just a steady stream of power. I wonder what it would take to stop that thing. Did you notice it never laboured once while we were threshing? Not even when I overloaded the mill enough for the governors to stop the feed belt. God! What a tractor."

We all went to the barn.

The fanning mill, the wagon, and the binder had been put outside while the threshing machine was here. We carried the fanning mill into the barn and shovelled the chaff from the floor into it. We saved the oats which fanned out into a bag. Then we fanned the other seed that had been shifted out onto the floor, under the thresh machine. We bagged it in a flour bag. We pushed the binder and wagon onto the barn floor where they would stay for the winter.

Threshing was over for another year, except for the dust and smut we would cough up for the next three days or more.

The t*hresher machine operators that I recall at our place were* (not necessarily in proper sequence).

John Kernohan. (Steam Engine)
Jim Minaker (Steam Engine)
.   *Gord Sharpless, (WD9 Diesel)*
Roy Kernohan (WD4 Gas)

The man who fed the machine had to be a very responsible person. It was not unknown for a loose fork to go through the mill, which would result in great damage, and heavy costs.

Every time the mill was overloaded by feeding too much grain at once, the governors would kick the feed belt out of gear, and the oats would go over the cylinder and into the straw mow. If it were under-fed, the threshing would last longer, costing the farmer more. A good steady line of sheaves going into the mill, end to end, headfirst, was ideal. For this reason, only certain men were selected to feed the machine. The owner of the threshing machine had the right to refuse any feeder who he felt was not suitable and to request a feeder from the crew.

The person who threw sheaves down from the mow to the feed table could be a great help to the feeder. They tried to have the sheaves land on the table, at the feet of the feeder, in the same place every time, with the head toward the mill. This allowed the feeder to maintain a rhythmic motion. However, there were times when the sheave would glance off a beam, or other obstruction, and would land right on the feed belt. If this happened, the feeder would attempt to spear the wayward sheaf with his fork, and hold it, until there was a suitable space for it to go through in proper order. Two sheaves on top of one another would overload the mill. Two sheaves side by side were also not desirable. However, these things were allowed, if there was any chance that his fork may go through in an attempt to rectify the problem.

Feeders in our neighbourhood were; Fred Barry, Doward Johnson, Nelson Archer, Dad, and later myself. I remember following the threshers into other neighbourhoods, as a hired hand, if I were available. In most cases, I would be chosen to feed the mill. This was a great advantage as it kept me away from most of the dust.

The owner of the farm, where threshing was taking place, would always be in charge of the granary, as he would want to put oats of different quality, into separate bins for storage.

There is a threshing mill, much like the one featured in this chapter on display in the grounds at the Minden Hills museum.

The little farms are gone now from Haliburton County. The only ones that remain, are along the banks of the Gull River, south of Minden, and a few around lakes, where the soil is deeper and more fertile. Our farm, between Minden and Kinmount, has been allowed to grow up entirely. I contacted the present owner early in 2004 and took a walk through the fields. Trees with trunks a foot through now stand in what were once cultivated fields. The barn is now in the middle of a forest.

Any grain that is grown now is cut and threshed in the field, in one operation, with a combine. The straw is now baled with a baler. No one tramps straw any more. No one feels the itch of thistles down their neck, or the burning in the lungs from smut. No one coughs up chunks of dust for days. But then, no one feels the elation of hearing the mill slow down, knowing that it is over, at least for another set. How well I remember the camaraderie of being among those men who cared for me. Or the trust that I felt when I knew that Nels would catch me at the verge of a fall. It was a privilege to sit at the table, among men I admired, and eat pumpkin pie. I sit here today, with tears in my eyes, as I go remember a hard time, but a pleasant time as well.

Fred, Nels, Gord, Doward and Dad are all gone now. But the memory of that threshing brings them back to me.

GLOSSARY

Blower- This was a tube, about eight inches in diameter, that led from the back of the mill into the mows. This actual blower itself was a large fan that blew straw and chaff through the tube. It hinged in the middle by pulling a pin on one side, which allowed it to be swung in small areas. Then, with the end of it headed into the mow, the tube was straightened and the pin reinstalled. There were wheels and cranks to assist in this operation. It could be raised, lowered, and swung with these wheels. It was telescopic, and could be extended to almost twice its transport length. It had control ropes, to turn the hood at the end, and to pull the hood back, allowing straw to be directed anywhere you needed it. However, when it was just peeking into the mow, as in this instance, the hood was turned by hand. Straw could not be allowed to build up in front of it, or it would plug. Damp straw could occasionally plug the blower, and it would sometimes be plugged when a lazy worker held a fork in front of it, wanting a rest. When it plugged, a major shut down was required, as the mill had to be opened and all the straw forked away.

Feed table- This was a platform, or what we call a scaffold now, that clipped to the side of the mill and had legs that reached to the barn floor on the other side. The mill was positioned so the table would reach from the wall of the mow to the mill, providing a good area for the feeder. It would move with the mill, and was sometimes hard to ride while the mill swayed as it gained speed. There was an area on the side of the mill for it to be transported from set to set.

Mow- The word was used in those days all the time in reference to what we would now call a hay loft.

Set- Threshers would charge a set fee for the first hour, which was referred to as a set. This was charged to give the mill owner compensation for short thrashings. The rest of the threshing was charged by the hour. The complete threshing would also be referred to as set as in 'a three hour set' or 'a five hour set'.

Scaffold- This can be a little confusing. The scaffold referred to in this chapter, is an area directly above the barn floor. Poles reached across, from beam to beam, above the barn floor. They were pushed back against the wall when not in use to allow crops to be hoisted into the mows at the side. If they were needed, (in a good crop year), they were brought out to cover the area above the beams providing an extra area for crop storage. They were usually arranged to provide a blower hole for threshing and were usually used to store grain.

Entries in Our Diaries
From October 20th 1951 to November 29th 1952

1951, October 20: Demonstration Here of IEL Chainsaws. Floyd Bought One. *This was a large one-man saw. It was purple metallic.*

October 22: Started working at Kilcoo Camp preparing things for winter. *My First Real Job*

October 22 Floyd Moved to Woodview to Cut Timber for Bagshaw Lumber. *Bruce Bagshaw had a timber limits at Woodview, near Buckhorn Ontario. Floyd and Marg, Dad, and Marg's Brother Harold Coulter went to take the logs out. They stayed in a farmhouse on the property and Marg cooked. The horses were trucked to Woodview but Harold drove them back when the work was completed. He left there at 6:30 A.M. on January 8th 1952 and travelled 55 miles with the team and sleighs. He stayed the night at Faulkner's, south of Kinmount, where they had room to stable the team, and arrived home at 12:30 noon on January9th. The shoulders of the highways were usually snow packed, with just a bit of bare and sanded area in the centre, so sleighs had a place to travel. There was quite a lot of horse traffic on the highways, in this area, so no one paid much attention to them.*

October 25: Cut Wood for Basil Hewitt with Two-Man Saw. *Doward ran the saw and I was on the little end. I spent the day climbing over brush and carrying this damned thing with the exhaust blowing in my face. When I arrived home that night, I was so sick I thought I would die, and there were times when I wished I could. Mother made me chicken broth with raw onion and gave me a slice of raw onion as well. Then, she put me to bed with a dose of Rawleigh's Red Liniment in hot water with a spoonful of honey. As she left my room, she stated in no uncertain terms, "If Doward ever asks you to do that again, tell him to talk to me." I did operate the saw many times after that, but it never bothered me the same.*

November 7: Snowed Ten Inches. *Snow came early sometimes.*

1952, January 21: Dad and I to Lindsay, Dad Bought 1948 Chev Stylemaster. *This was a good car. This model had a very stiff gear-shift lever. When Dad found out that some had a vacuum assist, he asked Fee motors why his did not, and was told that it was an option available at extra cost. He didn't think it was worth the money, so we just forced it from gear to gear. The car was the last one Dad owned, and was sold at the auction, after Dad died, seven years later.*

April 29: Mabel had baby boy 7 pound 8 and half ounces named AJ.

June 16: Started to Work for Bagshaw Lumber Piling Slabs

May 18: I bought 1950 Fargo Truck My First Vehicle

October 21 Dad Bought Cockshutt 60 Tractor from Russ Benson and Rod Shewfelt.

October 6: Worked 18 hours Planing 13,000 feet of Lumber at Bagshaw Lumber in Lindsay.

October 11: Gareth Cut Foot I was Home for Thanksgiving so I took Him to Doctor.

October 15: Hurricane Hazel

November 29: Fired from Bagshaw's. Jack Wiles said I was dead from the arse hole both ways

Bagshaw's Mill

Bruce L. Bagshaw came into the area when I was very small. The first I remember of his presence was a truck that had 'Hotton and Bagshaw' on the doors. I remember activity near Denna Lake at one time, but I can't remember just where, what or why. I do remember the mill being at Lawrence Terranie's, on Lackey's Creek, near Kilcoo Camp. Then it was moved to it's final destination, three miles south of Minden, on Highway 35, where Prentice Power Sports is now located.

Bruce also planted pine seedlings in the field next to the mill yard in 1950. That field is now part of the subdivision known as 'Lutterworth Pines'.

He was an honest little man, who didn't pay high wages for the time, but your money was always there. He created a lot of much needed work, and in his own words at a reunion in 1987, "I put food on a lot of tables, not a lot of food, but food none the less."

He was always in a hurry. He drove Chev cars, and had a habit of leaving the car in gear, turning off the ignition, opening the door, and stepping out before the car actually came to a full stop.

I had worked for Kilcoo Camp from April 25 until June 14, 1952, burning brush for fifty cents an hour.

On June 16, I was hanging around home being bored, when Bruce drove into the yard. As usual, he was out of his car before it had actually come to a full stop, and approached the door in great haste. He tipped his hat to Mother as she appeared inside the screen door with me right behind her.

"Good morning Mrs Miller is Milt in?"

"No... He's working at Kilcoo Camp."

"Damn, I was afraid of that. I started the mill this morning, and need help badly. Okay Mrs Miller. Thanks anyway." He turned and was out of the yard in a flash.

In a very few minutes, he drove in again. Mother and I went to the door as he approached.

Without any greeting this time he said, "Mrs Miller, could the young fellow there work in the yard piling slabs, maybe? Now, he is too young to be covered by Workman's Compensation, but he shouldn't be at a lot of risk in the slab yard, and Floyd is driving the slab truck."

"Oh ... he will be alright then Bruce."

Looking past her at me he said, "Do you want to do that then Ray?"

I wanted to work and was excited. I said "Sure do."

"Then come with me right now." He said turning toward the car, and I followed.

As we turned onto the road, he said, "Thanks for coming Ray, it helps me a lot. You will be piling slabs and tying edgings into bundles. You will be paid five dollars a day, and your dinner. If a married man with children to feed were to apply for work, he will take your place immediately. Okay?"

I cheerfully agreed to this.

When we arrived at the mill, he drove me right to the slab yard, where Floyd was piling slabs right off the truck.

Without even saying good morning, Floyd said, "I am going to dump the rest of this, as I am running behind now. You pile the rest of the slabs on the pile. Then put the edgings in that hopper there and tie them with the cord hanging on the end." He raised the hoist on the red 1947 Chev truck with no doors, and sped off toward the mill. By the time, I had finished piling slabs and tying the edgings, he was back with another load. I climbed up into the truck box and we threw slabs off the truck onto the pile, with Floyd watching the slab hopper at the mill intently. Suddenly he said,

"Okay, I have to go now," and he climbed into the cab, dumped almost half the load, and was gone. This procedure was repeated several times, until I heard the mill slow down and stop. It was time for dinner.

We left the truck in the slab yard and walked across a pathway shortcut to the camp. We went to the bunkhouse, where men were gathering from the mill and were getting water from the nearby well to wash outside the door.

Floyd said "Did you bring a towel and some soap."

"No."

"Well use mine today, but don't forget to bring one tomorrow."

We washed up and went into the bunkhouse. Men were sitting on their beds and some were kidding around with Floyd. I already knew Jack Barnhart, one of the truck drivers, and he said, "Come over here and sit on my bed if you want." Just then, the bell rang at the cookery. We all headed for it.

Dust flew as two of the log trucks, that had been dumping logs onto the rollway, came charging across the valley and right to the gas pumps near the office. I knew both drivers, when they got out, and came running to the cookery door behind me. They were well-seasoned truck drivers, Keith and Wren Hughes. Before I could think Wren picked me up, all 129 pounds of me, and threw me into a nearby pile of sawdust and said, "Welcome to camp life kid."

Everyone laughed, as I picked myself up and, brushing myself off, I said, "How much do you weigh you big bastard?"

"185 pounds of solid muscle. Why?"

"If I ever get to weigh 185 pounds I will hunt you down, wherever you are, and kick the shit out of you." Everyone laughed loudly as we entered the dinning room to eat.

Mrs. Jean Stewart (the millwright's wife) cooked for Bagshaw all the time the camps were there. She was the kind of cook who could feed you the same thing, day after day, and you enjoyed it immensely every time. Bruce believed that a well-fed man worked harder, so he always provided the best ingredients. There were always thick slices of beef, smothered in gravy, with two choices of vegetable, potatoes, bread, and lots of butter, milk, coffee, and tea. This was followed by three kinds of home-made pies, and juicy syrupy tarts for which men would die. I was a fifteen-year-old boy. I had worked hard all morning, and boy did I eat!

"The kid can take the place of a man at the table," Wren teased.

Bruce and Wes Allen came in from the office and before Bruce sat down at his place at the end of the table he said, "I guess most of you know the lad who is trying to devour the whole plate of tarts. For those who don't, he's Floyd's brother, Ray."

Keith Hughes spoke up, "I know him, He's a pain in the ass guys, believe me." The rest all mumbled some kind of greeting between mouthfuls of pie and gulps of tea or coffee.

Men trickled back to the bunkhouse where they lay on their bunks picking their teeth, burping and making other contented sounds.

Most of these fellows I had known all my life. There was Ken Bowron, Daryl Thompson, John Harrison, Keith Hughes, Wren Hughes, Jack Barnhart, and Nelson Archer. Others I had met before were Ted Johnson and Stan Scarlet. I would get to know Stan Stewart, Jack Wiles, Herb McGee, Bill McFarland, Charlie Stewart, Harold McFarland, Harold Suggitt, Morley Pickard, Jim Casey, Vic Robinson, and Glen Briggs. These were all very willing and capable men. Glad to have work, they never complained.

The sawyer and millwright never came into the bunkhouse at noon, but went straight from the cookery to the mill. There, the sawyer would file the big saw and the millwright would do millwright things. At five to one, the big diesel motor started and everyone hurried off to his post.

The day's work ended when the mill shut down at five o'clock. Floyd drove me home. The following day I rode my bike to Floyd's, and hitched a ride with him to be at work by seven.

On Saturday morning about nine-thirty or so, I saw a young fellow playing along by the cookery. When Floyd returned, I asked him who it was. "That's Stan and Jean's boy, Jackie," he said, referring to the cook and her husband the millwright, Stan and Jean Stewart. The next load brought another surprise. Every job has a perk here and there, and this one was in the form of a little blond girl. Riding with Floyd was Joyce Stewart, Stan and Jean's daughter. She didn't go back when Floyd left but stayed, sitting on the slab pile, talking with me while I piled slabs. She was very pretty, and I just couldn't help but notice there was a lot of girl inside those tight fitting jeans. Life was good. Good God! Life was good.

Bruce paid every Saturday, but always one week late. The following Saturday I picked up a pay envelope with a cheque for $27.22 in it. The slip read:

5 1/2 days @ $5.00 = $27.50.
UIC Stamp   .28
Total $27.22

In a few days, we got into some straight hardwood, so things slowed down for us in the slab yard. Floyd, knowing that I had driven the truck around home, began to let me take the truck, empty the sawdust bin, and bring back more slabs, every now and then. I was proud to do this.

As I passed the office with a load of slabs on the morning of August 4, the foreman Jack Wiles stopped me and said, "You like driving this thing, don't you?"

"Yes I do"

"Well, the job is yours. When you get to the slab yard, tell Floyd I need him in the log yard. You should be alright, as long as we are in hardwood, but if you get behind, just dump a load or two over there against the woods." The next day Gord Ruttle was hired to help me. I drove the slab truck every time I worked for Bagshaw from then on.

On May 21,st 1953, Bruce announced at dinner that he had purchased 500,000 feet of softwood from the International Cooperage in Eagle Lake. It had to be transported immediately. The Cooperage had closed and this was the left over stock. Bagshaw's four trucks were designated to haul the wood to the mill, along with the two Leary Brothers, Nelson, and Dean. Floyd went to run the jammer. These small spruce logs began to arrive late that afternoon.

These logs had been cut for making barrelheads, not lumber. The result was that many only produced one two by four, two at the most. They were cut live, I was swamped with thin slabs and lots of sawdust, and trimmer ends.

On March 18th, 1954, Jack Barnhart drove into Bagshaw's yard with the biggest truck I had ever seen. A green 20 ton Mack, belonging to some guy in Buffalo, New York. It was the first tandem in the country with a four-wheel type trailer. It had been brought to the new yard in Lindsay and he drove it from there, as the driver was afraid of the roads beyond there.

I went with them, when the rest of the operation was moved to Lindsay on May 12th, 1954. It still operates under the name of The Co-Op. The mill shut down at noon that day forever.

On Sunday, May 16, 1954, Dad moved me to the home of my second cousins, Marie and Walter Bacon, behind the studio of CKLY radio, to board, until I could find other arrangements. On Monday, May 17, I drove Bagshaw's light delivery truck, and that evening I purchased my first vehicle, a 1950 Fargo pick-up truck for $850.00 cash. There was no sales tax in those days.

The next night I drove it home, to show my family, and stayed overnight. The following morning I drove back, to be at work by seven.

That night, I moved to the home of Roy and Muriel Hadley, at 41 St. Peter Street, to board where Daryl Thomson was boarding at the time.

I worked right along with the rest all summer, driving every truck they owned, delivering large and small loads throughout Lindsay and the surrounding area.

On October 6, 1954, that same Green Mack tandem truck that Jack drove last March, was sitting in the yard when I went to work. There was an old long box Dodge truck on the trailer. The pickup was green, with one black door and one black fender. The driver wanted to know where he could unload the pickup. They told him to back up to a gravel ramp that had been put in the yard earlier that year, to assist in unloading machinery for the new planeing mill . He unloaded it, and left for the mill in Minden, to get a load of lumber. This time he wasn't afraid to drive it there himself. At quitting time that evening, some of us were asked to come back after supper, as that truck would be back and the load was to be planed and re-sawed into bevel siding through the night. It arrived with 13,000 feet of two-inch pine on the truck and trailer together. He rolled the trailer load off onto the ground and went to a motel for the night driving off in his pickup.

Jack Wiles said, "Okay Ray, take the trailer around to the other end."

"Me?"

"You're the only truck driver here, and you will build the load as it arrives from the mill."

I took the trailer around to the other end, where the finished product would be coming up a ramp from the re-sawing machine. I unhitched and returned the truck to the other end where the load could be rolled off, as soon as the lumber on the ground was finished. When the trailer load had been planed and re-sawed, and I had piled it onto the trailer, I chained it down and went around to the other end, as the rest of the guys rolled the load off the truck. I brought the truck around and pulled the trailer out of the way. Then I backed the truck to the end of the ramp. We worked all night. They gave me the next day off, so I drove home to Minden and rested there.

Author's Note *There was no space on the trailer for that old green pickup truck with the lumber, so it was left on that gravel ramp for years, and years.*

As I drove to work on Friday, October 15th, the sky was very black. Ugly clouds were coming in low and seemed to be churning. Wind was building and it was quite dark. One of the International trucks was in the shed with, what I recognized to be, the material for a complete cottage. There was lumber on the bottom. Shingles on top of that, and doors and windows roped on top, including a picture window. At the dispatch desk, Jack handed the invoices for that load and said, "This is a cottage for Dalrymple Lake. Turn up a road by the Bolsover store there somewhere and go through cow pastures for about five or six miles. Ask the store owner where it is - he apparently knows. Be sure you close all gates behind you, both ways, as there are cattle pasturing all the way. There will be a sign where you are to roll off the lumber. Unload the windows and doors first. There is supposed to be a rope there to tie them to a tree. See you early afternoon. Goodbye."

When I got to the store at Bolsover, it was raining steadily. Wind was building all the time and it wasn't at all pleasant. The store owner was helpful, and directed me with quite precise instructions.

I followed a trail made by farmers, who had cattle pastured in those fields through several gates. I found the little sign at the south end of South Dalrymple Lake. It was raining hard now, and the wind was getting serious. I untied the ropes, slid the windows and doors off the back of the load, and leaned them against a tree. The wind gave me a lot of trouble before I got them lashed securely. Then I released the 'bear traps', unhooked the chains and removed the back one. The front chain I left laying across the top and hanging loose on both sides. I was soaking wet now. I put a couple of planks from the load under where the load would land and reversed the crank. I rolled the load back to where it was about to tip, hooked the loose chain to itself under the load, replaced the bear trap, and tightened it as much as possible. I then gave the crank a couple more turns, the load tipped, and the back end dropped to the ground. I got into the cab, released the brake, allowing the truck to roll ahead and out from under the front of the load. I undid the bear trap and unhooked the chain that was still around the load. I fastened one end of the chain to the truck platform and drove ahead, pulling the chain free. I fastened the front roller down with the chains and tightened them with the bear traps. I stuffed the invoices under a bundle of shingles and got back into the truck. I was soaked to the skin, cold and lonely.

I had never before, or have ever since, seen the rainfall or the wind blow as hard as it did when I started back toward the road. It was very dark. The clouds seemed to lay right on top of the cab. A small tree, complete with roots, met me and rolled away. Cattle were trying to walk against the wind without much success. I was very afraid.

The landscape there is mostly flat limestone and scrub trees. There was water everywhere sometimes two feet deep. The wind was so strong, I had to hold on to things the best I could, whenever I got out to open gates. International trucks had a habit of conking out when they got wet, and my truck did just that. In the middle of nowhere, it decided to take a rest. I got out, raised the hood and the wind nearly blew that away. I removed the distributor cap and dried the inside with my handkerchief. I then removed the fan belt in an attempt to stop the water being blown back over the distributor. It worked. I got back to Bolsover at three in the afternoon. I went into the store where I bought a roll of stovepipe wire and a dog dish. I fastened the dish over the distributor with the wire in such a way as to prevent water from blowing over it from the fan. I replaced the fan belt, and was on my way back to Lindsay. Trees were being blown down all along the road and water was running fast along the ditches. At four in the afternoon it was nearly as dark as night.

There had been eight hurricanes in the Atlantic that fall. This one was called Hazel.

Author's Note *Hurricane Hazel had been predicted to lose most of it's fury as it crossed the Allegheny Mountains, Instead it joined a low pressure cell, took in moisture from it and the Great Lakes, and packing winds of 70 miles per hour, it dumped 300,000,000 tons of water on the city of Toronto in 24 hours. 81 people were killed and 4,000 were left homeless. 14 homes on Raymore Drive slid into the Humber River. The dikes broke at Holland Marsh, causing homes to float away,* *some ending up on service roads miles away. A ladder truck with five volunteer firefighters on board, was swept away. It was found 35 years later on the bottom of Lake Ontario, five miles from where it was last seen. Forty highways in the Toronto area were under water.*

Younger people laughed, as I fretted when Hurricane Isobel appeared to be following the same path in September 2003. They weren't with me when, as a young man only 17 years old, I experienced only the edge of Hazel, in that cow pasture, miles from anyone.

I made some mistakes during that summer. The first was on June first. I was sent to the mill yard at Minden for a load of lumber. Nelson Archer was handing lumber to me, as I built a load of two-inch hemlock on the truck. Harold Suggitt was scaling it, and as it approached five o'clock in the afternoon Harold said, "Okay, that's it." There was 4000 board feet on the truck. I thought he meant that was all I was to take, so I chained it down and drove to the yard in Lindsay, then went home to Hadley's. The next morning, Jack met me at the door of the office. "What in hell happened to you yesterday?" he said.

"Why, what do you mean?"

"You came back with half a load. You only had 4000 feet on for Christ sake."

"Harold said that was all, Jack."

"That was all for last night. You were supposed to stay at your parents and put on another 4000 feet of hardwood this morning."

"I'm sorry, Jack," I said, feeling very bad "I wasn't told."

"Harold would have told you. You just weren't paying any attention, that's all."

The second was on November 27. A barn had burned down just the other side of Manila and was being replaced by one of the very new Quonset buildings. The contractors had called for some hemlock planks, a few nails, and a bag of cement. The lumber was loaded on a 1952 three quarter ton truck, used for town delivery, but the cement had to be picked up downtown, at the former Lindsay Coal building, that Bagshaw also owned. I didn't notice the cement on the invoice, until I arrived at the building site. I told the contractor I would bring it back using my own truck. It was Saturday and I would be off work for the weekend when I went back. He said that would be fine and signed the papers.

When I arrived at the office, Jack said, "I noticed you didn't go down town to get the cement."

"No, I didn't notice it on the invoice, but I told the guy I would bring it out this afternoon with my own truck before I go home."

He mumbled something I didn't understand, as he walked the other way. I signed out for the weekend, got in my truck, went to the other warehouse, and picked up the cement. I drove to Manila, delivered it, cut across the Thunder Bridge to Highway 35 and went home for the weekend.

When I arrived for work on Monday, Jack met me in the yard as I got out of my truck.

"What the hell are you doing here?" He asked angrily.

"I came to work. Why?" I asked.

"I fired you on Saturday."

"Fired me? Why?"

"Because you are dead from the arse hole both ways." he said as he turned and walked away.

To be fired from a job was quite disgraceful in those days. I was broken-hearted and very ashamed to go home and tell my parents and Floyd.

Author's Note: *I really can't imagine that I would be fired because of these two misunderstandings. Others made mistakes that summer. Another driver piled a truckload of cement on top of two aluminium garage doors, crushing them beyond repair, and another lost two passage doors from a truck. They worked there for years after that. I have concluded that there was some personal reason for him to take this action. He did have a beautiful young daughter and I was a young man.*
As a matter of interest, anyone who drives through Manila, on the main street, looking straight ahead heading west, can see the Quonset still there.

Bruce organized a reunion of Bagshaw Mill employees in 1987 at the church in Norland. I now weighed 240 pounds. When Wren Hughes saw me, he walked over and stuck out a shaking hand. "I guess this is where I get the shit kicked out of me." he said, trying to be serious. "I couldn't find you when I weighed 185 pounds," I said. "And it wouldn't be fair now." Wren spent his life in the army. He had lifted weights all his life, and I am very sure he could still have thrown me into the sawdust pile. He has passed away since. Keith worked for Blair Construction and is now retired. He lives between Haliburton and Minden.

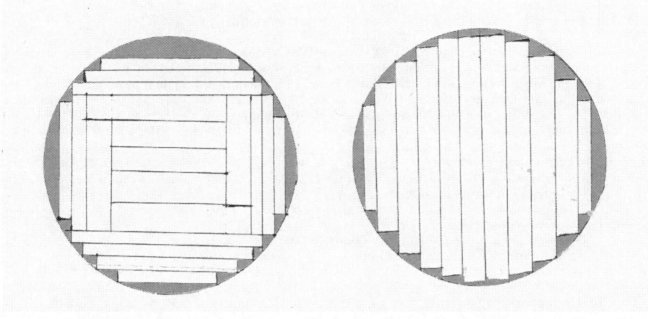

Hardwood   **Softwood**
The log is turned to acquire the best grade.   **Cut live, as there is no grade.**

These drawings shows how logs were cut. Softwood has no grade, so it was cut live, meaning, the log was put on the carriage and only turned once. The big saw cut one and two inch slabs about the middle. It was turned over, and cut until the log was gone. The edger edged, the trimmers trimmed, and another log was brought up.

Hardwood has grade. The outside rind of the log is white and clear. It is used for finished product like furniture, so it brings a better price. The heart is dark, and is only suitable for truck platforms or floor planks and other rough applications, so it brings a much lower price. The log is turned between almost every cut so the best grade is acquired. A good sawyer can make his boss money; a poor one can break him.

If you will follow the drawing on a following page, I will attempt to lead you through the process of cutting logs into lumber.

Logs were dumped on the end of the rollway, either by simply dumping from the trucks right on the rollway, (called hot logging), or pulled up from the pile by Floyd and Jim on a sloop behind a jeep.

They were rolled onto the carriage by the sawyer and canter, and clamped there with three sharp dogs. The sawyer then made the first cut. By pushing a lever; he caused the carriage to move ahead into the big saw, cutting off a slab.

That slab fell onto live rollers that carried it away to the slab saw, where it was cut into four foot lengths, and thrown into the slab hopper.

By this time, the sawyer had pulled on the same lever, causing the carriage and log to return to the starting position. He then pulled a lever on the carriage to advance the log toward the saw. One pull for a one-inch board and two pulls for a two-inch plank. The sawyer repeated the first operation but this time, when the slab fell off the log, the edger operator slid it over to the edger. By moving a lever under his worktable, he set the width of the finished board, and by giving the slab a push between live rollers, it went through to the edger tailer. The person tailing the edger, then jacked the board over to the trimmer operator and put the two edgings that has been cut off the sides onto the live rollers, that took them to the slab saw where they were cut into four-foot lengths and thrown into the hopper.

The trimmer operator puts the board onto the trimmers where two saws cut the ends to a perfect length. The lumber then falls onto the board way where the operator puts it in the right pile. The lumber truck can pull it off and take it to the lumber yard, where it is strip piled, to dry. When dry, it is a rough board, ready for market. The trimmer ends and sawdust was transported by endless chains to hoppers. The yard truck is backed under the hopper, when it is full, a tripped gate allows the material to drop onto the truck. The same truck would back under the slab hopper and take them to the slab yard where they were piled and when dry they were sold for firewood.

Slabs were in great demand, to fire the furnaces and boilers of industry. Bill McFarland drove a 1947 K8 International truck that he kept immaculate, inside and out, at all times. He put a sun visor on it and kept the wheels clean and painted. It was a single axle truck with no dollies. It carried eight cords of slabs to places like Silverwoods in Lindsay and Peterborough, Lindsay Coal and Wood Products, McKnight's Wood Products and many others. He would often load his truck in the evening, to get an early start the next day. He didn't get extra pay for this, he just had the satisfaction of getting the job done. He seldom did anything else.

Lumber was sold locally and shipped by truck and rail all over the country. Ties were sold to the railroad, and square timbers to mines, barn, and bridge builders. The hardest day's work I ever experienced was loading ties into a boxcar at Kinmount on July 21, 1953. These ties are made from elm wood. They measure eight by eight inches and are eight feet long. They weigh between two and three hundred pound each. One person would walk out onto the truck, pick up one end, carry it into the car, up to the end, and drop it in place. Then go back and get another. When I had done this for nine hours, I didn't need any rocking to go to sleep.

John A.C. Kernohan operated the mill for a few seasons before it was demolished and the land sold to Prentice's.

Entries in Our Diaries
From July 1st 1952 to February 6th 1954

1952, July 1: <u>Aunt Mabel Arrived from Saskatchewan</u> *She arrived by train. I had never seen her before.*

July 13: <u>Reunion at Lindsay 40 People there.</u> *A large family gathering while Aunt Mabel was back.*

July 19: <u>Dad and I Bought 1942 Chev Truck after Bargaining Since August 26 1951.</u> *This was a former Muskoka Construction truck. It had somehow come into the ownership of Lawrence Terranie. The gearshift lever was worn so badly in the transmission tower that the lever would swing all over the cab. Someone had put water in the hydraulic brake system and ruined most of the seals. There was no booster on the brake system, so you had to stand hard on the pedal, especially with a load on. It was a dirty, dull green, so we painted it blue with a paintbrush. However, it was our pride and joy. Dad died sitting in this truck seven years later.*

October 23: <u>Dad and I Started to Build Garage</u> *I remember it getting very cold and wet before construction started on this building. One afternoon I was up on the scaffold, nailing rolled roofing onto the gable end of the garage while Dad was cutting it. The supply of roofing material was getting very low. Dad had ordered just enough, so every piece counted. I was painting tar around the edges as I waited for another piece to nail. I mistakenly went around the edge of the last piece I had nailed instead of the edge of the next piece. That mistake is still evident on the building to-day. The people who own the property now live in this garage, which has since been enlarged.*

November 4: <u>Grant Stamp Drove into River in Minden and Drowned.</u> *The roads were getting straighter, and the cars were getting faster. Some people say that Grant just got going too fast, as he drove down the hill from the fair grounds, and missed the curve onto the old iron bridge at the north end of Minden's main street. Others say that there was a grudge race and the other car went across the bridge, but there wasn't space for both. Either way, a fine young man lost his life that night in the cold fall water of the Gull River.*

November 26: <u>Dad and I Started to Build Vincent Todd's House.</u> *Dad and I constructed a lot of buildings around the country.*

Xmas: <u>Sold 115 Trees to John Mason for 20 cents each.</u> *Many farmers would cut a supply of trees and pile them near the road for sale. Brokers would see them, and purchase them for city tree lots. Before artificial trees were invented, this was a good and profitable market.*

1953, May 18: <u>Daryl Thompson and Floyd Broke Bagshaw's Truck on Bright's Hill.</u> *The hill is near the southwest end of county road one. It was narrow, crooked, and very steep in places. Floyd and Daryl had loaded lumber at Uncle Arnold MacElwain's place near Gelert. Daryl changed gears on the face of the hill and the rear axle broke loose. It ended up under the front wheels. The load broke loose and spread all the way down the hill. What a hell of a mess that was to clear away. All the men from Bagshaw's mill were there until dark piling it onto another truck.*

May 19: <u>Stan Scarlet Upset Bagshaw's Truck on Scotch Line Hill.</u> *Some say that bad luck comes in threes. Sometimes that seems to be true. Bruce Bagshaw lost two trucks in two days, but he was very happy when he arrived at this mishap. The Scotch Line hill is still steep, but it is not nearly as steep as it was then. It also had a sharp bend and a switch back in it. Stan Scarlet was an experienced truck driver, one of the best, but he lost control coming down the hill with a full load of logs. He went over the edge of the switch back and rolled down over the cliff. There was* *an axe lying loose under the front of the seat. That axe left an imprint of its sharp blade in the back of the cab, right beside where Stan's head would have been. Stan walked away.*

May 21:   Bagshaw Lumber bought 500,000 feet of Logs from International Cooperage. *The Cooperage closed forever.*

May 28:   I Passed Driver's Exam Got Operator's Permit. *There were only two classes of driver's licenses then. One was Operator's that allowed you to drive any vehicle as long as you weren't paid to do so, and Chauffeur's, which allowed you to drive everything. I went to Jim Smith's Barbershop. I had to wait until he finished with the customer in the chair. Then, with his shop full of customers, he came out with me. We got in the car, and I drove around to the backstreet, through it to the corner, along the river to the main street at the bridge, back to his shop, and parked. He signed the paper. I had to go to the police station where they verified that I was not wanted for anything. I signed the paper and became a licensed driver.*

July 3:   Got Chauffeur's License. *I was driving Bagshaw's yard truck on this Friday afternoon. As I approached the office, about four-o-clock in the afternoon with a load of slabs, foreman Jack Wiles came out of the office and flagged me down. "Bruce wants to see you in the office," he said. I went in, and after finishing a conversation with his office clerk Wes Allan, he turned to me and said, "You would be a lot more value to me if you had your chauffeur's permit, Ray, so I will take you to town so you can get it."*

"You mean right now?" I asked.

"Yes, let's go." We went to Jimmy Smith's and followed the same route again. I had to have a picture for the application for this permit, which I cut from a picture in my wallet. I could now drive anything anywhere.

July 21:   Loading Ties in Boxcar for Bagshaw. *This was very hard work. I weighed 129 pounds at the time. The railroad ties weighed an average of 150. (See chapter, 'Bagshaw's Mill')*

August 11:   Dad and Uncle Stewart Started to Build House in Lindsay for Uncle Arnold. *Uncle Arnold McElwain was a section worker on the CNR railway line in Gelert. He was transferred to Lindsay as freight traffic began to dwindle over this line.*

August 21:   Aunt Leona Died of Cancer. *Aunt Leona Miller, (my uncle, Herb Miller's wife) had been to so-called "healers" in a city somewhere. She returned by train in very poor shape, and soon succumbed to her illness. Uncle Herb operated Herb Miller Electric in Haliburton.*

October 12:   Floyd and I Started to Cut Logs and Pulp Wood for Angus and Harold Coulter at Scotch Line. *It was actually a little north of the Scotch Line, on the west side of Bobcaygeon Road. We parked our vehicles in Sammy Barton's yard, and later walked the horses there, where we stabled them at Sammy's. Sammy fed and watered them for us on weekends.*

November 14:   Rover Shot. *For a reason known only to him, Rover always ran to where there were gunshots. On this morning, the rest of the men were hunting. I had seen a 1953 Chev Belair drive into the old campgrounds. Two men got out with rifles. I went to the barn to do chores and Rover went part way with me, but when he heard gunshots at the campgrounds, he responded to the sound and went up there. The guys were target practising and used Rover as a target. Mother's illness often caused her to lose her balance and fall. She had to crawl to a piece of furniture in order to get up. When Rover would see her fall, he would go over and backup to her. She would grab him by the fur on his hips and he would walk forward, helping her to her feet. He was missed.*

November 27:   Uncle Herb Had Party Here With Everett Fearry and Bill McKnight playing music and singing. *After Aunt Leona died, Uncle Herb purchased a small sound system and put on some house parties to help get through a lonely time. He later married Teresa Blair.*

December 1:   Floyd Hit Holly Stevenson's Car at Rogers. *Each morning, Floyd would go to Sammy Barton's early to feed the horse an hour before daylight, so they would have an hour to eat before Dad and I got there. Just north of the cemetery, there were some sharp corners in the road. As we approached these corners on this morning, we saw Floyd running toward us. His face was covered with blood and he was waving frantically. Holly Stevenson had lost control of his car and came to rest with his vehicle cross-wise on the road. He then went to sleep in the car. When Floyd hit it, Holly woke up and ran down the hill to Rogers place. Floyd had already notified the police and they arrived a short time later. Holly had no insurance, so Floyd's insurance paid for repairs to his truck. Floyd's nose soon healed. There was no further litigation.*

December 6: <u>Marion McDowell Kidnapped from James Wilson's Car in Toronto.</u> *This should be in Ripley's Believe It Or Not because believe it or not, crime was rare even in Toronto then. It was rare enough for us to include this case in our diaries. We would require a scrapbook the size of a city newspaper to record the crime now.*

December 17: <u>Floyd and I finished Coulter's bush 1300 Logs and 17 Cord of Pulpwood</u> *Dad skidded the logs out to the Queen's Line where they were sold to Bagshaw and hauled to the mill the next spring. The pulpwood was piled there too.*

December 20:. <u>I got lost in Patty's swamp.</u> *It had snowed six inches on Friday, and there was a cold wind blowing that snow around. Hazel and Doward left for home, so Floyd and I decided to see if there were any deer in the swamp to the north of us, on the east side of the road. This property had belonged to Patty Mack and was now Elmer Kellett's, but it was still called Patty's swamp. Floyd told me to stay at a certain place, he would go up to the north side of the swamp and come down through. He said, if there were any deer in the swamp, I would see them from there. He told me to stand there for a half hour and if I saw nothing, I was to go to the house. He would cut across from where he was, and would be at the house by then. I stood there for the half hour, then I headed home. It had started to snow. It was late and beginning to get dark. Not being good in the woods, I was soon turned around. However, I had chased cows through his darned woods lots of times, so, I just took off in what I thought was in the direction of the house. I didn't see anything familiar and was getting a little panicky, when I came across footprints in the snow. Thinking they were Floyd's and would lead me out, I followed. I soon came to footprints leading in from the left and wondered whose they were, but trod on the same tracks. I had followed these tracks for long enough to be at the house, when I came upon more tracks. It looked to me as though I was to spend the night in the bush, as it was now getting quite dark. I began to run. I went through a thicket and a hand touched me. It was Floyd. "Come with me," he laughed. "Look over your shoulder," he continued. I looked, and I could see the chimney of our house. "I stood there and watched you go past me twice," he said. "You were following your own tracks." I have never wandered far into the woods again without a good path or road leading home, or a rope tied around my waist with the other end tied to the doorknob!*

December 24: <u>Floyd went to Oshawa with Truman Wright to check GM plant.</u> *Now this may be hard to believe, and was then as well. Truman was working at General Motors in Oshawa. It was Christmas Eve. As I recall, the whole, plant was closed for Christmas, but someone had to go in to fill something or start something. Oshawa was a long distance away, over the roads that existed then. Floyd went with Truman. Mother worried.*

December 31: <u>Floyd and Mervin Barry drew Pulpwood from Coulter' woods to Kinmount.</u> *They put tire chains on Mervin's truck. By shovelling and charging the snow banks with Mervin's truck, they broke their own trail through the snow to get to the pulpwood on the Queen's Line Road. Seventeen cord of pulpwood just filled a small railroad car.*

1954 January 10:. <u>Sunday, Nelson Archer's House burnt to the ground at 10:00 A.M. Nothing saved but washing machine a table and chairs.</u>

January 15: <u>Mabel had baby girl 8 lbs.</u> *Derinda was born at the Haliburton hospital. Canoe FM Radio station now occupies that building.*

February 6: <u>Worked half day at Bagshaw's mill with Dad's truck. At Nelson Archer's house in afternoon.</u>

Nelson Archer

If this publication were to mimic the TV series 'Little House on the Prairie', my Dad would be Charles Ingalls, and Nelson Archer would definitely be Mr. Edwards. Nelson's stalwart appearance and kind but strong character, matched that of Mr Edward's to a tee. .

He was a large, strong man wearing a wide brimmed felt hat. He was very hardy and tough as nails. He was a hard worker and, although he was set in his convictions, he was as honest and true as any man could ever be.

Nels was born, and lived his entire life, in the house on the south end of Archer's Flats, just three miles south of Minden, on the west side of Highway 35

He inherited the so-called "farm" when his father Robert passed away on December 22, 1942. None of these little farms were very fertile, but the soil on the flats was especially sandy and inclined to grow broom grass* and very little else.

He met and married a lady named Nelly, (unfortunately, her maiden name eludes me), who had a daughter, Bessie, whom Nels adopted immediately. Nels and Nelly had three children, a boy, Robert, and two girls, Susan, and Dorothy. None of these children married.

Because of his rugged appearance and somewhat withdrawn demeanour, he seemed at first to be a little backward, but it was a lucky soul who had the opportunity to even be acquainted with him. Those who employed Nels could expect, and received, a hundred and ten percent of his abilities. He often helped, and sometimes was employed by, Dad, Doward, Floyd, or Murray. I was privileged to work with him on many occasions.

Nels was a big part of my life ever since I was old enough to recognize him. He was humorous, kind, gentle and very clever. It was actually a challenge to match his skills. I once assisted him in building several cribs for docks at Kilcoo Camp, using nothing but an axe and a bucksaw. He would measure logs using his axe handle, then cut them to length with the bucksaw, and notch them with the axe. They would fit perfectly. As I watched, I realized that he could very well build a log cabin using the same technique.

One time when I was just an early teenager, I was working at Kilcoo Camp with Nels. Doward had gone to town during noon hour and Nels and I were in the workshop eating, when I picked up one of the camp's 22-caliber rifles and a box of shells. I went to the diving tower, to target practice. I only intended to fire a shot or two, but with every shot, I figured I could hit the target with the next one. This went on until I had shot almost the whole box. I went back into the shop and said, "God almighty Nels, I am in trouble."

"What have you done now?" He grinned.

"I fired off nearly all this box of 22 shells. Doward will kill me."

"Let me see the box," he said, reaching toward me.

Knowing that Doward would indeed scold me for wasting bullets like that, he reached into his pocket and pulled out a box of shells, and filled the box from it. Handing it back to me, he said with a chuckle, "There. You never fired a shot."

Another time, we were splitting wood for Kilcoo Camp, on the other side of the road, half way up the hill from the camp. Doward had just replaced the handle in one of the dago axes that morning. I over-hit the block of wood, just as Doward came in sight walking toward us, and broke the new handle. Nels reached past me and took the broken piece from my hand. When Doward got there, he was holding the broken handle in his hand, looking at it. "This Christly thing had a serious cross grain," he said, as he handed it to Doward. "One over-hit and it split like glass."

He had saved my bacon again.

I would bet my life on Nelson Archer, and did as recorded in the chapter 'A Tight Squeeze', when I jumped, knowing he would catch me.

On Sunday, January 10th 1954, at 10:00 am., Nelson's house caught fire and burned to the ground. It had been very cold, with a stiff southeast wind the day before, but this day dawned cold and still. These old houses, with no insulation whatsoever, were very hard to heat. Everyone would maintain a roaring fire during the cold spell. As I recall, Nels had a good fire going before he went to the barn to do the chores. He noticed the house was on fire and ran to save his family. The timber in the house was tinder dry, and with all the space between the walls, flames spread quickly. The family was only able to save the kitchen table and chairs and the washing machine.

There were no phones in the area, so word spread slowly. Neighbours arrived as soon as they heard, but there was little to be done but fold* the smouldering timbers back into the open basement, so they would burn completely and there would be only ash to remove before starting to rebuild. Art and Rita Hodgkinson sheltered the family at the Wagon Wheel Motel until a new house could be built. Clothing and food supplies began to arrive from neighbours immediately.

I was driving Dad's truck at Bagshaw's mill on Saturday, February 6th.. The transmission had given out on the old red company Chev. the day before. We only worked half a day on Saturdays, so when the mill shut down for the day at noon, I ate dinner at the cookery, and then hurried to Nels' place. There was a work bee to start the new house. There were quite a number of men on hand when I arrived and they had laid the beams and floor joists. We laid the sub-floor and erected the walls and partitions in place. Then we nailed the Donnacona* on the outside.

As we were loading, our tools into our vehicles to leave, Art turned to Nels and said, "Well Nels you can see what your new house will look like."

"I sure can. You guys are all so wonderful. I really can't believe that you all turned up to help today. We got so much done. I don't deserve this." Nels said.

"You have always been there to help any of us, Nels. We are just starting to pay you back you know," Dad added as he headed for his car.

As I drove out of the yard, I looked back. It was now pitch dark and Nels was lighting the coal oil lantern and heading to the barn and tend to the cattle.

The last time I talked to Nels was at the Kinmount Fair a few years before he died. His family had taken him there so he could enjoy an event that he had attended many times before. I saw them sitting under a tree, so I went over to talk to them. Nels was not well and was not able to talk much. It was hard for me to see this undeserving man suffer like that. I said goodbye, knowing I would not likely see him alive again.

Nels died on June 15th 1990, after a long illness had reduced him to a fraction of his former self. I couldn't attend his funeral as I was out of town.

I knew Nelson Archer. I am a better man because of it.

Robert died in 2003 of cancer. Nelly and the girls still live in the same place.

*Broom grass. *Broom grass was the name given to a useless plant that resembled a stalk of oats, with a tall hard shiny stem, and a small broom like head. Even though it grew to twelve to eighteen inches high, there was no part of the plant that was of any value as animal food. It was too hard to lend comfort for the animals, so it was ineffective as bedding. I expect there is a fancy name for it, but to us Haliburton rednecks, it is broom grass.*

*Fold the burning timber back into the fire, *When a building caught fire, it would usually burn completely because the fire department was poorly equipped and staffed. All anyone could do was try to save as much of their personal property as possible before it became unsafe to return to the building. They would return any burning timber to the fire, in order to burn it completely. This made it easier to clean up afterward There would only be ashes in the burned out basement to dispose of, .instead of a lot of charred wood.*

*Donnacona. *This is a brand name for a type of siding in common use in the 50's.*

Walter McKelvey

In an area where no Provincial Police are present, justice is swift, and sometimes severe, you will often find a gentle giant of a man who just seems to fit in anywhere. A man who can sometimes quell the anger in an aggressor with a gentle, but firm grip around the neck, or settle a raging fist fight by merely banging a couple of heads together, accompanied by a broad and friendly smile. Standing six feet seven inches tall and weighing a muscled three hundred pounds, Walter McKelvey was such a man.

Although I never saw it myself, I was told by more than one person he was able to snap the handle of a pick axe by driving the blade under a rock and giving the handle a snap with one hand. At fairs, there were sometimes lifting contests. They would use a set of platform scales, found on many farms to weigh out bags of grain and carcasses of meat, with a handle on each side. The handles could be adjusted to accommodate the best lifting height of each contestant. Participants would stand on the scales, adjust the handles, then lift and hold, until the operator could slide the balance weights to measure the amount lifted. Walter was said to have lifted more than seven hundred pounds at age eighteen. It was before my time, so I can't verify this, but I do know he was a powerful man.

Walter was kind, gentle, and very slow to anger, even when called upon to settle a fight.

He lived on the South Lake Road, where it now crosses the Minden bypass. He would walk with a slow powerful gait to the downtown, where he would sit on a bench in front of the Dominion Hotel for hours, where he was greeted by all. He would go inside to join a friend for a glass of beer, but I never saw him drink more than one, or be under the influence of alcohol.

I worked with him at Kilcoo Camp. He told me that there was going to be a large 'settling of the ways' between some guys from Toronto and the local Kelletts and McKelveys. He had a nephew, Claude (Skelly) McKelvey, whose mother was a Kellett.. Skelly looked like his mother's side of the family and like all the Kelletts, he didn't pick a fight, but was quite willing to oblige anyone who wanted one. He usually ended right side up and not looking to much the worse for it.

I asked Walter what the beef was between these guys.

"Apparently, Skelly and some of his cousins were working somewhere near Toronto, and dated some girls. When they left, the girls were broken hearted." he said.

All of the Kelletts are good-looking men, charming, and well built and Skelly was no exception, so I could readily believe that story.

"Apparently, some relatives of these girls have taken it upon themselves to come up here this weekend and make the boys pay," he continued.

"They will have their hands full doing it. I want to see that," I said.

"Well, they have sent word for the boys to be at the Dominion, on Saturday night, to receive their comeuppance," he smiled.

"I'll be there."

Saturday evening came, and I joined Walter in front of the Dominion where he was cheerfully greeting people as usual. Some of the Kelletts were inside, including Elmer who was slinging beer at the time, as well as Skelly, and his brother Morris (Cooney).

Soon, a car stopped on the street. The driver looked at the sign on the building then drove behind the Hotel to park, followed by another.

After a while, great banging and crashing could be heard from inside the hotel.

"Are you going in?" I asked.

"I think the boys can handle themselves," he said with a broad grin.

A couple of strangers crashed through the front door. They immediately returned, to join the war raging inside. A woman came out of the alleyway between the buildings and said, "There's a guy in the back yard, laying on his back quivering."

"Look like a Kellett or McKelvey?" Walter asked.

"No," she replied.

"Then he don't count for anything," he laughed.

After a while, he looked at me and said, "I think I will go in and introduce myself."

He went through the front door and I heard him announce loudly, "Hello, I'm Walter McKelvey."

He returned in a minute, with a head under each arm. The door wasn't wide enough for the bodies attached to those heads to come through at the same time, but that didn't slow him down one bit. The stress on those necks must have been severe, as the bodies wedged and finally squeezed through. He stepped back, banged the heads together, and stood the two fellows against the wall, where they slowly crumpled into a heap on the sidewalk. He looked at me, smiled as he went through the door, and said in a low raspy voice, "I'll go get some more."

It got considerably quieter inside. Walter returned shortly. His right hand was holding the belt of another man, who was dangling upside-down. He dropped him on his face on the sidewalk, looked at me and laughed silently.

The Kelletts and Skelly filed out the door. Most of them assisting a limp starry-eyed guy. They gathered them together, took them around to the back where their cars were, and picked up the fellow that the lady had seen lying on his back, stuffed them all into the cars, and wished them well with a fist to each door as they left.

I looked the fellows over. Some of the Kelletts had scratches and there was evidence of an odd black eye. Skelly looked as though he would survive. Morris was a little the worse for wear but he would heal. Walter walked off toward home. Justice prevailed.

If such a fracas was to happen today lawsuits would abound. Court cases would last for months, with liability being paid in the hundreds of thousands of dollars.

The term 'slinging beer' refers to what is now known as 'waiting on table' or 'serving beer'. If you were to drop into the Dominion then, then you would no doubt be served by the owner Steve Rastall or beer slingers Elmer Kellett or Arnold Reynolds. All of these men were quite capable of removing anyone from the premises, should the need arise, and it frequently did.

The reason I had to witness this event from outside the premises was because I was too young to enter. You had to be 21 then, I was 17.

Cutting Ice

Before refrigerators and a dependable electricity service were available, iceboxes could be found in most cottages and some homes. This generated a need for a good supply of block ice in the area. Ice houses, an outbuilding big enough to hold several hundred blocks of ice with a thick layer of sawdust all around it, were dotted throughout the area. These were located behind general stores in town and at various places where cottagers could purchase ice as needed. Ice blocks were around twelve inches square and as deep as the ice happened to be in the lake, when they were harvested in winter. They were cut and loaded by hand, with ice tongs, and hauled by team and sleigh to the icehouse. The work was very strenuous.

Ever the inventor, Doward designed and built an ice cutting system, (in the early 1950s) using the motor from a two man chain saw and a circular saw, with the teeth* specifically filed to cut ice. This was a well-built machine mounted on a short sleigh. It had an adjustable depth guide, that set the depth of the cut, and a width guide that set the size of the block being cut. By raising the handles of the chain saw engine, the frame rocked over the sleigh, lowering the saw into the ice. Since it was important that the saw didn't cut right through into the water causing water to enter the kerf*, the depth gauge would be set about an inch less than the depth of the ice.

He also built an "ice elevator" from aluminium tubing, to load the ice. It was powered by a Johnson portable engine. The whole damned contraption loaded nicely into the back of his pickup

This machine eliminated the drudgery of cutting and loading by hand and was very popular.

Although I had been involved in ice cutting and packing for a year or two, the winter of 1955 became a time when I would become experienced in the operation of this machine.

Ern and Don Berry lived in the house on the west side of Highway 35, next to the Portage Bridge. They had an icehouse there and sold ice to customers on Horseshoe and Mountain Lakes.

Entries in our diaries related to this chapter read:

February 9, 1955: I helped Ern Berry pack ice at his place.

February 11: Art Hodgkinson and I packed ice at Ern and Don Berry's.

February 14: Art and I finished packing ice at Berry's at noon and then started to pack ice in the icehouse behind Sam Welch's Store on the main street in Minden.

February 15: Finished packing ice at Sam Welch's at noon, then rode with Dad as he hauled ice from Mountain Lake to the University Camp west of Minden. I helped load and unload.

February 17: Worked for Doward shovelling snow off ice at Mountain Lake in the morning, then drew ice with my truck to Wright's Ice House.

February 18: Drew ice to Sun Valley Lodge.

February 22: I took Doward's machine and Nelson Archer to Devil's Lake to cut ice. Clutch on ice machine broke.

February 23: Nelson and I cut 352 cakes of ice on Devil's Lake.

February 24: Nelson and I cut 270 cakes for Rackety Ranch, then went to Deep Bay where Floyd Pogue took us out onto the bay where we floated a block* up for Black Bear Cottages.

February 25: Nelson and I cut 405 cakes for Black Bear Cottages and 215 for Teddy Pogue*.

This brings me to a memorable incident that I would like to expand on.

Dawn lay on the horizon of a cold February sky as I drove up to Nelson's driveway with Doward's truck loaded with all the ice cutting equipment. It was 7 am. Nels came running from the barn, and stopped at the door of his house, where Nelly handed him his lunch box.

He ran to the truck and opened the door.

83

"G'day," he said, as he put his lunch on the floor of the cab and climbed in.

"Cold, eh?" I responded as I slipped the truck into gear.

"Yeah, but it looks like it's going to be sunny. How's Hazel?"

"I haven't talked to her this morning, but it won't be long now."

"I hope not. It's always good to get it over with."

The sky brightened steadily as we drove along Highway 35, heading south. We chatted about everyday things. We were soon crossing the Moore's Falls bridge, and turned onto the Deep Bay Road. The road was very well ploughed, but only as far as Teddy Pogue's. I was goofing along, chatting to Nels, and not paying too much attention to what I was doing, as we turned the corner in front of Leary's driveway. The load was a little heavy to the rear, with the ice elevator hanging away back. The front wheels were light. The road was hard packed. I turned the wheels, but the truck went straight into the snow bank.

Nels was looking at me at the time. He looked back, and all he could see were snow-covered fields beyond the fence, which was right in front of us.

"What the devil are we doing here?" He said looking around. "We can't cut ice here," he continued, as he tried to open the door. Snow blocked it. He pushed the door into the snow enough to get his head out and look back. "Lordy it's a long way to the road," he laughed, as he pushed the door open and climbed into the thigh-high snow.

By the time I had battled my way out of the truck and reached the rear, Nels had taken a shovel out of the back of the truck and was starting to dig a way back to the road.

I got another shovel to help him when, I heard an engine start at Leary's barn. "I guess we should go and see if someone can come and hook onto us with a tractor." I said.

The sound of the engine got closer. Then a tractor turned toward us from the driveway. Steam rose from the exhaust into the clear morning air, as the sun peered over the horizon.

Nelson Leary drove up and turned around.

"Morning fellows," he said, as he backed to the edge of the ditch and slowed the engine down. "I saw you go past the driveway, and then I heard the thump. Where's Doward?"

"Hazel is looking for a baby, so he is staying close to home," Nels said.

"Oh yeah, I forgot. When's the baby due?"

"Any day now," I said, as I hooked the chain from his tractor to the rear axle of the truck.

"Okay, get back into the truck and I'll give you a little tug," he said as he tightened the chain.

I climbed through the snow, got into the cab, and started the engine. I was soon back on hard ground. Nels unhooked the chain and wrapped it around the draw bar of the tractor by the time I got to the rear of the truck.

Nelson Leary waved and drove back to his driveway.

When we came into sight of Teddy Pogue's house, we could see that someone had horses harnessed and hitched to the sleighs. They were standing just outside the door. Floyd Pogue emerged from the house and came toward us, along the road. The horses' feet made a clopping sound, as steam rose into the cold air from their nostrils. He pulled up beside the truck.

"Good morning guys. Where's Doward." Floyd's voice was deep but gentle.

"He wants to stay near Hazel," I said.

"Oh yeah. I forgot about the baby." The horses moved ahead. "Whoa!....how's Hazel?"

"She seemed a little uncomfortable the last time I saw her," Nels said.

"I hope everything turns out okay. It's been a while since their last baby was born. How old is the other girl now anyway?"

"Ten," I said as I untied the elevator and give it a pull.

"Well I hope the baby comes alright and they are both okay," He got down from the sleighs and started toward the truck. "Back up a couple of steps." The horses backed up exactly two steps.

"Where's your father?" Nels asked, as we moved the machines unto the sleighs.

"He went over to Black Bear Cottages to tidy the ice house up a bit."

We loaded the machinery and climbed onto the sleighs. "Okay lads," Floyd said, picking up the lines. We headed out onto the lake.

The lake cracked and moaned under the weight of the team, as we went out to the middle of the bay. These sounds were normal, so no one paid much attention. Flakes of frost glittered in the sun as the moisture from open water down at Moore's Falls rose, then froze in the cold morning air, and fluttered to the ground. I could hear Pogue's dog bark back at the house, over the clink of the chains on the harness tugs, and the squeaks and squeals of the sleigh runners on the snow. I looked back at Nels sitting on the rear of the sleighs with his feet hanging over the edge. I wondered how he could stand to have his ears exposed beneath the wide brimmed felt hat he wore winter and summer.

I stepped up beside Floyd, standing holding the reins. "It's nice out here on the lake," he said. "I always like it here when the sun is shining like this."

"Yes, it's great to-day." I answered.

"A young fellow like you must have a lot of girlfriends," he said.

"I am going with Audrey Harrison right now."

"He likes Joyce Stewart though," Nels yelled from the rear.

"She's a nice girl," Floyd said, as he chirped to the horses. "I saw her last night in Norland. If I was younger I would be interested in her myself."

"You're too old for her Floyd," I said, as I grabbed his shoulder to regain my balance as the horses broke into a trot.

"I could act young for a pretty girl like her though."

"Yeah, sure, just stay away from her."

"I am going to Norland tomorrow; I think I'll look her up. Whoa!" He reined the horse back, as we approached the block of ice, "Whoa!" We pulled up beside the block and began to unload the equipment.

Nels scraped the snow off the floated up piece, as I cut a hole in the ice for the elevator, and a channel, a little wider than the cakes of ice, to feed them onto the elevator. Then he took the manual ice saw and completed the cuts. He and Floyd used a pike pole and an ice pick to push the ice from the elevator hole under the ice out of the way. They put the elevator in place, as I started to cut cakes from the block. The ice measured 29 inches, so I set the gauge at 27 and a half. This way the power saw won't quite cut through and bring up water. The lengthwise pieces are then cut through easily by hand, and the crosswise ones can be split away with an ice pick, as they are pushed onto the elevator.

I started the elevator engine. The belts danced and the endless chain began to move. Floyd drove the horses past the end of the incline where the cakes would slide down from the top of the elevator onto the sleigh. He picked up his ice tongs. I deliberately set the throttle much faster then usual. I went to the rows of ice Nels had pushed up into the channel. There were ten or more cakes still attached to each other by the inch and a half of ice at the bottom. I broke them apart with the ice pick, then started to push them onto the elevator. The engine governors opened up to compensate for the load, as every crosser of the elevator carried a block of ice. Floyd was soon buried in ice. "Hold on," he yelled, as he jabbed at the cakes with his tongs, "I can't pile them this fast."

"Are you going to stay away from Norland?" I asked, as I pushed several more cakes onto the jack ladder.

"No, I won't," * he said, as he piled ice as fast as he could. Nels laughed and shook his head.

I slowed the engine down to a normal speed and climbed onto the sleigh to help him catch up. Nels fed the ladder at a regular pace. When the sleigh was partially loaded and it would be easier if it was ahead a bit, Floyd said, "Ahead two steps, lads." The horses moved ahead two steps.

Floyd drew the ice to Black Bear cottages and Teddy packed it there, then we started filling the ice house at the Pogue's.

We cut 405 cakes of ice for Black Bear Cottages and 215 for Teddy Pogue. Doward's inventions were a lot faster and easier than earlier methods.

Hydro lines were built around lakes soon after this making the icebox, and Doward's machine, obsolete.

Floyd was a wonderful teamster and very gentle. His horses seemed genuinely to love him.

__Kerf.__ The Path of a saw cut.

* ***"No, I wont"*** *Nels and I often laughed at Floyd's response since then. I didn't see Floyd for more than thirty years. Then I was talking to him while I was living at the Staanworth apartments in Minden. He was living in another building there. I mentioned it to him and he remembered.*

*Floated a block up; *If there was water on top of the ice, we would cut a block of ice big enough to cut cakes of 12 x 12 inch ice for a customer first. This involved cutting nearly through with the power saw, then finishing the cut all the way around with a hand saw. When this was finished the whole block would float. This allowed us to be on top, and cut the cakes without being in the water and slush.*

*Teeth especially filed to cut ice; *The teeth on a wood saw are designed to cut the fibre of the wood on both sides of the kerf and the centre splits away with the grain of the wood. Ice has no grain so the teeth must chisel the centre of the kerf out.*

*Teddy Pogue; *This is the same Teddy Pogue, who 22 year old Mabel Boyce was staying with, when she was drowned in early 1920s. Mabel was a relative of the Pogues. She left to gather the cows for the evening milking and never returned. There had been a heavy summer storm that fateful Saturday night. It was believed that she lost her way in the darkness brought on by the storm, and, taking a wrong path, she tumbled from a cliff, into the waters of Gull Lake. She was found three days later by some of the Gull River Lumber log drivers* who were working nearby.*

*Log drivers; *Many logs were floated from lumber limits in the north, down the lakes and rivers, to sawmills in the south. I never witnessed 'the drive' myself, but there were many stories of the spectacle these brave men created, as they drove thousands of logs through Minden and out into Gull Lake every spring. They were as comfortable on floating logs as they were on dry land. I am told that some would burl a log* as he went through town, just for the fun of doing it. Logs would sometimes jam in the narrows, rapids, or falls. Many stories and songs still exist about the men who would go out onto these jams and free them. When the key log was found and removed, the whole pile of timber and the water that was dammed up behind it, would race down stream. These were very agile workers. They were accompanied by a floating cookery/bunkhouse, and a boat, called an 'alligator' for herding and towing the large booms of timber across lakes. The river drivers were always ready to provide valuable assistance with any emergencies along the way.*

*Burl a log; *the art of spinning a log in the water and running crossways on it just fast enough to stay on top.*

Cutting Wood

Dawn came early for me on March 24, 1955. John Kernohan had arranged for Doward to cut wood for him, but Doward was very busy with his new Mall chainsaw agency, so he asked me to do the work for him.

John lived at the end of what is now called Lutterworth Road One. During the winter, that road was always re-routed along the top of the hill between Albert Pogue's and Kernohan's, as the main road went along the river and was hard to keep open. We left the road at Albert's gate and went through his yard and barnyard, around the barn and across the field right along the top of the hill. It had been lovely weather for days with cold nights, so the field was bare. The plan was for Doward to be across the field on frost in the morning and John would pull him and his truck back through the mud with the team at night.

The early spring sun was already warming things nicely, as I turned the corner past the barn, and headed across rutted road toward the line fence. I could see that the earth was darkening in the sunny areas, indicating that the soil was turning to mud. I put my pickup into first gear and just let it moan its way along the ruts.

As I approached the line fence, I dropped into a deep soft rut with both wheels and that was it as far as the truck would go. I could see that John and Vic Alsop were already leaving the house to come and meet me. I went to the back of my truck and found that all my tools had shifted to the front of the truck box, so I climbed in to retrieve them. John and Vic arrived at the back of the truck just as I climbed down.

Vic said, "Good morning Ray. How are you?"

John eyed me up and down and said, "Where's Doward?"

"He's busy with the shop, so he sent me." I replied, as I lifted the chainsaw out of the truck and set it on the ground at my feet. (Mall had just produced this new model OMG chainsaw. It was very small and delicate looking, but it was a fierce little thing in the woods for its size).

John looked at it. Then he looked me right in the eye and said, in no uncertain terms, "I hired a man with a chainsaw, not a kid with a goddamned toy. Load that Christly thing back into the truck and forget it."

Turning to Vic he said, "Will you look at that thing? It has a bicycle chain on it for Chrissake. What in hell can anybody do with a thing like that?"

Then he turned to me and said "Load the stupid thing up and get out of here. I am going to give Doward a hell of a talking to when I see him."

Vic was standing there grinning through all this, then in a cool voice he said, "John, I think you should give the lad a chance. Garnet Stevenson told me in the Dominion, the other day, that Ray here cut ten and a quarter cord of wood for him in seven hours a week or so ago."

"How long had you and Garnet been in the beer parlour before he told you that yarn?"

"Well, Morris McKelvey was there to help Garnet, and he told me the same thing. And Morris doesn't lie John." Vic picked up the toolbox and gas can and nodded his head, indicating I should follow him, as he headed for the house.

I picked up the chainsaw and my axe. John brought the oilcan muttering, "This kid can't fell trees, for Chrissake. He needs to fell trees, Vic." John said.

"Milton Miller can fell trees. Floyd Miller can fell trees. Doward Johnson can fell trees. I will lay odds with anyone that Ray Miller can fell trees too," Vic said, in a 'that's enough of that' tone of voice.

When we got to the house, Vic headed toward a couple of dago axes and a basket of wedges lying against the drive shed, opposite the house.

"You won't need those. For all the wood that is going to be cut today I could split it with my jackknife," John started up again.

"Let's take them just in case," Vic humoured him, picking up the basket and nodding for John to get the axes.

Just then, Mrs Kernohan appeared in the kitchen door and asked, "Lunch at twelve be okay John?"

This touched him off again. "Set the table for Vic and me only. This lad won't last for five minutes, before I fire him and send him the hell home. I never thought Doward would send a kid like this and expect me to pay for him. Look at the damned thing he is carrying Lil. It's a piece of damned crap. Look at the size of the motor, and that has to be half a gas tank Vic."

Vic laughed and said, "And there's an oil tank in there too."

"It's no wonder it only has a bicycle chain on it. It can't have enough power to drive a bicycle," he said, as we followed Vic toward the barn and up over the hill.

Crows cawed. The sun shone. A few clouds drifted across the sky. There was no wind and the temperature was a little above freezing. The few patches of snow lying around the flat plane on top of the hill had turned to crystal with the constant freezing and thawing of the last few days. I kicked some snow crystals out onto some bare ground, as I followed Vic toward a tree that he and John had felled the day before. I laid the things I was carrying on the stump, and, looking the tree over for areas of bind, I removed my coat. Deciding that it would be better to start at the top, I stepped up onto the trunk and, as I walked toward the top, I started the saw. I dropped into the limb area and started to cut. I limbed it back to the trunk, then started down toward the stump. Those little machines could cut wood. I was young, agile and strong. Sawdust flew. Blocks rolled away. Soon I was back at the stump. I shut the saw off, straightened up, turned around and there was John. Absolute awe was showing all over his face.

"I owe you an apology," he said taking my gloved hand in his two hands. "I have never seen anything cut wood like that."

Vic was grinning, as he split wood near the top of the tree.

I had cut up the trees they had felled, brought down some more, and had six or seven cord of wood cut by the time we went for lunch.

"How did your morning go?" Mrs Kernohan asked when we walked into the kitchen.

"Did you notice the sun went in this morning at one point?" John asked her. "Well, those weren't clouds Lil... that was sawdust, flying from this young man and his chainsaw. I have never made such a damned fool of myself as I did today. I don't like eating crow, but by God, I need to now. I have never seen such a small machine cut wood like that!"

The rest of the day went well. John harnessed the team and followed Vic and I to the truck, where he hooked up, and pulled me around the field in a big circle and back to Albert's barnyard. Later he paid Doward for cutting 'a good fifteen cord of wood'.

Dollo Brothers

Maybe I should have entitled this chapter, "1955", as there were lots of things happening during that year, but working at Dollo's was most of it.

A few significant things happened, like my niece, Joy Johnson, being born on February 27th, (the family hasn't been quite the same since), and my nephew, Royce Miller, on May 12th, (he has tried to offset the effects that Joy has had on the family ever since, but has never quite achieved that!).

Morley and Keith made some maple syrup that spring and had sold some to a guy by the name of Dan O'Connor, who lived alone on what is now the old road near Kilcoo Camp. The boys rode their bicycles down on June 10th to deliver his syrup and found him dead under his car. He had been working under the car, with it up on jacks and the wheels removed. The accident occurred about a week earlier.

A fire started in Snowdon on the Schroter place, behind our beaver meadow, on July 23rd. It took 100 men three days and nights to bring under control.

July 12th, Ken Mar Lodge burned to the ground.

I have been wandering around the calendar here a lot, but I wanted to deal with some of the events of the year, before I settle down to the main part of this chapter.

Pete and Joe Dollo were both war veterans. Pete fought in France and Italy. While serving overseas, he met and married a Scottish girl, Christina Barkeley, who was serving in the Auxiliary Territorial Services in England. Joe was in the navy.

They arrived in town in 1946, driving Ford Anglia cars. Joe's was blue, Pete's was green. Joe lived in McKayville and Pete lived across from where Don Finn's Law Office is now located on Newcastle Street. Pete and Christine had two children, Marian and David. Joe and Florence had Joan, twins Angie and Louise, and Rosie.

They opened a fruit store, on the east side of Minden's main street, in a new building that had been built since the fire. This building housed Easton's Meat Market, the Minden 5c to $1.00 store, which Ken Currie had just brought to Minden, as well as Dollo Brothers Fruit store. They boasted, and indeed provided, the best fruit and vegetables around. They would rather be out of stock on an item than sell poor fruit or produce.

By 1955, the 5c to $1.00 store had moved across the street, into the former E.A. Rogers store, where Stedman's is now located. The partition was removed between the little meat market and the 5c to $1.00 store, and that portion of the building became Easton's Red and White.

Charlie Plewman, CEO and founder of Kilcoo Camp, was going to build a cottage on the property for himself, so Doward hired me on April 13th to clear the trees off the site and burn brush. I worked there until the cottage was finished and, knowing that I would be laid off when the campers came after school ended, I began to look elsewhere for work for the summer.

Marg was working in the store for Dollo Brothers, and told me that they were looking for someone to help on their truck, so I went into their store one day. Joe was there. I approached him.

"Can I get you something?" he said expecting a sale.

"I want to talk to you about the truck driving job." I said nervously.

"We have decided on hiring Brian Todd." he said as he turned to straighten some fruit in a display.

"Oh, okay, I guess I'm too late."

He wiped his hands on his apron and turned back, throwing his head back a little in an inquisitive manner.

"Have you driven truck much?"

"Around the farm, since I was nine. I drove for Bagshaw Lumber last year."

"I know you drove around Bagshaw's yard, but have you driven much on highways?"

"Oh yeah, I drove their lumber trucks on delivery around Lindsay and Oshawa some."

"You have never driven in Toronto, though."

"No, but I want to learn."

"Why aren't you still with Bagshaw then?" He straightened some more display.

"I got fired last fall."

"FIRED... What for?" He looked me straight in the eye.

"He said I was dead from the arse hole both ways."

He turned around and leaned against the display. "Well, at least you're honest. Why would you tell me that when your looking for a job?"

"It's better that you hear it from me, than from someone else, when I'm not here to defend myself."

"What was that about anyway?"

"I really don't know. I think there was some other personal reason. I made some mistakes but others did also, and they're still there."

He looked down at the floor. "Well that can happen. Why do you want to work here?"

"I want to drive truck."

He lifted a case of trimmed celery off the floor, put it on a stand, and started to place it on a display.

"You're working at Kilcoo Camp right now, aren't you?"

"Yes, but I will be laid off as soon as the campers come in ."

"What about wages. You likely want more than we can pay."

"Well, I'm making fifty cents an hour, four dollars a day at Kilcoo."

"We have to pay by the week. The hours on the truck are too erratic. You would be going to Toronto, and delivering to lodges. That means strange hours."

"That's okay."

"We can only pay $15.00 a week and your meals on the road."

"Sounds good to me. When can I start?"

He looked at a calendar, "June 27th , that okay?"

"What about Brian."

"We haven't told him anything definite."

"What time on the 27th?"

"Be here at nine, when the store opens, okay?"

"I will be here. Thanks Joe."

They had a well-kept dark green 1947-48 Chevrolet truck, with a sixteen-foot factory built wooden van body. There was no reefer*, just two little dropdown doors on the front above the cab and one on the back. This let cooler air blow through as you drove, but didn't do much when the truck wasn't moving.

I went to work on June 27th at 9a.m. They sent me to Joe's, where I was to shine the truck and check under the hood. I was to bring it over to the back of the store and load empty six and eleven quart baskets, basket racks and dividers. Then go home for supper and return at 7pm to go to Toronto.

I was very excited. I had not been to the city much and this was going to be an adventure.

I drove to Steven's Market at Myrtle, Ontario, where Pete stopped to talk shop with the owner. Then Pete took the wheel, as I had never driven on the new, four-lane 401. That portion of the 401 was just completed from Oshawa to Kingston Road at Toronto. Highway 2 was still the only through route along the lakeshore. The 401 put us right onto Kingston road at that time. The bypass around Toronto had been cleared of buildings, and work was progressing but far from finished. All traffic from the east went in on Kingston Road, to either highway 2 or 5 to get to the west end.

We arrived at Pete's parents around 10 p.m. He backed into the lane between their house and Pete's sister's. These houses were so close together that only the body of the truck fit between them. The mirrors, even though they were only little four inch round things on a stick, wouldn't go, so the cab stuck out in front of the houses.

Momma Dollo, a pleasant typical Italian lady was on the front veranda, as we walked across the lawn. She gave us both a mighty hug, then led us into the dining room, where the whole family was waiting to meet Pete's new helper. There was a great hullabaloo as the whole gang hugged, kissed, shook my hand and patted my back. Some of the family members were beautiful young ladies, and I must admit, I was quite shaken by the time it was all over.

In two lively and confusing minutes I met Pete's Dad, his brother Frank and his wife and children who lived there, his sister Teresa and her husband who lived next door and their daughter (a gorgeous young lady who I still can envision in my mind.)

Then a full course meal was served with lots and lots of Mazola Oil. (By the end of summer, I swear, I sweated Mazola Oil). There were all kinds of vegetables fried in Mazola Oil, salads, pastas, and Italian sausage fried in Mazola Oil. This was a fantastic meal and only the first of many I enjoyed during the summer. Being an eighteen-year-old guy, I cleaned off several platefuls.

Teresa and her family went next door about midnight. Frank and his wife went down the hall and upstairs. Papa Dollo disappeared somewhere. Momma Dollo made me a bed on the chesterfield and said goodnight with a big kiss. Pete trundled off down the hall at 12:30a.m. only to return at 3:00a.m. and shake me awake. I sat up, burped a couple of times, tasted Mazola oil, and said, "Huh?"

"Come on, we have to be at the food terminal, when it opens at five, to get the good stuff."

"Food terminal...good stuff...five...huh?"

He gave that silly crooked grin that belonged only to Pete Dollo, and said, "Aw jeepers," and went into the bathroom.

I sat up, yawned, scratched what needed scratching, and waited for him to come out.

We went outside into the hot, humid, still, morning air, heavy now with the smells of the city. A street sweeper went past, and traffic could be heard nearby.

We climbed into the truck. Pete eased it out of that tight slot and onto the street. I can't remember the name of the streets we took, but it was a little way along until we pulled into a driveway leading to a brand new building with "Ontario Food Terminal" on the roof.. Pete showed a pass to security and we drove in.

I had never seen so many transport trucks. There were trucks there from all across Canada, Florida, California, Texas, Prince Edward Island, and anywhere else I could think of.

He drove around the building, where trucks like ours were lined up side by side at a dock, found an empty space, and backed in.

There was lot of rollup type doors all along the back side of the long dock. None was open yet, but there was a lot of shuffling, crashing and banging and yelling in different languages going on beyond them.

We went into a brand new restaurant right on the dock. There were a lot of guys in there having breakfast. Pete bought me ham and eggs, toast and coffee. I didn't think I was hungry after the meal I had the night before, but once I started to eat, I found I was able to polish it off quite nicely.

When we returned to the truck, it was almost five. He showed me how to pack open six-quart baskets, and then counted the empties. We unloaded them and put them on the dock against the open tailgate. The dock was filling with people preparing their trucks and some standing around with clipboards in their hands with the look of warriors about to attack. There was a thermometer outside the restaurant door. It was ninety-four degrees.

The light of dawn teased the night darkness on the horizon as the roll up doors opened and all hell broke lose. There were sellers and buyers all over the place. Pete started to bargain with fellow selling cherries in one of the nearby stalls. There was a lot of discussion, both by speech and show of hands, then a slip was placed in a basket and another guy pushed a hand powered forklift under the skid jacked, it up and brought it to the truck.

"You Dollo?" he said.

"Yes, Dollo."

"You get thirty baskets." He said in broken English, as he piled thirty baskets just inside the tailgate. He then took thirty empties from the pile, had me sign the slip, and left.

I piled them against the head rack, using racks and dividers, the way Pete had shown me.

I never saw Pete again for the next three hours, but man, did the fruit and produce arrive. There were potatoes, turnips, carrots, peaches, pears, radishes, tomatoes, corn on the cob, oranges, lemons, lime, parsnips, every kind of fruit and vegetable you can think of. The truck was filling up. I was sweating buckets and sand from the potatoes was sticking to my arms and clothing.

I looked out between our truck and the one next to us. It was now broad daylight. The sun was appearing on the horizon threatening another hot day. The air was heavy, humid, and smelly.

I looked up and down the dock. There was produce piled behind every truck. Some had people piling it into their trucks, others were just piled high.

Confusion definitely prevailed. There were all kinds of people talking in different languages. They were arguing over prices. Buyers were criticizing value and quality, and racing from stall to stall. Forklifts and loaders threaded their way among stacks of fruit and vegetables with their operators yelling and making gestures with their hands. .

The truck was full from end to end and right to the roof. Nothing had arrived for a while, so I was about to close the tailgate when a fellow came along the dock toward me pulling part of a skid of cabbages. He looked at the load, looked at me and said, "You're Dollo."

"Yes."

"You get three of these."

What the hell was I going to do with three cases of cabbage and a full truck?

Pete came along, looked at the truck, looked at the cabbage, and said, "Aw Jeepers."

He opened a case and took a cabbage out. He forced it along the roof on top of the load, and then another and another until all three cases were empty. He threw the boxes in the garbage.

We went back to Mom and Pop Dollo's where breakfast was waiting. There was toast, coffee, eggs, and sausage, fried in Mazola Oil. I was hungry, the food was good, and I ate like a horse.

"It's good to see the young man eat," she said.

"He can eat," Pete answered. I just kept on eating.

We went out into the back yard, where Pete's Dad was working on his plants. We said goodbye and drove to Steven's at Myrtle.

There was a blonde girl working at the stand. I looked her over and I really couldn't see anything out of place. Everything was there and quite ample where it counted. She caught me looking, and a smile broke out on her pretty face. I went over and talked to her while Pete was talking shop with the owner.

Life was good.

I drove from there and arrived in Minden late afternoon. I blew the horn as I drove past the front of the store on the main street. Joe was waiting at the back door as I backed up to it.

"How did he do?" Joe asked as Pete approached him.

"He packed the whole load, so we will see when we unload." Pete answered.

I started to hand things down, and Pete and Joe carried it to the cooler. Bill Coneybeare was working next door.

"I see you got a new helper Pete." he called.

"Yeah."

"Is he any good?" He joked.

"Aw, Jeepers," Pete said with the crooked grin.

Some things should have been packed differently, which resulted in some damage. They showed me what I had done wrong, and what to do to avoid it.

When the truck was finally empty, Pete said, "We don't usually make two trips to the city back to back, but we are down in product, so we are going to go down tomorrow afternoon. You can come in the morning at nine and we will show you how to clean and display fruit and vegetables. Then you can get the truck ready after lunch and we will leave."

We arrived at Mom and Pop Dollo's before dinner this time. It was hot. We waited for Frank to return from work. He came in complaining loudly about the heat, and described vividly how all the parts of his body were sticking to other parts, while Pete's Mom loaded the dining room table with plates and bowls of food and a spare jug of Mazola Oil. Pete's Pop came in from the back yard. They did a lot of talking in Italian. They all seemed to be upset with each other, but I learned to know that they weren't; It was just their way of communicating. Frank's kids were called in from the street and we ate.

After dinner, Frank turned to Pete and said, "Let's take the lad to a show or something."

Pete turned to me and asked, "Would you like to go to a show?"

"Okay."

We went out the front door and got into Frank's multi-coloured, Dodge van standing at the curb. I guess it was mostly blue, so I will call it blue. I got into the back and sat on a box.

Downtown somewhere, as we were sitting at an intersection waiting for the light, Frank and Pete were deep in conversation and Frank let his foot off the brake, just as an elderly fellow was shuffling across in front of us, in the crosswalk. The truck rolled ahead and the front bumper touched the gentleman knocking him off balance and he toppled over. Both Pete and Frank jumped out and helped the poor old boy up. They were dusting him off and apologizing profusely, when a bunch of people who had seen it happen, joined them. There was a lot of discussion going on, and at times, it looked to me as though the brothers were going to lose the battle, but loud language and a few hand gestures eventually won out, and they returned to the truck. The old gentleman toddled on.

Soon we were standing in line at a place called Casino Royale to buy tickets. I noticed that the whole line was made up of men, but not wanting to appear a Haliburton County Hick I didn't ask. We went in and watched a movie. Then a comedian appeared and told a bunch of bad jokes. A voice on the speakers said, "Now gentlemen. It is time for you to meet Myra."

Onto the stage walked a tall blonde, dressed in red from the floor up. She wasn't too bad looking, and seemed a little on the heavy side, but with all those clothes it was hard to tell.

A band in the orchestra pit struck up a thumping tune. She looked down gave them a smile and a wave and began to dance and remove clothing. She had a lot of red feather boas and layers of thin shawls with feathers all over them, so it took her a while to get to the good stuff, but when she did it was well worth the wait.

This lady had a pair of pasties with six inch tassels, that she could do everything with, but tie them together. She spun them both to the right, then both to the left, then one each way. She bent over and let them hang to the floor. She stood on her head and chewed on them. She went over and put her foot up on a chair and I could see the promised land! That lady got this backwoods kid into a terrible frenzy. She disappeared into the wings, the band started a slow building drum roll, at the end of which she appeared, and flashed a totally nude body. The house lights came on, I tried to stand up, but my knees wouldn't hold me.

Life was good.

When we unloaded in Minden the next day, we did it a little differently. We left some things on board such as potatoes, cabbage, turnips, carrots, and things that don't need to be in the cooler.

The next morning we loaded some perishables and empty cases on the truck and drove up Highway 35. We stopped at all the businesses that prepared food from Minden to Halls Lake. Pete would go into the kitchen and take orders. Sometimes he would call out for me to bring in a bag of potatoes or half case of something. He would finally return with an order and we would make it up, put it into a case and carry it in. Then we would go to the next stop.

We always left Minden on this lodge run as soon as we could get away in the morning and never finished much before 6:30 or 7:00p.m. One night it was 9:45p.m when we finished. We had made three trips to Toronto that week and worked 81 hours.

A routine started now that lasted all summer. Work in store on Monday morning, and then go to Toronto. Load and come back and unload Tuesday. Go to lodges Wednesday. Work in store and go to Toronto Thursday. Load and come back and unload Friday. Go to lodges Saturday. This may look like a boring job, but the only thing that was boring was the heat. That summer could very well be the hottest summer I have experienced. The days were sunny and humid. The nights were hot and humid, with never a breeze. It rained hard in the city on July 15th , but it just came out hot and even more humid as soon as it was over. The remnants of Hurricane Connie went through in the afternoon of August 13th. Lots of rain, but the heat never let up. Residents of Toronto were concerned about this storm because it had not been a year since Hurricane Hazel caused so much death and destruction.

The first thing to break the monotony, was a truck break down at Pickering. The engine started to knock, so Pete shut it down. I don't remember how we got it to a repair shop at stop 27 Kingston Road, but that is where it was to be repaired. Pete made some phone calls from his parents home, and arranged to have Ontario Produce deliver a load to Minden for us the next day. Pete took me to Fenelon Falls the next night, to borrow one of Fenelon Produce trucks to use to deliver to lodges on Saturday.

We went to Toronto on Sunday with Gareth Kellett. He was attending some kind of teacher's class or seminar at the time.

While hanging around Mom and Pop Dollo's the next day, we made a call to the garage and were told that there was strange pitting on the bearing throw of the defective engine rod. They had changed it and the truck would be ready very soon. Pete called a taxi and we went out to the garage. There were tiny etchings on the surface of the bearing insert, like tiny rivers leading to the edge, letting the oil pressure escape from the bearing, causing it to knock. The mechanics there suspected something in the oil was the cause. The oil had been changed not long before I began to work there and had been switched to one of the new multi-grade detergent oils just coming on the market. Phone calls were made, and both General Motors and the oil company showed great concern. They took the bearing for analysis and told us to drive the truck, but watch the oil pressure closely. Two weeks later, they called and asked to have the truck back at the same garage, so they could replace all the inserts including the mains, flush the engine and replace the oil with another kind.

Pete and Joe had cousins who operated a transport company. It only moved cookies from the factory to a warehouse. All these brothers had a truck of their own, and a new one was purchased for each boy as they reached a certain age. They had a new, 1955 International sitting in their yard waiting for the brother to come of age. It had never had a load on it. They loaned it to us for one trip, while our truck was in the garage. I remember their name was Tarranova; the name of their transport was Regent Haulage. Boy, I enjoyed driving that truck.

The next break in routine, was a night when it was terribly hot. In an attempt to survive the sweltering heat of the city, all windows, and doors were open. I slept in the living room on a chesterfield, right below a window that opened to the driveway between the houses. City lights filtered through the blinds, casting a low glow throughout the room.

Pete's niece, who lived next door, was alone. Her parents operated a business of some kind at Washaga Beach in summer. She sang at a nightclub somewhere in the city.

Around 2:30a.m., a scream that would wake the dead, penetrated the whole neighbourhood.

I sat upright, just as I heard the screen door slam next door, and footsteps go toward the street. Our truck blocked the way, so they turned and headed toward the back yard, just as I saw the figure of a well-muscled young Italian race through the room heading for the back door with another one right at his heels. The footsteps outside quickened, as the screen on our back door slammed back against the wall. There was a flurry of yells, puffs, and pants as feet trampled Pop Dollo's precious plants in the yard, then three crashes against the six-foot high board fence.

Momma appeared in the room, talking over her shoulder to Frank's wife, as she headed for the back door. Frank's wife reached for the phone, as Pop showed up. I fell in behind Pop.

In the pale light of the yard, I could see Pete and Frank dressed only in pyjama bottoms pacing back and forth along the fence, looking very much like hounds that had just lost a coon. I guess the intruder had more incentive to clear that fence than they had. I know I would have, with these two guys at my ass.

The women and children gathered around a vision of true loveliness. Standing in the middle was the tall, long black haired, dark skinned object of the attempted home invasion that had just occurred. Dressed in pink baby doll pyjamas, she was a vision of every man's fantasy. Visibly shaken she laid her head on her grandma's shoulder and cried.

There was a knock on the front door and I turned to answer it. Two police officers were standing outside the screen as I approached.

"Someone called about a home intrusion."

"Yes come through here they are all out back."

They followed me through and began their investigation.

By the time things were settled a bit, it was time for us to go to the terminal to start our day. When we came back for breakfast, we learned that the intruder had probably followed the young lady home from the club. Bare foot tracks, wet from walking through the grass, led from right inside the basement window, straight to the steps leading upstairs and directly to the young lady's bedroom. The police thought the intruder had been in the home before, as it appeared he knew the layout of the house. No one ever discovered who he was. I don't know if there was any follow up to the investigation.

Pop was busy repairing his trellises and trying to save his plants, when we went to say goodbye.

For a change in pace and to see his parents from time to time, Joe would go with me sometimes. The first time he went, I drove to Myrtle as usual, but when we went to go on, I got in the passenger side. I was sitting with the window down and was talking to the blonde girl, when Joe came to the truck. He walked up to the passenger side and said, "Get over."

"You want me to drive?"

"You're as good a driver as I am, and you have to start sometime, so get over."

In ten minutes, I was pulling onto the 401 as the radio played 'Cherry Pink and Apple Blossom White'. I drove all the way, both ways, for most of the rest of the summer. Every time I hear the song, I think of driving down the 401 for the first time.

I have never been afraid of the four lanes since, and prefer four lanes to two-way traffic to this day. When I think how close we are to a head on collision every time we meet another vehicle on a two lane highway, it makes me shiver We miss each other by mere inches every time. When we travel at the speed limit of say 50 miles an hour, and the opposing vehicle is going the same, the collision would be like hitting a cement wall at one hundred miles an hour.

There are pileups on four lanes, but at least they are all going in the same direction, originally.

Business slowed down as the Canadian National Exhibition opened in late August. Our loads weren't as heavy now and it was finally getting cooler.

On September 3rd, we went to the lodges for the last time. This was the very last time Dollo Brothers delivered to lodges, as they were on the move now.

Unknown to most of the townsfolk, their store had become an affiliate of the Independent Grocers Alliance group. On September 5th 1955, I began to clear the lot between the 5c to $100 store and Sam Welch's General store for their new store on the main street. Inquisitive bystanders gathered as I removed the beige picket fence, along the front, and watched as I took down a large tree, that was hanging over Sam's store. I did this by climbing the tree and fastening a rope from it to the truck. I cut the tree almost through, then drove the truck ahead. I received a glorious ovation from the crowd, as it hit the ground. I cut it into pieces and took the body to Dad's, where he cut it into firewood. The limbs I took to the swamp across the back street, where Keaney Chrysler is now located.

On September 13th, Joe and I went to Toronto. He bought a black 1952 Ford car, with a red top, he named 'The Red Bird'. He was very proud of that car, so he had me build a garage for it at his place. He put his blue Ford Anglia up for sale.

During the next month, I helped Frank Bowron haul tie logs to Burnt River for Floyd, helped Dad dig potatoes, took a load of pigs to Peterborough for Floyd, helped Floyd put a roof on his house, traded my truck for a 1953 Ford at Deacon's garage in Minden, made several trips to Toronto for fruit, worked in the store, and built a garage for Joe's car. I recently (2004) drove past the house where Joe and Florence lived. The garage still stands.

The lot for the new store had been excavated in the meantime, and on October 11th Harry Cummins and I started the foundation for the new store. Various sub-contractors came and went, but Harry and I were the only steady workers, until November 22nd, when Jim Trumbull joined us. On November 28th, the steel beams arrived for the roof along with a crane to hoist them. By December 19th, we had the roof sheathed and the roofers completed their work in the next two days. It was 32 below zero that day. My new car wouldn't start, so Dad had to drive me to work. How embarrassing!

I worked until noon on December 24th. When I was packing my tools to go home, Pete told me to go over to the store. They gave me $10.00 and a large basket of fruit for Christmas. This was the first time that anyone I knew ever got a Christmas bonus. Wow! Was I proud?

By February 25th, the store was finished and they had started to stock shelves. Joe wanted me to take a meat-cutting course and be their head butcher, but I wanted to drive truck, so I went looking elsewhere.

The store operated for several years at that location, and then was moved to a new bigger building around the corner toward the bypass, then to the present location on the bypass in 1986 and was extended in 1998. Pete's son, David, now operates a huge IGA that employs from 40 to 75 people.

Having served the community well, and being a loyal and faithful confidant to everyone he met, Peter Dollo died, a local legend in 2003. There were pages of his accolades in the local papers.

Reefer; The refrigeration system used to cool the cargo area of a truck. It is the unit you see hanging on the front of the cargo body above the cab.

History of Highways in the Area

It is hard to believe, that when I was born in 1937, there were no highways, but then there were not many cars either. Those in existence, travelled so slowly that bumps, sharp turns, steep hills, and a few logs in the way didn't really matter. Cars were also unreliable and considered more of a nuisance than they were worth by most. Without modern explosives and machinery, roads were hard to build. Rock was drilled by hand and moved by horses. Pictured on the right, my Dad is sitting proudly in his Model T Ford.

Highway 35: In 1931, a piece of road from Lindsay to Fenelon Falls was assumed by the Department of Highways of Ontario and assigned number 35. In 1934, it was extended to Rosedale. Then, in 1937, it was extended all the way to Huntsville. Then it went south from Lindsay to Highway 2 at Newcastle, in 1938. The only paved part of this southerly extension in 1938 was from Orono to Newcastle. I recall the highway being paved from Lindsay north in the late 1940s. However, for some reason, the part from Norland to the Haliburton County boundary, was not paved until 1954. I recall seeing graders working on that piece of highway, attempting to smooth out the washboard caused by the increasing traffic, just before I drove for Dollo Brothers, in 1955. The section south of Lindsay, to Highway 115 at Enterprise Hill, was gravel until 1958.

Even though the traffic through the main street of Minden became horrific on weekends, many people criticised the new bypass around the town, which was completed in 1954, calling it an unnecessary expense. Fenelon Falls was also bypassed, the following year. The Lindsay was bypass was built in 1959, Newcastle in 1956. Southbound traffic on Highway 35, was automatically directed up the ramp onto the westbound 401. There was nowhere else to go. Likewise, eastbound traffic on the 401, down the ramp onto Highway 35 north. There was nowhere else to go for four years, until the 401 was extended east to Port Hope, in 1960. Pontypool was bypassed in the early 1960s.

The portion of Highway 35 &115, north of the 401, was upgraded to four lanes during the mid 1980s.

Highway 115: In 1953, the Department of Highways decided a road, linking Peterborough with Oshawa, Whitby, Ajax, and Toronto, was needed. Prior to then travel between these points was via Highway 28, south to Port Hope, then west along Highway 2. The alternative was along gravel roads, running east and west south of Lindsay. Highway 115 was built, using a portion of Highway 28, south of Peterborough, to link with Highway 35 at Enterprise Hill. I recall several terrible accidents occurring at the intersection of 115 and 28. The road was straight for nearly a mile from Highway 7A west, and vehicles were travelling too fast to negotiate the sharp ramp, part of the cloverleaf. This deathtrap was eliminated in 1979, when Highway 115 was extended to Highway 7, at the Peterborough bypass, and a full cloverleaf was installed at Highway 28. Highway 115 was extended along Highway 35 to the 401 in 1961, and became a four-lane highway in 1990.

Highway 118: When I moved from the area in 1969, the road heading west from Highway 35 at Carnarvon, Ontario only went a short distance. It turned north, and came out again at Buttermilk Falls. I was very surprised, when I visited the area in the late 1970s, to find that a road had been punched through the rocks and swamps to Bracebridge. On a later visit, in 1982, I found that this road had been upgraded and was now part of Highway 118. This was a great boost to the area, as it was a short cut to Highways 11 and 400, which lead to the industrial areas at Barrie and Orillia, and to Toronto. I predict, that this road will become greatly improved, and might even become four-lane, as the Muskoka cottage area is almost full, and people are beginning to look to the Haliburton Highlands for lakeshore property.

On May 1, 2003, Highway 121, East of Haliburton to Paudash, was renumbered 118.

Highway 121: Highway 121 originally began at the junction of Highway 35, then referred to as Powle's Corners, south-west of Fenelon Falls. It wandered north, through the town of Fenelon Falls, the hamlet of Burnt River, Kinmount, past our house, joined Highway 35 again, two miles south of Minden, and terminated at Minden. This section was taken over by the Department of Highways in 1955. From Minden, it then went east, through Haliburton, and on to the junction of Highway 503 at Tory Hill. This portion was taken over by the DHO in 1956. I remember driving, on a part near Loon Lake that was still gravel, when I was employed by Hewitt Transport. That portion wasn't paved until 1959. Most of this highway was paved with cold tar mix* at the time.

The part of the highway from Fenelon Falls to Powle's Corner was rerouted to meet Highway 35 west of the town, when the Fenelon Falls Highway 35 bypass was opened in 1955. Prior to this date, Highway 35 went right through Fenelon Falls.

A road, heading east from Highway 503, between Tory Hill and Wilberforce, had been completed through to Paudash at Highway 28. That road was paved and was taken over by the DHO in 1964.

In early 1998, the responsibility for many highways in Ontario was downloaded to counties and townships. The portion from Fenelon Falls to Highway 35 at Minden, was renamed 'Kawartha Lakes Road 121; and the part from Highway 35 at Minden to Haliburton, was renamed 'Haliburton County Road 121'. Early in 2003, the last part of Highway 121, from Haliburton to Highway 28 at Paudash, was renumbered Highway 118.

*Cold tar mix; *This road material was mixed on the job, with the use of graders. The 'A' gravel was spread along the side of the road by truck, then a portion was levelled with graders. Cold tar was then spread over the gravel and another few inches of gravel spread over this by the grader. This was continued until all of the gravel was levelled. Then the entire mixture was rolled back into a windrow of partially mixed asphalt, along the side of the road. The graders would spread a thin layer of this on the road bed, and the entire process would be repeated, until the engineers declared it ready to spread permanently. It was levelled across the entire lane and sealed in place by a heavy roller. This provided a nice smooth road. Unfortunately it was thin and not very durable. Cracks would appear during the first winter, and sections would lift with traffic. Patching was usually necessary by the end of the second year.*

Mabel, Floyd, and Hazel ready to go to town. The license plate reads 1935. Notice the fill cap for the gasoline tank is right in front of the windshield, in the middle. That was where the tank was located. Your feet were under it, so it was right in your lap. The placement of the tank did little to enhance the safety of the vehicle.

I don't know why Mabel was upset at the time, but I am sure someone got a good swift kick in the shins, as soon as the picture was taken.

Entries in Our Diaries
From September 6th 1954 to
January 31st 1956

1954, September 6:   Doward, Hazel, and I Went to Toronto Exhibition in Toronto. *We drove to a car pool area near Whitby, then took a bus from there to the Exhibition. Doward and Hazel took the bus back to the car. I attempted to take a TTC bus to Mom and Pop Dollo's place, where I was to meet Pete and bring a load back the next day. I got on the bus going west instead of east and wound up in Oakville, then returned and got to Dollo's late, embarrassed and confused.*
September 15:   I Bought 1953 Ford from Deacon Brothers.

It was metallic green when I bought it. I had it two-toned green and cream, while I had it back in Deacon's to have the left rear fender repaired, after the accident on March 29, 1956.

September 24:   Mother, Dad, Morley, Keith, Phyllis, and I went to Lindsay Fair. I Lost Wallet. *I had quite a lot of money in my wallet, as I was planning to purchase snow tires for my car. I paid our way at the fair gates, and because there were a lot of cars behind us, I laid my wallet on my lap, and drove on to the parking lot. I forgot the wallet was there, and when I got out of the car, it fell out beside the car. An hour or so later, there was a call over the public address system for me to go to the office. When I got there, they asked me if I had lost my wallet. I said "No". I reached for it, but my pocket was empty. I described it, and they gave it to me. Absolutely everything was still in it. A couple from Sunderland had parked beside me, and when she got out she saw the wallet laying there. They turned it in and waited. It is unfortunate, that kind of honesty is getting very rare.*
October 29:   Floyd Went To Kirkland Lake for Hydro. *Floyd hired on with Bob Young's construction crew. He went to build hydro lines in Northern Ontario.*
November 17:   Snowed 2 Inches. John Harrison and I got Floyds Cattle from Ranch. *Floyd had cattle at all over the place. They had to be stabled at various places, where people were to winter them. He was up north, so John and I began to bring them in.*
November 18:   Floyd Home from Kirkland Lake and helped John and I with rest of Cattle *He came home unexpectedly that night. The three of us completed the job.*
December 15:   Joliffer Simpson stayed here, tramp walking on road. *Prior to this time, it was common to have a homeless man appear at the door needing food and shelter for the night. There were also often signs that someone had spent the night in our barn. Sometimes, there*

would be footprints in the snow or the shape of a person pressed into the loose hay of a mow. Joliffer Simpson was the last tramp to stay with us.

December 16.:   <u>Went to Gareth's Concert at Blairhampton School</u>. *Gareth was teaching school at Blairhampton. This was his first Christmas concert. I went with Elmer and Gladys.*

1956, January 31:   Ross Dugan Pulled, <u>Arm Off in Lumber Camp</u>

Tragedy in the Woods

It was Tuesday, the last day of January, 1956. Snow had been falling for several days. S.G. Nesbitt was jobbing for Hay and Company, cutting logs on limits near Kennisis Lake. My cousin, Ross Dugan, was operating a bulldozer for Hay and Company.

Drivers were having trouble keeping trucks under control going down a hill with their loads. Sand had been applied several times, but was being covered by snow and was of no avail. The company placed Ross at the top of the hill with his bulldozer, so he could let the trucks down the hill with the winch, at the rear of his machine.

The cable on the winch had been replaced the day before, and the new one still bore the shape of a larger coil than the spool of the winch. As a result it was not reeling back onto the spool smoothly and would pile up. Each time a truck would be let down the hill and unhooked, Ross would put the winch in gear, and letting the engine idle slowly, he would get down from the controls, go to the rear of the machine and guide the cable back onto the spool. He was wearing long sleeved underwear, a heavy long sleeved shirt, a sweater, a heavy parka jacket and leather gauntlets.

He really didn't know if there were a broken strand in the cable, causing a barb to stick out that caught his left glove, or he just simply put his hand too close to the spool, but he found himself being wound into the machine. He felt the slow turning spool begin to crush his hand. He frantically tried to free his hand from the glove, but the cable was wrapped too tightly. It crushed his wrist and his sleeves were caught. His forearm was being mangled, as he was drawn into this mighty, unsympathetic machine. He knew that he had to do something or he would die. He yelled, but there was no one near enough to hear. The engine idled on unfeelingly. He felt the elbow separate, and the bone between the elbow and shoulder break. As the bone broke the second time, he placed his right arm and shoulder against the fuel tank of the tractor and pulled. His clothing separated at the shoulder. Also his arm, mid-way between the elbow and shoulder, but he was free from the monstrous machine. He was a stalwart man, and it was believed, if it weren't for his colossal, adrenaline-driven strength and stubborn determination, he would have died in the snowy woods that day.

He looked at the fragmented stub of his arm sticking out of his shoulder. He was surprised that there was very little blood. He doesn't know why he did what he did next, but he climbed onto the machine, and shut it off. He then walked down the hill to where a crew of loggers were working. They took him out the crooked, hilly log road to West Guilford and on to the Red Cross Outpost Hospital at Haliburton, the same building now occupied by Canoe Radio. Dr Carroll looked it over and determined the arteries had stretched out, then snapped back, tying themselves off by the force of stretch and the recoil. That is why he bled very little. The doctor bandaged the stub and, using what drugs were available to him at the time, he made Ross as comfortable as possible.

Five days later, on February 5th, when the nurses went to change the bandages, gangrenous gas was released. Dr Carroll phoned Toronto immediately to have serum sent. In two hours and fifteen minutes, a police car raced through Haliburton's main street. Siren wailing and its one red revolving light flashing, it turned right at Curry Motors, then left at the town hall and screeched to a stop at the front steps of the hospital. The siren died. The drivers door opened and an officer raced up the front steps and into the building. In his hand was the lifesaving substance. The serum was applied and the gangrene treated. The Ontario Provincial Police had alerted all the detachments between Toronto and Haliburton and relayed the medication through.

Ross was taken to Lindsay, three weeks later, to have what was left of the arm removed at the shoulder.

He operated a log jammer* for a year, and then went back to driving the same bulldozer that had taken his arm. He was later transferred to Searchmont, Ontario, where he lived his life working for Hay and Company and then Weldwood Limited.

He was fitted with an artificial limb, but threw it away after trying to use it for two years. He said that it was only in the way. He learned to do everything he needed with one hand, and was a perfect marksman with a rifle. I have heard those who have hunted moose with him, tell of the amazing way he could throw his lever action rifle over his shoulder, racking another shell into the breech. It was said he could rapid fire with the best of them.

Ross was originally married to Alice Trumbull, and has a daughter Gayle. They divorced, and he remarried Maureen Howard.

His sister Irma, Mrs. Ron Little, suffering from cancer, went to visit him, when she knew he didn't have long to live. She said that they had a wonderful two weeks together.

He died in a Sault Ste. Marie hospital on May 17th, 1993, at the age of 66.

Irma also succumbed to the illness two years later after a hard fought battle.

Tragedy struck the same logging operation the day after Ross was hurt. Cecile Bacon was throwing a wrapping chain over a load of logs, when a log was dislodged from the top of the load and fell on him. He died of his injuries.

When I was preparing to write this chapter, I called his brother Carl on the phone to verify some things. Carl is a stalwart individual. He has suffered more than one mishap in his 80 years. He is still very active. Just a year or more ago, he was working alone in the woods when his family began to worry. He was late for an appointment, so they called Mike Newell who lived across the road from the woods in which he was working. Mike found him pinned beneath a tree that he had fallen. He had lain there for many hours. Responding emergency personnel, pried him loose and he was taken to Haliburton Hospital broken, and quite bruised. He spent a few weeks in hospital. He is back working in the woods, cutting wood and logs as I write. Friends and neighbours will not allow him to be there alone. I heard that one friend told him, if he was determined to be in the woods alone, he was going to shoot him, so he wouldn't get hurt and suffer!

Log Jammer; A pole and cable lifting device used to load logs.

The Minden Monarchs

I remember the old skating rink, in the middle of a swampy area, where the municipal buildings are now in Minden. It was open air, with four-foot high boards around it and a couple of strings of bare light bulbs over it, giving very poor light at night. When it would snow, the skaters would shovel the snow over the boards. There would be a pile of snow as high as the boards by spring.

Then they launched a campaign to raise money for a community centre. The drive was successful, and with the help of many volunteers, the building was erected in the same location. I am not sure what year that was, but I know it was prior to 1951, as Marg and Floyd held their wedding dance there on September 18th of that year. That building was very modern for the time, with a regulation-size ice hockey rink, player dressing rooms, ticket wickets, a heated snack booth, and a large auditorium upstairs, complete with stage.

A huge frost heave formed in the southwest corner of the ice the first year, which caused some unusual deflections of the puck, but this was still a big improvement over the open-air rink. The soil was removed during the following summer, and replaced with proper gravel.

The ice surface was scraped, during intermission, by rink rats* and the snow shovelled over the boards by hand. I don't remember the first ice makers, but Les Winch and Walter McKelvey served in that capacity at a later time. This was a touchy job, as there was no artificial ice system, so it depended solely on the weather. Most of winter was below freezing, but there were times, toward spring, when the ice would be soft and covered with water. There was no Zamboni so the ice was flooded on a cold night and nature was allowed to do the rest.

Permanent fixtures at almost every game were the Minto Twins, Winnie and Mae, and their mother, Ethel. Seated on woollen blankets, to soften the effects of the cold, hard, wooden seats, and covered with other blankets against the bitter cold, they sat beside the players box on the south side of the arena, and cheered the home team. They could also be seen at some out of town games.

By the mid 50's, the country was opening up. Roads were being built and hydro lines were strung to the back shores of lakes. This brought many new hydro and construction workers into the region. I recall the names of some: Larry and Len Lonsberry, Gerry Gartland, and Eston Watt. There were others, but their names escape me at this time. These were capable young men. They were also hockey players.

Mark Vasey was manager of the Minden Monarchs. The team was made up of local boys, such as Glen, Gary, and Hugh Vasey, Morris McKelvey, Doug Pritchard, Grant Hewitt, Roy and Junior Windover, Lawrence and Stafford Yearwood, and others. They played against the Haliburton Huskies, and the Bobcaygeon Bobcats.

The new workers were introduced to the team and along with the originals, they produced a calibre of local hockey far superior to anything we had ever seen in this area. In 1956, this team went into the play-offs, which took them, and many followers, to places like Beeton, Huntsville, and Napanee.

Entries in my diary during the winter of 1955 read;

January 6: Helped Dad in barn swamp*, to hockey match tonight.

January 11: Helped Dad cut logs and pulpwood* across the road. To hockey match in evening. 4-3 for Minden, (No mention of who they played against that night.)

January 29: Cold. Fixed heater in my truck. Helped Dad tear engine apart in his truck. To hockey match.

February 8: Helped Dad in workshop. I painted a tractor wheel. Snowed. To hockey match.

February 22: Lovely day. Nelson Archer and I to Deep Bay. Cut ice on Devil's Lake. Clutch on saw broke. To hockey match. 7-1 for Minden. (No mention who they played.)

March 3: Cut ice for Doward at Nelson Leary's. Cold raw East wind. *Hazel home. To hockey match. 10-4 Minden. (No mention who they played.)

Entries in my diary winter 1956;

January 26: Worked eight hrs For Dollos. Audrey Harrison and I to Haliburton to hockey match.

January 28: Worked 9 and a quarter hours for Dollos. Audrey and I to hockey match. Rain and freezing tonight.

February 3: Worked eight hrs for Dollos. Audrey and I to show and hockey match.

February 14: Worked eight hrs for Dollos. To hockey match.

February 15: Worked eight hrs for Dollos. To Little Britain to hockey match. Audrey & I, Mervin & Sylvia, Ferne, and Marlene.

February 21: Cold. 10 below this morning. Audrey and I to hockey match. Worked eight hrs for Dollos.

February 24: Rain and freeze. Worked eight hrs for Dollos. To Uncle Will's to see about Uren Construction job. Audrey and I to hockey match in Sutton.

March 1: Painted second coat on woodwork in kitchen. To hockey match in Minden. Rain at night.

March 8: Snowy. Floyd and I to Peterborough. Audrey and I to hockey match.

March 15. Lovely day, but cold east wind. Went to Bobcaygeon to hockey match. Took Audrey home from work.

March 17: Lovely day. Went to hockey match in Minden. Took Audrey home after work.

March 20: Lovely warm sunny day. Audrey and I to hockey match.

March 24: Lovely day. Audrey and I to Bobcaygeon, (hockey match). Floyd, Beverley Kernochan, and Murray Gartshore went with us.

March 29: Cloudy. Misty all day. Snow in evening about four inches. Went to go to Huntsville (hockey match) but ditched car.

Buses were not available, so we travelled what were then considered as great distances, in cars to cheer on and support our Monarchs.

On March 29th ,1956, Joan Hewitt, Louie Trapanier, Robert Lazere, several others and I embarked on one of these trips. It had snowed about four inches that day, and was still snowing when I left to go to Huntsville for a hockey game. It was getting really slippery and hard to see for snow flying, when we got as far as Camp Kandalore, so I decided to turn back. There was not enough traction to climb Partridge Lake hill, (it was much steeper then and the highway has since been re routed) and I slid back into a guard post. There was a big dent in the right rear panel, behind the rear door. Hugh Taylor upset his car that night.

April 12: Lovely day. Audrey and I, Gareth, Mervin and Sylvia, Morley and Keith, and Floyd to Bobcaygeon to hockey match. (*Eight people! What a hell of a load that must have been*).

April 14: Hung around. Audrey and I, Gareth and Shirley Cox, Mervin and Carol O'Neill to Napanee to hockey.

We started to plan this trip, as soon as we learned that the Monarchs would be in the play-offs against Napanee. I had finished at the construction of Dollo's store and had looked for work at Uren Construction, a company working out of Uncle Will's gravel pit in Lochlin. I was doing nothing at the time, so I decided to take my car and we would go. Mother worried.

The day was bright and sunny, as I recall, with a strong wind blowing from the north west. I left home shortly after noon and went to Len Hamilton's, where Audrey was boarding. We picked up the rest in the parking lot at the arena. My 1953 Ford was not the best in snow, even though I had Goodyear Suburbanites* installed, but one thing it did have, was a superb heater. I remember Mervin yelling from the back seat, just as I was slowing to turn onto Highway 121. "Turn that heater up, Ray, we have to get these women out of these winter clothes." He was sitting between Carol and Shirley as Gareth was in the front with Audrey and I at the time.

When we started on the short cut from Bobcaygeon to Emily Park, we began to encounter some heavy drifting, where the wind had drifted snow two feet deep, all the way across the road. We found ourselves stuck in the middle of one of these drifts more than once, but I had a good shovel and a box of sand in the trunk, so with a little exercise, we forged on.

The construction of the 401, in the eastern sector, was patchy to say to least in 1956, so our route took us south from Peterborough to Highway 2 at Port Hope, and then east. The journey was long. We stopped somewhere for food and a washroom, but I don't remember where, and arrived just as a line up began to form at the arena. There were a lot of Minden people at the door. One of them was Shirley Cox's father Lyman. This was a little funny, as she didn't know he was taking a load down also. Apparently, some people had approached him with the idea after she had left.

When the doors opened, we went to the washroom, and to the snack bar for food, then to our seats. I don't remember what the score was that night and it didn't appear that I recorded it in my diary. I do remember, though, that the trip home was uneventful. The wind had dropped. The roads had been plowed, and the moon was out. It was daylight when I arrived home.

April 16: Snow and Rain. To Bobcaygeon tonight to hockey. Audrey acting the bear.

April 18: Snowy. Audrey, Mervin, Harriet Lazere, Joan Hewitt, Lola Stevenson, and I to Napanee to hockey.

April 21: Snowy. Went to hockey in Bobcaygeon. Ernie Uptergrove here to hire me to go to Toronto.

April 28: To Minden. Rainy. To Bobcaygeon to hockey. Audrey and I had a little difference of opinion.

April 30: Worked for A.N. Richmond. To Beeton to hockey match.

May 4: Worked for A.N. Richmond. Quit at Richmond's. To hockey at Bobcaygeon and fireworks at Minden. (*The ice must have been very wet and sloppy for these last few games, as there was no artificial ice*).

I have included all these entries, to show just how devoted we were to the Monarchs. We hardly ever missed a home game, and travelled as much as time and money would allow supporting them. Besides, it was damned good entertainment. I am not a fan of hockey at all now. I would much rather watch the Monarchs of the 1950s than any NHL game I have ever seen.

I happened to see Larry Loughheed the other day at Keanny Chrysler. It was good to see him, and do a little reminiscing about those times.

Oh... Just in case anyone was following my love life in the diary entries and wondering what happened: Audrey and I broke up, after attending a show at the Molou Theatre, in Haliburton, on May 5th. I took Joyce Stewart out the next day.

On May 20th , 1956, I took Mervin's sister Ferne Cowan home from town. This was the start of a rocky courtship that led to our marriage three years later.

*Rink rats: *Several young male skaters would push snow scrapers around the ice during intermission piling the snow into windrows. Then they would get out large scoop-like scrapers, and scoop the snow into these. They would then take it to an area where there were no seats and an adult would shovel it over the boards. Zamboni were not available then.*

*Goodyear Suburbanites: *Goodyear Tire and Rubber Co. had just invented a winter tire that was considered to be the only winter tire anyone would ever need. It was a wonderful invention as it replaced the need for tire chains, which had been an almost permanent winter fixture up to that time. They took a good grip on packed snow, but unfortunately, they were not as effective on ice as tires are now. That is why other treads were invented.*

*Barn swamp: *This refers to the swampy area south of the barn where spruce and balsam grew thick. It was the source of many logs and pulpwood at that time. It is completely grown in now, after not been harvested for nearly 50 years.*

*Pulpwood: *Pulpwood is cut from softwood trees, spruce, balsam, or poplar, in four-foot lengths and shipped by rail to paper plants.*

*Hazel Home: *Refers to Hazel arriving home from Haliburton hospital with newborn baby. Joy.*

Entries in our Diaries
From March 8th 1956 to May 20th 1959

1956, March 8:   Ray and Floyd took Floyd's pigs to Peterborough. *Floyd was raising quite a few pigs at this time. When they were ready for market, we would load five or six into his pickup and take them to the feed mill either at Fenelon Falls, or to Peterborough. Floyd didn't like driving in Peterborough, so I would go to do the driving. We would unload at Canada Packers in Peterborough where Holiday Inn now stands on George Street.*

      March 13:   Bank of Montreal and Dollar Store Burnt in Haliburton

      March 25:   Elmer Kellett Took a Stroke. *Elmer was found unconscious at the water hole, where he had gone to chop a hole through the ice, so his cattle could get water. It was first thought that he had suffered a stroke, but it was later diagnosed as a brain haemorrhage.*

      March 27:   Ray Helping with Elmer's Chores. *Neighbours thought nothing of caring for each other's animals in an emergency. I was very familiar with what had to be done there as I had helped many times before.*

      April 2:   Ray Went To Oshawa GM to Look for Work

      April 5:   Elmer Kellett Died 46 Years Old

      April 23:   Ray Went to Toronto to Work

      December 27:   Telephone installed. *Our first telephone was installed this day. There were phones elsewhere, but the lines that went past our house were all long distance and couldn't be utilized. The Burnt River telephone company put its line through from Kinmount and everyone hooked up. Our number was 23R21.*

1957, January 15:   Ray Went to Cutler to Work

      February 15:   Ray Home from Cutler

      March 29:   Dad took fainting spell 8:45 pm

      June 19:   Started to haul meat from Toronto for Hewitt Transport

      August 14:   Dad went to Toronto with me on meat truck

      September 7:   Worked for Hewitt Transport this morning. Ferne and I to Lindsay this afternoon. Bought new car. *I bought a new Meteor Rideau 500 from J&W Motors in Lindsay. It was green and cream. This car cost $3,485.00. There was no tax.. There was a clock on a display in the showroom that fit this model. I asked what it cost to have that installed. It was $15.00, so I purchased it bringing the total to even $3500.00. This car proved to be a bit of a disaster. It was fine mechanically, but the metal of the body was so thin, that when they drilled the fender to install the radio aerial, they drilled through more paint than metal. I sold the car to Boris Plutt, when I needed money to start the house in 1960. He hit a rock, near Gelert, and the whole body became a honeycomb when the rust had fallen out. I have never seen a 1957 Ford done up as a classic car. Maybe there just aren't enough of the bodies left to rebuild. It came with Dunlop Gold Seal tires, that kept separating from the cord. Randy Welburn of Welburn Tire and Battery in Burnt River kept replacing them under warranty but the replacements did the same. I finally installed something different and had Dunlop supply me with a set for my truck.*

Later that year Ferne and I took Mother and Dad to see the Hunters at Leamington. There were only small parts of the 401, west of Toronto, near London. We travelled Highway 2 most of the way. The trip was good and the car was a pleasure to drive.

      October 4:   Sputnik Launched 184 pounds. *This was the first exploration into space. (The satellite portion of this publication starts here). Although this program was greatly*

criticized, in this part of the country we have benefited greatly from the over 2500 satellites now in space. Many people don't realize the things we enjoy to-day that wouldn't be possible without them.

1958, November 8: <u>Bought 1953 Chev half ton truck.</u> *I can't recall where I bought this truck, I think it was Fee Motors in Lindsay. I do know that the name O.C. Childs, Fenelon Falls was on the box. The name had been erased, but I could still see the letters in the sun. I was working for Reg Hicks Construction at the time. We worked on the new Lutterworth School, (now Acorn Furniture), the second floor of the Hardware Store on Minden's main street, (the store was operated by Walt and Mabel Wideman), and the addition to the United Church in Minden.*

December 30: <u>Worked at Floor In Front Room.</u> *Ferne bought me a Dermeyer power hand saw for Christmas. This was the first power handsaw the family had ever owned. Dad though it was amazing. We used it to replace the entire floor in the front room. I recall mortising beams with it.*

1959, February 13: <u>Ray Started to Build Trailer Cabin</u> *I began to build this trailer, as I had a contract to erect pre-cut cottages for Peterborough Lumber, around Peterborough and surrounding lakes. I found an axle and the irons for the tongue. I built it from the ground up. It was 8'x16' and made of plywood.*

February 18: <u>Ray Went to Peterborough to Work Early This Morning</u> *Joe Sullivan, salesman for Peterborough Lumber, called me to erect a pre-cut somewhere.*

February 24: <u>Mrs. Hulbig Died.</u> *Imagine the terror and insecurity this woman felt when her husband, Lou Porter, was murdered near Kilcoo Camp. She was faced with the responsibility of raising five children, in backwoods Ontario, in early 1900s. Lou's brother in law, Hector Ellis, confessed to the crime, and spent time behind bars, before being released to die of a terminal illness. Conflicting stories abound, some blaming Ellis and others praising him. Some say Porter had it coming to him because he was an evil man, while others very strongly disagree. His body was found by Chester Kellett, nearby was a hat the he had won from George Kellett in a poker game. Ada later married John H.Hulbig Sr. She had another son, John S. Hulbig, a lifelong citizen of our community and author of the book 'Whispering Pines'. After John Sr. died on January 22, 1942, she and young John carried on with the farm. I was privileged to have sampled the hospitality of this lady on many occasions.*

March 15: <u>Wind Blew my Trailer Cabin Over</u> *The trailer was sitting on snow. When the wind hit it, one of the wheels sank into the snow and it toppled onto its side. The only damage was a broken window.*

March 16: <u>Got my Trailer Back on Wheels. High Winds and Snow. Lot of Highways Blocked</u> *Dad put a chain over the trailer, and using his chain blocks, fastened to a nearby fence post, he pulled the trailer back onto its wheels. This is the last time I remember the roads being plugged. It didn't last for long as there was more powerful equipment by then and the roads were easier to clear.*

March 17: <u>Got my Trailer out Of Snow Bank</u> *We shovelled snow from the trailer to the road. I took it to Haliburton, where it was weighed and got the license from George Brennan.*

April 10: <u>Lena Kellett Buried</u> *Lena was a hard working lady. She and her husband, George, raised 11 children on a farm no bigger or more prosperous than any of the others. As a result of the children being raised with an iron hand, all of them grew to be respectable citizens and went on to become successful in their careers. The youngest were twins, Glen and Craig, with whom I attended school. Glen formed up a large hydro line maintenance company, 'K-Line Maintenance', that works all around the world. Glen died in 2003 of pancreatic cancer.*

May 12: <u>Dad Died.</u> *Mother wrote in his diary, "This book was Milton's. He passed away this evening with a heart attack, 64 yrs. 12 days. In at Dick Hylier place. His Grandpa Schroter's farm".*

May 20: <u>I Married Ferne Cowan</u>

Searching for Work

In the late 50s, work was hard to find. Most individuals drew unemployment insurance during the winter and helped with barn chores. There was always wood to cut, split and pile, and some equipment repairs, if you were fortunate enough to have a shop.

When the first spring warmth was felt, we would get a strong urge to find employment for summer and make some money.

I always wanted to drive truck, but when there seemed to be no hope of that, I would look for anything that was available.

Mervin Cowan and I had spent some time together going to hockey matches, helping our fathers in the woods, and making maple syrup. We decided to look for work further afield and put our names in at factories in Barrie, Toronto, all along the lakeshore, at General Motors in Oshawa, and Canadian General Electric and Outboard Marine in Peterborough.

We spent a few days doing this, and wound up at Mervin's Aunt and Uncle Carmen Sutton's in Peterborough. Carmen had just traded his gravel truck for a new one, so I had a good look at that.

While we were waiting patiently for work, Ernie Uptergrove, a travelling used car salesman made his annual trip to the area. He was a good friend of Mervin's parents, and called on them one day while I was there. He told us that an estate owner in Toronto was looking for help for his gardener. We were interested. He made a phone call, and the following Monday we were working on the grounds of a property owned by a VIP at Toronto's northern limits.

This was a fairly large place, with acres of lawn and flower beds, a large horse stable, but no horses, a lot of roads and pathways. There was a separate dwelling for the head gardener. A creek ran through the property with a dam. We were not allowed in the main yard, but we could see there were several large cars in a garage. We had a full compliment of tools and equipment at our disposal, including a small farm tractor and wagon.

We spent a lot of time planting flowers and raking winter debris from the lawns and, on the first Friday of the job, we put several stop logs in the dam. Weather forecasting wasn't what it is today, so we had no idea that there was a spring storm on the way. It rained hard during the weekend and the creek overflowed, depositing a lot of silt and debris on the lawn. It was a heavy job, raking it all away.

Ernie came around one day to see how we were doing, and during the conversation, he told us that there was a playoff hockey game in Beeton, between the Monarchs and the Beeton squad. Ernie had sold cars to some of the players and indicated that he would like to see the game. Beeton wasn't far from where we were, so he said that he would come by, and we could follow him out of the city. The night of the game came and he arrived. We pulled out behind him, and followed to the first light, where he sped through on the orange. We never saw him again until we arrived after finding our own way out of the city.

We boarded with an elderly lady who the head gardener knew, just a few blocks from work. That lady took a liking to Mervin, but wasn't fond of me at all. Once the diverter in the bathtub was left on 'shower', and when she went to run some water into the tub to clean it, she got her head wet from the shower head. I heard about that at dinner. Another time Mervin and I were wrestling for fun in the bedroom. One of us landed on the bed and broke it. I got hell for that also. I don't know to this day what she had against me. I think she just liked Mervin, and so someone had to catch it and I was handy.

We must have planted a million roses, and many other plants during the next two weeks. We both decided that this was not for us, so we tendered our resignations and returned home.

On May 18th ,1956 I found work at Hewitt Transport and worked there seasonally for four years.

Mervin and I in 1956

Wolves

Sam Crawford and Jumpsey Austen lived at Brady Lake, several miles north of Minden, in an area that was very much isolated, before Highway 118 was punched through from Carnarvon to Bracebridge.

These were hard-working men, who raised large families during very hard times, by utilizing all means available to them. Although they were well versed in ways of coaxing crops from rough and rocky land, a good deal of their livelihood depended on what the woods had to offer.

Marksmanship with firearms, and the ability to acquire a fish dinner with a stick, a piece of twine, a safety pin and a worm, was instilled in their children from the start. An acute sense of direction in deep woods was essential for male and female children alike.

Although schooling was not readily available, these men did everything possible to acquire as much education for their children as they could by boarding them out with families near a school*.

This, coupled with a keen sense of ethics, produced a character second to none. The men who came from Brady Lake and entered into the work force had a level of intelligence, decency, and honesty, I have not seen in some well-travelled professors.

Their ability to exist in close proximity with animals in the wild was second nature to these families.

Sometime between October 22nd and November 15th 1956, I experienced the fine character of one of these men first hand.

Two of Sam Crawford's sons, Murray and Elmer, were very valuable workers for Prentice Roads. They had become very talented operators of heavy machinery. The rule of thumb in a construction crew is, the loader operator is foreman in the pit, and the 'dozer' operator is foreman at the dump, whenever the owner is not present. With Murray usually operating loaders and Elmer usually operating bulldozers, Morgan and Bill Prentice could leave the job site with a high degree of comfort that all would be well in their absence. They knew that all decisions would be made with the highest level of common sense.

I had been laid off from Hewitt Transport for the season on August 18th, and hired on for the first time with Prentice Roads on August 21st.

We worked locally until September 11th, when we transferred to Algonquin Park, where we built roads around Tea Lake for two weeks, then moved to The Forestry School, (now known as the Frost Centre), to build roads around Miller Pond.

On October 22nd we moved to Port Severn, where we boarded at Camp Rawley Lodge.

The extension of Highway 103*, northward from Port Severn, to meet with Highway 69 at Foot's Bay, had been started the year before and was ready for the sand cushion, but work had been suspended until spring. The tendered portion built by the construction company, north from Victoria Harbour, ended in the middle of a rock cut, which meant the road ended in a sold rock wall.

Another company was putting in guard posts along that portion and had a camp a mile or so north of Victoria Harbour. This was a crew camp in a field, with coal oil lights for lighting.

The Department of Highways had sent an inspector by the name of Sing Fergus from Huntsville to oversee the roads we built into and around Six Mile Lake.

This was tough country in which to build side roads. The only fill available were pieces of sod which grew over solid rock. Murray would pull these pieces of sod (which we affectionately called porcupine hides), down off the rocks, and load them into our trucks. We would then go to the dump where we would dump them over cliffs and into boggy areas to make a road bed. When we had built a piece of road, we would go down the new, partially-built highway to a pit, and haul gravel back, to make a poor, but passable, cottage road. There were no cottages on these lakes yet, but with the highway opening the area, there soon would be.

With all of this work on bald rock, the cantilever arm on the Drott loader became bent. There was a possibility the pin, holding the unit together, could spring out, bringing work to a halt.

It began to rain just before noon, so we all headed back to Rawley Lodge for a day of rest. After lunch, we were in the lounge. Some of the workers were planning to have a rest then a drink at the beverage room across the dike.

Murray came into the lounge and said, "I am going to remove that arm from the loader and take it to the machine shop at Waubaushene to have it straightened. Who wants to come with me as I can't lift it alone?" There was some mumbling among the guys, but no one jumped at the chance to work in the rain, even though there were rain coats available, so I said, "I'll go Murray."

We were using an old, black and turquoise Ford car, that Jack Prentice had rolled, as a crew shuttle. The lights and everything required to make it legal had been repaired, but the instruments on the dash were nowhere near accurate. We climbed into this contraption and headed up to the job site.

The arm on the loader was removed easily. We took it to the shop, where we had to wait a while for a mechanic to be free. It was a little difficult to straighten the arm and have the pin holes all line up properly.

We returned to Rawley Lodge just in time for dinner. After dinner we went to install the arm, so it would be ready for morning. The rain quit, and it was beginning to get colder. We used the headlights of the car and a flashlight for illumination as we installed the arm. The motor was kept running so the battery wouldn't die.

Murray said at one point, "Don't let me forget to fill this thing at the skid tanks* before we head back." I assured him that I would remind him.

Part way back to the village, he said, "We didn't fill the tank before we left. Oh well, hopefully there is enough to get back in the morning." Just then the motor coughed, "Maybe not." It went along for a few more yards then died. "Have you been paying any attention to where we are?" asked Murray

"No, I have no idea."

"I think we might be closer to the construction camp than the skid tanks."

"I have no idea."

"We'll head for their camp."

We got out and he dug out the flashlight. He turned it on. It was about as bright as a match, then went out entirely.

The sky was beginning to clear, with the moon popping out from behind the clouds occasionally, but it was dark when it went in. We had just started to walk, when I thought I heard something on the road bed behind me. Then I heard what seemed to be a small stone rattle on the gravel.

"We have company." Murray said.

"Who?" I said looking over my shoulder.

"Don't look back, and don't stop talking, just walk normally. Don't run. It's a wolf."

I heard a slight panting sound, and more paws on the gravel.

"We have a pack, now don't worry, I don't think they are hungry." he said.

"Oh! Good."

"Now, they can detect nervousness, and you are more nervous than I am, so you are going to have the most behind you."

"I'll take three, you can have the rest."

"That's good Ray. Try not to be nervous."

There was a bit of a howl from farther back, then a lot of quiet chirps near us.

"The leader has joined them. We have a full pack now."

"Wonderful - I'm pleased that they have supervision."

The moon came out and they fell back. Murray said, "Don't look back. If you look a wolf in the eye he will take it as a challenge and attack. If one attacks, they all will, and we are goners."

The moon went in and the wolves closed in again. There was a loud howl from a rock on the side, followed by another chorus of chirpy yips. Man!, I was scared.

Murray said "Oh good."

"What the hell do you mean, 'good?'. I'm scared to death."

"That was the leader calling young ones up."

"Great, they are going to have a family picnic, with me being the main course."

"No. This is only a practice run. They are calling the younger ones to a practice in stalking. They won't attack unless we run. Then it would become a game, and we would be it."

We rounded a curve and saw the light from the coal oil lights at the camp. The wolves set up a chorus and dropped away into the night.

Someone was outside the door of the camp as we approached.

"Was that wolves I heard?" he asked.

"Quite a large pack," Murray replied, as though he was talking about a flock of geese..

"I didn't think there were wolves in this area. Anyway what can I do for you?"

"We need gasoline and a can. We ran out of gas up the road there a piece."

Knowing that the road ended just a short distance away, he queried, "What were you doing up there?"

"Oh, we're Prentice Roads and Excavating; we're building roads around Six Mile Lake." Murray answered.

"Oh yes, I saw your trucks go by. I'll get some gas and take you back." He disappeared into the trailer and returned with a can which he filled at their skid tank. We crawled into the cab of his pickup and returned to the car. After we put the gas in the car, we went back to the skid tank and filled it up.

As we rode back to the lodge, Murray told me how he would lay in bed at night at Brady Lake and listen to the wolves howl. He said that he could tell when they were hunting for prey and when they were only teasing by the commands from the leader.

When we reached the Lodge the rest of the guys were relaxing in front of the fireplace. They had been to the beverage room and some were really relaxed indeed.

I had not experienced any close encounter with wolves before. If Murray hadn't been there to prompt me, I would no doubt have broken into a full run, only to be brought down by the heels.

Murray's son Rocky, a small child at the time, became a four time classic angling champion and now travels, showing others how to catch fish. He has also been interviewed on many TV sports shows.

There have been a large number of studies of wolves in the past few years. Some of the studies may contradict some points in this chapter. The Crawford and Austen families were born into an area where wolves were plentiful. They practically lived with them. I tend to believe personal experiences before studies of wolves in captivity.

Boarding them out with families near a school; *During the school year of 1952-53, Sam Crawford's daughter Carolyn, and Elmer Crawford's daughter Joan, boarded at Floyd and Marg's, so they could go to school at SS #5. A special arrangement had to be worked out between the township of Anson Hindon and Minden and Lutterworth Township, so school taxes would be transferred to pay for their education.*

Highway 103 *was completely assumed by Highway 69 in 1976. It no longer appears on any modern road map of Ontario. It is now part of Highway 400.*

Skid Tanks; *A holding tank for gasoline used on construction sites.*

Cutler

Photo courtesy of Bill Prentice.

Dunc Prentice (Foreground) Herb Cox (Middle) and Bill Austin (Background) ready to leave for Cutler, Ontario 1957

I had been laid off from Prentice Roads on December 1st 1956. I was drawing unemployment insurance and helping Dad in the woods, while looking for work. Work was scarce during the winter in Haliburton County in those days, so the prospects were not good everywhere I applied.

Sunday, January 13th, 1957, was a normal day at our house. It was sunny and 20 below zero Fahrenheit that morning. The day went slowly, with not much to do except help Dad with the chores. Hazel and Doward came down in the evening for a while.

Monday morning dawned cold and clear. It was 30 below, making the frost whistle under our feet as we walked along to the barn to do the chores. I was glad to hear Dad say, "Too cold for the woods today, Ray," as he walked ahead of me on the narrow footpath. We did the chores and settled into the house for a lazy day.

Just after lunch, Morgan and Bill Prentice drove into the yard. They got out of the car and came to the door. Morgan was ahead, and when Mother answered the door, he tipped his hat and said, "Good afternoon Mrs Miller - cold isn't?" Bill was standing behind him, and smiled and nodded to Mother. I had been eating an apple at the table in the kitchen, and went to join them at the door, as Mother replied, "Good afternoon Morgan, Bill, come on in out of the cold."

As she stepped back and opened the door, Morgan saw me standing there. He said, "Oh, hi Ray, you're the one we want to see. Is your Dad in?"

Dad came out of the front room, as they entered the washroom and said, "Oh, hello Morgan, Bill. Come on in." They went to remove their footwear, but Dad and Mother said almost in unison for them not to worry about it.

Me in fall 1956.

As they came into the kitchen, Dad pulled out a couple of chairs at the table. Mother asked if they would like a cup of tea.

They sat down and after the usual, "Cold isn't it?" and "What have you been doing Milt," pleasantries were over Morgan said, "I am glad you are all here, as we want to make sure that you, Mrs. Miller and Milt, know and approve of what we are here for."

Bill looked at me and said, "We don't want to seem to belittle you Ray. We know that you are a good man or we wouldn't be here, but this is a little different, and we want your Mom and Dad to know exactly what we want to happen, and a few details as well."

"As you all know, we have a crew working up at Cutler, Ontario for Cape Construction, building a sulphuric acid plant for Noranda Mines," Morgan began.

"Oh yes, I read about those mines in the paper. Uranium or something, at Elliott Lake, right?" Dad interrupted.

"Yes that's right," said Morgan. "They are going to use the sulphuric acid to process the ore. There is a lot of work going on up there. Bill and I went into Elliott Lake the other day. They are improving the road, and they are beginning to build a town for the workers at the mine. It's big stuff Milt."

"Anyway," he continued, "Herby Cox sort of fell out of one of our trucks, backing down a hill the other night, and injured his groin area really bad."

"Oh! Poor Herb, I hope he is not too bad," said Mother.

"Well, he's pretty bad. There's a doctor at the camp. He took a look, and said that we should bring him down here, and have it looked at properly." Morgan replied, showing great concern.

"What happened, Morgan?" Dad said, alarm and awe in his voice at the same time

"Well he ran a hill and started to spin. You know how we have to open the door and put our foot out on the running board to see to back up Milt? Well his foot slipped off the running board and he came down on his privates, on the corner of the seat."

Dad sort of flinched, as he replied, "Good God, that would hurt. How did he get the truck stopped, with him out of it and hurt?"

"Well, he had a couple of guys in the cab with him. The one in the middle slid over and stopped the truck."

"I wondered," Dad seemed relieved.

Morgan said, "Dunc called this morning and he said that Herb's injury is swelling pretty badly, so we have to bring him home right away, which brings me to why we are here."

Bill turned to me and said, "We want you to take his place Ray. Now once again, we don't want to hurt your feelings and we know you have a good head on your shoulders, but you are only nineteen, and I don't think you have stayed in a construction camp before, so Dad, Mom, Uncle Dunc and I have talked about this. You all need to know, there are over five hundred men working there. There is every nationality on earth, and for all we know, there may be criminals of all kinds. With that many lonely men in one place, we have to know there are prostitutes and a lot of drinking."

"They are staying in Crawley McCracken Catering camps Milt, ten men to the room. Dunc is our boss, and Bill Austin, and Don Sedgwick are there." Morgan interrupted.

"I heard that Crawley McCracken camps are good." Dad said.

"They are clean and warm and that's the main thing," Morgan replied.

"So what do you think, Mr. and Mrs. Miller? If Ray agrees, are you content to have him taking Herb's place?" Bill said, expectantly.

"We'll take good care of him," Morgan said, nodding his head assuredly.

"He'll be alright, as long as he stays off the corner of that seat," Dad laughed.

We all laughed. Then Mother said, "If he's not a man now, he never will be. It's up to him entirely."

Bill said, "Will you go Ray?"

It was a little scary. It was a long distance away, and even though I had been away from home before, I had always been able to come home on the weekend or through the week, if I got lonely.

"How long does it take to go up there?" Dad asked, as I pondered.

"Eight or nine hours Milt, maybe longer, depending on the weather." Morgan answered. "We always leave in morning, around five or five thirty, to get there in the middle of the afternoon."

"You could hit a storm, too," Dad exclaimed...

"Well, we haven't on any of our trips yet, but if we do, we will have to find a hotel or somewhere to stay." Morgan replied.

Turning again to me, Morgan said, "Well, what do you think lad? We are paying a little extra to be away from home. You will get one dollar and ten cents an hour and your board. There is a commissary right there, and the little town of Cutler is right up the road."

"What will I be driving and what will I be hauling?"

"You'll be driving that long wheelbase international, with a wood platform on it. It's a good truck. We'll put a radio in it if you like. You will be hauling steel with Bill Austin during the day for Cape, and bringing in drinking water and taking garbage away at night for Crawley. The water and garbage is usually finished by midnight or so, then you can sleep. It's a cost plus job that Cape is doing, and lots of days you don't do much at all. At night, you will haul food supplies, sometimes from the railroad station at Spanish, too. You are forbidden to get out of the truck, except in certain areas. You will have two helpers with you all the time, so you don't load or unload at all. Oh, did Dad mention, you will be paid for 24 hours a day, seven days a week?" Bill answered.

Morgan looked surprised, as he looked at Bill and said "Radio, Bill?"

"Ed can get one cheap from Walkwoods. We can take it up the next time we go or send it on the bus. Ray can install it himself." Bill said, looking at his father a little puzzled.

"I know, I know, I'm only kidding." Morgan laughed.

It was very exciting, and I liked the money, so I said, "Yes, when will we go?"

"We will pick you up at five tomorrow morning. Take some warm clothes, but don't take much money. We will send money to you every week. You can set up how much with Lola, after you get there and figure out how much you need. The rest we will put in the bank here in Minden, and it will be there when you come back home."

I have to admit that the words, "come back home," sent a little chill up my spine, as I thought of how long it could be before that happened, but I would be making more money than I had ever made before.

"Oh, don't forget to take all your Prentice Roads uniforms. You wear a medium shirt, don't you Ray?"

I said "Yeah - medium."

"Okay, laundry is a bit of a problem up there, so we have some extra medium shirts we will give you. We have some more of your 'Ray' badges. Mom, or someone, will sew them on this afternoon." Turning to Morgan, he said "Don't let us forget to do that Dad."

"We won't!! We won't," Morgan assured him.

They said goodbye and left. I phoned Ferne and told her of my going, then headed for Minden to do a little shopping. I went to Sam Welch's store and purchased a bomber jacket, some heavy underwear, a pair of high backed overalls, a sweater, a pair of insulated winter work boots and some woollen socks.

When I got back home, Mother had gone through my closet and had put some clothing out on my bed. I sorted through this stuff, and put some of it into a pillow case. When I went down stairs, Dad had my new stuff all out on the kitchen table, admiring it. He said, "My God man, look at all this stuff. I have never seen so much new clothing in my life. By the way, do you know that you will be pulling in a hundred and eighty four dollars and eighty cents a week? I think you should stay at home and I'll go."

Mother being Mother, had already figured out something to worry about.

"I just hope you don't get too tired, working all those hours."

"Dunc will see that he doesn't." Dad said.

We took the tags and things off everything and put what I wouldn't be wearing in the morning into the other pillow case, and settled in for the evening.

The trip to Cutler.

I heard Dad putting wood in the stove during the night. I checked my alarm clock and it was ten after three. The alarm was set for four, so I stayed awake and waited for it to ring. Before it went off, I heard Dad and Mother's alarm go.

In those days, most men slept in their underwear in winter, so all I had to do was pull on a pair of socks and the Prentice Roads uniform, I had placed beside my bed the night before. I strapped on my watch and headed for the stairs. When I got to the kitchen, Dad was stoking the fire. Mother was already breaking eggs into a frying pan.

I said, "Good morning" as I pulled on my new boots and rushed out the door, into a clear, cold, very still, moonlit, thirty below morning. Frost squealed beneath my boots, as I headed for the toilet.

As I came back through the kitchen door, Mother said, "I hung a clean towel on the door there. The pump is frozen, so you can wash up there at the counter," nodding toward the door and kitchen counter top.

I dipped some warm water from the reservoir on the stove into a hand basin and washed my hands and face and shaved. I put my shaving kit into the pillowcase and headed for the table.

By now Mother had placed fried eggs on a plate in the warming closet, and was toasting bread over an open lid on the stove. We had an electric toaster of sorts, but I always liked toast that way. It seems to taste of the wood smoke, and is quite different.

We finished breakfast with quite a bit of chat, mostly from Dad, as he sort of went over what I would be doing again in his mind. He asked me things like, "Have you driven this same truck for them before?" And, "They said that you never get out of the truck. Why is that I wonder?" I answered, "I think it has something to do with safety or insurance, or something like that."

I placed my 'turkey', (the name given to the pillowcase luggage men packed to go to work camps. This was done so the man would have clean pillowcases with him also), along side the washroom door, went to the toilet again, and put on my coat and hat at five to five.

Right on time, as Prentices always were, there was the sound of tires whistling through the snow. I said goodbye to Dad, gave Mother a kiss and hug, and went out and got into the car.

"Good morning," Morgan said, as I threw my turkey and bomber jacket into the back seat and climbed in.

Bill looked into the back seat and said, "Damned cold isn't it?"

I said, "It sure is," as Morgan backed out and headed the car toward the road.

As we turned toward Minden, I said, "Did you bring my shirts?"

"They are on the counter in the office," Bill said, "We have to go in on the way past and get some papers and other things."

Bill and his Dad talked of business things as we went along. We sped along the old highway 35 north of Minden. It was still crooked and hilly, and we leaped over frost bump after frost bump.

It was breaking daylight as we turned unto Highway 60 at Dwight, and fully daylight at Highway 11 at Huntsville.

I sat up and started to look at the country side now, as I hadn't been over this piece of road before.

I had heard guys talk of places like Novar, South River, Burke's Fall, Powassan, and Trout Creek, now I was going to see them.

We stopped for coffee somewhere along the road, but I can't remember where.

It was around Powassan that we stopped for lunch. Bill took over the driving.

We drove into North Bay. I had never been there, so that was exciting.

I started thinking about the work ahead of me and wondered why I was going to have this twenty four hour a day pay, while Dunc or Bill Austin, who had been with them longer than I had would not be getting it. So I asked them.

Morgan turned in his seat and said, "Well Dunc is on salary. He is looking after the paperwork and stuff, so he doesn't want it. Bill does some overtime, in the evenings sometimes, and does a little operating for Cape at night. And of course, as you know, Don Sedgwick owns his truck. He just flies our colours. Your truck is the only one with stake pockets for side boards. They need that for water and garbage, so it just kind of leaves you to do it."

We turned west onto Highway 17 and headed for Sudbury.

It was getting colder now. The side windows of the car were starting to fog up badly. Noticing this Morgan peered past Bill to a little thermometer he had on his radio aerial. "Its getting colder out there lads," he said. Then "By Gad, it's 35 below."

We went through Sudbury. I marvelled at the smoke stacks and the barren land caused by the acid from the mines. The trees were just scrubby little things that would never amount to anything at all.

Somewhere between Sudbury and Massey, we saw a large snow machine come across the field and stop on top of the snowplow cone. It sat there, waiting for us to pass. It was a large thing, with skis out front, and there were wide drive tracks under it and a large cabin type cab. It had the insignia of Canada Post on its side. Morgan said that it was built by Bombardier for Canada Post and it runs daily from a town north of there. I had never seen one before.

The side windows were starting to frost up now and Morgan looked at the thermometer. It was 42 below.

As we passed Spanish I knew we were getting close, as I had heard Bill and Morgan speak of Spanish. Bill pointed out a little road to the right soon and said, "Up that road is where Herby got hurt Ray."

We were there.

My arrival.

We rounded a curve in the highway. I could only look through the windshield, as the side windows were frosted all the way to the top.

I saw a convenience store on the right as we slowed and signalled a left turn. As we turned, I could see tall, half-built steel and concrete buildings, towering above a little village of Crawley McCracken bunkhouses. Each bunkhouse held forty men. There was room for five hundred men.

There were two, very high, crane booms reaching toward the sky, beyond the bunkhouses.

Smoke and steam rose from everywhere, blowing off to the southeast by the wind. Men and machines were everywhere. I could hear a dull roar from salamanders, heating sand and gravel, even as I sat inside the car.

Mild excitement quickly gave way to sheer panic. I was downright scared. We drove over the railroad track and through a new page wire fence, where a guard shack stood at the gate. We stopped, and a small window opened. A man in uniform stuck his head out into the bitter north west wind.

Bill told him who we were and he issued each of us a pass card.

We drove through the gate.

Straight ahead were roads leading between the bunk houses and toward the tall structures. To the left and right were wider roads. Bill turned left, toward a bigger building. It was long and green and had a sign on the door that read, "Crawley McCracken," and on another door, "Cape Construction".

We got out and immediately felt the wind. Wind-chill was unheard of so I have no idea what the temperature felt to the skin

It was noisy. I could hear the ping, ping, ping of hammers driving bolts into steel, far up in the half-built structures. A tractor trailer went roaring past us toward the highway and stopped at the guard shack. A little car with "Security'" on the side went by.

This was to be my home.

We entered the office and a man greeted Morgan and Bill, with a degree of familiarity.

Somebody introduced me as a replacement for the injured man. "Yeah, I heard about your guy there," he said.

Then turning to me he said, "You need to meet our truck foreman - Ray is it?" I nodded. "Yeah, well Ray, that guy over there in the corner is Pete Adamchuck."

"Pete! Here is the replacement for that guy who was injured at the spring."

A tall slender man stood up and came toward me. He was well bundled up, with layers of clothing and wearing a hard hat.

Sticking out his hand he said, "Welcome aboard lad."

Turning to Bill he said, "Young isn't he?"?

Bill said, "Don't worry, he has been with us a while now. He can handle a truck."

"Well, that remains to be seen" he said, dryly.

Bill said, "Where will we find Herb, Pete?"

Morgan was talking to the man behind the desk.

"He is up in front of the first building, with steel on board, waiting for a crane to unload him. I trust you want to relieve him as soon as possible. The poor lad is in a lot of pain," he said.

Morgan finished talking to the Cape man and turned to go.

"Don't forget to get meal tickets from Crawley," he called after us.

"We are going there now," Bill said.

"Let me know when you are ready," Pete commented, as we went out the door.

We went through the other door. Several people were there. A couple of ladies were working at desks, and one was behind a counter. A man could also be seen through a door, in another office.

The lady at the counter got up and asked what she could do for us.

"We are Prentice Roads," said Morgan. "We will need a bed for this fellow, and we will be taking a guy out in the morning. We will also need two beds, for Bill and I, overnight tonight, and meals for us all."

She said, "Okay" and turned to her desk.

"Now, you need a bed for three extra people for tonight, is that right?"

"We have a worker here now who has been injured. This man will be taking his place, and we will take the injured guy away in the morning. So we need beds and meals for everybody tonight then just for Ray here after that."

She looked at some charts, went over to talk to another lady and showed her. A conversation ensued between them, ending with "Okay." Then she returned.

Looking at the chart more intensely, she said "Okay, we have a little problem, but we will be alright. The new man will have to be put in the back of the cookery, with the cooks, at least until the injured party is gone."

Bill said, "He can't be with our other drivers? Why not?"

"Well, that room is full, until your other guy leaves tomorrow," she explained.

"You will move him after that though, won't you?"

"Oh yeah," Turning to me she said, "Just remind us."

She sorted out the meal tickets for Bill and Morgan until tomorrow morning, and mine for a week.

"Be sure to turn in any left over tickets the other man has before he goes, so we can reimburse you for them," she said.

"We will definitely do that," Morgan replied.

She handed me a little card, with a letter followed by a couple of numbers.

"What's this?" I asked.

"That's your bunkhouse, room and bed number," she said. "It's right behind the cookery," waving her hand over her shoulder.

We went back to the truck foreman.

He said, "Everything fixed up okay?"

I nodded.

"You have a turkey with you I hope?"

"In the car" I replied.

"Okay. Get it and let's go. I'll take you to your bunkhouse first, so you can leave it there. Where did they put you?" He reached for the card still in my hand, and took it.

"That's the cook shack" he said in disbelief.

"It's only for tonight," I explained.

"You won't like it there," he said, "Too noisy."

We went out to a green pickup that was idling outside. It had a large, revolving orange light on top and "Cape Construction" on the door.

We drove past a lot of men working and stopped near a large green plywood building, that I would later learn was the dining hall, to the east of most of the other buildings. Steam rose over it, swirled in the wind and then simply evaporated in the cold.

"It's the only one through there," he said pointing to a narrow laneway between buildings.

"Be sure you put your stuff on the right bed or you'll find it outside when you return" he added.

The bunkhouse had a long hallway through the middle, with rooms on both sides, just inside the door. Beyond that, there was a washroom on one side.

There was a large space heater, right in the middle of the building. Then rooms on each side again, and a door leading outside at the other end of the hallway.

I looked at my card and found the right room. The beds were numbered and I found the right bed. I put my things on the bed, and returned to Pete in the truck

He drove around some men and machinery, up a little grade and there, parked beside one of the tall, partly-built buildings, was my truck. It had two long 'I' beams on it. Herb was in the cab, laying over into the corner.

Pete said, "Don't get out of the truck until I say to."

He went up to the Herb's truck and knocked on the door.

Herb roused and turned the window down. I had turned my window down, so I could hear.

"I have your replacement here, Herb," Pete said.

Herb flinched with pain, as he sat up straighter, and said, "I'm glad of that."

"Where's your riggers," Pete asked.

"They walked around to check on the crane." Herb explained.

"Okay, let's go," Pete said.

He turned to me, as Herb eased himself down out of the truck.

"It's all yours lad," he said. "There will be two high riggers show up here in a while. Don't get out of the truck anywhere but your bunkhouse and the cookery. There's too much high rigging going on overhead. A crane will come along and unload these beams, then you are finished for Cape for today. After dinner two other guys will come to your bunkhouse and get you. You will work for Crawley, with them, during the night. I do hope Prentices told you that you will be working all night did they?"

I nodded and climbed into the truck.

I said, "How will the night guys find my bunkhouse."

"Crawley knows where you are." he said, closing the door to his pickup.

I looked around the truck. Herb had set the throttle so it was running at a fast idle.

I heard the sound of chains and cables clanging against the side of a crane boom and the sound of a heavy motor.

I saw the crane slowly turn the corner behind me. It was the tallest boom I had ever seen. It must have been nearly seventy-five feet high, with about a twenty foot tipping boom on top of it.

It got closer and I wound the window down, as a guy walked up from behind the truck wearing lots of clothes, a tool belt full of various wrenches and pry bars, and a safety belt. Another man was walking a few feet behind him, and to the other side of the crane.

"Can I have you move ahead about ten feet Herb?" he said without looking.

"No problem," I answered, as I pushed the throttle in, and stepped on the clutch.

Hearing a different voice, he looked and then called to his partner, "Look Charlie, we have a new driver."

Watching the crane rigging as it approached, he walked backwards beside me as I moved ahead. He said, "They took Herb away, did they?"

I said "Yes, just a few minutes ago."

He said, "That was a hell of a thing, getting hurt like that. Okay hold it there, we will take it from here."

"What's your name?"

"Ray."

"I'm Bert and that's Charlie."

"Okay Ray, now I'm going to be leaving you, going straight up as soon as we hook up. When you know that the beam is free from your platform, drive straight ahead from under it. We don't want to drop it on your head."

I watched through the back window, as they slid odd looking things over both ends of one of the steel beams. I could see that it would clamp into the top lip of the steel, when it tightened.

He signalled the crane operator to lift, and I felt the truck rise as the weight left it. I pulled ahead fifteen or twenty feet. Then he signalled again, and the beam went fifty or sixty feet into the air, with my two riggers standing, one on each end, hanging onto the cables.

The crane turned and they disappeared over top of the building.

I could see a man at the edge of the roof signalling. The crane hissed, as air valves opened and closed. It twisted and swayed.

Soon, the riggers appeared, hanging on the ends of the cables, with their feet through the hooks.

The crane turned, until they were over me again.

It let them down on the ground, and one came to my truck.

He said "Okay Ray, from now on, when we have a second beam on the truck, like that, and they are letting us down, the crane operator will hold us just above the height of your platform. Then you back under us, and he will drop us right on the platform. That way, we don't have to climb back on to the truck."

"I understand. I didn't know," I replied.

They took the other beam away, but this time he told me, "As soon as the beam clears your truck, you are free to go for the day. I'll see you in the morning, at seven. Just sit in your truck, until we come to you, regardless if it is noon when we get there."

The beam lifted, I drove to the bunkhouse and went inside.

My first steel hauling job was complete.

Settling In

It was a little after four when I entered the bunkhouse again. There was no one in the entire building at the time. I assumed all the cooks were busy making dinner.

I looked things over a little closer now.

Nailed to the inside of each entrance door was a notice which read.

Crawley McCracken Catering
Building and Eating Rules

BUNKHOUSE RULES

You are totally responsible for your own bed.

Sheets and blankets can be purchased from the office for a nominal fee which will be refunded upon returning the goods. These can be turned in for clean ones on or after one week from the day of issue. You must supply your own pillowcase.

You may purchase one bath towel, one face towel, and one face cloth from the office at a nominal fee which will be refunded when towels are returned. These can be replaced with clean ones free of charge on or after one week from date of issue.

Keep your area clean and tidy.

Use garbage containers in hallways.

Use hot water sparingly at all times.

Do not leave water taps running.

Clean basins when finished with them.

Please report loud noise or rowdy behaviour to security.

Please report any unusual spills or mess to office at once.

DINING ROOM RULES

All meals will be served for meal tickets only. You are responsible for obtaining meal tickets from your company or purchase them from office. No tickets will be sold at the dining room door.

Dining room hours:

```
Breakfast:      5:30 a.m. Red passes only.
                5:50 a.m. Green passes only.
                6:10 a.m. Blue passes only.
                6:30 a.m. Black passes only.
                6:50 a.m. White passes only.

Lunch;          11:30 a.m. Red passes only.
                11:50 a.m. Green passes only.
                12:10 p.m. Blue passes only.
                12:30 p.m. Black passes only.
                12:50 p.m. White passes only.

Dinner:         4:30 p.m. Red passes only.
                4:50 p.m. Green passes only.
                5:10 p.m. Blue passes only.
                5:30 p.m. Black passes only.
                5:50 p.m. White passes only.
```

Check with your foreman for your dining room pass colour.

Each person is allowed twenty (20) minutes in the dining room from ticket presentation. Dining room staff and security personnel will enforce this rule without exception.

Have your meal tickets ready before you enter the building.

ABSOLUTELY NO TALKING will be tolerated in the eating area at any time. Security will remove all offenders immediately without exception.

All plates and cutlery must be given to the dishwashing staff as you exit Exit at exit door only.

Mid morning and afternoon break snacks will be available from 8:30 till 10:30 a.m. and 2:00 till 4:00 p.m. for half regular meal ticket on first come first served basis.

Late evening snack will be available to those who are working only from 9:00 p.m. till 10:00 p.m. for half regular meal ticket.

I read this and went to my room.

AUTHOR'S NOTE
There was a reason they were so strict about talking in the dining room. Talking slows eating and with only twenty minutes of eating time for each pass, it was important to get the men fed. Also, one hundred men talking make an unbearable din in any room.

There were two steel bunk beds on each side of each room and one across the end. Between the side beds and on each side of the door, there was a locker made of plywood. The lockers on the side had four compartments each. There was one locker for each bunk and the number on the door matched the one on the bed.

My bed was a top bunk. I found a locker that matched my bed number, and was busy putting my things into it, when Dunc and Don Sedgwick walked in.

"There you are," Dunc said. "Good to see you again."

Then he said, "We'll get you in with us tomorrow, when Herb leaves."

"It is only for tonight," I answered.

Then, "Hi Don, it's been a while since I've seen you."

"How are you? Yes, it's been a while, hasn't it?" Don said.

"Where's Bill?" I asked.

"He'll be along in a minute. We just wanted to get you settled." Dunc said, going over to my locker and looking for a lock.

"You'd better lock this up right away, or they will steal you blind."

"I didn't think to bring a lock," I admitted.

"That's okay, you can get one from the commissary, but do it before you go out tonight, or you could be sorry. Did you read the rules on the door yet?" said Dunc.

"Yes, I did. I don't know about a pass though; they didn't give me any pass."

Pulling a red pass from his pocket and handing it to me, he said, "As you can see, it is red which means we're up first and being as it is almost four-thirty we had better go."

As I followed them to the door, Dunc explained "We got the early shift because you have to work nights. This way you will have a little time to yourself each night, to shave and things like that, before you are to start at seven."

It was 45 below, as we trundled out into the late afternoon air.

A slight breeze blew things more gently. The sky was clear and cold.

"It's going to get damned cold tonight," Don said, from behind me as we walked out to the narrow lane between buildings.

When we came to my truck, Dunc quickly turned to me and said, "You shut your truck off!! Don't shut your truck off in this weather kid, it will cool off in minutes and the oil will thicken enough to make it hard to start. It takes forever for it to warm up again. Give me your keys and I'll start it up again."

I gave him the keys, as I asked, "But how can I lock, it with the key in the ignition?"

"But you see Ray, Herby gave me the door key as I left the bunkhouse just now. Now you can leave it running and lock it up too."

He started the truck, set it at a fast idle, and turned on the parking lights.

As we walked to the dining room door it opened and a few guys with red passes were allowed to enter. Standing outside in the cold, even briefly, I quickly realised the extra clothes I packed would certainly be useful.

Bill Austin came running from the direction of the clump of bunkhouses to the north of us.

With his usual silly laugh he joined us, as he greeted me for the first. He fell in behind us, as we approached the door. Men converged on the entrance from every angle. Many languages were being spoken.

We entered the building through a hall designed, I suppose, to keep the winds from entering the building directly.

There was a man standing behind a counter to the right, just inside the main door. Dunc showed him his red pass, and gave him a meal ticket. Then taking a plate he walked on. I was handed a stainless steel plate and I picked up some cutlery.

Ahead of us, on the right, was a long counter, behind which were several men, all dressed in white aprons and caps. There were several kinds of meat, boiled or mashed potatoes, two or three varieties of vegetables, gravy, and bread.

I watched Dunc closely, and soon caught on to the fact that, if we wanted a helping of anything, we would put our plate down in front of it. One of the servers would place a helping on the plate. If you wanted more, you just left it there for a second, and he would add more, until you moved it. You didn't have to speak his language or he yours, and the rule of "no talking" in the room was enforced right from the start.

I chose roast beef, mashed potatoes, carrots, a slice of white bread, and gravy.

At the end you could choose tea or coffee, by simply picking up a full cup. The cups were also stainless steel. I found myself with a full plate, as I turned to the left around a railing, and there was a large dining room.

The tables all had stainless steel tops, and the wooden benches were fastened right to the table like some picnic tables. I assumed that was so the benches would stay in place at all times. I also noticed that the tables were fastened to the floor also so they couldn't be moved.

The floor was very clean, considering that five hundred men had already been fed twice in this room today.

I followed Dunc to the table of his choice, as we were almost the first for this shift, and stepping over the bench, I sat down. Don and Bill came along and sat beside me. There were stainless steel bowls of sugar, cream, butter, mustard, ketchup, and any other condiment you could ever want, all lined up, touching each other, the full length of every table. No one ever seemed to move any of these, as they were in easy reach of those on both sides of the table. You just took what you wanted using the little spoon standing in it, and poured it into your coffee or whatever. There were also pepper and salt shakers within reach.

The place was filling up real fast, and the sound of steel on steel, as plates were placed on the tables, was the only sound to be heard.

It didn't take me long to finish my meal, and rinse it down with tea. I looked up, and there along each wall, every twenty feet or so, was a security guard. These were big, burly bastards, complete with uniform, night stick, and handcuffs.

I waited for Dunc to finish, and picking up my plate and utensils, I followed him to the exit which was different from the one we had used to enter the dining hall. Standing beside a roller system, leading into a different room, was a man, whose job it was to see you put the dishes in the right tray. When a tray was full, he would push it along the rollers, through an opening in the wall to another room. I suppose that was where they were washed.

I watched, as Dunc put his cutlery in a sort of tank, his cup into a special tray for cups, and his plate in another. I did the same, and received a nod of approval from the man as I passed.

We had just passed through the entire meal in ten minutes.

Dunc said, "Before you go back to your bunk, I want to take you over to the commissary, so you can get a lock for your closet."

I agreed, and he got into the driver's seat of my truck and we drove off.

We wove through the cluster of bunkhouses. He stopped at one saying "This is ours here."

Our other three trucks were sitting in a line, idling with lights on. Steam rolled up through the bodies and rose into the still night.

We went in. Herb was lying on one of the bunks. "How are you feeling now?" I asked him.

"No good, I'll tell you." he replied. "I'll be glad to get that trip over tomorrow, and get something done for it. How'd you get along this afternoon?"

I said, "Okay."

"Those are good guys working with you. I hope they can stay with you."

"Yes, I think they seemed okay."

"You're going to be fine," he said reassuringly.

We went back out and got into the truck. Dunc drove around the cluster, to some separate, smaller buildings. One was marked "Laundry". He told me that that was where we took anything we wanted washed. "The cost isn't too bad," he said, as we got out of the truck. The other building had "Commissary" on the door. The windows were frosted up to the top, so I couldn't see in from the outside.

They had most things a working man might have forgotten and all the confectioneries anyone could ever need. Candy, gum, soft drinks, tobacco products, cough remedies, matches, shaving accessories etc.

I asked the man for a padlock. He got one and, as I paid him, I asked how late he was open. "From nine in the morning until ten at night," he answered.

As I dropped Dunc off at their bunkhouse, he reached into his pocket and put part of a package of cigarettes in my shirt pocket. "You'll need those," he said. "Believe me."

It was not until I went to put a pillowcase on my pillow, that I realized that I didn't have any towels or bedding. I thought about going to see Dunc about this, but I realized the Crawley office was likely closed by then. I wouldn't be in my bed for long anyway, because I would be starting my first night shift in a short while.

There was still no one else in the building, so I decided to take a closer look at the washroom, as it had been a quick visit before dinner. It was a long narrow room, with a counter along one wall. This counter had several hand basin type sinks, with hot and cold water at each. A small mirror hung above each sink and wall plug for electric razors. There was a towel bar on the face of the counter, in front of each sink. Several signs had been placed above the taps saying "DO NOT DRINK TAP WATER."

On the other wall were several stalls, with toilet bowls in each. A galvanized hot water tank, with an electric heating band around it, stood behind the door, and there was a cream can, with a tap on it, on a shelf.

None of the exterior walls were lined in any of these buildings, and the partitions were only lined on one side. The walls were bolted together to allow for fast erection and removal. These were very much, temporary living quarters.

My First Shift

It was a little after seven p.m., when two Indian guys walked into my room. They were heavily dressed against the cold.

One of them said, "Are you the new Prentice Roads driver?"

I said, "Yes that's me."

"Well I am Jim, and that guy over there, he's Tony, and we are your helpers."

They seemed very friendly, so I stuck out my hand and said, "Great, I'm Ray."

"Okay, we had a time to find you. We went to the other shack, where Herb is and they sent us here."

"Pete Adamchuck said that Crawley would tell you."

"Yeah, well, what does he know? He works for Cape." Jim said with a laugh.

"Well the sooner we start, the sooner you can get some sleep. How long have you been up today?" he continued

"Since four this morning" I replied.

"You'll be ready for bed by the time we finish then. Let's not mess around tonight then Tony. Let's go," he said, as he started for the door.

We went out into the still and very cold night. The truck was idling so the cab was warm. Jim climbed in beside me, and Tony followed.

I popped the truck into gear and said, "Where to?"

"Go to the end of the cookery and turn left around it. We will go to your oil shed, and put on the side boards. That is where our shift will start every night."

I drove where they directed me. Up on a little hill, to the very extreme southwest of the compound, was a small building silhouetted against the moonlit sky. Leaning against the side of it was a pair of wide planks, with a series of stakes crudely nailed to them. I backed in beside them, the guys got out and fitted them on each side.

They got back in and directed me to the back of the cookery. There I saw a hurriedly erected frame, with plastic over it, in front of the door of the building. It was big enough for me to back right in, as the guys held the flap up, to clear my truck. Inside this 'tent' were two salamanders, blowing heat toward a pile of metal garbage cans. Tony directed me right back to the pile and said. "You should turn your engine off in here," which I did.

They loaded all the cans that would stay on, and then directed me back out, as they held the tarp up again. As we pulled up to the guard shack at the gate, an arm came out the window and waved us on without stopping.

They told me to turn right, and about a mile or more down Highway 17 we turned right onto a little road. This led to a garbage dump.

After telling me where to park, they got out, and taking each can separately, they dumped them over the side until they were all empty. Even in that short time, some of the garbage was frozen to the inside of the can. As a result they banged the cans on the edge of the truck platform in an attempt to knock the garbage free. I realized now why the tent was over the garbage at the back of the cookery, and the salamanders were running to keep the cans warm.

After the third trip from the cookery, we took the empty cans to the tent. Then we went to the offices, the commissary, and all the bunkhouses and gathered up cans from each of them. We took them to the dump and emptied them. As we drove around putting the empty cans back into the various buildings, they began to bring five gallon cream cans out, and, emptying any water in them, they were loaded onto the truck. I recognized them as being the same as the one I had seen in the bunkhouse.

When we had a full truck of these empty cans, we went back out to the highway and turned right again. This time we turned left up the little road Bill had pointed out to me, as being 'where Herby got hurt'. We drove along a short flat, then the road went straight up a steep hill. It was well plowed and sanded.

We climbed the hill and turned around at the top. There was a pipe sticking out of the bank, with a good stream of water running out of it. They got the cream cans down off the truck, one at a time, and started filling them under the pipe.

I had turned my headlights off, and the glow of the moon on the snow, gave an illusion of pure grandeur. A vehicle went past on the highway below, and a sphere of light rose up from its headlights as it went. I got out a writing pad I had brought with me, and began to write the first of many letters to Mother and Dad.

I remember vividly how that letter started.

Dear Mother and Dad;

I just climbed the hill where Herb got hurt. It is quite steep, but they have it well sanded tonight. I am sitting here in the cab of my truck, while two Indian guys fill cans with water from a spring.

It is 45 below here now. I've just seen a car go by on the highway below and there was an unusual beam of light rising up from its headlights toward the sky for twenty five or thirty feet. Do you suppose it might have something to do with the northern lights?

The trip up was great and the people here are okay so far.

The letter went on to tell about my day.

After I finished the letter, I laid my head back in the corner of the cab and fell asleep. When they had finished filling the cans, they woke me up and we took the cans back to the buildings in the compound. We had three more trips, then we went to the oil shed and took the side boards off. We were finished for the night. It was 12:30 when I got back to the bunkhouse.

There were men sleeping throughout the building when I entered this time. One guy was in the washroom. I used the washroom briefly, then went to my bed. There was all kinds of snoring from all four rooms. The smell of cigarette smoke and sweat filled the air. I stripped down to my underwear, put my clothes in the bottom of my locker, and climbed up into my bunk on top of the mattress. Remembering that breakfast was at five-thirty for us red passes, I set my alarm for four-thirty. The room was nice and warm and I was soon fast asleep. It had been a long day and I was tired.

My first full day at Cutler

Pete Adamchuck was right about one thing: this place was noisy.

At four-o-clock in the morning, it seemed as though all hell had broken loose. There were men all over this damned building and not one of them was speaking anything I could understand as even close to English. They were in all stages of dress. Some were in the bathroom. Some were in the hall. Someone, near the door, seemed to be upset with someone else. When I sat up in bed, one guy came over and said something to me in a foreign language. I shrugged my shoulders and shook my head. He hit the side of my bed, said something else, and left.. I went into the washroom, ran a basin full of hot water, and shaved. I was going to have a sponge bath, but remembered I had no towels, so I wiped the lather off my face with my underwear sleeves.

It wasn't far to the cookery, so I didn't put on too many clothes. My uniform, my sweater, and a vest seemed adequate. I checked that I had my dining room pass and meal ticket. My truck was sitting where I had left it, idling away in the steam from its exhaust. The sky was clear but no wind. A thermometer at the dining room entrance read 48 below as I joined the line up.

The door opened and we went inside. They served scrambled eggs, fried eggs, omelettes, home fries, bacon, ham, toast, coffee, juice, milk, and tea.

As I turned to go into the dining room, with my scrambled eggs, ham, bacon, toast and coffee, I looked back and saw Dunc and the boys just starting into the buffet. The place was filling fast, so I knew there was no chance that we would be able to sit together. We couldn't talk anyway, so I just sat down at the first empty seat I found, ate and left.

There was no one in the building when I returned, and my shift wasn't to start for over an hour yet, so I climbed back up on my bed and fell asleep.

I was awakened at seven-ten by a hand shaking by arm. Bert and Charlie were standing beside my bed with their tool belts in their hands and their safety belts on. They said Pete had dropped them off.

As I jumped out of bed and started to dress in outdoor clothing I began to apologize. "I'm sorry guys. I'll just be a minute."

"Don't worry," Charlie said. "There isn't anything to do for an hour or so, but we thought we would show you around the place, so you have an idea what it is all about."

Bert was standing beside my bed and noticed that I didn't have any bedding. He asked "What happened to your bedding?"

"I was only here for one night. I have to remind them in the Crawley office to move me today, so I'll pick it up while I'm there then."

They put their heavy tool belts on the back of the truck while I unlocked the door. I checked for fuel and discovering it to be less than half, I said, "I wonder where I get fuel?"

When we pulled around to the Crawley office, Morgan and Bill were just pulling away with Herb in the back seat. They waited, said goodbye, and asked how things were with me. Then they left for Minden. Dunc's truck was there, and when we went into the office, he was talking seriously to the lady. "He is supposed to be moved around into Herb's vacant bed today," he said. "Herb has left so what is the problem?"

"Someone put someone else in that bed last night," the lady explained.

"Well get that person out of there. Ray Miller is to take Herb's place in our room, today. Someone here promised us that last night," Dunc said in a stern voice.

"We'll do what we can, but we can't be moving people around all the time. The person who is in that bed now is going to be annoyed."

"Well too bad, lady, I'm annoyed now."

Dunc noticed us behind him then, and turning to me, he said "I'm sorry Ray, there has been a mix up. How was it last night?"

"It was pretty hairy around four this morning," I said. "Oh, I didn't get any bedding or towels last night."

"My God! Well, welcome to shanty life lad. We have really been booting you around, haven't we?"

He turned to the lady and said, "We need a bedding and towel issue for Ray here."

She got them and he signed for them. Bert said we had better go, so Dunc said, "I will drop by and put these things on your bed for you Ray."

"Okay, but where do I get fuel, Dunc."

"I'm really on the ball, aren't I?" He said, disgusted with himself. "You have to go to the station in Spanish. Do you need fuel now?"

"It's a little under half." I said.

"Herby usually gassed up the first time out the gate at night. If you don't think you will have enough until then, tell Pete."

We went out and got into the truck. Bert directed me along the front of the buildings toward the north. This was the first time I had seen the place in daylight, except when we arrived.

As we passed the clump of bunkhouses, I noticed Bill's truck up ahead, parked against the fence on the right. Opposite it was a tractor trailer load of long reinforcement rods in bundles. A crane was unloading the rods and placing them on square timbers on the ground.

In the field to our left and behind the rods, was an area where men were using torches to bend and cut these rods, to be used in the construction of concrete beams. Inside a crudely built tent with salamanders heating it, carpenters were building forms of different shapes, sizes and lengths, into which concrete was being poured by bobcats. The rods were nestled in and more concrete was being poured. Just outside the opening in the tent there were three large concrete mixers. These had large trays, that would lie on the ground to be filled with gravel and cement, and then they would be raised and the ingredients would slide into a rotating drum to be mixed. The bobcats were getting the gravel from a pile with two salamanders heating it. When we arrived Don Sedgwick was just dumping a load. The bobcat would then go into the tent, where a pile of cement was located. I asked the guys where the cement came from, just as a tank type tractor trailer drove past us and backed into the opening. It was evident the cement was being trucked in.

"We call this the concrete area, so when we tell you to go to concrete, you will come here and wait like that other driver, until we come to you," Charlie instructed me.

Over top of the tent, I could see the boom of a crane moving and was about to ask what it was doing, when Bert told me to drive ahead.

As we passed the end of the tent, I could see an area of steel beams piled on timbers. Workers were bolting ends, and other attachments, to beams all through this area. Moving on a roadway between the steel, was a small crane carrying a short beam with two riggers walking beside helping to guide it along. We sat and watched as it turned toward us and swung its load to the side. The two riggers motioned to Bill, he turned his truck around, and backed under the steel. The riggers signalled the crane operator, and he lowered it onto Bill's truck. The riggers then got into the cab with Bill, and they drove away slowly. Bert said, "This, we call the steel area, okay?"

We went past the steel, and turned left. An open field on our right was piled high with snow. I guessed they brought it here with trucks or simply pushed it along with plows. It was 20 feet high in places. I could see tracks of machines on the side of the pile.

Ahead of us was a little hill, that levelled out to what I first thought was some kind of road. Well it was, but it was a railroad. Men were laying ties, and further to the north, they were laying rails. This was to soon be a spur line for railroad cars to be parked, while waiting to be loaded or unloaded.

We turned left again, and started south along this railroad bed. On our left was a narrow area piled with fittings for steel. Bags of bolts, rivets, and short pieces of angle iron had been pushed aside to allow the construction of the railroad siding. A little farther along, I could see large pieces of steel, about eight feet each way, that were curved. I could only imagine that these were sections of some kind of tank or silo. On the right rose two tall buildings. They were at different phases of completion. Some walls were closed in, and I could see that some floors were in place. Two large cranes turned and swayed, as signal men waved orders to the operators.

I said, "It's noisy here."

Bert turned to Charlie and asked, "He can get out of the cab here, don't you think? There's no high rigging going on overhead right here."

Charlie agreed and said to me, "Pete no doubt told you not to get out of the truck anywhere but the bunkhouse and cook house area, right?"

I said, "Yes, he was adamant about that."

"Yeah, well, he is a little over cautious. In fact, as long as there is nothing over your head that could fall on you, it's okay. Staying in the cab in dangerous areas, saves you having to wear a hard hat all the time," he explained.

"Get out, and listen to the sounds right here, if you want."

I stepped out onto the running board and stuck my head up above the cab.

The crane controls were operated by air valves, and the constant hiss of air escaping from the lines, was loud. The big diesel engines roared and belched black smoke. The main booms stand nearly upright on these machines, so cables and chains clashed against the side of them constantly.

In the bowels of the buildings, the ping of hammers on steel could be heard, and inside the building, as all over the grounds, was the low roar of salamanders providing heat.

"This is building two," Charlie said, "and the next one is building one."

We drove off the end of the railroad bed and turned right, up the hill. I recognized our oil shack as I passed, and then we turned right again, behind the building. As we turned here, I could see Georgian Bay, a little distance away.

We drove down, along the back, where various air compressors and welders were humming away, doing their work in the cold winter morning.

As we turned right again, Bert said, "Now I want you to go to steel and wait by the fence. At four o'clock you are off duty with Cape. Don't wait for instructions, just go, and we will see you tomorrow. Are you comfortable with the layout now ,Ray?"

I told him I was. They got out and took their tool belts off the back of the truck, strapped them on and went into building two. I drove down to the steel area and parked beside the fence.

The drawing is not to scale.
BH = Bunkhouse. Highway 17 runs along the bottom of the drawing, (right hand side of the page), parallel with the railroad track.

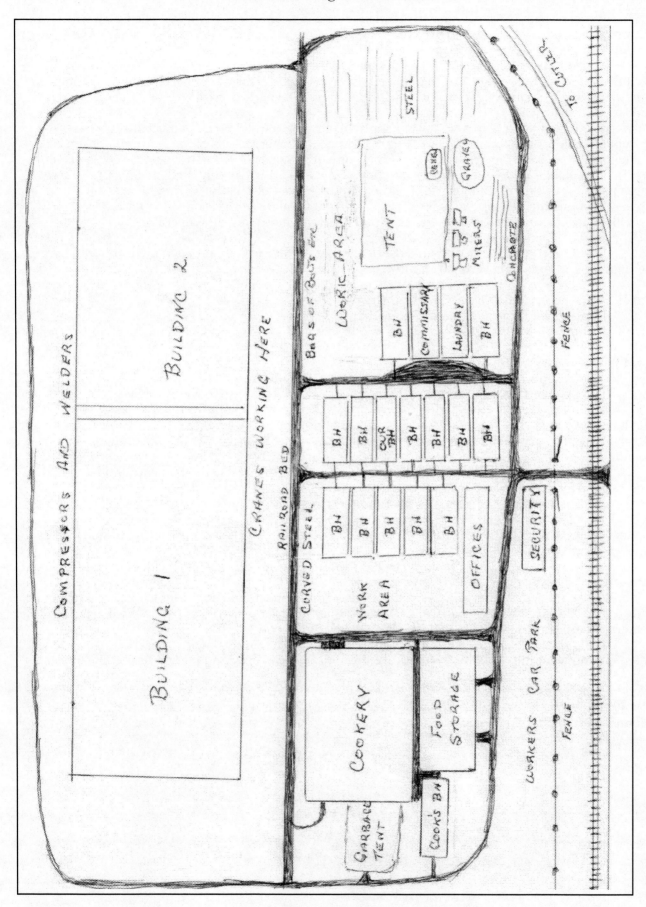

Trouble!

We hauled some steel that day, water and garbage that night. Things looked to be becoming repetitive, except for one thing.

The next morning, when the cooks were getting up and causing a lot of noise, the man I now recognized as being the fellow who was sleeping on the bunk below me, and had spoken to me the morning before, approached my bed again. He spoke in a language I didn't know. When I couldn't respond favourably, he hit me a backhander on the shoulder, and I believe he cursed as he did it. A conversation ensued between him and several other men that I didn't understand, but one guy seemed a little angry with him for a minute, then it all settled down and they left.

The following morning was different. After the rest had left, he approached my bed and spoke.

I said, "I'm sorry. I don't understand what you want."

He went to the bottom of the bed, grabbed it by the foot, at the top, and upset it sending me flying onto the floor. Then he walked out, saying something to himself. Someone had been sick, where the foot of my blanket landed on the floor and some vomit got on the blanket.

I picked myself up, put the mattress back on the bed, replaced the sheets and blanket, and changed the pillowcase. It was dirty from sand that had tracked into the room. I turned the blanket, so the vomit was at the bottom of the bed. I went into the washroom and got some water on a towel and tried to remove it from the blanket, but it didn't come off very well.

I was starting to get a bit lonesome for home by now, and this upset me enough for Dunc to notice across the dining room, at breakfast. I had just got back to my room, and was trying to clean up the mess when he and Bill and Don walked in. He saw the mess and said "What the hell?" What happened here Ray?"

When I told him, he turned to the others and said, "Look at this mess would you."

As he stripped the blanket and sheets from my bed, he said, "Pack up your things boy, you're moving."

I said, "What!! There's no room for me anywhere else."

"There is now,.. I'll trade places with you if I have to. Nobody working for Prentice Roads has to put up with the likes of this. We will go to security right now," he said, his voice now breaking in anger.

I don't think I have ever seen anyone as angry as Dunc Prentice was right then.

By now, I had taken my shaving kit and all my extra clothes out of the closet and put them in the pillowcases along with my new lock.

"Give that to Bill and follow me," Dunc said as he headed for the door. Over his shoulder, to Bill, he said, "Take his turkey to our room, and tell that Gary guy who is in the bed Ray should have, what has happened. We are going to try to get him moved out and Ray in. He seems like a reasonable guy and I think he will understand."

I can still see him, as he walked ahead of me through the narrow alley between the cookery and the food storage building. He was wearing his Prentice Roads uniform and a vest. It was cold and dark. The steam from his breath circled around his head and rose toward the eave of the buildings. His feet made a crunching sound in the frost.

As we turned onto the roadway heading toward the security building, and I stepped up beside him, he said, "This is my fault you know lad. I should have seen that you were moved before."

"But you tried Dunc. How could you know that I was being picked on?" I reasoned.

"Well, we are going to get this straightened out, and right now. Was there anyone in that building who spoke English?"

"No not that I ever heard."

"Are you getting lonesome Ray?"

"Yeah, a little," I answered, feeling a little immature at that moment.

"Well it's no wonder, being in a room where you couldn't even talk to anyone."

We reached the security building and went inside.

It was six fifteen. There was no one in the office, but I could hear voices in the back room.

"Is there anyone here?" Dunc yelled.

A man dressed in uniform appeared at the door.

"Yes! What can I do for you guys?"

Dunc put the pile of loosely folded bedding on the counter, and dug out the soiled part with the vomit on it.

"I have been trying to get Crawley to move this young man, from the bunkhouse behind the cookery to our room, where he should have been, from when he arrived on Tuesday. He is stuck down there where no one speaks English. One of the fellows has been picking on him, and this morning he dumped him and his bed onto the floor, where some bastard had puked. Look at this blanket. He is going to be moved in with us, or I will take his place in the cook's house, and just let that prick pick on me. You will have a major fight to settle then." I could hear anger grow in his voice as he spoke.

Two other security officers were now standing behind the first.

"I see that you are one of the Prentice Roads men... what is your name and position sir?"

"Sorry... I'm Duncan Prentice the foreman, and this is Ray Miller one of our drivers."

"Well, it seems like this is a problem between you and the Crawley office. What is it that you think we can do for you here?"

"I think it would help to get this lad moved in with us, if you were to send an officer to Crawley with us, and back me up. There are going to be security problems, if I have to take Ray's place in that damned cook shack," his voice raising as he waved the blanket around in front of him.

"Okay Mr. Prentice. Calm down, and don't be waving that disgusting blanket around. I get the point."

The officer thought for a minute, and then he turned to another officer, and said, "I think we should try to do something, before this goes any further. One of you guys go with them and see what can be done, before Mr Prentice here, explodes."

The camp was beginning to come to life, as we walked across the road to the Crawley McCracken office. I looked to my right, and could see that several tractor trailers had arrived overnight and were lined up beside the road, by the steel and concrete beams yard, waiting to be unloaded. We had to wait for a meat supply truck to pass, heading for the food supply storage building. A bread truck was already backed up to the building. Steam seemed to rise from everywhere into the still, cold morning air. The constant roar of salamanders filled the air. Off toward the half built buildings, a crane snorted, as the operator revved the engine from its overnight idle. Heavily dressed men headed toward their posts in hard hats and protective gear. Dunc's stride signalled determination in every way, as he led the way. The guard walked behind me, with an air of authority.

We climbed the steps of the Crawley office, but when he went to open the door, it was locked He sort of bounced back and exclaimed, "When does this stupid place open anyway."

"Six-thirty." said the guard, looking at his watch. I guess someone was inside and heard, as the door opened. A woman, dressed in a Crawley McCracken uniform, said in an annoyed voice, "I wasn't looking for anyone this early." Seeing the guard behind me, she continued, "My goodness, what is the problem?"

Her comment angered Dunc even more. He followed her in and, putting the bedding on the counter, he said, "Lady... it is you who has the problem. I have been trying to get this fellow moved from that silly cook shack, where he was put on Tuesday, to our room, where he belongs. He should never have been put there in the first place. He was down there, where no one spoke English, and this morning, some son of a bitch dumped him out of bed into a mess of puke. Look at these blankets. If you can't move him now, I will take his place, and I don't think anyone will be happy with that."

The guard stepped past me, and placing himself beside Dunc, he said, "You have to calm down Mr. Prentice."

Stepping back and thinking for an instant, Dunc said, "I'm sorry, lady. Please excuse the language, but I am very serious about this," his voice rising again slightly.

The guard said to the woman "There has to be something done, as I understand the young fellow here has been picked on for some reason, maybe just because he doesn't speak their language, no one knows, but the cooks are your people, and if this happens again, we will have to step in. I know you are crowded, but there are men coming and going all the time. Juggle them around and get this chap into the proper room, before it becomes an issue for all of us."

She looked at Dunc, then at the Guard, then at me. "I remember you now. You were only supposed to be there overnight, right?"

I said, "Yes, but someone put someone in my bed, before you could put me there the next morning."

She looked at Dunc. "What is the guy like who is in your room, in this guy's place now. Do you think he will be annoyed at being moved so soon?"

"He seems very reasonable, and my boys are talking to him about this now. We have told him, ever since he came, that we were trying to get Ray moved in, and he seemed to understand."

"He speaks English, does he?"

"Broken English," Dunc answered.

"If we just make a switch, we will likely have the same problem," she said, looking at some charts.

"Okay... Mr. Prentice, you go ahead with your day's work. Put Ray's things in your room, and we will do something today, I promise."

"That will be fine," Dunc said. Then, "We need clean bedding for this chap."

She looked at the date tag on one of them, then said, "But they haven't been issued a week."

Dunc's eyes narrowed, as he said "Listen..."

The guard stepped up and, looking her right in the eye, he said, "Under the circumstances, I think you can overlook that fact....Can't you?"

She went into the storeroom and got me a clean issue. Handing them to me, she took the soiled ones and, saying to Dunc, "This will be resolved today" she turned and went to her desk.

Going out the door, Dunc took my bedding from me, and turning toward his bunkhouse, he said, "You go and get your truck and bring it to our bunkhouse. I'll get Pete to tell your riggers where you are."

I walked back and got into my truck, idling by the cookery. I drove it to our own bunk house and parked. When I went inside, Bill's riggers were there. They went out to go to work. Dunc was still there, and said, "They put your things on my bed there," he nodded toward my pillowcases on the top bunk. "Bill sleeps under me, so you can use his bed, until your own is free. That's yours, there, when they move the guy out." He looked toward the top bunk at the foot of his and Bill's. "Don is below you."

It was good to be with friends.

My riggers soon came. Another shift started.

Dealing With Homesickness.

During the nights, through the week, a skeleton crew worked, keeping the salamanders fuelled, and some other things going, but not much work was done after about eleven o'clock. The weekend came, and on Saturday, there was little to no work, as those who lived nearby went home some weekends. Others spent time in Sault Ste. Marie or Soo, Michigan.

Once, when a large Polish chap returned from Sault Ste. Marie, he asked me for a cigarette. I took out the pack Dunc had given me when I arrived, and gave him one. He thanked me, went to his bed and sat down. Later, after he had left, another man said, "You were lucky you had one to give him. When he is drinking, he only asks once. If you don't give him one, he just hits you." Good old Dunc had come through for me again.

Some men's religion would not allow them to work on Sunday, so it was very slow. We still had to take the garbage and bring in drinking water, but time was on my hands, both Saturday and Sunday. I went to the commissary, wrote a letter to Ferne, and laid on my bed a lot.

I had been getting quite homesick, as each day went on. It was nearly a week since I left home. By dinner time the feeling had grown. By the time we had climbed the hill to the spring and the boys were filling the water cans that night, I got thinking about my parents and home. I wrote a letter.

Dear Mother and Dad;

I had a little trouble with the man who was sleeping in the bunk under me, in the bunkhouse behind the cookery. He dumped me into a pile of puke, one morning at four o clock. But don't worry. Dunc took care of that in good style. I am in the bunkhouse with the rest of Prentice Roads men and things are okay now.

In fact, for a while, I thought I had landed in hell. I was going to tell you, if anyone asked where I was, you could honestly tell him to 'go to hell', that's where he would find me.

I have spent a lot of time in the room alone today, as the others have been coming and going, tending to their laundry and trucks etc. I guess I was alone too much, as I got very lonely for you guys at home. It could be a long time before I go home, so I guess I will have to deal with it somehow.

The radio hasn't arrived for my truck yet.

I arranged to have ten dollars a week sent up for things from the commissary, but I don't need very much, as I don't smoke or spend money on drink.

I hope you are both OK.

Ray

We finished early that night and, when I got to bed, I was still unhappy. I didn't sleep much and, the next morning, I really wanted to go home.

The riggers came, but they only moved me to the beam area, and didn't do anything more. I sat in my truck and began to really feel sorry for myself. I contemplated going to Dunc, and have him phone Morgan, and have me replaced.

Then I got very cross with myself. I am a Miller, and Millers don't quit.

I sat there in a truck, in the middle of a large camp full of men, looking out toward a field full of piles of snow and I had a little talk to myself.

'I am here. I am nowhere else. I can only be in one place at a time and this is where I am right now. I won't be happy if I go home because I will have let many people down, but most of all I will have let myself down and I will hate myself for the rest of my life. Home is where you are, wherever you are. What is home anyway? It is just a place. I have three very good friends here who will stand up and fight for me, as they have shown very plainly this week. I don't have to go home. I am at home'.

I thought about what I had said to myself, and after I reconsidered it a few times, it made a lot of sense.

Things started to look a lot better. I thought: **'I am having an adventure here. I am earning money while I'm having an adventure. I can learn so much here, if I just smarten up and enjoy the ride'.**

In a few minutes, the terrible hurt had left me. I laid my head back in the corner of the cab, and was soon asleep.

I have never been homesick since. Yes, I have missed people at home, but I have never hurt like that since.

A Package Arrives.

My riggers woke me up, and we moved some things around the yard.

The weather had warmed up some. Overnight lows were ten to fifteen below now, with day time highs a little above zero F. Men were beginning to wear fewer winter clothes.

We had just unloaded some parts of machinery, when Pete Adamchuck drove up. "There are a couple of packages in my office for you," he said. Drive around and pick them up when you have a chance." Charlie said, "Let's get them now."

The man at the office gave me two packages from Walkwoods in Lindsay. They were addressed to

Ray Miller
Cape Construction
Prentice Roads & Excavating
Cutler Ontario Bus Stop

"What did you get?" Bert asked, as I got into the truck.

"I think it's my radio," I answered. I was wearing a large grin, as I began to open the big one. Inside, was a through-the-dash radio, and two five by seven mirrors for my truck. In the other was an aerial.

"Wow!! That will make your wait for us guys more pleasurable" Charlie said.

"Yeah, and the long waits at night, while the boys fill the water cans at the spring, too," I said happily. "All I have to do now, is find time to install it."

"Do you have tools?" Bert asked.

"Sure... up at the oil shed."

Looking at his , Bert said, "Why don't you slip around there now, and put it in? We can look busy for the rest of today."

I said, "Great."

I went to the shed and got out some tools. This was a new type of radio at the time called 'through-the-dash'. To install it, all you had to do was find a flat area in the dash where there was space behind for the chassis of the radio, which wasn't very big. There wasn't nearly as much equipment behind the dash on those old International trucks, as there is now, and there were plenty of flat areas in front as well.

You had to drill three, seven sixteenth holes through the dash, to accommodate the two knob posts, and a light in the middle one to light the dial. They sent a template, to help get the holes exact. The chassis of the radio was placed behind and the knob posts were pushed through the holes from behind. A bracket, to hold the dial, was then placed over the posts, and then nuts to hold the radio in place. The dial housing was fastened to the bracket with screws, and you had a nice radio that looked like it was part of the dash.

I found a suitable area, close enough for the driver to reach, with enough space behind. I peeled off the backing from the template and stuck it on there.

I drilled the holes, dangling upside down, with my head under the dash, fitting the posts through when Bill drove up in his truck.

"What the hell are you doing," he said, as he walked up to the open door. "Oh, you got your radio. How did that get here?"

"Bus," I said, as I pushed the radio into place.

"Where are the nuts?"

"There, in the box on the seat."

"Here... I'll put them on for you. Hold the damned thing still."

He put them on hand tight, and by the time I had crawled out from under the dash, he had taken the aerial out of the box and was looking at it. "It looks like it needs a five-eights hole. Where do you want it mounted? Left side or right?"

"I don't know... Left I think."

"You get back under there, and while you're hooking up the power wire, I'll drill a hole in the fender, and feed the aerial wire down to you."

He went into the shed, looking for a five-eights bit, and I climbed back under the dash. There was an in-line fuse block in the power wire, and it wasn't hard to find a place to tap off power in those days. The back of the ignition switch had several posts. I found the one that accessories were wired to, so the radio would turn off with the ignition.

"You'll need this," Bill said poking me on the shoulder with a pair of pliers.

While I was loosening the nut on the post, I heard the sound of a centre punch, and then the whirl of a drill. I wrapped the bare wire around the post, and was tightening the nut, when the drill came rattling through the cowling, and into the area above me.

"Can you push this contraption up from the bottom?" he said, tapping me on the side with the aerial.

I pushed it through the hole and held it up, while he positioned it. Then I wrapped the excess wire around some other wires and things, and plugged it into the radio chassis.

I got out and tightened the knob post bolts, then fitted the dial housing, and secured it with the screws provided.

I turned the switch to 'accessory' and fired that baby up.

It gave a couple of unpleasant squawks, and a squeal or two, as I turned the dial back and forth.

"Oh...I should have told you. You only can get a French station from Quebec up here," he giggled. "The music ain't bad, but the lyrics are terrible."

About then I found a station, and then another. It was fine. There was no such thing as FM, and AM signals would wander off sometimes, but it would sure be a pleasure, when I had to wait for the riggers and helpers so much. We went down to the room where Dunc and Don were getting ready for dinner.

"Your radio should be coming soon," Dunc said.

"Its here and already in his truck," Bill said.

"It didn't come through me."

"No, Walkwoods sent it directly to me, in care of Cape Construction," I said.

"Is it okay? Does it work well?"

"Yeah... Its great," I said as I headed to the washroom, with my towel over my shoulder. Life was good.

Now it's the Big One

Work was routine for a day or two. We would haul steel or concrete beams and some machinery around by day, and take the garbage out at night. But, every now and then, I would hear Bert and Charlie refer to 'the big one'.

I heard such comments as "That will have to be after the big one," or "The day of the big one,"

I got a little curious, so I asked them what "The big one" was. They laughed and told me not to worry, I would know all about it when it happens.

As I walked back to the bunkhouse from breakfast one morning, I could hear the sound of air brakes on the highway. I didn't pay much attention at first, as there were a lot of transports bringing in machinery and supplies everyday. But then, I noticed that this was not the usual braking and gearing that accompanied highway trucks. This was louder. The squeal of air being released was also intermittent, with the roar of a heavy diesel engine, as it geared down several times.

The winter morning was just breaking. I could see a great stream of exhaust against the morning sky, over the roofs of the bunkhouses, in time with each roar.

I thought "My God this is the big one."

I ran to where I could see the gateway, along the road between our bunkhouse and the next row. Turning into the driveway was the biggest truck I had ever seen. It was puffing smoke half way to the early morning sky. It shook, and the front bumper rose, as the great engine took on the task of turning thirty four tires against their will, as they slid sideways under the weight of a huge crane. The load finally straightened out behind the cab, as it pulled up to the guard shack and sat there panting loudly. The load bed was extended out onto supports that had been turned out to provide extra width. The trailer was extended to ten feet, but the crane hung a foot or more over both sides. I didn't even see the chase car, that entered the compound ahead of it, but there it was, looking like an ant sitting in front of an elephant, with its little lights flashing.

The guard came out as a second tractor trailer pulled in beside the big one. I recognized the load as being pieces of crane boom. Then another pulled off to the side of the highway with more pieces. Another chase car pulled in behind that load with its little lights flashing.

I was standing at the pathway that led to our building, and I'm sure my mouth was hanging open in awe, when Dunc and Bill came up beside me.

"It's a God Damned Autocar," Dunc said. "Would you look at that thing? It's got to be eleven or twelve feet wide."

"I was looking at the little car," Bill giggled.

The chase car turned right and went toward the steel yard. Then that thing started to howl. Smoke bellowed skyward from the two large exhaust pipes. The front of the tractor rose a foot, as the engine cranked the large wheels into action, then settled heavily on the front axle as it started forward. It moved slowly and very deliberately, as it turned to the right and followed the car.

We could see the side of the crane now. The tracks were easily twenty feet long, made of pads that were thick and huge. The crane house was big enough to sleep ten people.

My riggers appeared, and I said, "Yeah... Now I know what you were talking about."

Bert laughed, and said, "No, Ray. That is big alright, and it is here because of the big one, but it is not it."

"You're kidding." I said, as Bill's riggers joined us.

"Let's watch them unload that thing," Charlie said, looking at Bill and his riggers. Then, "Bill you and Ray can go in his truck, so you will have something to sit in while you watch. We will walk."

We drove up and rounded the corner. The float was sitting, just barely around the corner. The two transports were squirming into position, some distance ahead of the float, and the chase cars were both parked in the field of snow piles. The drivers were walking back toward the three trucks and their huge loads. A small crane was coming out of the alleyway, between the concrete beams. A bobcat zipped around, it seemed aimlessly.

I drove up beside the monster and backed up, so not to be in the way. We watched as the whole thing began to take shape.

The Autocar driver and some helpers lowered the front of the trailer onto the ground. "What the hell are they doing?" Bill pondered. "They can't take it off that end, can they?"

"I have no idea." I said, in absolute awe.

They unfastened two hooks, and the tractor lifted the gooseneck part of the trailer right off and drove away with it.

"Guess they can now," Bill said.

The two car drivers had walked back and climbed onto the trailer, then up into the house of the crane. In a minute, they slid the two back doors aside, revealing a small gasoline engine.

"Christ almighty, that little thing doesn't run that does it?" I questioned.

"That's the starting engine," Bill laughed.

"What do you mean? That is just the starter?"

"Yeah, I read in a magazine, Caterpillar Diesel came out with that system a year or so ago. It must have a big cat in it."

"Yeah… well keep that cat away from me."

They started the little engine up and let it run for a few minutes. Then they pulled a lever, and blue smoke started puffing out of a six or seven inch pipe at the top of the house. Then, with a mighty blast, it roared into action. Smoke filled the air. It settled down a little, then idled out to a humming, hissing throb. The operator climbed into the seat, and reached down by his foot as if to release a lock. He revved the engine to a steady high idle, pulled and shoved some levers, and we could hear the sound of gears and shafts tightening. It started to move forward, very slowly. Those huge track pads lowered at the front and lifted at the back, putting me in mind of some prehistoric monster's feet. It just crawled down onto the ground, drove ahead about thirty feet, and sat there.

The tractor backed in around it, hooked up the gooseneck, lifted the front of the trailer and backed away, down by the food shed. The driver started lifting the planks off the extensions and folding them back in, making his trailer eight feet wide again.

Meanwhile the crane reversed to about where it was, when it was on the float. The first transport backed up, until the rear of his load was about even with the front of the crane's house. The small crane crawled into place and started to unload the sections of boom. The first section was forty feet long and had two large pin holes, on legs about eight feet apart. The little crane lifted the section into place and held it so the pinholes lined up with the two holes in front of the house. Two riggers, using their pry bars, with the help of the operators, were able to drive the four inch by foot long pins into place. The first section was attached.

The transport and the crane moved to the end of that section and lifted and fitted another length into place.

A bobcat moved into position and some riggers fastened a chain to the end of a cable, wrapped around a big drum inside the house. The cable was pulled over pulleys, on a frame above the boom, and the other end went to the bobcat. It struggled, as it backed away, pulling out the cable beside the boom. It stopped just before the cable reached the end of the boom.

That transport pulled away and parked beside the cars. The second transport pulled up beside the end of the boom. The crane lifted off a thirty foot length and it was fitted it onto the end of the boom. The bobcat pulled the end of the cable up to there.

Next a thirty foot tipping boom was lifted off the transport. The transport pulled away to park beside the cars.

The little crane placed the tipping boom on the end of the main boom. Riggers pried it into place and fastened it.

The bobcat then pulled the cable beyond the end of the boom. Then came all the way back, and they fastened a smaller cable to it. It pulled that cable past the end of the boom, returned for another one, and did the same with it.

Riggers climbed into the booms at the end. The bobcat went to one of the transports, where they rolled a big ball, with a hook on a swivel on it, into the bucket. It brought it back and dumped it beside the boom. There was a great deal of activity as they threaded the cables through pulleys as the bobcat pulled the cable.

One of the workers yelled up to the operator sitting in the cab, "Okay Bob, take her away."

The engine awoke from its idling hum. Black smoke poured from the stack, as the big cable began to move, ever so slowly. It finally tightened. The steel boom groaned, pins tightened on their locks and the end of boom lifted off the ground, one hundred and ten feet away.

The far end of the tipping boom still rested on the ground, until the main boom was twenty-five feet off the ground. The main boom stopped, and the second cable began to move. It tightened, and the tipping boom lifted. The third cable just tightened as the steel ball cleared the ground. The main boom began to lift again, and continued to do so, until it was standing straight up and resting against supports.

It stood one hundred and fifteen feet tall. With a tipping boom on the end, it could reach another twenty feet. Hanging on the end of the tipping boom was a steel ball that gave it weight to pull the cable down with a large swivel hook on it.

The four riggers came over to my truck at ten-thirty in the morning. One of Bill's riggers said, "Bill, get your truck and bring it here."

Charlie and Bert motioned for a loader to follow them. They went into the tent, as workers began to remove the plastic from the tent frame. They soon returned with something that looked like the front bolster on Dad's sleighs. It was a turntable device about eight feet across. They drove up to the side of my truck, lowered it in place, and began to clamp it to the platform. Bert looked at me through the back window of my cab and smiled. I am sure the wonder showed on my face.

They went back into the tent and soon returned with a second turntable. Bill had pulled up behind me, and his riggers clamped it on to his platform. They told him to turn around and position his truck back to back with mine.

They motioned for the big crane to follow them. It started to trundle along, with riggers walking all around it. It turned, and barely missing things on each side, it entered the now topless tent.

It stopped. The big ball came down inside the frame, the cable was drawn as tight as a fiddle string. The great boom swayed in the air, as it positioned itself over the load and began to lift. With much swaying about, a large long concrete beam appeared above the tent frame, with guy ropes held by riggers to stop it from spinning. The beam was fifty feet long, a foot wide and a foot and a half deep, with eight foot steel beams fastened, crosswise, on each end. It weighed eighteen tons.

Charlie walked up to my truck and said, "Pull ahead Ray, beyond the road there. You and Bill are about to meet 'the big one'."

I pulled past the road, and sat there watching, as the crane carried the beam toward us. As soon as it cleared the frame, they let it down to where it just cleared the beams on the ground. Riggers guided the main beam on each end, holding it parallel with our trucks. When it reached our truck, it was lifted so it would clear our platforms. They backed Bill's truck so the cross beams on the end was directly above the turntable. They did the same with me. Our trucks squatted under the weight, as the beam was lowered, and the cross beams were clamped to the turntables. There we were; back to back, clamped together, fifty feet apart.

When everything was lashed in place, Bert stepped onto my running board and said, "Now, this is how this is going to work. The truck driving forward will be the one providing power. The other truck will be in neutral and free wheeling in every way. Both drivers will pretend they are facing forward, so when I say right you will turn your wheels to your right and the same for left. We are going to weave our way through the buildings, up to building one. All turns and swing areas have been measured. Now, to start, Bill will be the power unit, so you put your transmission into neutral. Don't touch the brakes and steer where I tell you. Okay?"

"Okay."

He signalled the riggers on Bill's truck, and I started to move backward.

I am not going to bore you with all the turns, left and right, as you can imagine, there were many. But I am going to say, we never had to reverse direction because of poor instructions. These guys knew exactly what they were doing.

When we reached the driveway to the highway, Bill turned toward the highway. As he proceeded, the beam started to pull me sideways. Bert signalled the other riggers and told me to put the truck in reverse. I did, and Bill went into neutral. I backed up, pushing Bill ahead, until I was on the intersection, and turned facing the roadway, between bunkhouses. They then instructed me to forward. I put my truck in first-low, and started ahead. When we reached the little rise, onto the railroad bed my wheels began to spin. Bert yelled back to the others to tell Bill to go into reverse and give us a push. This worked, and I was soon up on the railroad bed. We negotiated the turn there, much the same as the first, and stopped on the railroad bed, where we waited for the crane to catch up.

They unfastened the beam from the turntables, hooked up the cable, lifted it enough to clear our trucks, had us drive out from under it. With two riggers standing on each end of the beam holding on to the cables, it went one hundred feet in the air, and was swung over the building. Bill and I were finished, so we went to our bunkhouse and washed up. My night helpers wanted to see the crane that night. It was sitting, idling alongside building one. The lights of the camp illuminated the house, but the boom looked as if it went right up to the sky.

A Night to Remember

Things were quite normal for a few days, then true to form in Cutler, another adventure, so to speak, maybe I should refer to it as a happening. Anyway it was different.

Just as Jim and Tony arrived for the night shift, a bad stomach cramp hit me. I rushed to the bathroom with a bad case of diarrhoea.

When we were at the garbage dump later, I had to head for the woods.

While we were loading up the water cans, I had to rush to the bathroom again, and found that many others were doing the same.

It wasn't long until I realized, all five hundred men were running to the bathroom. Line-ups formed, and some had to resort to alternate accommodations - for instance a snow bank! The situation was serious.

After doubling back a few times, we finally got to the spring, where I stayed as long as possible because there I at least had a degree of privacy. Jim and Tony were not having any problem, so they sat in the truck, while I made several trips to the woods.

Around midnight, it seemed to settle down, so we went back down to the camp. As we passed the offices, I noticed the lights were on in the Crawley and Cape offices. There was activity in both. We unloaded the water cans and I had to use the bathroom in another bunkhouse while we worked. Things seemed to be settling down. There were not as many men using the facilities.

We finished our work around one in the morning and I went to bed. My sleep was interrupted several times either by having to go, or someone else in the room moving about.

In the morning, after much discussion about the night before, we went to breakfast, only to find a notice on the dining room door. It was closed. It advised everyone to return to their bunkhouse and wait for further notice. It also said, all work was suspended.

We returned to our room and Dunc headed for the offices. He returned to say that the health department inspectors were there, and they were carrying out an investigation into the overnight problems. The kitchen was closed until food and water could be analysed.

An hour or so later, a truck, with a loud hailer on it, drove around announcing that the kitchen was open again, and for everyone to proceed, using the same pass arrangement as usual.

It turned out that the kitchen had started using a type of dishwasher detergent that had been substituted by the supplier, because the regular one was unavailable. This detergent was intended for a model of washer with an extra rinse cycle. As a result, a deposit had been left on the dishes causing the problem. The solution was to put each load through the second time, until another delivery arrived, and everything returned to normal.

It was said that Pete Adamchuck, who had a rented house in the village of Cutler, never made it past the halfway point that night. Each time he tried to go home, cramps overtook him and he had to rush back to the bathroom. He slept as much as he could in a chair in the office.

The reason that Jim and Tony weren't affected: they were local guys and ate at home.

I Get in Trouble With Security.

One night, as my shift was about to start, Pete brought two French Canadian fellows around to our room. One was tall, the other short. He told me Jim and Tony had been transferred to high riggers. These fellows would be taking their place as my helpers. Jim and Tony told me that they applied for the positions. Heights didn't bother them and it paid a lot more money.

Pete said that these fellows didn't speak English, but, since that I knew the routine, he thought we could work it out.

Everything was all right, until we arrived at the spring to fill the cans. The short fellow was sitting beside me, and when he slid across to get out, he hacked up something nasty and spit it on the dash of my truck.

I thought that this was probably unintentional, so I got a rag from under the seat and cleaned it up.

When he got back in he did it again, and this time it hit the inside of the windshield, almost in front of me. In a fit of rage, I grabbed him by the back of the neck, and banged his head on the dash. He took a half dazed swing at me. I grabbed his arm and hit him on the ear a couple of times with my fist. By this time, the tall fellow was out of the truck, and soon, so was the short guy. He wandered around out there in the cold for a minute or so, while I cleaned up the mess, then the tall lad got in beside me, the other one following on the outside.

We finished our shift without incident, and I went to bed.

The next afternoon, Dunc pulled up beside me and told me that security wanted to see me before I started my night shift. I was to go to the office at seven that evening.

When I went to the office, the tall man and someone else were sitting there.

An officer came out and said, "I hear you had a problem last night."

"Yes, I did sir." I said.

"I hear you hit a guy a couple of times."

"Yes, I did sir, and I am not sorry either sir."

"That guy got fired because of this."

"That's good sir. I'm glad."

The tall fellow said something to the officer in French. The officer answered, also in French.

"Well, he says that if you hadn't hit him, he would have, as it was about to turn his stomach."

"Yes sir, it was bad."

He pointed to the other fellow, who I hadn't met, and said, "This guy will be taking his place with you. You're pretty tall aren't you?"

"I'm six feet, sir."

"How much do you weigh?"

"I'm one hundred and thirty pounds, sir."

"If you ever fill out you will be a big man."

"I've been told that ,sir."

"Well until you do, you had better leave the fighting to us."

"Yes, sir."

"Oh, and before you leave, and strictly off the record... I don't blame you."

"Thank you, sir"

When we went to pick up the garbage from our bunkhouse, Dunc and Bill were there and Dunc asked, "What was it with security Ray."

"Well, I had a little trouble with one of the new fellows last night."

"Oh... What happened?"

"Well, he spit on my dash, and then on my windshield, so I banged his head on the dash."

"I don't blame you, but you might have gotten hurt. He might have taken a swing at you."

"He did, but I managed to block it. After a few pecks on the ear, he settled down and didn't do it any more"

Bill laughed, and said, "Watch it Dunc, you could get your head banged on the bed there."

"It's the few pecks on the ear that I am worried about," he laughed.

Going Home

There had been great change since I arrived here just one month earlier. The railroad siding was complete, two huge vats have been installed, between the end of the siding and the building, and the buildings were now completely closed in.

The vats were now full of a sulphuric liquid, with paddles constantly stirring the mix. Tanker type railroad cars stand at the end of the siding, full of sulphur, and two empty transport trailers stand in another location, ready to be loaded with acid. The air smells of sulphur. Our clothes smell of sulphur.

Most of the roar of salamanders had been replaced by the cur-ching, cur-ching of huge pumps moving liquid through thousands of feet of pipe.

There was no need for drinking water to be brought from the spring, as the water system had been switched to potable water and we could drink right from the taps.

Garbage removal had been contracted out. So I now only work day shifts, hauling machinery from the railroad stations on occasion. Sometimes I moved machinery around the compound and do various other clean up jobs.

It was February 14 and Dunc had been talking to the office in Minden by phone. He drove up to me and said, "I have been talking to Morgan. Herb is on his way up, with that short wheelbase International. They want it to haul some ready mix concrete around here for a few days."

"That box will never hold concrete, will it Dunc? The tailgate doesn't fit tight enough for that. It will spill concrete all over the place."

"Well apparently, Ed has reworked it, and it is tight enough now. So, it looks like you will be going home tomorrow."

Herb appeared late that afternoon and it was sure good to see him looking so much better.

Late in my shift, they loaded some machinery on my truck. They didn't have time to unload it so the next morning I had to wait until about ten thirty when they took that off. Dunc came by and said, "I won't be seeing you again before you go, so I want to say that you have done a good job, and don't forget to get your spare tire, jack and that stuff from the oil shed. You are to call the office in Minden, when you get to South River. Elmer Crawford has a fourteen dozer working in the Park for a lumber company there. They are going to take the blade off his dozer and install a skidder. Ed wants the blade home, to do some work on it, so you may have to go into the camp there and pick it up on your way. Pete Adamchuck wants to see you in the office before you go too."

I packed up my things from the bunkhouse, and then went to the office.

Pete shook my hand and said, "Well, I want to tell you, I didn't think you would work out that first day I saw you, but they told me that you could handle a truck. You proved them to be right." He stuck out his hand again, and said, "I'll not likely see you again, so have a good life and goodbye."

I mumbled my goodbyes, and headed for the oil shack where Bill and Don were sitting waiting for instructions, and to help me load my spare wheel. We shook hands and said our farewells.

I had never worn my new bomber jacket during my stay in Cutler and had hung it in the oil shack, to make more room in my locker. I saw it there in the last look around. I remember taking it off the nail and heading toward the truck. I must have laid it on the platform of the truck and left it there. I didn't have it when I got home. I remember to this day as that was a nice jacket and I regret my being careless enough to lose it.

I pulled onto the highway then immediately parked on the shoulder of the road. I looked back at what had been my home for the last month. I remembered the highlights of my stay and the great guidance that I had received from the riggers, Dunc ,Bill and Don, as well as Morgan, Bill and Mrs. Prentice. At that moment I felt that I had come here as a young, and inexperienced boy, and I was leaving much more of a man.

I popped my trusty steed into second gear, released the clutch and I was on my way home.

It was much milder now. The sky was clear. The sun was warm, as it shone through the back window. It promised to be a lovely trip home, or at least as far as South River. I was relaxed and happy.

A few miles down the road I saw a hitchhiker ahead. He had a backpack and a satchel of some kind, which made him appear to be going somewhere important so, I pulled over. He thanked me for stopping and asked if I was going as far as North Bay. I said, "Yes, but I turn south onto eleven there."

"Great," he said, as he climbed into the cab, pushing my turkey over beside me on the seat.

We pulled out and were on our way again.

Just as we passed the road to Espanola, I felt the wheel begin to pull to the right. My front right tire was loosing air. As we pulled over on what was by now a flat tire, I said, "Thank God you are with me, to help me change this damned thing."

He never even answered me. He just gathered up his things, got out, ran up ahead and started trying to thumb traffic.

I got the jack, loosened the wheel, then got up onto the platform and dropped the spare off between the truck and the snowplow cone. I removed the flat, installed the spare, tightened the nuts, let the wheel down until it touched the ground, then tightened them as tight as I could.

Now...I had a problem. How was I going to get the flat tire and wheel up onto the platform? I could sure use that bastard's help now.

My truck had quite a bit of overhang, and the snow bank was higher than the platform, so if I could roll the wheel onto it, and back the truck up at an angle to it jamming the platform into the snow a little, I would be all right. I tramped a ramp of sorts along the bank. Rolled the tire up it, and then backed the truck over to it. The front of the truck was sticking out in traffic a little, but not enough to cause any problems for a minute. I rolled the tire onto the platform, pulled the truck around onto the shoulder properly, and got back out and chained the tire down.

About a mile or a little better down the road, I came upon the same hitchhiker. He smiled all over his face as I slowed, but his smile vanished as I sped on by.

Life has a way of righting things sometimes.

I didn't stop until I reached South River. I had a quick meal there and found a phone. I called the office and Mrs. Prentice answered.

"Prentice Roads and Excavating, Lola Prentice speaking, how may I help you?"

"Hello Mrs. Prentice... this is Ray Miller."

"Oh... How are you?"

"I'm fine."

"I bet you're glad to be on your way home. Did you get lonesome?"

"Yes, at first, but I'm okay now."

"Well, they're going to keep the blade on Elmer's dozer for a few more days, so you come right on home. Oh...and Ray," she continued, "You don't have a car here, so when you get back just take the truck right on home and bring it back tomorrow. I'll call your parents and tell them you are on the way."

"Thanks Mrs Prentice. I'll see you tomorrow then."

I hung up and drove on.

My truck was working well, and I made good time, arriving home a little before ten that night.

Dad and Mother were expecting me, so they knew it was me when I drove in. Mother met me half way to the truck with hugs and kisses. Dad went right on past me to look at the truck.

"How long is this damned thing" he said.

I laughed and answered, "The platform is eighteen feet long."

"We could get a lot of hay on this bastard, couldn't we?"

"We could get a lot of anything on it Dad."

After a bit of chat, I went to Cowan's and brought Ferne back for the weekend. The next day, she followed me with my car when I took the truck to the yard. Then we went to see Hazel and Doward and Floyd and Marg.

It was nice to be home again.

In 1971, we purchased a new Plymouth Valiant, from Don Earle Motors in Peterborough, for $2800.00. We started on a trip out west with our two children, Laurie, 10 and Scott, 8. As we went through Spanish, I was telling the kids that we would soon be to Cutler, where Daddy worked 14 years ago, building a big sulphuric acid plant. We passed the road where Herby was hurt, and I said, "Now right around this corner on the left you will see two big buildings. That's where I worked." We rounded the corner and there on a bald rock, in an open field, stood a seagull and nothing more. While the children laughed and Ferne made remarks, a state of absolute confusion came over me. I felt as though I must have had a dream. It was as though a part of my life was suddenly missing. It was not usual in those days to destroy an expensive building, that had been built so recently. I pulled off the road for a few minutes in order to get a grip.

In late 1981, I overheard a fellow talking about a time when he was in the Army. They had demolished some big buildings up at Cutler, Ontario. He spoke of using them for target practice, and implosion exercises. I realized he was talking about the buildings I had worked on 24 years before.

In 2002 Caryl and I camped at the KOA in Spragge and went to the site. There is a native art studio and souvenir store there now. I drove around the field and visualized where everything had been.

Back for Bulldozer Blade

After returning from Cutler, I learned that Prentice Roads and Excavating had signed a contract to haul ore at Elliot Lake.

On Wednesday night, February 20th, Bill approached me just as I was picking up to go home, and said "Ray... I guess you have heard that we are going to be hauling ore at Elliot Lake."

"Yeah... It is all over town."

"Well, we have bought some new R190-4 tandems for that job from Boice Motors and two of them are at North Bay. They are supposed to drive them down here, but they only have one driver available, so we are going to supply the other. Max Boice will pick you up here tomorrow morning to go up and drive one of them here. Okay?"

I was excited. I was going to drive a brand new tandem.

I said, "Sure...I will be ready."

The next morning, Max and another fellow picked me up, and we drove to the International Harvester dealer in North Bay. We pulled into the yard and there they sat. All bright red and shining like candied apples. There was no body on either of them, just cab and chassis. Max went into the office to do the paperwork. I climbed into the first one and looked around. I had driven one of Prentice's older tandems at Port Severn the fall before, but this was brand new. WOW! What a difference. It had the same two transmissions; one five speed, and one four speed, but all the instruments on the dash were different, and everything worked!

Max came out and said, "Okay lad, you're on your own. I am needed back at Haliburton, so I'm not going to be waiting for you."

The trip back was interesting. I played with everything that wouldn't affect my driving, and arrived at the yard, after everyone had gone home for the day.

The next morning, when I arrived for work, there was a lot of interest in the new truck.

Morgan, Bill, Mrs. Prentice, and Ed were looking it over, as well as a few other workers.

I got out of my car and walked over. Bill turned to me and said, "We are starting to draw sand across the lake to Shuyler's Island this morning, Ray. I want you to help Ed take the sander off the 1700. Then go to Walker's and pick up two 4x12 elm planks. Then go to Ben Davis's pit - the rest of us will be there."

The sander was a spreader that hung by two hinges on the very back of the box. An endless chain went from there to the rear wheel of the truck on the right side, where a clutch engaged and disengaged the spreader whenever the operator wanted to spread sand. There was a steel plate between the sand spreader and the box of the truck to prevent sand from going between the box and the body of the spreader, as the hoist was raised. A wire disconnect supplied energy to the stop, turn, and clearance lights on the spreader, as the whole contraption covered the regular lights on the truck.

Ed had built a stand on casters to help remove this thing. I backed the truck into the garage, while Ed brought this stand out and placed it under the spreader. "Okay... raise the hoist," he yelled. As I did, the overhang of the box lowered the sand spreader onto the stand. "Hold it," he yelled again. I shut the engine off and went back to help him. He was already removing the bolt in the hinge on one side and said, "Take that bolt out on your side there." I did, and he went to the centre, reached over the spreader and disconnected the wire. He removed the chain and we pushed the thing along on its casters, over against the wall, as he said, "Now don't forget to get those planks at Walker's."

I gassed up and went to Walker's Lumber. While I was loading the planks, I noticed that we hadn't removed the plate that goes between the spreader and the box. Thinking that it would

141

probably get damaged during the day, and that it covered the signal lights at the back, I decided I should return to the shop and take it off.

As I stopped for the stop sign at 121 and 35 Highways, I saw a car pull up tight behind me. I watched it in my mirrors, as I slowed to turn into the yard. I knew the driver couldn't see my signal lights. I looked ahead where I was going and looked again in the mirror. I couldn't see the car at all, and figured it was in behind me, waiting for me to turn. WRONG. It was already passing me and was in my blind spot.

I turned, and it caught my running board just ahead of the back corner. The collision took the dust cap off the front wheel, and bent the front bumper at the frame, turning it straight out.

It drove into the snow bank between the two entrances to the yard.

The driver was a school teacher from Haliburton by the name of Max Archer. He was taking a car load of students to Toronto for a school outing. No one was hurt.

Mrs. Prentice came running from the office and Ed was right behind her. Mr. Archer was most concerned that the children would miss the function, as they didn't have much time. In true Prentice fashion, Mrs. Prentice loaded them into her car and was on her way to Toronto with them almost immediately.

By the time the police had been there and we took the plate off the back, Morgan had called to see why I hadn't arrived. They needed the planks to bridge a soft spot on the road to the lake, and everyone was held up.

When I arrived at the lake, Morgan and Bill looked the damage over, asked why I had gone back. No one was very happy, but the day's work finally got under way.

Laverne Cowan was the regular driver for sanding at the time. I don't think he was very impressed, when he came in and saw what I had done to his truck. After all, it was brand new.

On February 27th, they sent me to South River to get the bulldozer blade. The trip was somewhat uneventful. It was a nice day, after some warm wet weather that had caused us to loose a day's work at Shuyler's Island the day before. It was clear and colder. I was happy, as I was doing what I have always loved to do; drive the open road in a truck. I had the same truck I drove at Cutler, so I had the radio and life couldn't be any better.

If you look at a map, you will not see a road leading from South River into Algonquin Park. In order to harvest a stand of timber, the lumber Company had built a winter road, for 13 miles across frozen swamps and through the woods. This was a single lane road, with turn outs, where trucks could pass. When a driver met a loaded truck, the empty one would back up to the nearest turn out, in order to get off the road, and let the other one pass.

The lumber company had a fleet of green Mack tandem trucks hauling logs out to a mill on the highway. They were the same as the ones that Jack Barnhart had brought to Bagshaw's in 1954.

At one point, not far from South River, the road crossed a swamp, for about a mile or more. It was at about the middle of this swamp I came upon one of the Mack trucks, lying on its side, in the ditch, with a full load of logs on it. There was no sign of the driver, so I squeezed past and continued. When I finally got to the camp, I was told that the road had softened the day before, and the shoulder of the road had given way, under the weight of the load.

They loaded the blade on my truck with a loader. I had my lunch there and headed back out. When I got to the upturned truck, a crew was there with a heavy duty tow truck from North Bay. They had released the bindings to let the logs go onto the frozen swamp, and were beginning to hook onto the truck to right it. I had to wait for a few minutes, while they winched it out. It appeared not to be damaged, but they told me they would take it to North Bay, to have the frame checked for twisting.

I followed the crew out to the road and drove home without incident.

On March 2nd, we were hauling sand across the lake and dumping it on the ice at Shuyler's Island on Horseshoe Lake. It would go through the ice in the spring, and make a sand beach. Ben Davis was caretaker for the island. He was directing us to where the sand was required. I do not like being on a frozen lake, never have and never will, so I was very nervous.

The lake was quite smooth. It had "watered up" and froze again earlier. There wasn't much snow on it at all. We were not carrying full loads. We were also travelling with the driver's door open, to facilitate a speedy escape, if things went wrong.

By mid morning, we had finished a bay, and had moved around a point to another little bay, where they wanted a sand beach.

As I rounded the point, I saw Ben on shore waving for me to come to him. I headed that way, but what Ben hadn't noticed, was a place just off shore, about four feet wide, where two pieces of ice had gone over top of each other during the thaw. It was about a hundred feet from shore. This had caused an air space between them, which insulated both from the frost, so neither had frozen again. This flaw carried my front wheels fine, but when the rear wheels came onto it, the ice gave way. I immediately bailed out the open door. Ben said I passed him on shore, like a bat out of hell and away up into the bush.

Earl Toye was driving one of Francis Thomas' trucks, and could see me from a long way behind. He drove to within a hundred feet of me and stopped, to distribute the weight of the two trucks. Another truck stopped a hundred feet behind him.

After I had walked back from the woods, we looked the situation over. The water wasn't very deep. The truck was sitting with its rear wheels on bottom and the front wheels on the ice. The tailgate was still out of the water.

Morgan and Bill had noticed that trucks were not returning, and came to see why.

They approached the whole mess with a bit of caution, and finally drove up close and got out.

"What the hell happened here?" Morgan asked.

"Not having a good day are you Ray." Bill grinned.

We unhooked the tailgate, raised the hoist, and let the load go into the lake. Then we hooked long chains between several trucks, and the front of my truck. They put wheel chains on any that had them. They pulled it at an angle, which caused my truck to spin around in the hole. It was now facing out towards the lake, with its front wheels on the ice. The rear wheels were already part way up the load of sand. Another pull, and a bit of chopping ice, brought it up on top.

"You had better get it back to the shop, so Ed can drain the rear end, and remove any water before it freezes." Morgan said. He was not at all his usual jolly self at this time.

Word had spread that one of Prentice's trucks was in Horseshoe Lake by the time I arrived. Ed came out of the shop, when I drove up to the door. "Who is in the lake?" he asked worriedly.

"It was me."

"You should never have gotten out of bed this morning."

"I know."

"Well, I'll open the door, you drive it in, so we can see what has to be done."

We straightened the sander brackets at the back which had been bent out of place. Drained the rear axle and refilled it with grease, drained the water from the rear lights, and mounted the sander, so it would be ready if needed that night.

You can well imagine the look on Mother's face, when I walked into the kitchen that day, and she asked if I had a good day. "Well...I put a truck into Horseshoe Lake."

The next day, Ferne and I went to Lindsay, where I spent the money I made at Cutler. I dealt my 1953 Ford on a 1955 Chevrolet at Fee Motors, and bought a diamond engagement ring.

Sanding the roads in 1957

Sanding roads in 1957 was far more dangerous than it is today.

As I wrote in a previous chapter, there was a spreader hung on the back of the truck. The spreader was a trough across the full width of the truck, with a rod, about three inches through, all the way across the bottom. It looked like some of the lawn fertilizer spreaders we see today. On the right side, there was a six inch sprocket, with an endless chain connected to the right rear wheel of the truck. There was another, smaller sprocket, mounted on the wheel, with a clutch that could be engaged by a rod that connected to a handle mounted on the running board. When this clutch was engaged, the chain activated the spreader, causing sand to be metered out along the road. If we needed to spread a little thicker, we had to get out with an adjustable wrench and adjust a spring loaded nut on each side, which increased the opening at the bottom of the spreader.

In order to sand the roads we had to set our tailgate spread chains so it would only open about four to six inches, otherwise we would dump the entire load on the road when we tripped the tailgate. Then we would raise the hoist, until the front of the gravel box was about even with the top of our cab, and we would head out down the road. When we needed spread sand, the driver would reach out of the window, grab the trip rope to open the tailgate, and the person on the passenger side would open his door, reach out and pull the handle on the running board, engaging the spreader. Usually, this would result in a nice even flow of sand sprinkled behind us.

The key word here is 'behind'.

You see, the sand was sprinkled 'behind' the truck, leaving the truck itself on the slippery road <u>NOT</u> on a nice controlled layer of sand, like the twirling under body sanders do today. We travelled on slippery surfaces, with a dump box flailing around, standing on its end, on highways that twisted and turned and went up and down hills like very few side roads do today. When I consider this, I have to wonder why I heard of several sanders being destroyed last winter (2003) by slipping off hills into a ditch.

Grant Hewitt was the supervisor for the Department of Highways, Minden Division, with the yard being between where Rusty's Auto Service (which was Ward's Auto Body then) and Home Hardware is now.

My first experience with road sanding came on March 7th, 1957. I had worked all day in the shop at Prentice Roads, getting equipment, house trailers, and other things ready for the move to Elliot Lake.

Laverne Cowan had been the regular driver on the sander, but for some reason he had not been available for a while. The truck was the 1956 S1700 International that I had driven at Shuyler's Island.

It had snowed quite a bit that afternoon, and when Grant called for the sand truck, Morgan asked me to take it. I sanded all that night and all next day without stopping. It cleared toward evening. I had the weekend off.

On Monday, the two new tandems were back from having hydraulic dump bodies installed, and we were sent to Leslie Coulter's, where we hauled field stone to the Ox Narrows Bridge. The rock was used for a retaining wall. I wasn't going to Elliot Lake, so the drivers who would be driving the trucks there were trying them out on that haul, and getting used to them. I remember Doug Eastman driving into the field that morning, with one of the new 190s and, as he climbed down out of the cab, he exclaimed, "She's too damned big for me." (Doug later mastered the skill very well).

I went with the first load, and spent the day placing stone into a wire crib by hand.

The sky clouded over late that afternoon, and by the time I had my supper, it began to rain. The temperature was just slightly below freezing, and it soon became ice. At six o'clock Mrs. Prentice called to tell me that Grant had called. He needed the sander right away.

It was getting awfully damned slippery, as I made my way to town. Salt from previous sanding was breaking the ice up on the highway somewhat. When I drove into the yard, my car wouldn't climb the little grade to the shop. Instead, it slid back and only stopped when the back bumper encountered the snow bank. The sander was always kept in the shop. Always fuelled and checked before it was put away. I raised the shop door and drove out. It is a good thing that it was backed in, as there was no way I could have turned it on the slight slant of the yard, on the ice. As it was it slipped and slid sideways and every which way as I drove to the highway. At one point I was afraid I was going to slide right into my car.

I drove carefully along the bypass, to Ward's Auto Body, then turned toward Minden. That road was already quite slippery.

Chester Loucks was operating a small loader in the yard that night. He had sprinkled a little sand around the yard from the open pile. He drove into the pile and backed out with the bucket high, indicating where he wanted me to back under, so he could load my truck.

I went into the office, and Grant said, "Hell of a night."

"Damned slippery out there, I didn't think I was going to get out of the yard."

"You have Halls Lake tonight Ray. Doug McKelvey is in the washroom. He will be your helper."

I went back outside just as Chester finished my load.

Doug came out and said, "Grant just said for us to sand this road to the highway, as we go."

I popped the hoist in gear and raised it to the top of the cab, holding the trip rope in my hand out the window. It was really raining now, and ice was forming on everything including my arm. I put the hoist out of gear and the transmission in second lo. As soon as we were moving Doug reached out and engaged the sander. We sanded from the sand pile to the highway. We went along the bypass, and across the Gull River Bridge near Horseshoe Lake Road One. There I stopped and raised the hoist some more, making sure there would be a supply of sand in the spreader for the hill ahead. The drive wheels spun a little in places, but going up a hill we always had our sand to back onto, if we couldn't go any farther forward.

It was now raining so hard that the wipers couldn't keep up, and every damned drop was turning to ice, made even slicker by a heavy coating of water. On the elevated corners, the back wheels would slide down against the snowplow cone.

Before we went down the Mountain Lake hill, I stopped and raised the hoist some more, so we would be okay climbing the other hill. I only geared up to third hi and we started down the hill. The motor would retard, and the back wheels would slide. I would kick the clutch, to let it straighten out, then speed the motor and release it again, to try to keep as much control as possible.

Taking hold of the door handle, and bracing his other hand on the dash, Doug said "I wish this ******* thing would settle down."

I squeaked, "Me too," as I shifted into fourth lo and headed for the other hill.

I had only gone up the hill about a third of the way, when I started to spin. This is nice with a hoist waving around in the air! Thank God, this truck had the new west coast mirrors, and they had installed a bright backup light.

I kicked the clutch, went into reverse, and backed onto my own sand. Even then the wheels slid. At the bottom, I went into second lo, and then split shifted into second hi, clutched and split back into third lo. Before we went off the end of our sand, I went back to second hi..

This time we went about fifty feet farther and spun. Back down the hill we would go and start all over again. This time we cleared the top. (Remember, these hills were crooked and very much steeper than they are now).

By the time we got to the hill at Ogopogo Lodge, it was as slippery as I have ever seen in my entire life. It was raining very hard and freezing, but not tight. The skim of water just polished the ice. We slipped and slid on every curve and grade all the way.

I said, "I think we should check to see how much sand we have." The hoist was nearly all the way up now.

I stopped in the middle of the road, as every time I had got off the crown, I would slide to the snow bank, and continue along it until we could climb back to the middle.

I stepped down off the running board, went flat on my ass and started to slide toward the front of the truck. I caught the front wheel as I passed, and saw Doug go down the hill on his back. I stood up, soaking wet from the iced pavement and rain. Doug rolled to the side of the highway and got a grip on something. He was twenty five or thirty feet away, but he couldn't stand up. Every time he tried, he would go flat. I told him to stay there, and I would sand my way to him. There was always a round mouth shovel or two, stuck in the crossers under every dump box. I got one out and, hanging on to the truck, I got around to the back of the spreader. I sanded my way down to where he was sitting, cold and awfully wet. Then we both carried sand and spread it down the hill. I would let the truck to the end of the sand and we would do it again.

The Rotary Club had a dinner in the lodge at Ogopogo that night and it was breaking up about this time. We had the truck just below the driveway so we threw some sand under some of the cars, to help them get moving. Harold Deacon came along and rolled his window down.

"Terrible night fellas" he said.

"You are telling us!"

"You know, your backs are covered with ice?"

I gave myself a shake "No I didn't know that. I know it is cracking and breaking off our arms every time we move."

"You guys have sanded all the way into Minden haven't you?"

"Yes, but I imagine it is coating over some, so watch it," Doug said.

Harold and some others pulled out, spun their way over the top, and out of sight. Some others were going north. They wanted to know if they could get past the truck, so they could go home. I said, "You won't go anywhere, anyway, as it is slippery ahead of us."

One of them made a comment about having driven longer than I had been alive, and, squeezing and sliding along the snow bank, he got past. We saw his headlights ... then his taillights; his headlights again, then his taillights; his headlights lighting up the woods at the side, then his headlights as he went twice the length of his car backwards into the snow, on the curve at the bottom.

Several times, while we had sanded our way to the bottom, I noticed the lights on the truck would dim. With all the lights on for a while, and even though I had it on fast idle as much as possible, the battery was losing power. In those days, vehicles had a mechanical solenoid type voltage regulator, that controlled the flow of current from the generator to the battery. This thing was a source of constant trouble. I really didn't need this extra hassle that night.

When we got to the bottom, there were three or four cars behind us and, of course, the smart guy in the ditch! Nothing was coming toward us. It was too slippery there with no sand.

The driver of the car nearest us said, "We will just follow you along and we will be alright, all the way to Carnarvon, right?"

"No. Unfortunately, I am just about out of sand," I replied. "I will try to take you to the top of the next hill, but stay the hell back until I'm at the top. I expect I will have to back down a time or two."

I raised the hoist all the way to the top, to shift all the sand down against the tailgate, and then lowered it part way. The box fully raised was above the thirteen foot, six inch limit and would catch overhead wires. The lights were getting quite dim, with the occasional bright spell, as the regulator would cut in and out.

We sanded along Hart Lodge, (now Twin Lakes Resort), and across the bridge, with the wheels spinning any time I stepped on the throttle.

"I'm going to get her going as fast as I can for the hill," I said, as I stuck it into fourth low.

"Wherever you go, I'm right beside you," Doug answered brushing ice from his arms.

I was moving fairly well as we approached the grade, then I heard it, the thing I didn't need. The chain had came off the wheel sprocket and there was no sand behind us to back onto. I hit the hoist valve lever, to let the box down fast, lowering the centre of gravity, in case we went sideways. At the same time clutching and going into reverse fast. Back we went to the bottom, where we got out and replaced the chain, (it was always hanging on the back sprocket when it came off), raised the hoist again, and started up the hill.

Just at the driveway to Ellencliffe Lodge (now Heather Lodge), we ran out of sand. I lowered the box and backed into their driveway, turned, and headed back to town.

I have no idea what happened to the cars. They wouldn't go very far on their own and Ellencliffe wasn't open in winter.

As we headed back south, the lights were dim more then they were bright. Of course, the strain on the system was less, as I had turned off the flashing blue and orange lights. I pulled up in front of Ed's house about ten-thirty, and walked along the edge of his driveway kicking my feet through the ice at the side to get traction. The rain had slackened off some.

Ed saw the truck, and turned the outside light on. He came out onto the front veranda and said, "Is that you Ray."

"I have a problem Ed."

"I see it. Your voltage regulator is acting up."

"Yeah. Is there a new one at the shop I can change or should I just play with the solenoids while they load me again and see if I can get it going?"

"No, there's none at the shop. I put the spare on that other International yesterday and Walkwoods haven't come yet." Thinking for a minute, he said, "Listen Ray, why don't I take over for the rest of the night? I think I can keep it going. You go home and then you will be fresh to take it back over in the morning."

Going back into the house, I heard him say, "Rhoda, I'm going to take the sand truck over for the rest of the night," as he put on his hat and coat.

We walked along in the footprints I had made on the way in.

When there were no Prentice people around, Ed McKelvey, chief mechanic, shop and equipment manager was in charge. I didn't argue one bit, just slid over and let him move in behind the wheel.

He let me out at the yard. I got some ashes from the trunk, as my car warmed up, and sanded my way to the highway.

I found that the patrol truck had sanded all the way to the boundary at Norland, and to the lower Dutch Line without incident, as the ice was not as bad below Minden.

I couldn't get up the hill at home, so I left the car at the bottom.

When I reported for work the next morning, Ed still wasn't in. They were still somewhere near Hall's Lake. It was warming up and the ice was beginning to melt when he pulled in about eight-thirty.

Climbing out of the cab in front of the office, he declared in a definite tone, "I have never had such a hell of a night in my life, and I hope I never do again."

Bill met him and Ed said, "You know Bill, where the highway is close to the lake, at the road that goes in to the old Hewitt place, at Hall's Lake?"

"Yeah," Bill said.

"Well, I came down that hill, lost it, and slid off the highway, and sanded a loop right out onto the ice on the lake and back."

"You must have got the voltage regulator to work though?" I asked.

"Yeah, I kept sticking a piece of wood under the back side of the solenoid clapper, whenever I needed it. It worked alright, but that has to be changed Bill, and we should check the battery before it goes out again."

"You'll take care of that, won't you Ed," Bill said, as he turned and went back into the office.

Author's Note:

This method of sanding was a great improvement from what was available before. That was a hopper trailer, with a turntable at the bottom of the hopper, to broadcast the sand. Two men stood on the back of the truck and shovelled sand into the hopper with round mouth shovels.

And before that, two men would simply throw sand in broadcast style, out onto the road. This didn't work very well as it was uneven, and when it melted into the packed snow, it created deep, bone rattling holes for vehicles to hit.

And before that, no sand was put on the roads in winter, as it interfered with the horse drawn sleighs. It was not good sledding on sand.

During the next three years, I drove sand truck for Prentice Roads again, and for Roy Kernohan. They invented the hopper turntable and twirler that, although there are various versions, is still familiar today. This was a great relief to sand truck drivers, as it put the sand ahead of the drive wheels creating traction as they drove forward. By adjusting controls, right at the drivers reach they can put sand from shoulder to shoulder, and even throw it up ahead of the front wheels.

Imagine the difference it would have made that night, if we had this method then, almost fifty years ago, in 1957.

This is a good example of the rapid change that had taken place in the first twenty years of my life, and is one of the things that convinced me to write this book

Swift Canadian Meat Run

In 1932, Alex, Earnest, and John Hewitt formed Hewitt Brothers Transport. They operated from the old livery stable, which was located just north of the bridge, in Minden, on the east side. This building was built for horse and wagon and was not entirely suitable for trucks, but served well until it was sold to Harry Campbell and Bud Barr in 1956. These men didn't know the country whatsoever, so Earn stayed on for a few months, and he and Harold Coulter were still very much in charge of dispatching, when I started to work there on Friday morning, May 18th,1956.

Bud soon sold his share to Harry, who changed the name to Hewitt Transport. (That name continued until it was sold to Freightmaster, sometime after I left Minden in 1969.) Harry immediately commissioned Murray Hewitt and Amos Brubacher to build a new terminal on Bobcaygeon Road, just past the fair grounds. That building still stands, although it is now no longer a transport garage.

By spring of 1957, we were getting larger shipments of meat, from Swift Canadian in Toronto, for delivery throughout the Haliburton Highlands. The meat was being shipped on regular, mixed freight runs at the time and was included on the same trucks with every other type of freight you can imagine. This was not a good arrangement, as frozen items were nearly thawed by the time of delivery, and some items, such as quarters of beef, were occasionally in close proximity to freight that could be toxic.

Negotiations had been hammered out between their office and ours during the spring.

In order to make a full load, deliveries to areas such as Lindsay to Bobcaygeon and Fenelon Falls would have to be included. This area was outside the license under which Hewitt Transport operated, so permission had to be negotiated, with the authorities, to have a special license granted for those deliveries. Hearings had been held, with representatives from opposing transport companies present, and the license was finally granted in early June.

The transport purchased a used truck, had it painted the company colours and it had been sitting in the yard for a few days. I came in from a run on Monday, June 17th, just before 5p.m., to find the truck backed against the dock, with the Dollo Brothers old truck body on it. Earn Hewitt was lining the body with a fibre insulation board, and placing quarter inch poplar underlay over that. There was a forty five gallon drum sitting near the head rack.

I said, "Is this the new meat truck?"

"You're about to find out," he said. "Harry wants to see you in the office."

I went into the office, and Harry said, "Ray, as you know we are putting a special on the Swift run. Earn is insulating the old Dollo truck body now. We are going to put a drum up front, with a fan over it. That will be filled with dry ice and the fan will blow the cold air back over the meat."

"I'm sorry sir, but that won't work. Cold air falls, and will be trapped in the barrel. Very little will be used. You will wind up with a hot truck and a drum full of dry ice at the end of the run. It should be suspended from the roof, on its side with both ends cut, and screened in, and the fan blowing through it."

"EXCUSE ME!" he said, with a look that told me to keep my young mouth shut and listen. "Earn says this WILL work."

"Okay," I said, holding my hands up in surrender.

"Anyway, the run starts this Thursday, and you are going to be the driver." Harold joined us then. He continued. "On Wednesday, you will come in at five in the morning as usual to help unload the trailers. Someone else will do your usual Wednesday run, and you will do town. Then you will go home and sleep. You will come in again at seven in the evening and leave for Toronto.

Your dock time is eleven o'clock. You will load and come back to Lindsay. You should have time for a little sleep in the truck there. You can't start delivering before six, because there will be no one at your first lodge, at Sturgeon Point, until then. We will put Cooney McKelvey on with you when you get here, and take Minden, Lochlin, and Gelert off. We'll deliver that from here. Do you know where Swift's is in Toronto?"

"No. I've never been there."

"Okay, Harold will be doing the late trailer run this Wednesday, so you follow him. He will lead you to Swift's. Do you have any returns or pick-ups on your truck now?"

"No."

"Turn in your bills and C.O.Ds to Jack, and come in at five in the morning. We have three trailers coming tonight."

Wednesday, June 19th, happened just that way. I worked on the dock and delivered town just as planned. Then I went home and tried to rest. At 7p.m. I followed Harold out of the yard, and we headed to Toronto.

He was a little way ahead of me as I approached the big hill, before we turned onto highway 12, at Sunderland. It was raining hard and thunder and lightning was all around. The sky grew dark and ugly. The clouds were so low, I thought I was going to drive right into them as I climbed the hill. The light of late evening turned into almost complete darkness. As I turned on my lights, I remembered my experience with hurricane Hazel in 1954. Suddenly, a funnel formed to the south and left of me. It dropped to the ground ahead and to the left and I could see debris flying through the air. Then, it lifted back into the clouds.

I turned onto Highway 12 and went toward Sunderland. Where the highway turned right and went up through the main street, there were parts of the cement block wall of a repair garage and an overturned farm tractor partially blocking the road. Roofs were torn off and trees were down everywhere. Stunned residents were just coming out of homes to look at the damage. I threaded my way through hydro wires and downed poles and out the other side of town. Down the road, Harold was sitting on the side of the road. I pulled in behind him.

"I'm glad to see you," he said as he walked back to my truck. The rain had lessened some.

"The town is in a hell of a mess," I said.

"I know. I could see it in my mirrors. I nearly got caught in some telephone wires as they came down beside me."

"I could see the funnel as I climbed the hill on seven."

The tornado had passed through between our trucks and caused neither of us any harm.

We had great stories to tell the dock crew when we arrived at the trailer terminal on Bridgeland Avenue.

Harold switched trailers and led me to Swifts on St. Clair Avenue. He stayed for a few minutes, until my load began to come down to the dock, then he left. He had to be in Minden before five in the morning.

They filled the drum with dry ice, and then they started to throw packaged and boxed meat to me from the dock. I caught it, piece by piece, and dropped it into place. By the time I had dropped one, another was on its way toward me. When quarters of beef or halves of pork were being loaded they would carry them right in and place them for me. The truck was soon filled, to just above the height of the drum, from front to back. Powdered dry ice was sprayed over the whole load and the tailgate closed.

I watched as a clerk tallied up the weigh of my load on a comptometer. I had not seen one of these things before. It was about the size of a shoe box and would weigh about 8lbs. (no way you could carry it in your breast pocket as you do calculators today). I was amazed at the speed the operator ran this thing.

He handed me a master bill of lading and I checked the weight of my load. It was just over nine tons. I signed the bill and was on my way.

My truck was licensed for just five and a half tons. I knew if I went along the 401 and the new weigh scales at Ajax were open, I would be in trouble. I cut north instead and went by Highway 7 to Highway 12. There was a police officer sitting in a parking lot up, but he just looked at me, and I travelled on.

The debris had been scraped from the highway when I came back through Sunderland and crews were at work on telephone and hydro lines.

I got to Sturgeon Point at 6a.m. after trying to rest in Lindsay for a little, but to no avail. The first time you deliver to any place takes longer, as you have no idea where the receiving door is located. I delivered to Sturgeon Point, a store in Dunsford, some lodges at Greenhurst, and Thurstonia, then into Bobcaygeon. When I finished the stores and restaurants in Bobcaygeon, I cut across and did Fenelon Falls, then onto Highway 35. I stopped at all the lodges, restaurants, stores, and camps between Fenelon Falls and Minden.

Back at the depot they took the local deliveries off my truck, and fuelled it. Then with Cooney on board, we did Highway 35 north all the way to The Forest Ranger School at St Nora's Lake, now known as the Frost Centre. We doubled back to North Shore Road and went through Maple Lake delivering to Maple Lake Lodge, Maple Lake Store and all the lodges there. We delivered to the stores in West Guilford and Eagle Lake. At Silver Maple Lodge we turned toward Haliburton. We did all the stores there then went to the lodges on the south side of Kashagawigamog Lake to Ingoldsby. Out to highway 121 and in to Wig-A-Mog Lodge and Locarno-on-the-Lake. (There was a swamp where the multi million dollar Delta Pinestone Resort now stands).

We went through Haliburton and headed out 121 east, to the Drag Lake Lodge turn. I had a key to a locked box there. We put their order into the box and locked it. Then we travelled on to Findlay's Store in Tory Hill, Agnew's Red and White in Wilberforce, Harcourt General Store, and Highland Grove General Store.

Now we turned back to Agnew's in Gooderham, then the General Store in Irondale, and ended up in Kinmount where Bill Scott met us just before midnight at Scott's store.

We unloaded and returned to the yard in Minden. Harry was there to take the money from my C.O.Ds.

"How do you like that run?" He said.

"It's long and hard and I'm tired."

"You'll get used to it. You don't need to come in at five. The guys will unload the trailers and load your truck for your usual run. You can come at nine and do it. Oh, it will be a little heavy tomorrow for you. There are some deliveries that today's driver wasn't sure of the location . They will be on board with the rest waiting for you"

I had driven more then 450 miles, delivered to 76 stops, and handled nine tons of meat twice, (some of which were quarters of beef weighing as much as I did). I had been on the job for 29 and half hours straight. And, just as a matter of interest, I still had over half a barrel of dry ice.

We punched a clock as I was paid by the hour. To mention overtime in those days would mean unemployment, no matter where you worked in this country except Ontario Hydro or the Department of Lands and Forests, (now known as The Ministry of Natural Resources). With time lost the day before, and the four hours the day after, it really didn't mean much of a boost in my pay cheque.

I did that run every Wednesday night and Thursday, right through until it ended in the fall, with not much change, except a few incidents that held me up making me even later.

One time, when I was going south on Highway 12, a transport in front of me, grew tired of the elderly chap in front of him slowing and speeding up all the time. The transport driver gave his air horn a little jerk, just as we approached a railway crossing. The elderly fellow thought it was a train and hit the brakes. The transport tapped him on the back a little.

All the delays didn't happen on the road. The invoices were transferred to the loading dock, from offices upstairs, through a tube. One night the system clogged and a maintenance crew had to be called in to dismantle it. I was a couple of hours late all day.

Later in the season, the same police officer who had watched me all summer, helped me to recover when a switch-over from one fuel tank to another went wrong. There were two tanks on the truck, so the complete trip could be made to Toronto and back to Minden without refuelling. The fuel pump was not an electric one, right in the tank, that we have today. This one hung on the side of the engine itself and was powered by a lever, that rubbed on the side of a cam, inside the engine. These things were subject to vapour lock, when they ran out of fuel. The trick was to switch the valve just before fuel run out of the first tank. However, that tank had no gauge, so I didn't know how low it was. I used all the fuel, from both tanks, every night, to get safely back with the heavy loads I was carrying, so I would wait until the engine sputtered, then change. Usually this would happen on a flat stretch of road. The vehicle would coast far enough for the pump to pick up its prime. I should have changed before I began to climb a hill on Highway 7. I knew it would be running dry soon, but I wasn't thinking properly. Half way up the hill it sputtered and quit. The truck was pulling hard in second gear and it stopped right there. The cranking of the engine caused the battery to fail before the pump picked up its prime, even though I doused the lights immediately. I turned the parking lights on and let the truck back down the hill. Remember there were no west coast mirrors then, so this had to be done by hanging out of the door.

At the bottom of the hill, I was sitting there, the hood up, with a flashlight and wrench in either hand, trying to loosen the gas line at the pump to allow gas to flow from the tank, when a police cruiser pulled in behind me. He assessed my predicament, and then held the light for me.

When most of the air had bled out, I tightened the fitting and tried to start it, but with the lights being on for this long, the battery wouldn't turn the engine over. He pulled the cruiser around, and drove up to the front of the truck, connected his booster cables, and it started right away. I have always felt a degree of comfort, when I am on the road alone at night, and I see a cruiser.

Easton's Red and White ordered 50 turkeys for a special event during the summer. These would normally have been shipped with me the following Thursday, but somewhere between ordering and shipping, another zero was added, making it an order for 500 birds. This size order was transferred from Toronto to Swift's plants in either London or Kitchener. They were shipped by refrigerated railroad box car to Union Station in Toronto, then by non-refrigerated car through Lindsay to Kinmount.

Turkeys are shipped in heavy cardboard boxes each containing four birds to a box. The turkeys are heavy, and if handled too much, the corners of the box will give way, even though they are bound each way by either wire or straps.

By the time they arrived at the station in Kinmount, the turkeys were partially thawed, the boxes were wet and they were not in good shape. Many boxes were already tearing.

Harold Coulter was driving the truck sent to pick up freight from the station that day. Knowing that Easton's would not likely be needing this many turkeys and not wanting to get Hewitt's in the middle of something unusual, he wisely made a call to Easton's before releasing them from CNR to Hewitt's responsibility. Bill Coneybeare said that they would take 13 cases, but not the whole shipment. CNR would not release part of a shipment, without authority from the shipper.

Not wanting 125 cases of thawing turkeys in his station, the agent got the phone number from our office in Minden, and called Swift's in Toronto. After a lot of haggling, they agreed to let Easton's have 13 cases, if Harold would accept the whole shipment, and store the rest at Stouffer's cold storage in Minden, until my next run. Arrangements were made for me to take them to Union Station and ship them from there back to sender by refrigerated car.

By the time I loaded them the following Wednesday, they had been handled three more times. Most of the boxes were damaged. When I reached the station in Toronto, the turkeys were all loose. The agent in Toronto looked inside my truck and said, "No way."

Here I was with 448 turkeys rolling around in my truck like loose footballs, at 10p.m. and I have a load of meat to pick up across the city at 11p.m.

I called Swift's, and after much conversation, they instructed me to shovel them onto the dock at Union Station. They would send some people down with new boxes and wire and repack them.

I got away from there about the time I should have been at the dock for my load. Being from the backwoods, I managed to get myself thoroughly lost before I got anywhere. I was in a residential area, where signs clearly said 'no heavy trucks'. Seeing a corner service station, I pulled in to look at a map.

Apparently someone had called the police, because a cruiser wheeled around and pulled up beside me.

"Were you just down that street now?" the driver asked without even saying hello.

"Yes, I was."

"There are no heavy trucks allowed on that street, buddy."

"I saw that, and got out of there as fast as I could."

"Are you lost?"

"Yes I am looking for Swift Canadian. Can you help?"

"Mister, step out of your truck and look above the service station." He laughed and drove off.

I got out. There above the service station, was a huge brightly lit sign that read "Swift Canadian."

A highlight of the run occurred on August 14th ,when Dad went with me. He hadn't been to Toronto since his mother died. He was amazed at the changes and had never seen a highway clover leaf before. The first time I went around a cloverleaf, I remember seeing him turn his head, to follow the moon as we completed the loop. He finally said, "Do you have any idea at all where you are going?"

"Pretty much, why?"

"That moon has been on all sides of us in the last two minutes."

He helped me all the way to Minden the next day.

Highway 401 north of the city of Toronto was finished then, but was only two lanes each way. Don Valley Parkway was in the planning stages.

A weigh station had been installed at Bowmanville, on the westbound lanes, and at Ajax, on the eastbound lanes. The police officer who watched me all summer, must have known I was overloaded, when he saw how heavily laden the truck was and could very well have made me follow him to, and over, the scales. I think what he saw instead, was a young man trying to make a living.

I always carry an adjustable wrench in a vehicle. I even have a very small one hanging on my key chain. They have got me out of so many pinches in my lifetime, that I feel strange without one.

A regular load of freight for delivery through Haliburton each day would consist of several deliveries to homes from the T. Eaton Company, or Simpsons. I had several deliveries to lodges and camps around Kashagawigamog Lake, deliveries of biscuits etc. to Easton's Red and White, Eddy Miller's Store, Steinberg's, appliances for Black's Hardware and Newbatt's Appliances. There might be shingles and hardware on board for Emmerson Lumber. There would likely be truck parts for Boice Motors, and body parts for Curry Motors body shop. Plumbing supplies were delivered daily to Whitfield Plumbing, and T.A. Irwin Plumbing. Rae's hardware was very busy then, so I would be there almost every day with supplies. Cliff Elstone may get some tires, and oil or anti-freeze. Bella Bernstein was always getting big bales of clothing, and I usually had something for Harry Brohm.

I would hurry on to Stan's Shell with tires, batteries and a few cases of oil. Paradise Lodge then Drag Lake Lodge would take me away off the highway and back. There may be more Eaton's deliveries, to homes along the highway to Tory Hill. Once a week there would be Dare Biscuits for Findlay's General Store in Tory Hill, which he would always refuse, because his brother operated Findlay Transport then, and he wanted to give him the business. Dare Biscuits shipped to all the stores in the area, and when our truck was there, they always included Findlay's order with ours. He would refuse them, we would take them back, then a few days later they would come by another Transport to Lindsay, and be loaded onto his brother's truck there. They would then arrive at Tory Hill, all battered and bruised, but I guess someone had made a point. The next week it would happen again.

After delivery to more houses, I would arrive at Tallman Brothers Plumbing and Heating in Wilberforce. Gary Agnew's Red and White would always have a lot of general supplies. Wilberforce Veneer might have drums of glue or drums of varnish, sometimes machine parts.

A couple of Eaton's deliveries were left at the Harcourt General store. Occasionally I would have to take a side trip to Harcourt Park, and sometimes to Elephant Lake Lodge and/or Martin Lumber.

My load was getting lighter, and it was a good thing, as it was probably well after the supper hour by this time. Highland Grove Lucky Dollar may be the last stop, but quite often I would have plumbing supplies for Mack Peters.

I would then go back to Wilberforce Veneer, where I may pick up a full load of chair seats and backs, or sometimes bowling alley gutters. I would then point the 1952 International for home and floor it, arriving home for supper by nine or ten-o-clock.

I would be at work at five a.m. the next morning, to help unload and sort three tractor trailer loads of freight loading it onto three delivery trucks. I would probably be routed through Carnarvon and Eagle Lake to Haliburton this time. Then to Tory Hill and down through Gooderham where I would deliver to Ross Agnew's Red and White, Sisson's Texaco, and my then good friend Cliff Stoughton* of Stoughton Electric. There was always a smile from Cliff. He would often volunteer to take deliveries to cottages around the local lakes for me. This would save me snaking through the trees on a cottage road, with the big truck, and allowing me to get home hours earlier. There was no road from Gooderham to Buckhorn, or from Gooderham to Haliburton, so I would have to go to Kinmount or back to Tory Hill, to get home from there.

I drove a truck with eight by sixteen-foot platform, six-foot high racks and a tarp. The first thing I would do in the mornings, was go all along the sides of my truck and untie the tarp ropes. That way, we could push the tarp up for tall items so it would hold more freight. The truck was always full from head rack to tailgate and higher than the six foot racks. My days usually started at five in the morning and ended whenever I got home at night, usually around nine or ten. The same work is now done with several smaller trucks owned by Muskoka Delivery Service, Purolator, and United Parcel Service. Most building and plumbing supplies are delivered by company trucks.

A truck backed into our yard just before Christmas a year or so ago at four-thirty. The driver was in a terrible rush, because he was going to be late. He said that he would not be getting home until five-thirty or six , so his supper was going to be late. Times have changed.

I worked for the transport company seasonally, from May 18th 1956 to 1963. I was laid off in the fall, when freight loads would become lighter, and delivery routes would be covered every other day, or once a week, depending on freight demands. During the winter, I would work for Prentice Roads and Excavating, and/or drive for other truckers, such as Roy Kernohan.

Near the end of my employment at Hewitt's, I spent time in the office. When the first trailer arrived around three in the morning the driver would telephone me and get me out of bed. I would go to work and start typing delivery slips from the bills of lading for that load. Jack Philips and Harry Campbell would join me around six. There was an average of one hundred deliveries in a trailer load of freight, so that meant there had to be three hundred bills typed and rated, before the dock guys had sorted and reloaded the freight for delivery usually by nine thirty or ten a.m. Sometimes I couldn't see Jack for carbon paper.

One morning, I was shaving when I felt a sharp pain in my right shoulder. I went to work, but soon found that my right hand wasn't functioning properly. I had to leave work and, after a visit to a doctor, soon found myself in Toronto General Hospital. They discovered a break-down of the nerve in my shoulder. The nerve just needed time to heal, so I suffered for several months at home.

Lyle McKnight of McKnight's Haulage and Excavators, came to my house one morning and asked me if I could operate a backhoe. We thought, maybe my arm could rest on the console, and I could work the levers. I went over to their yard and tried it in a sand pile there. It seemed okay so I went to work digging spur lines for the water system in Minden.

Charlie Shaw was my safety man. One afternoon I was digging a trench across the back yard of the Dominion Hotel. The trench had to be at least six feet deep, so frost wouldn't reach the water pipes in winter. The soil there is sandy and prone to cave in. Charlie was laying the copper pipe along the trench as we went, so if there was a cave-in, the pipe would be in place. Half-way across the yard, his hat blew off and landed in the trench. He climbed down to get it, and the bank caved in on him, covering him to his armpits. Loose sand is like a boa constrictor. It holds you until you breathe out, then it tightens around you and restricts your breathing in. The sand was tightening around Charlie.

I swung the hoe to dig beside him, but when I removed sand, it pushed him aside, and I was afraid of hurting him more. There was a company truck there, with a couple of round mouth shovels on board. I ran into the beverage room and yelled that I had buried Charlie. Several men came running out and we dug him free. He was almost out of breath by then, and had very sore ribs for several days. They now use steel cribs to prevent this sort of cave-in.

Scott Gartshore was a cute, little curly headed guy running around town at that time. He would see the loose spoil from my digging and he would go home, get a little truck, and play in the soil. Sometimes he would get too close to the hoe, and Charlie would chase him away. Scott later became a long distance trucker, and is a grandfather now. My son is named after him.

McKnight's Haulage was located where Sears Floor Covering is now, on County Road 21.

Cliff Stoughton. *I see in a local paper that Cliff has invented a positive trailer hitch, to keep trailers from separating from the tow vehicle. It looks like a hell of a good thing and I hope it becomes mandatory. If it does, he could become a millionaire. I hope he does. No one deserves it more.*

<u>Not a good time</u>

Dad. in front of garage and tractor shed, with the trailer I built on the right. Taken on March 19th, after a storm had blocked all highways in the area

I had worked for Stuart Harrison for part of the year before, assembling pre-cut cottages around Chemong and Gold lakes, for Peterborough Lumber. Stuart was unable to continue doing this, so their salesman, Joe Sullivan, had asked me if I was interested.

I took on the contract, and built an 8X16 plywood trailer, which my men and I would live in while on the job. We had moved to Anstruther Lake, near Apsley, on the Friday before where we were to erect several cottages

On Monday, May 11th, 1959, at 6:30 a.m. I was waiting for Keith Aggett to arrive, so we could go to work, when Dad came around from the implement house with the seed drill behind the tractor. He rented his Grandpa Schroter's place from Dick Hillier the year before, and was preparing the fields for planting. He stopped beside the tractor shed, and began to carry seed oats and grass seed from the shed and load it on the front of the seed drill. While I was helping him, Keith drove in, so I said, "I guess we had better go, if we are going to get anything done today at all."

"I had better get going too," he said.

We said goodbye. I climbed into my truck. Waved goodbye to Mother, and left.

In Apsley, we rented a 14 foot aluminium boat, a motor, and a boat trailer, and then drove several miles off the highway to the landing. We crossed the lake to the first cottage site, but discovered that the material wasn't there. I knew where another cottage was to be built, so we crossed the lake to that site. We found a cottage package there, but it belonged to the lot across that lake. I went back to the dock, drove out to Apsley, and called Joe. He told me go ahead, erect the piers for the second cottage, using the blocks available, and he would contact the people who floated the material across the lake, and have them correct their mistake. We started the job and returned to our camp for the night.

Joe arrived at our camp before seven the next morning and accompanied us across the lake. He told us the raft would be coming to move the material to the correct lot during the morning, so we could prepare the lot, and be ready to start building as soon as it arrived.

We worked late that afternoon, and completed the floor and two walls. A wind had risen by the time we crossed the lake, waves were splashing against the side of the boat, and extinguished Joe's cigar. We teased him about that. Joe left for Peterborough. I prepared dinner. Keith read as I studied the plans for the next cottage. Just after dark, about ten o'clock, I noticed he had gone to sleep, so I went out and shut off the generator and put it into the truck. I looked out over the lake, where a loon was calling, and marvelled at the reflection of the moon on the still water, then entered the trailer and went to sleep.

I awoke at 11:45, to the sound of a vehicle driving right up to the trailer door. Two car doors slammed and Keith answered a knock on the door. He was in his underwear, and stepped back as the officer stepped in. The only light we had was from the headlights of the cruiser.

"Are you Ray Miller?" the officer said, as the other officer stepped in.

"That's him there," Keith replied, nodding my way.

The officer turned to me and said, "I have a message from Joe Sullivan that your father has passed away."

Mother had been ill for a time and Dad had been so well just the day before, so my reaction was, "No, Mother maybe, but not Dad."

He looked at his pad and said, "It says Father here."

"What happened, was it an accident?"

"I don't have any details, Where are you guys from?"

Keith said, "Minden."

"Will you be going there tonight then?"

I said, "Yes, right now."

I guess I looked a little pale, as he shone his flashlight on my face, and turning to Keith, he said, "Don't let him drive, will you?"

Keith said, "No, I'll take him home."

When I arrived home, at 1:45 a.m. Doward, Morley and Keith were in the kitchen.

"What happened," I asked, expecting he had been involved in an accident of some kind.

"Griffiths said it was his heart." Doward answered.

"Where's Mother."

"She's in the bedroom."

As I passed through the front room where Floyd and Marg were, Floyd jumped up and came to me saying, "Are you alright."

"I'm fine," I said, as I went on into the bedroom.

Mother was sitting on the bed, between Mabel and Hazel. One of them moved over, and I sat down and put my arms around her. "What happened, where was he, where is he now?" I asked trying to be strong for Mother. With help from the girls, she sobbed out the details.

Dad had left that morning to work in the fields at the Schroter place. This farm is in Snowdon Township, and well over a mile up a side road. The road leading there was axle deep mud for the tractor and truck at this time of year.

Ferne and Mother and Marg had gone to Lindsay that day, to arrange for some things for our wedding, which was planned for May 20th , just over a week away. Bill Brown, a neighbour living between Kinmount and us, had passed away a day or so before. As they passed by the

Brown residence on the way home, Mother had said, "I feel so bad for Ada, it will be hard for her to be alone." She kept saying that she had said this and, "I didn't know I was coming home to the same thing." This broke my heart every time she repeated it.

They said, Dad wasn't there when they arrived at our place, but no one paid much attention, as he was in the habit of working until dark. The girls dropped Mother off and went on home.

When darkness came and Dad hadn't come, Mother became worried, but waited for a while longer, knowing that the tractor had lights, she felt he perhaps was working by headlights to finish a field.

Around nine o'clock she phoned Doward.. He and the boys came immediately and went in to the farm. Doward told me later they had trouble with the mud, and had to reverse several times and try a different rut. Finally, they turned into the gate and the headlights of Doward's Volkswagen Van picked out Dad sitting in the truck. He said to the boys, "Be prepared for what we might find here."

They drove up to the truck and Doward opened the door. Dad had been rolling a cigarette. His head had fallen back into the corner of the cab and his hands dropped onto the steering wheel. He still had a cigarette paper in one hand, and tobacco in the other. Doward spoke dad's name and touched him. He was cold.

They drove back out to the house and told Mother, then called the police, coroner, and undertaker, then Floyd, and Mabel. While they were waiting for the police and coroner to arrive, they found Joe Sullivan's number among my things and called him. He called Bancroft OPP.

Apparently the police arrived, then the coroner. The officer was quite adamant that he would take the cruiser into the scene, but Doward argued strongly that no car could ever navigate that road. Half way in, as Doward battled his way through deep ruts, the officer agreed that he would not have made it with the cruiser.

Dr. Griffiths examined the body and estimated the time of death to be around six that evening. They brought the body out with them to the highway, where Gerald Coulter was waiting with the hearse.

Dad had a habit of looking back at the end of each day to admire his day's work, before he left the scene. He had done a huge day's work that day, and I believe he was sitting there in his truck looking out over the finished fields, while he rolled a cigarette to enjoy as he drove home. The attack struck and it was over.

After I had learned what had happened, I asked Floyd to drive me to Cowan's, to get my car. It was near morning when I woke Ferne's parents, and told them and her.

My aunt Mabel lived in Vantage, Saskatchewan. She wanted to come to the funeral, but travel wasn't as easy as it is now, and it would take too long for her to get here by train.

Funeral chapels were not available then, so the funeral was held from the house. The house was full of relatives each night, so I slept on the chesterfield, at the foot of the casket, each night it was there.

There were many people coming and going over the next days, but one man stands out in my memory. Dick Kirkwood entered the front room. He greeted the family, then I accompanied him to the casket. He stood there with his hands behind his back, as he bowed his head for a minute. Then he reached down and touched Dad's folded, white hands and said, "Goodbye, my good and faithful friend. You were a good and honest man; you never took on a task that you couldn't finish. You will be missed by friends you didn't even know you had." He turned, with tears running down both cheeks, and with head down, he walked through the front room to the kitchen, through the washroom to the yard, got into his car, and drove away.

Aunt Gertie* played hymns on our old organ. It had only one bellows functioning. Reverent Hugh Robert MacDonald preached the service. Then Dad was laid to rest in the Cemetery at Minden.

Pallbearers, left to right. Gordie Kellett, Frank Bowron, John Harrison, Bert Bowron, Jack Hounsell and Fred Barry.

Uncle Stewart and Aunt Gertie went to where he had been found, before they went back to their home in Whitby. They took the following pictures of his machinery just as he had left it.

Dad's brother Stewart. *Note wheel chains on the truck.*   **Where he left his machinery.**

  In late 1956, Mother told us about Dad having some kind of spell, that had turned his skin as white as skimmed milk. Apparently he had pain in his chest, but also in his rectum. On March 29, 1957, mother called me from my room, saying, "Dad is having another spell." I went down to the front room, where he was lying on the chesterfield. He was an ash blue colour. His skin seemed to be transparent: I could see the roots of the hair on the backs of his hands. I spoke to him and he answered, but barely and very faint. On September 7th, 1957, he entered in his diary, "Had another bowel spell." On December 12th, 1957, he wrote, "I had another attack." They called Dr Griffiths, and he came to the house, but by the time he got there, Dad had improved. He said for Dad to come to his office in a few days, when he felt better. On December 14, 1957, he went to the doctor's office. He looked him over and said it was probably sciatic neuritis of the lower spine. He gave him an electrocardiogram and said he had a strong heart and would never die of heart failure. That same doctor pronounced him dead of a heart attack just 18 months later. He said the whole heart had been in distress and the bottom had simply blown apart. Death was instant.
  He was 64 years and twelve days old.

*Aunt Gertie played hymns on our old organ. It had only one bellows functioning
That organ was purchased years before, for Hazel, when she was very young. It was passed on to her when Mother gave up housekeeping. Hazel gave it to her daughter, Phyllis Sisson, who donated it to the museum in Minden. It is in the Bowron House there.

We Got Married

On May 20th ,1959, just eight days after Dad's death, Ferne and I got married in the United Church, in Minden. Mervin and Dorothy Cowan stood up for us, and Reverent Hugh Robert McDonald officiated. The ceremony was on Wednesday, which was a bit unusual, but Ferne wanted it to be on the anniversary of our first date.

Original plans were for the reception to be at Matabanick Inn on Boshkong Lake, where Ferne's sister Doreen was working at the time, and the dance was to be at Medley's Dine and Dance in Carnarvon. When Dad died, we decided to go ahead with the wedding as we felt Dad would want that, but to cancel the dance. No one thought to tell Muriel and Stanley Archer, operators of the lodge at that time, about Dad not being at the dinner. When time came to sit for dinner, Mother sat down, and there beside her setting was a place marked, 'Father of the groom'. Naturally, she was upset, and broke down for a bit. She struggled back heroically and soon was able to carry on.

We honeymooned at the residence of Mabel and Earl Ryall, in Leamington. The Ryalls had hunted with our hunt party. We then went on to Mr and Mrs Elwood Zaibze's, cottagers on Horseshoe Lake, who lived in Lorraine Ohio.

When we returned, we lived in the trailer I had built. I continued to erect pre-cut cottages for Peterborough Lumber. We would stay at Ferne's parents on weekends.

Later that year, we placed the trailer on the site of the old camp grounds, across from home. We soon moved it to Lot 30, then onto a lot we purchased from Holly Stevens, on what was then Highway 121. It was two lots east of McKnight's Haulage, which is now Sears Floor Coverings. We lived in the trailer the first winter.

We were expecting our first baby, the following September, so I began to build a house during the summer of 1960. Laurie-Lee was born in Minden hospital, on September 28th, and we didn't move in until December 18th, so we all lived in the trailer for three months.

Our son, Scott Ray, was born on November 6th, 1962.

I have no pictures of our wedding. Ferne either kept them all or threw them out when we divorced, thirty six years later.

A Night at The Dominion

In March 1961, the army had a platoon of soldiers at Brady Lake, testing some new winter gear. They had been there for a week or more, and had been seen in town from time to time, with large personnel carriers and other vehicles with tall aerials.

Ferne's uncle, Morris Holland, was at our place. He and I decided to go to the Dominion Hotel for a beer. We had to wait at the bridge in Minden for several of these army vehicles to cross in front of us. It had been mild that day and I suppose the lads were in need of a night in town. With aerials waving in grand array, they trundled through the intersection and some turned into the back yard of the Dominion, the rest going through town to the Rockcliffe. By the time we had parked and entered the beverage room, there were quite a number of army lads already sitting down. Among them were two or three Military Police, (MPs).

I saw Murray Hewitt at a table. He waved for us to join him. I was not one to frequent beverage rooms in Minden, as Ferne didn't like that.

"Am I ever surprised to see you here," he said, as we sat down and ordered a beer.

"We might not be here long," he continued. "These army guys have been in that camp a while and may get a little rowdy after a few beers. I see they have some MPs with them, so they are expecting something."

Murray was a vet of World War Two so I believed him.

I looked around the room. I saw Joe Rivers playing shuffleboard over against the wall behind the back door and nodded to him. He smiled and returned the nod. Tom Sawyer and Tom Harrison were both there. These two elderly men couldn't agree about anything, and usually had words whenever they were within shouting distance of each other. Their verbal challenges would often lead to fisticuffs. The owners of both hotels could usually keep things under control, by simply chucking them out the door. Steve Rastall owned the Dominion then. He was a well built man and could handle himself well in any altercation that might arise. A very handy asset indeed, when you owned a beverage room in those days!

It wasn't long before Tom Sawyer yelled an insult at Tom Harrison and received a stinging reply.

"Don't start Tom," Steve said from behind the bar.

"Go ____ yourself" Tom replied.

Steve came around the bar and picked this little old man from his chair by the arms, as if he were a doll.

Joe opened the door.

Steve stood Tom on the doorstep outside.

Joe closed the door.

As usual, in a minute Tom reappeared at the front door. Licking his lips he returned to the table and sat down.

Steve eyed him from the bar.

It wasn't long until the two Toms were yelling at each other again.

"Settle down fellows or I'll have to throw you both out," Steve shouted.

Now these two fellows also had a habit of closing ranks against a common enemy, and that is what happened here. They both stood up and headed toward the bar.

"A softer job would suit you a hell of a lot better," one of them said, as Steve came around the bar.

It wasn't much of a challenge. He simply grabbed them both by the scuff of the neck. They were both drunk, both old, and neither resisted much as he headed for the back door.

Joe opened the door

Steve pushed them out.

Joe closed the door.

This time Steve turned and came face to face with a large Sergeant.

"You like pushing little old men around, don't you?" he said. "Well, let's see you put me out."

Joe opened the door.

Murray took a look around and, spying an empty table in the corner, he said, "Grab your beers and come over here, we don't need to be involved in this." We followed him, as Steve took hold of that soldier.

The MPs sprang between the other soldiers and the two fighting men at the door, before they could join in. The altercation moved away from the door enough to knock a few tables and jar the shuffleboard.

Joe peeked from behind the open door.

Several attempts were made by uniformed men to join the row, but were held back by MPs. Fights started all over the room. Local guys were standing along the wall, as more tables were tipped and beer spilled. Steve got that big guy headed out the door and pushed him through, with a well placed kick in the ass.

Joe closed the door.

Steve began to stand the tables back up. His shirt was in shreds and one arm was bleeding from a scratch.

The MPs herded their guys out the door and apologized. The roar of army vehicles could be heard, leaving the backyard.

Joe played shuffleboard.

In the early to mid 1900s, Haliburton County was 'dry'. This was an issue in several elections. There were no liquor stores, and no beer stores. This fostered bootlegging in great volume.

Bootleggers could purchase as much hard liquor as personal licensing* would allow in stores in Peterborough and Lindsay, and resell it at greatly inflated prices, doubling and sometimes tripling their initial outlay. They did not bootleg beer. It was too bulky to transport and store discreetly.

The only place you could get 'a cold one' was in the beverage rooms at the Dominion and Rockcliffe hotels in Minden. The returning war vets could drink at the Legions in Haliburton and Kinmount, but admittance there was restricted to members only and strictly enforced.

Many people, including my parents, could not understand that this arrangement actually contributed to family anguish and broken homes. Many men needed a beer after a hard day's work. There was none at home, so they would drop in to the beverage rooms for one, before going home for dinner. Most of them really intended to have just one or two, but everyone knew everyone and it was easy to be 'captured' by the camaraderie of the group. The result was, in many respects, devastating.

A well-intentioned stop on the way home, would turn to a night of drinking with friends, until closing time at ten-thirty. Then a stagger or drunken drive home to a cold supper, an irate spouse, and the children already in bed. More times than anyone wanted to admit, these evenings would become abusive. In some cases, the day's wages would be spent in the beverage rooms. This would put the family in financial distress and separation would soon follow.

Today these fellows go home and have a beer from the refrigerator, and have dinner with their family. They can then spend the evening doing things around the yard or house, and help their wives tuck the children into bed. Yeah.....well some do!

* Personal Licensing; A license was issued to individuals allowing a certain number of bottles of liquor over a period. The number of units, and period, often varied, as the law changed. Liquor was not displayed in stores, as it is today. Instead, there was a list of available spirits at the government- operated stores. You wrote down the identification numbers of the spirits you wished to purchase on an order form, with your license number. The attendant marked the purchase on the back of your license and brought the bottles to you in a plain brown bag. (This method was still used for some years after personal licensing was discontinued). As you would expect, there were many attempts to falsify these licenses, and some were very successful.

Sanding the Roads for Roy Kernohan

Roy Kernohan was as honest and hard working as any man you would ever want to meet. He operated a farm, at one time owned a grain separator and threshed all through the area, had a gravel truck, logged, and trapped. Like most men he also liked beer, but scarcely ever did he allow this to interfere with his work or social activities.

He had a way of adding the phrase, "son of a whore", and, "of ours", to most conversations. This made him unique.

On a late fall day, I received a call from Roy that went like this.

"Hello"

"Hello...Ray?"

"Yes."

"This is Roy Kernohan."

"Hi Roy, What can I do for you?"

"Well...I got myself in a bit of a jam."

"Oh, what happened?"

"Well, I put in a bid on that son of a whore of a sand job, and I also applied for a trapping license, thinking I would get one or the other but, I'll be a son of a whore, if I didn't get both. I was wondering if you could drive this son of a whore of a truck of ours, on the sand job, whenever I can't. Now, I want to drive it myself, when I can, but when I get tired, maybe you could take the son of a whore over for me. Also I have a camp up at the Snake Lakes, and I will be up there sometimes, taking care of the trap line, so you would drive it then."

"I can do that for you, Roy."

"Okay Great. Now, I'll pay you a dollar and a half an hour. Is that OK?"

"Yeah, that will be fine."

"Now, they have changed things around a little this year. They only allow you twenty minutes now, from the time they call you out until you sign in. Then there will be a penalty. Now, on a dirty night, this may be a problem for you to get here and then down there."

"It might be, if I have to check the oil and everything and fuel it."

"Either myself or Glenn and Jean will have the son of a whore ready, don't worry about that."

"Okay Roy, that should be fine."

"Good." Click.

I took it over from him a few times between then and Christmas. One night, in January, I got this call.

"Hello."

"This is Roy Kernochan."

"Hi Roy. What's up?"

"Well, I was in and set my son of a whore of a trap line the other day, so I have to go in and work it for a day or two."

"Okay Roy. You want me on standby while you are gone?"

"Yeah Now, they are going to call here and Ethel will call you, alright?"

"I'll be here, Roy."

"I know you will." Click.

Ethel called me in a day or so, about four in the morning. It was snowing and they needed the sander right away. It wasn't snowing hard, but just kept on coming down. Dunc Prentice and

Frank Wright were on the plow for one shift and Laverne Cowan was driving the other. I can't remember the name of his wingman. Gordie Kellett was on the patrol truck.

I sanded all that day, throughout that night and all the next day. When I went to Roy's place to get fuel and check the truck around three in the afternoon, I reminded Ethel I had been going quite a while. I asked if Roy was planning on coming out of the camp that night. She said she was expecting him any minute, and he would take over, as soon as he arrived.

I was heading out with a load to do toward Hall's Lake about eleven that night, when I met a car flashing its lights, right at the road to Doward and Hazel's, which is where the Go cart track is now. I stopped, hoping it was Roy, and it was.

Now... you have to visualize the scenario here. Roy had been in his little trap line camp for a few days. He headed out to relieve me, but went into the Dominion Hotel for a quick beer. Roy was well known and well liked. Others would offer him a beer, and he would buy one for them. Next thing he knew, the beverage room was closing at the usual time of ten-thirty.

He got out of the car and came over to the truck.

I rolled down the window. In a drunken slur, he said, "Ethel tells me you don't want to drive the son of a whore no more." He sniffed a couple of times.

"I just don't want to drive it any more tonight, that's all, but Roy... You have had a little to drink. Maybe you had better go home and rest for an hour or so."

"You think I can't drive the son of a whore, don't you?"

"Sure, you can drive it Roy. You're a better driver than I am, but you have been drinking. I think I am in better shape than you are to drive right now."

This made him mad.

"Get out of the son of a whore, get into that son of a whore of a car of ours and go home and stay there. You're fired."

I drove his car straight to my place. I had been working for forty-four hours straight and boy did that bed look good, but it didn't last long. The phone rang at six thirty.

"Hello," I said half asleep.

"This is Grant Hewitt. What are you doing home?"

"Trying to sleep, Grant, why?"

"You're supposed to be on the sand truck. We never signed you out. You can't just go home like that. Where's the truck anyway? Do you have it there with you?"

"No. Roy took it over last night at eleven."

"Well look, Ray, the boys called me out because we can't find it. You signed it in and no one signed it out, so it's our responsibility. You had better come in and we will see what we can do."

It was breaking daylight as I broke over the hill where Roy had taken over the truck. I saw it It was on its side, in the east ditch, part way down the hill. It was mostly snowed over. The plow had gone past and thrown some slush on top of it. I went over the bank to look, but there was no sign of Roy and any tracks he made were snowed over. I suppose the snowplow operators were watching the road as they passed, and didn't see it in the dark.

"I found the truck." I said, as I entered the office.

"Where?" Grant asked.

"It's on its side, in the ditch, up there by Doward's road."

"I was just thinking, he took over just after the beverage rooms closed. He was drinking, wasn't he Ray?" Grant said.

"Yes, he was."

"You shouldn't have let him take over in that state."

"I tried, but he almost pulled me out of the truck. In fact he fired me for giving him trouble."

Grant sat there deep in thought for a minute, and then he said, "If we report this to the Department, there will be all kinds of hell to pay. More damned paper work than enough, and Roy will never be able to apply for the job again. He's such a good man, Ray, I don't want to report this. Let's go up and take a look."

When we got there, Grant stood looking at the truck for a minute, then went down and looked closer, and said, "If we put a cable from the snowplow down here to pull, and hold it upright, while at the same time pull it back out on its own track with the grader, I think we can get it out of there. We'll wait until the plow comes in and do that."

It worked. They parked the patrol truck on top of the hill, to slow traffic, someone flagged the other way. I steered the truck, as it came out onto the road. We looked it over. It had gone into the ditch quite slowly, and only tipped after it had come to a stop. The mirror was ripped off and there was a small dent in the fender, but not a lot of damage at all. We towed it back to the yard and put it in the garage, where they checked out the sander motor. I checked under the hood. It hadn't even lost any oil or anti-freeze.

We put another load on it and I spread it, wherever it was needed, down the Kinmount road. The storm was over, so I was signed out. I left Roy's car there and took the truck to his house. Then I went home.

I got a call that evening around eight-thirty.

"Hello"

Silence for what seemed like a minute. "Ray?, Roy Kernohan."

"Yes."

"I owe you an apology."

"That's alright, Roy."

"Will you still drive for me?"

"Sure Roy. Don't worry about that."

"I guess I owe Grant and the boys a vote of gratitude too."

I drove the sander a couple of times between then and spring. The mirror was replaced immediately, but the dents remained until the sander was taken off. Before he put the dump box back on, he had the body work done.

Author's Note. *Readers may think that I made a lot of money that time, with overtime and all that. We didn't even expect extra compensation back then. We went to work, and stayed until the job was done.*

<u>Ray Miller Heating</u>

I ran a backhoe for McKnight's, off and on, for several years. I did all the excavating for the tile beds and septic tanks at the new Legion Hall in Haliburton, and dug a lot of wells through the area.

Employment was very much hit-and-miss, during the winter months in 1964. I would work for McKnight's for a few days, then for Prentice's for a while, sand roads for Roy Kernohan, and then Dave Stamp wanted me to drive a school bus for him. I agreed, and a bunch of us went in one of Dave's buses to Lindsay, to try out for our school bus license. The other drivers included Basil Hewitt, Mervin Barry, Ron Martin, Bruce Dudman, Dave and myself. We all passed. We were all going to be drivers for Dave's fleet, except Mervin Barry. Mervin* had a bus of his own.

I started on the school bus run, from Kinmount through what is now County Road 1, to Haliburton, that fall, with a 47 passenger 1958 GMC bus. A wheel came off that darned thing, just as I came down off the hill, onto the flat area East of Donald, and I took a full bus load of children for a ride on three wheels. No one was hurt, but that didn't stop word from racing back to Kinmount that half of them were killed, so there was much confusion about nothing that night.

Dave had purchased the local White Rose tank truck business from Bob Ewers. Shell Oil merged with White Rose Oil, and dropped the White Rose name.

The so called "free service" for all oil burning customers, had came into effect, and mandatory oil burner licensing also came about. On our way back from Haliburton High School, after we had all made our runs, Dave said, "Ray, Shell Oil is putting on a course, at the Empress Hotel in Peterborough, to train people for this new oil burner license that has come into force. Would you be interested in going and becoming my burner service man? We have a lot of clean outs to do immediately, and I thought maybe you would do them between school bus runs."

"Will I have to pay for the course?"

"No, Shell will pay for it."

"That sounds good to me Dave."

"Good, they are starting right away. Bruce is helping me with the chores on the farm, so I'll pay you good and Bruce can help you. You will have to supply your own tools, and I guess you will need a special vacuum cleaner or something. You'll get five dollars a cleanout and you will make money on any parts you might sell."

The Shell Oil instructors didn't put the course on in Peterborough until the next summer, but I started doing cleanouts right away. I didn't have much idea what in hell I was doing, but I had worked for J.O. Jackson Heating from time to time, and had picked a little up from him. My license was issued on July 10th 1965.

Dave got right into the business and sold Bob Young, who lived south of Kinmount, a new furnace. Keith Hughes, who lives on the highway to Haliburton, also bought one. He had no idea whatsoever how to size a furnace to be compatible with the heat loss of the house, so he just sold them the biggest one he could get. These were through Shell Oil and were made by Gurney Foundries. As it turned out, these were both big old draughty houses, so that was alright, but he had no one to install them, and just kind of thought I would do it. The only agreement I had with Dave was to do cleanouts for one year.

Bruce quit doing Dave's chores in the spring, and was slinging beer at the Dominion. I had quit driving bus for Dave, and had purchased Holiday Laundromat across the bridge in Minden, where Minden Collision Service is now located.

I decided to use the skills I had picked up working for J.O. Jackson, and put these two furnaces in for Dave. I examined the installation locations, went to Quality Utilities in Lindsay and ordered the necessary plenums, ducts, boots, take offs, perimeter pipe and transitions. Quality Utilities was a wholesale business only selling to the trade, so I had to own a business in order to purchase from them. I made up the name, 'Ray Miller Heating'.

I hired my nephew, Keith Johnson, and we installed the two furnaces. I fired them up. Both customers were happy with the results and my work.

Dave's son, Sid, got out of school, took over the oil business from his Father and called it Sid Stamp Fuels. I did some work for Sid, both driving oil truck and doing service work. Sid died years later, but his sister Dorothy and her husband Brian Black, carry on the business under the same name today.

A salesman began calling on me from Quality Utilities every week, and then Duomatic of Canada, a furnace manufacturer, contacted me looking for a dealer for their units. I looked over their design and found it to be a good unit. I signed up, studied methods for sizing furnaces on individual home heat loss, and began to sell furnaces.

I hired Bruce full time.

My business grew, and soon I was working full time at promoting and making sales. The heating business kept me busy from September till May, and the Laundromat got very busy in the summer.

One day a man drove into my yard and got out of his car. He walked up to me and said, "Are you Ray Miller?"

"Yes?"

"I am Jack McGuinty, representing Canadian Petrofina."

"Oh yes, what can I do for you?"

"I would like to talk to you about doing some furnace cleanings for XXXX."

"Okay."

He came into the house and we worked out a deal.

About a week later there came a knock on the door as I began to eat my supper. I went to the door and found Jack there.

"Oh, hello Jack. Come on in. I was just starting to eat."

"Well, may I wait in your living room until you finish? I have a lot I want to talk about."

I finished my supper, then went in to where he was sitting. "Okay, what do you want to discuss?" I said, expecting it was something about the work I had been doing for XXXX.

"I want you to take over the oil tank business for this area for Canadian Petrofina."

"XXXX does that, does he not want it any more?"

"XXXX won't be doing it from now on."

"But why...I mean ....why not?" I was stunned and very confused.

"It's like this, Ray, if you don't do it, someone else will, or there will be no Fina agent here."

"But, XXXX has a lot of customers here. What will happen to them if you pull out of the county?"

"That is just the point, Ray, I am desperate. Will you take it?"

"But XXXX is a friend of mine Jack. He has a family what will he do?"

"That is not your problem. I must repeat this... XXXX will not be doing the Fina Agency here any more, whether you take it or not."

"It would fit into my heating business very nicely right now Jack, but I don't know?"

Before he left for Peterborough near midnight, we had all but signed the papers. He was back the next morning. I turned the days work over to Bruce, and we sat down. I became the Fina Agent for the area that day. I was to buy XXXX's truck so he took me to XXXX's place and I brought the truck home. Jack told me that Prentice Roads, and Hewitt Transport both needed fuel the next day. They were both getting low, so he suggested I get a load of gasoline from Orillia early in the morning and split it between them, until we could fill them both. Then he went home to Peterborough.

After giving Bruce a crash course on delivering fuel, I sent him to get a load. Jack had just arrived at the house, when the phone rang. I answered.

"Ray Miller Heating."

"Hello Ray, it's Bruce."

"What's wrong, Bruce?"

"I'm down here at Prentice's, and every time I open the valves to deliver fuel, there is gasoline running out under the truck. Stupid me I am likely not doing something right."

"Okay Bruce, I'll be right there."

Both Jack and I went. XXXX's truck was in need of new rubbers, in the joints of the pipes, from the main tank valves to the manifold valves, at the back of the truck. Every time we opened the valves, some of the joints would leak badly.

Jack looked under it and said, "You don't want this truck Ray. There's another one for sale at the pipeline terminal in Port Hope. Have Bruce take this one to your yard, and we will go and get it, if you are happy with it. Someone will take this off your hands soon."

I instructed Bruce on what to do that day, and we left for Port Hope. There was a 1962 GMC with a 1600 gallon tank and all the pumping and metering equipment. I purchased it for $3,500.00.

For some reason I couldn't get a load of fuel there so Jack took me and my truck back to Peterborough, where I loaded 1600 gallon of gasoline at the agent's pump station. Jack went to his home and I returned to Minden. I dropped 600 gallon at Prentice's and 1000 gallon at Hewitt's Transport that night

Laurie-Lee and Scott in front of the van, and beside the Fina Truck the day I brought it home.

By the fall of 1966, I had a 1964 Dodge pickup truck, a 1958 Chev station wagon, a 1965 GMC van, a couple of trailers, and the oil truck. I owned the Laundromat, Ray Miller Heating, and the Fina agency. Bruce became my right hand. My other employees included Mervin Cowan, Jack Shaw, Ken Fielding, and Porky Walker, part time. Harry Martin was full time. I dispatched the truck, and laid work out for Bruce and his crew every morning, then went selling furnaces. By the end of August, I had sold 13 to be installed in September. My brother-in-law, Murray, was temporarily out of work from Kilcoo Camp, so I hired him. I gave him and Bruce a crew of workers and we installed all those furnaces by the middle of October.

Meanwhile the Laundromat was flourishing. I replaced the eight top loaders with new ones, and added two front load washers. I replaced the three dryers with larger capacity, but narrower models, allowing room for five. I began to draw plans to enlarge the building, adding an office on the north end for my businesses. I had plans to put apartments overhead, and a warehouse at the back for my furnace supplies. This would have to wait until the sewers were installed in Minden. Then the tile beds behind the building would not be in use, and the property would be available. The sewers were being talked about by council, as the tile beds behind homes were beginning to overload. People had all the water they needed, since the water system went in, and were using more water than the beds would take. So sewers would be coming soon.

The extra washers became too much for the tile bed, so I hired Max McKelvey to help me and I enlarged the bed by two hundred feet. The washers all worked, because I repaired them myself. The place was clean and cared for, so people came. There were camps and lodges washing throughout the night. This overloaded the sewage beds, so I buried a 2000 gallon tank for overflow, bought a pump, and an old seized-up Shell truck from Cameron Fuels at Coboconk. Eldon McCracken and I transported the tanker by float truck to Walker's Texaco, on the bypass, and had Lloyd fix it up and paint it. I started hauling wash water away by the truck load, and dumping it on Joe Rivers' fields.

Things were going well. I was selling furnaces as fast as we could install them, the oil business was picking up all the time, Jack McGuinty put $25.00 down on a piece of land across from where John Frances Fuels is now on Archer's Flats, with intent to purchase the fields for a Fina oil distribution plant there. It looked like I was on my way.

Then things began to go wrong. The tile bed from the Laundromat began to smell. Neighbours complained. The Government sent inspectors, and even though I argued that the sewers would be in soon, they demanded I build a lagoon behind the place. This would mean purchasing land and a big expense. I went to Gord McKay, the bank manager at CIBC. He couldn't see lending money to put into a lagoon, when the sewers would be installed very soon. It was a classic 'Catch 22' situation. I was forced to close my coin laundry. I sold the building to Eldon and Harold Deacon, who built the Quonset that is still there. The washers and dryers were sold to Rex Boice, for use in his coin laundry, where Halco Plaza is now located in Haliburton.

My receivables got out of hand. People owed me over $30,000, a lot of money then. This would be equal to $300,000 in 2004 dollars. This put my payables in grave jeopardy. The cash income from the coin laundry had always carried me through the tough times, but it was gone.

Then Fina decided they wouldn't pay the transportation charges to haul oil from Orillia to Minden. They said my gallonage wasn't large enough to warrant putting a pump station here. I wouldn't be making enough money on a load of product, to be able to continue without haulage pay. I told Jack I was going to quit.

"But you can't. You signed a contract for five years."

"Mister, you already broke the contract, when you stopped paying haulage. I can't make any money this way. If you won't let me out I will just stop working. I won't deliver product."

I sold the truck to Glen Austin and Company in Haliburton, spent a while gathering 200 gallon Fina fuel tanks from customers, and shut the whole thing down. I struggled along until I had all my suppliers satisfied. I turned my accounts receivable over to a collection agency, but that did little good. There are still people that will cross the street today, so they don't have to face me. Some may think that I went broke in business and left town owing a lot of people. They were wrong. A lot of people owed me a lot of money.

I drove school bus for Mark Schell. The route that started each morning at Moore's Falls, went into Minden, up to McKayville, and back to the Dominion Hotel. Then express run to the high school in Haliburton. Albert LaRue had a run at the same time, which went through Maple Lake and Carnarvon, then down to Minden where he picked up students in front of the IGA. Then he had some pick-ups from Coneybeare's garage, where Pinestone is now. It was best if I got out of town first, so I wouldn't be held up behind him through those stops. If he got out of town ahead of me, he would hold up until I caught up. Then, at Coneybeare's flat I would pass him, if at all possible. Albert would slow to let this happen if necessary. Someone called the school and said we were racing with the school buses. Doug Hodgins was principal. He called us into his office one morning.

"I have been informed that you guys are racing with your buses," Doug said. He raved on for a while about safety of our children etc. Albert listened intently, then he could hold it no longer. "You poor, stupid man," he said. "Those damned school buses are all governed at 55 miles an hour. We couldn't race them if we tried. We are manoeuvring our buses to save everyone as much trouble on the road as possible, including traffic around us. You concentrate on teaching them; we'll bring them to you."

Algar Coach Lines approached me, to drive the regular line run from Haliburton to Lindsay every day. I remembered watching Albert Cox drive that run shortly after the war, and thought it was a prestigious job then, so I took the work. I was driving the same old 1947 clipper that he had. This thing was twenty years old. It had a four speed stick shift, sitting behind a straight eight Buick engine. No guts, no glory. The shutters on this bus would stick open on a cold night, and freeze everybody, or stick closed, and overheat the engine. I had to get out regularly and go to the back and hit the cylinder that operated the shutters with a hammer. I did the Haliburton run for a while, then they wanted me in Lindsay. I boarded with Ferne's cousin Marlene and Don Currie until I found a residence at 31 Pottinger Street. We moved there on March 15th ,1969. I drove school bus and washed buses, with some charter work. The money wasn't enough, so I got work at Uniroyal Canada, in the tire cord factory. The sound in that place seemed equivalent to at least forty jet planes taking off, so everyone had to wear ear plugs and muffs over them. We stood side by side at a machine and couldn't be heard if we wanted to talk to anyone. It was like milking cows for eight hours a day. This was driving me nuts.

*__Mervin Barry__ still drives his own bus. I was talking to Mervin in Haliburton in the spring of 2004. He had his bus there and I said, "Do you remember when we all went to Lindsay that time to get our license?"

"Yes I do." he said, "We could drive a bus with a chauffeur's license before that, but everyone had to get a special school bus endorsement before a certain date."

"You have been driving every since, eh Merv?"

"Over forty years now Ray, and according to the instructors and younger drivers at these seminars, I know nothing."

"You've never had an accident either have you Merv?"

"Never once, but that doesn't matter to them. Every time I open my mouth at these meetings, they just shoot me down and try to make a monkey out of me. So I sit in a corner and keep quiet."

That kind of experience should be respected.

Endicott Fuels

Lloyd Endicott rescued me from a boring job at Uniroyal in Lindsay, in the spring of 1970, by moving me to Peterborough to work for him.

I was on a 'no heat' call one night in January. It had been a relatively quiet night so far with no calls. I was getting ready to go to bed, when the phone rang. It was Lloyd telling me that the people at Trapper's Inn had no heat.

I went outside and started the truck. It was quite warm, and the air felt damp. There was the feeling of snow in the air. I went back into the house and put on my boots, hat and coat.

Snow began to fall as I went through Buckhorn, and was really coming down when I turned north at Flynn's Corners. The road from there had been plowed as well as possible, with the road as hilly and crooked as it was. There were a few places where improvements had been made, but those stretches were nowhere near finished, and were not accessible. The snowplow only went as far as Trapper's Inn, as the road was barely passable beyond there.

My little truck had good snow tires on it, and there was a fair amount of weight in the back with all the motors and parts on board. It wasn't long however, before the axles were dragging in places. The road was narrow and there were some God-awful hills and turns.

I arrived at the call, and found the problem to be a burner motor. I had one in the truck.

Every time I returned to the truck, I noticed the snow was getting deeper. There was no wind. The snow fluttered to the ground and stuck to the trees. It was as pretty as a Christmas card in the woods.

The snow was up to my knees, when I completed the call, at about one in the morning. I anticipated trouble on my way home, so I put on the snowmobile suit I always carried with me in winter. I got into the truck and had to rock it gently, before it would move. This vehicle was standard shift, so that wasn't hard to do.

The front bumper pushed snow as I drove out the lane to the road. I turned onto the road and shifted from first to second and pushed on slowly. I got into the rut I had made on the way in and tried to stay there. There was a lot of new snow in those ruts but it wasn't as deep as it was on the shoulders. Steering was a problem. If I wandered very far from the ruts I would catch the snow bank and would be pulled into the ditch.

I was using the skills that I had gained from years of driving in Haliburton County. I was really getting along fine, running the hills, and letting the throttle back as the wheels began to spin. The storm was letting up and I had covered a few miles. I was beginning to think I was going to be okay.

Then the trouble began. I could see a hill ahead, so I gained as much speed as possible, as I went down one hill and headed toward the next. There was a corner half way up; I was going too fast to turn, and my front wheels cut out of the rut and headed for the bank. I eased up on the throttle, and steered out of it, but I had lost too much speed. I had to back down to the valley. There wasn't enough traction to either go ahead or back.

I got out of the truck and looked things over. There really wasn't any value in trying to do anything under those conditions. I would only get myself in worse shape; maybe even get into the ditch. I got back in, and rolled both windows down most of the way. I knew that the cab would be cold, but I would have heat from the heater on my feet and legs, and the fumes would escape through the window. It wasn't really cold anyway. I looked at my watch. It was two fifteen a.m.

When I turned the headlights off, I could see that the moon was peeking through the clouds. It was starting to clear, and turn colder.

There was no two-way radio and no radio in the vehicle, so all I could do was sit there and keep warm. In an hour or so the wind began to blow. It was getting quite cold. I rolled the windows up a little, keeping in mind that I could die from fumes, if I closed them too much.

I got out and looked to see if I could shovel a little snow from the rear wheels and maybe start to move. I knew the tires would grip better as the night got colder. I got a shovel from the back door and was beginning to use it, when a wolf howled right beside me. It sounded very close, so I jabbed the shovel into the snow bank, and quickly got into the truck. I turned the headlights on, just as a deer ran out onto the road and up the hill. In a minute, a lone wolf followed its track. There was no pack, so I figured it was an old leader, kicked out of the pack by a younger one, and was stalking prey to survive.

I didn't venture very far from the security of my vehicle until daylight. It was very cold then. There was a lot of frost in the snow. I shovelled the snow from all my wheels and made a path ahead. I went up the hill and shovelled the rut, so it would catch my wheels as I turned. I got some sand from the truck and spread it in front of the rear wheels, and carried some up to the corner.

I drove ahead, and then backed past where I had spent the night. Then I went ahead a little farther, reversed again breaking trail and packing down a track. Then I went ahead, slipped into second gear and headed for that hill. To my surprise, the wheels stuck to the frozen snow like glue, and I cleared that hill with speed left over.

I had no more trouble getting to the highway. Someone had come out of a driveway just before Flynn's Corners and broke trail from there. Scarcely any snow had fallen south of Buckhorn.

I rolled into Endicott's yard at eight-thirty. There was snow half way up the grill and packed all under the truck. I went inside and was preparing to turn in the papers for my call, when Lloyd came out of his office. He looked at the clock and said, "We start at eight in the morning here Ray."

"That would be nice," I said. "I started at ten last night."

"What do you mean," he asked.

"I have spent the night between two hills on the road from Flynn's to Trapper's Inn."

"But there's no snow," he looked out the window.

"Eighteen inches fell north of Buckhorn."

"You're kidding. Well, you had better go and have some breakfast."

I was paid $2.00 for that call.

I was completing a service call a week later, in a crawl space under Reg Connelly's house. I was crawling on my hands and knees, with the burned out motor in my hand. As I reached the opening and began to rise up unto my feet, I twisted my leg and tore the cartilage in my knee. I was laid up until the following June. *In comparison, with the present advances in medicine, I would be off work with the same injury now, for a maximum of three days.*

While I was off work, the owner of the house we were living in, on Montgomery Street, became impossible to be near. He lived in the basement and was always drunk. There was a woman living with him and he would abuse her. We were kept awake at nights with her squeals. I tried to reason with him, but it was no use.

We made friends with Simon and Brenda Kloostra across the street

We purchased the house at 94 Greenhill Drive. I was planning to move on the first day of the month, but I overheard the owner tell someone that, on the last day of the month, he would charge us another month's rent if we weren't gone in the morning. I hobbled out of the house with my leg in a cast and went to get Endicott's pickup to start moving. I figured that Ferne and the kids could help me as much as they could, and we would work all night if we had to. Our car had automatic transmission so I had no trouble with it, but the pickup was standard, so I drove it along the curb, all the way home in first gear, and had to pull over and rest my leg, after clutching through each stop. It took a while for me to get back. When I turned the corner, there was a full size rented truck backed up to our front door. I drove up, and as I went through the door, a large man who I had never seen before walked out and unto the truck with my chesterfield chair on his shoulder.

"Hi," he said with a grin, "I'm Bill Uttley."

Ferne had told Brenda we had to move that night. Brenda called Simon at work. He rented a truck and brought it home. He called his friend and Bill came immediately. Ferne's cousin, and my lifelong friend, Grenville Harrison, and his wife Doreen, were there within minutes. We were gone by eight o'clock.

I worked for Lloyd a while, after my recovery, then went to Faulkner Fuels for a while.

Once again, the lure of the road overcame me, and I purchased a new 1973 Ford Louisville Tandem, from John Balldock at Holiday Ford. This was a nice truck to drive, and it was so good to have one of my own, but it had two faults. It had a 475 V8 motor with the two transmissions, but it had no power. Ivan Sweeting, who owned a 366 Chev, just loved to come up behind me and pass with a big smile.

It was also much too heavy. It tared in at 19000 lbs with full tanks, a full 3000 lbs heavier than the 366 Chevs. When paid by the ton, this meant the lighter trucks were being paid for an extra ton and a half each trip. When making ten or more trips a day, this meant a lot less money in my wallet at the end of the week.

The neighbour next door on Greenhill Drive, screamed blue murder when I would start my truck, at six in the morning, to go to work. So we bought a house at R R 2 Cavan and moved out there.

Gravel trucking slowed greatly in 1975, so I sold the truck and went back to burner service work.

Krescendos Drum Corps

Scott Ray Miller

The Krescendos Drum and Bugle Corps of Peterborough, Ontario, were formed in 1969. They were initially sponsored by the Kinsmen club of Peterborough, so their original colours were yellow and purple. They were later co-sponsored by the Peterborough Lions Club and always used the old Lions centre on George Street for their meeting rooms and winter practices.

They entered competitions throughout Ontario and the United States and became National Novice Champions in 1970 and then entered the Junior B class in 1971.

Laurie-Lee (pictured right) had been a member of a baton twirling group in Peterborough and then joined the Drum Corp in 1972-73.

Ferne, Scott and I boarded a chartered bus to the Canadian National Exhibition in Toronto, where the corps was in competition in front of the grandstand. It rained that afternoon and evening, then it became very cold in the evening, but weather never stopped drum corps competition and it didn't that day either.

Under the direction of Drum Major Valerie Bessey and Guard Captain Jane Bence, they marched to victory winning the Junior "B" National Championship with a score of 66.35*. Their closest competitor was The Flying Dutchmen from Kitchener, with 61.70. Other scores that day were The Cardinals of Precious Blood of Scarborough 53.75 and The Dutch Boy Cadets with 52.30.

Aboard the bus, on the way home that night, I asked Scott if he wanted to join the corps. "Not on your life, Dad, I would never walk around in the cold rain like that."

He joined within a year, and has marched with several corps during his young life, and it is still very much in his blood. He has many trophies.

KINSMEN KRESCENDOS DRUM CORPS
PETERBOROUGH, ONTARIO

The photo above only shows part of the corps that night. It was cropped so it could be used in a specific publication. You will notice that their feet are all in perfect stride. This is one of the reasons they won. Precision is a big part of what they are judged on.

Ferne and I became involved soon after.

Because of her excellent sewing skills, Ferne was appointed Wardrobe Manager, as well as chaperone, and I became equipment manager. With up to 120 members, between the age of 8 and 21, travelling every weekend during the summer months, there is a lot of management needed. I soon also wore the hat of Trip Master, and Transportation Manager and drove one of the buses as well.

We travelled in two or more Trentway Bus Lines school buses, a rented van for the executive, instructors, and first aid people and the equipment rode in a former Dempster Bread truck, which the members painted purple and christened 'The Purple Grape'. This truck would hold all the drums, horns, flags, rifles and the drum major's podium, but only if they were packed just so. That was my job. Uniforms usually hung in one of the buses.

I had the honour and privilege of driving the truck on most tours, with my dog Jenny (a very small pup at first) at my feet. The buses were driven by volunteer fathers with the proper licenses. If there were not enough licensed fathers available to drive buses, I would have someone drive the truck, and I would drive the one of the buses. Charlie Sweeting was a good and reliable driver. He and his wife Shirley were invaluable assets to the corps.

Under the capable direction of Corps Director Eric Hogg, with Bugle instructors Barry and Greg Hogg, Drum instructor Gerry Hemsley, drill instructors Bob Bond and rifle and flag instructor Diane Bond, the next four years took us to a lot of towns in Ontario, as well as tours into the United States. They marched in Christmas Parades, Fair Parades, and Grand Openings as well as doing very well in many competitions.

One year they marched in a Santa Claus parade in Barrie, when the temperature was -32 Fahrenheit. (I used a lot of alcohol in the horn valves that day).

That year, they were invited to the Festival of Lights in Fort Myers, Florida. There they were introduced as "The Krescendos Drum and Bugle Corps from Petersburg, Canada. These are a hardy group, ladies and gentlemen. A few weeks ago they marched in a parade where it was 32 below zero. They are here today and it is 94 degrees in the shade"

American announcers never once introduced them as being from any province, just plain old Canada.

During my years with the corps, many things happened.

We had several means of raising money for equipment, uniforms etc. We held walkathons in which Jenny, (a full fledged, duly initiated, corps mascot), participated fully. Wintario grants were applied for constantly, and we received at least one. The city of Peterborough gave us grants, and the service clubs did their share. Peterborough and district businesses also chipped in when needed.

The chaperones had to contend with many things on the road. The new, younger members would have to deal with being away from home. Some of the older ones had love affairs going on within the ranks, and would sometimes try things to be together, and, wherever we went, local boys would hit on the corps girls.

There was always medication to be administered, and cuts and bruises to doctor. Hyperventilation was common.

Once in Columbus, Ohio, one of the young ladies was hit by a car, and in Butler, Pennsylvania, a girl was stung by a bee. She was allergic and carried a kit, but hadn't had it renewed and the needle wouldn't penetrate. Gary Gauthier, who worked for the Ministry of Health, operating a mobile health unit, tried every needle in the kit then said, "We have to get her to a hospital, NOW!" The van was not available at the time, so we headed across town in a school bus. We weren't at all sure where the hospital was, but we knew it was downtown somewhere. I was driving, and I thought it would be to the left, off the four lane street we were on, so I pulled into the middle lane. Gary was studying a map behind me and trying to tend to the girl who was swelling dangerously. Up ahead, I could see a police cruiser coming toward me in the centre lane. I slowed, turned on my four way signals, and started to flash my headlights. As he got close I pulled tight to the centre line and began to wave my arm out the window. He stopped.

Eyeing my bus, he said "Can I help you in any way?"

"We have a girl here that has been stung by a bee and is allergic!"

His blue flashing lights came on even as I spoke. "Follow me," he said, as he began a three point turn in the street.

He led us to the hospital and right up to the emergency entrance. He rushed inside and came back with a stretcher and emergency personnel. He boarded the bus behind the doctor and nurses, and looked at her. She was very swollen and losing consciousness.

"I hope we made it on time," he said. "I need to go now, I was on my way to a call." He returned to his cruiser, turned off the blues and, with a toot of his horn and a wave, he was gone. The van arrived almost immediately with the director, the treasurer, and an instructor on board. I got in my bus and returned to the rest of the corps. They placed the needle from her kit under a microscope at the hospital and it was revealed that the points of all the needles had bent over at the hole, when we tried to make them penetrate. Apparently this is why there is an expiry date on the kit. Late that evening, as we were getting the corps settled in at Slippery Rock College, the director and treasurer and Gary came and told us that the girl was going to be okay. She would be released the next day, with a new kit and a stern warning to keep it up to date.

Parents would give members meal money, but some would spend it all the first day, then practically starve the rest of the trip. Chaperones got to know these people, and would have parents give them the money, so they could meter it out properly.

While performing in Butler the members stayed in the dorms at Slippery Rock College each year, while the drivers and executive rented a suite in a motel in Pittsburgh. But most of the time, everyone would sleep on the floor of gyms and arenas where washrooms were available. McDonalds was the restaurant of choice for meals.

Like all team competition, drum corps gets in your blood and is hard to shake. I sometimes think of the thrill when I would hear the announcer say,

"Are the judges ready," which would be answered by a salute from the judges on the field.

"Is the corps ready," followed by a salute from the drum major.

"Peterborough Krescendos you may enter the field in competition."

The Drum Major would turn to the corps and set the pace. Then turn and lead the corps onto the field. You could hear a pin drop in the crowded bleachers, as the field filled with precise color and music behind a Major who marched forward until the podium was reached, and without missing a step, climb the stairs and turn to salute the members. The horns would be lined across the entire field with the drums in the middle. The corps would then break and create one formation after another, until all the music had been played. The major would lead the corps past the grandstand, with the guard saluting to an appreciative audience.

The music for 1974 was "Camelot", off the line, then into "Puppet." The concert portion was marched to, "My Man Don't Rain on My Parade." Colours were presented to "Valiant Years," and they left the field to, "Music from Across the Way."

All the corps were brought back onto the field for the announcement of scores, with each guard saluting as their score was read out. Then each group would leave the field, crossing in front of the grandstand, with the lowest score first and the highest last.

For a year or more after we left the corps, we still followed it, whenever we could. There is a commercial on TV now, that features a corps and I still come from another room, each time I hear the music. I am very glad that I had the chance to be a part of a corps.

The corps fizzled out in the 80s. It began to fail when Eric Hogg resigned as Director. Eric had placed a great emphasis on discipline, which is a significant aspect of an organisation such as this. Directors who tried to take his place, put fun ahead of everything. Discipline breeds pride, and without the pride the corps soon failed.

The only corps that I know of that is still in existence today is The Kawartha Kavaliers of Lindsay, and every time I see them march in a parade or do an exhibition drill, I imagine I still can hear Eric yell, "Trim your lines guys, for God sake trim your lines and get in step or go home."

All drum corps in competition, are judged on the field by several judges. The members were instructed not to break their line or stride if a judge got in the way. "Just bowl him over and go on." I have seen the colour guard whack a judge royally, with the staff of their flag, or the stalk of a rifle. They never lose points for that, but would if they fell out of step.

I watched a corps from Anaheim, California put on an exhibition at a function in the United States. Even though this was for exhibition only, the judges announced that they would judge the performance.

The field lights were turned off for the start. All we could see in the semi darkness from the stands, were the white shoes and gauntlets.

A whistle blew and the corps began to mark time. All those white shoes moved with such precision, you would think they were all nailed to a plank. Then the gauntlets moved with the same precision. The lights came on, and they moved onto the field. I am sure everyone in the grandstand felt the same rush I did, as the whole field moved in perfect unison.

They moved as smoothly as a field of grain, swaying in the wind. They were so close together at one point, you would think they would trip each other, and then in seconds, they would fill the whole field, with lines as straight as an arrow flies.

Flags snapped from position to position so fast there was no visible image in between. They were down, then they were up. We couldn't see the motion, just the result.

Rifles flew high from one position and were caught several feet away, as the thrower marched under them.

Many horns played with such perfection, it sounded as though there was only one. Then with the direction of the Major, the sound would split, with far right and far left in stereo.

At first, the judges seemed to be in some kind of trance. They weren't moving, they weren't writing. I thought maybe they were just overwhelmed, but then I realized, things were happening so fast they couldn't get into position fast enough to check lines. But really, they had nothing to judge.

At the end of the evening, when the scores were read the announcer read them all, then said, "And by the way ladies and gentlemen, the Anaheim corps score 99.99. One judge had seen one thing that wasn't quite right."

Scott became a horn instructor for a little corps; formed in later years, called the Canadian Knights. He drove one of their buses for a while, and that experience was instrumental in getting him work with Trentway-Wagar Coach Lines, which became Coach Canada, where he has worked for over twenty years. During that time he fell in love with Kauru Sato, a Japanese interpreter who worked his bus sometimes, when he would be transporting oriental tourists. They were married in

2001 and in 2003 they made me Grandfather of a sweet little granddaughter, Sakura. They live in Kingston, Ontario. If he had never joined the corps, his life may have taken a different direction entirely.

Scott, Kaoru, and Sakura, taken Christmas 2003.

Drum Corps Scores; *All corps enter the field with a score of 100. There are several judges on the field. Every time they see an infraction, it costs the group a tenth of a point. The judging is always strict..*

Strano Foods

It was summer 1975, when I left Faulkner Fuels because of a misunderstanding at home. I had a mortgage to pay and a family to feed. Now I was without work, with absolutely no income, and no savings whatsoever. I went pounding on doors, seriously seeking work.

I found a job at Strano Foods and was so happy that I went home and hugged my dog Jenny.

That elation soon ebbed, when I found out what I was expected to accomplish each shift. This job proved to be the worst I have ever had. The pay was so lousy, I could barely get by on it, but it was income, so I stayed.

The work was horrendous. They would pack a truck from front to back, and right to the very roof with frozen food and produce.

There would be thirty to forty stops a day. Some consisting of a ton of flour, or a ton of rice. Others were as small as a ten pound box of hamburger patties. Rice and some other items came in one hundred pound bags. It didn't matter how difficult the delivery was, it was done on the dead run, in order to get back to the warehouse by nine or ten each night. I often ran up and down stairs with hundred pound sacks on my shoulder until I was totally winded.

My first delivery would be approximately six a.m., and usually two and a half hour's drive from the warehouse. This meant leaving my bed at three or three-thirty every morning, to be at work by three-thirty or four. I would check my truck, to be sure there was a hand cart, gasp when I saw the size of the load, unplug the reefer*, coil reefer cable and store it behind seat, circle check the truck, get invoices from office, and turn sick to my stomach when I saw the number and location of stops.

Lunch was eaten from my lunchbox, on the seat beside me, as I drove, and dinner was a plate heated in the microwave when I got home. To take any time for lunch or dinner, would make me that much later getting home.

To emphasize what a day's work really amounted to, I will provide an example: Suppose there was a truck parked in your driveway one morning, with a sixteen foot long, by eight foot wide, and six foot high body, filled to capacity with one hundred pound bags of rice, fifty pound bags of flour, seventy five pound bags of potatoes, ten pound bags of potatoes, cases of various vegetables, and small packages of frozen food. There are cases of frozen potato chips, rows of four gallon cases of pickles, ketchup, and mustard.

With the aid of only a two wheeled hand cart, you have to unload every bit of it alone, put the frozen food in a freezer, and the rest in the kitchen, or basement, before you can stop for the day.

I did that everyday, in addition to driving for four to five hours, manoeuvring the truck through city traffic, in and out of thirty to forty driveways. I walked the length of the truck fifty, to sixty times each day, to open and close the tailgate, to avoiding letting the cold air escape from the box. It is against the law to drive from delivery to delivery with the tailgate open.

Getting invoices signed can take as long as some deliveries. The person who signs for the order, may check every piece for accuracy and condition. Some deliveries were C.O.D., taking even more time. The money had to be collected. If I was short at the end of the day, the shortage was made up out of my own pocket.

This was not a one shot, extra hard day. It was everyday from Tuesday to Friday. Monday was different. I had time for breakfast.

Before I left for home on Friday night I would be issued pick-up slips for Monday.

178

I always hoped there was only one, at Rich's, in Fort Erie. Dock time there was usually seven-thirty a.m. If I was late, Strano Foods would be charged a fee because the load would have to be put back into the freezer, and retrieved again later. I would be required to wait, until another truck missed later in the day. Then I would load in that slot. If no one missed, I would have to return with an empty, and I would be seriously reprimanded.

For that run I would get up at three a.m. Go to work. Check my truck for pallets. Pallets were to be loaded by the dock crew on Friday night, but occasionally they weren't. Shippers will not give you pallets, if you don't have good ones to exchange. That necessitates piling the whole load of the pallets by hand. If no pallets had been loaded, or there were some poor ones among them, I had to unlock the warehouse, find a fork lift, and load them myself. They were only missing once, but I checked every time.

Then I circle checked the truck, and drive to Noone's Restaurant on Highway 35 and 115 just north of the 401 for a quick breakfast of bacon and eggs, toast and coffee. After, I drove hard to Rich's.

I was always backed up to the dock at seven-thirty. My pallets were counted, inspected, and set aside. My load would consist of individual coffee creamers, and some quiches.

I was always loaded by eight o'clock, then went to McDonald's for an Egg McMuffin.

Ever present in a trucker's world are the weigh stations, and, of course, the 'blue hairs' who insist on driving in my lane.

Why ever would I wish for this assignment when it carried such risks? Because, if all went well, I would be back to the warehouse by noon. Pick up drivers were allowed to go home when they returned.

If I didn't have the Fort Erie pick up I would have several in Toronto and Hamilton. Bick's Pickles, Burlington Meats, Lake Simcoe Ice, Sunny Orange, Monarch Foods, Federal Cold Storage, and Cliffside Bakeries come to mind. The first pick up was alright, as long as I got there early enough to be the first in line, which meant getting up damn early and sleeping when I got there. I usually had to wait in line for several hours, at each of the rest. This meant getting back to Peterborough late in the evening. Missed pick ups just didn't happen. I always got them all, or had a hell of a good reason why not; otherwise a lecture would have been in order, when I returned.

I recall once, when my first pick up was two pallets of margarine, at Monarch Foods.

However, the shipper began to load my whole truck full.

"No...No," I protested, "This is wrong! I only get two skids."

"You are to call your office, there has been a change of some nature," he said as he raced back into the building with his forklift.

I called the office and one of our buyers answered. "You are to take all you can get on, and head for Trenton Air force Base, as fast as you can. They are holding a Hercules aircraft there for your arrival. Apparently they are moving forces for exercises in the Northwest Territories, and that margarine is best for the colder climate."

"What about the rest of my original pick ups?" I asked.

"Earl Penny is on his way to take over your day's work, ignore all your first pick ups, but when you finish at the air force base, I want you to go back to Federal Cold storage and get a full load of frozen halibut."

By the time I returned to the loading dock, they had loaded my truck, and closed the tailgate. I signed the bills and pulled out onto the 401.

I had delivered to the base many times before, so I knew the drill there. No one gets beyond the gate without a security pass, a card that clips onto your pocket.

They were anxious to load the plane, so security came from the office, as I approached, and brought a pass to me. I signed the document. He told me to wait until a plane landed, before I could proceed onto the tarmac. A fighter jet roared across in front of me. Then he said, "Okay, get across in the next 90 seconds, then turn left, you will see the Hercules sitting in the field." Another jet screamed past behind me, as I cleared the runway.

As I rounded a hanger I could see the plane. It was facing away from me with engines idling, and its huge ramp lowered. When I got closer, I could see jeeps, and all kind of skids of cases inside. A fork lift emerged from a building, and the driver motioned me toward the aircraft. My entire load went into the plane. The ramp closed, and the crew raced the engines. The wash from the propellers nearly blew me away, as it turned, and started slowly toward the runway.

When it turned so I could see the flight crew through the windows, I looked up. The crew members appeared to be no older than eighteen. The giant aircraft stopped at the end of the runway, and sat there roaring.

A fellow walked up to my open window.

"As soon as they take off past here, you get across, very quickly, or you may get run over by a Hercules coming in. There is one due within minutes."

They took off to the east, and I crossed the tarmac right away. I could see my load circle over Lake Ontario, then head to the north over Port Hope.

I pulled up to the office and went in. I reached up to remove my pass from my pocket, but it wasn't there. "I hope you don't shoot people who lose their passes," I said jokingly.

"As a matter of fact, that is exactly what we do," he said, very firmly, "You will not leave here, until I have it in my hand." I had no doubt he meant what he had said.

He accompanied me to my truck. I searched the cab, then went to the back, and raised the tailgate. I was very relieved to find it just inside.

I returned to Federal Cold Storage, in Toronto, where they loaded the whole truck with halibut as large as kitchen tables. These fish swim on their side and are black on one side and white on the other. They can weigh over a hundred pound dressed. They were loose, frozen solid, and very slippery. When I opened the tailgate in Peterborough they spilled out, down hallways, into storage stalls and all over the place. Strano had people who worked in a large freezer, cutting these fish into portions with a band saw, and boxing them up for delivery. These workers wore snowmobile suits, all year round.

I mentioned a reefer somewhere in this chapter, but I really shouldn't have. Good ones were available by then, but the people who decided to use this type, didn't have much regard for the purpose. The reefer was driven from the power take off, and were designed for long haul use, not delivery. They didn't have their own motor to drive them constantly. Instead the compressor was mounted on the side of the frame, under the truck, and driven by belts from the power take off of the transmission. With the transmission turning at full speed on the highway, the compressor was operating at a good rate and thing worked fine. On delivery runs, where they were used the most, the truck was shut off a lot, while making deliveries, and they failed dismally.

I quit Strano, and went to work for Wayne Lucas for a while, doing burner repair work. Ferne and I purchased a motel, which is described in a following chapter, and I drove school bus for Trentway Bus Lines. But the urge to drive truck took over, and I returned to Strano Foods when they called in early 1981, to inform me that they were purchasing a new tractor trailer. Knowing I had experience with a semi before, they wanted me to drive it. I thought it would be used for warehouse-to- warehouse work, but I was sorely wrong. It was used for delivery, and I was right back into the hard work again.

The trailer was a 27 footer, which had been cut down from 45 feet. The reefer was sized for the 45 foot capacity. With only two thirds the area to cool, it was an exceptional combination. I once picked up a load of pitted cherries, in pails, at a place in Grimsby. They were hot from the orchard. In fact, I had to wait for a load to come in from the pickers. I had 'chilled the box' on the way down, and set the reefer to max. By the time I arrived at Peterborough, they were nearly frozen solid. They were to be blast frozen in our freezers, but I had already done most of the job on the way.

I drove this semi on deliveries, with my week consisting of pick ups on Mondays, then two day loads, to the Kingston and Smith Falls area, the rest of the week. My delivery loads would have over sixty stops, spread over two days. Tuesday would be deliveries to Kingston and Gananoque, then on to Brockville, where I would stay at the 401 Motel. I would arrive there at supper time, go up to my room and wash up, then to the dining room, where the waitress would bring two bottles of Red Cap ale. She knew I would want them. Having run upstairs and down all day with deliveries, I would guzzle the first right down, and boy did that taste wonderful. Then I would enjoy the other as I waited for my meal.

There were deliveries that had to be made that night in Brockville, because some establishments wouldn't be open until noon the next day, so I would eat dinner, then go back out and deliver until done, finishing around ten. I actually slept in the next morning until five o'clock as I couldn't start deliveries until six a.m. I had breakfast in the motel dining room, and then off to the stops in Spencerville. I called the office from there, and often would pick up at Trenton Cold storage on the way back, arriving home at ten, or so, in the evening.

Thursday's deliveries would start in Belleville, then on to Kingston, and up at Smith's Falls, where I would stay at the Mariners Inn. There were stops that had to be made that night also. The Psychiatric Hospital wouldn't accept deliveries after four-thirty in the afternoon. This caused a lot of tension, until I got there. Theirs was a large order, and if I wasn't on time, I would have to move that entire delivery to the side, in order to access the late deliveries that night. I would go to the hotel, and eat, then do the late stops, and get to bed around ten.

I would sleep in the next morning until five, have breakfast and finish Smith Falls, then go to the prison in Kemptville. I would call the office from there and most of the time I would have pick ups at cheese factories, on my way home, along highway seven, arriving in Peterborough around nine or ten.

I was receiving $255.00 a week for this. I asked for $300.00 and a helper. My request was refused so I turned in my resignation in June 1981.

Strano later sold to Sysco Foods.

There is a window above my desk that faces Haliburton Lake Road. I often see a Sysco semi, much the same as the one I drove, go past, on its way to Eagle Lake.

My back aches.

Unplug reefer. *The reefers on these trucks were plugged into hydro, after they were loaded at night in order to keep the load cooled. The cord, from the truck to the building, had to be unplugged from both the truck and the building and stored behind the seat.*

Melody Motel

That's me, standing at the office door. Circa 1980

Ferne was reading the Peterborough Examiner one weekend, in early 1979, when she came across an ad about a motel for sale. She read it out. We talked a little, and then she made a call. It was the little motel at the corner of Highway 28, and the Stony Lake Road. The gentleman on the phone said, "Its name is Melody, isn't that pretty?"

We went up that afternoon and talked to the people. It was somewhat grown in, with tall cedars around the door, some of the lights were in need of repair, and there were spiders everywhere. The two florescent signs were broken, and there were acres of uncut grass. There was also a large field full of stumps, and brush. It would need work, but the price was reasonable, so we made an offer. Money is hard to raise for a motel, gas filling station, or a restaurant. Banks are leery because these establishments depend entirely on day to day business. Poor management can turn customers away overnight. A business can show very substantial cash flow under the present manager, and be bankrupt in days with a new owner. We had some equity in our home on Western Avenue, but would have to sell it fast to realize it. We finally found a private financer, the bank gave us some, by placing the house in escrow, and we were soon the proud owners of an eight room motel, with seven rentable units and one we used for our residence.

I was working for Wayne Lucas Burner service, which gave me every evening off, so I went to work, clearing brush away from the building. This helped the spider problem right away. I also began to cut more and more grass, pushing it back from the building.

Our friends, Simon and Brenda Kloostra, and Grenville and Doreen Harrison, came the first weekend and willingly helped me clear away the stumps in the field. They worked hard and, by Monday, the field was looking a lot better. I had visions of building overnight cabins all along the lengthy driveway.

Scott, and some of his drum corps buddies, painted the upper part of the building white and Ferne painted the bottom.

I did extensive work levelling the driveway, and kept cutting more grass, until the three acres surrounding the motel, looked like lawn.

182

We installed a tall TV tower, with an aerial that, to quote the installer, "Will pull the birds right out of the sky." This also involved an elaborate cable system that was somewhat expensive.

Some of the TVs were not working very well, so we found some that were black and white and user friendly.

During the first year we changed some rugs, and replaced most of the shower cabinets. The place was looking pretty damned good.

Clientele began to change. We had a bit of a problem at first as the place had attracted a lower priced traveller. We had upgraded so the price now was higher.

Lakefield College, the private school that Prince Andrew attended for a time, was nearby, and this meant we were booked solid every time there was a parent's weekend.

We had 'no vacancy' throughout every summer, with the regular 'off road' traffic, as well as the noon hour 'quickies'. I have often wondered how many secretaries earned their promotion in our unit number four.

On of the funniest times I recall occurred when a fellow that I trucked with, showed up at our desk, all elated, with a girl on his arm who wasn't his wife. He was not from the immediate area, and hadn't heard that we had bought the place. His elation changed quickly when he recognized me behind the desk. I said, "Never mind xxxx, I am like Kommandant Klink of Hogan's Heroes, 'I see nutting'."

About once a month, a very expensive car would drive up and park in front of number three. A beautiful, middle aged woman would step out, wearing clothing and jewellery that was obviously very expensive. She would come to the desk and pay for a night, then return and stand inside the screen door, looking at her watch with frustration, until a beat up, rusted-out car would drive in. A greasy, dirty, young man would get out, she would open the door and he would rush in. They would be there for a an hour or more, and then he would emerge with clean face and hands, and leave. In a few minutes she would calmly return the key, and tell us we could rent the room again.

There were the spouses that would rent a room to get away from a drunken partner at home, and others, who had left their spouses permanently, who would use our establishment until they could find shelter elsewhere. Sometimes, the police would bring someone in the middle of the night and book them in until they cooled off, after domestic a dispute.

Needless to say, there were fights in our parking lot, and fights in our rooms. Some people would settle in with a giant ghetto blaster and turn it up to the max. They seem to think they have a right to do as they please, with no regard for the right of others to get a night's sleep. The O.P.P. was co-operative, but I was told more than once by them, that they were not 'glorified bouncers'.

Our dog, Jenny, would lay behind the counter and not make a sound when people checked in, except on four occasions. Each of those times, she went absolutely berserk, and wouldn't be shut up until they left the office. Every one of those four was wanted by police.

One was a burglar, who broke into cottages in the area. He was apprehended in Oshawa. He checked into our motel and would stay a week or more. I asked him one time what he was doing in the area. He said he was a window man. I guess he was truthful, he was breaking in through windows.

Two guys rented a room for the weekend and said they were fishing. Others joined them from time to time. I thought they were fishing buddies. As I was preparing for bed on Sunday night, at midnight, I heard someone run past the rear of the residence. Around three a.m. I was awakened by cars in the parking lot. I got up and saw men loading things from the room into a station wagon and a car, as well as the car that belonged to them. These were not items from the room. I called the police. One officer arrived around four. When he saw the register, he gasped. "How many are down there in the room?" he asked.

"I saw four, maybe more, as they were going in and out of the room."

He grabbed his radio and began talking into it using codes. He asked me to describe them. I did my best, but when I came to one description he just turned to the radio and said, "I need back up here."

He told me that they were not dangerous, but they were wanted for break and enter and could be rough, if they were cornered. He said that other officers were finishing a drug related arrest and would be a while. Ferne got us a coffee, while he had me draw a floor plan of the room. He asked if there were any way they could escape from the room, other than the door. I told him there wasn't. He wanted to know who was in the adjoining rooms. We looked at the register and he was satisfied.

He talked on the radio some more then said, "Okay... the others are lined up just down the road. They will come from both directions, and things will happen fast. There is not a lot of danger as they are robbers, except for one who we don't recognize. It would be just as well if you stay away from the windows, until I come back in." He turned to the radio and said, "Now," and rushed out the door, as the parking lot filled with cruisers.

Police ran with drawn weapons and I heard the door cave in. Someone shouted, "Police...Don't anyone move, or you're dead."

They brought all the occupants out in handcuffs and put them into cruisers. Then they went to the cars. Every vehicle was full of articles stolen from cottages around the lakes. The restaurant that adjoined us, had been broken out of on Sunday night. One of the guys staying at our place, had hidden in the washroom, and broke out with his loot after the restaurant closed. That was who I heard run past the building.

We couldn't rent the room for a day or so, because it was a crime scene, and I had a door to replace.

Another fellow Jenny didn't like, was wanted for passing bad cheques. The police took him away the same night. They had been looking for him.

The fourth was wanted for domestic violence.

I did some furnace work for neighbours, worked for Wayne Lucas, drove school bus for Trentway Bus Lines, did some charter work for them also, and drove trailer for Strano Foods while we were there.

The work was hard for Ferne. The place was almost too big for her to care for alone, and hardly big enough to hire help. It was also very confining. There had to be someone around the place, for twenty-four hours a day, every day.

Stan Hamblin, who owned the restaurant by the same name, made us an offer one day, and we took it. We left in 1981.

I was employed by the City of Peterborough Transit in December 1981.

Stan operated the motel and the restaurant together, until a spill of gasoline at the restaurant put them both out of business. The soil there is very shallow over layers of shale limestone. Thousands of gallons of gasoline followed the cracks and crevasses of the rock, seeping into wells and basements. The buildings were all removed and acres of land now rendered useless, stands vacant and growing in with brush.

I drove there a couple of years ago and parked in the driveway for a while. Another piece of my past was gone forever.

Post Offices

I was working for Wayne Lucas Burner Service in Peterborough, when I was called into the office. Wayne told me he had acquired the contract to inspect furnaces for efficiency, in Post Offices, housed in government-owned buildings, across southern Ontario. He wanted me to do the work.

He had just purchased a new Ford pickup truck and fit it out with a hydro type body. Ladders were placed on top and the side compartments were fully equipped, with everything I would need, a new vacuum cleaner and up to date efficiency test equipment.

The government had wanted to make sure all their buildings were up to standard. At that time, there was a lot of encouragement in the media for everyone to conserve energy.

I read the contract over with Wayne and found that I was to do the following.

>Test and record efficiency on arrival.
>Check heat exchanger for proper cleaning and clean if necessary.
>Check smoke pipes and replace or clean if necessary.
>Check and adjust draft regulator and replace if necessary.
>Clean circulation blower (if applicable).
>Check blower belt and replace if necessary (if applicable).
>Check air filters and replace if necessary. (if applicable).
>Change the oil filter cartridge whether it is needed or not.
>Check firebox and heat exchanger for damage.
>Change nozzle.
>Clean burner fan.
>Adjust choke.
>Adjust draft regulator.
>Adjust flame to most efficient setting.
>Test and record efficiency when finished.
>If, after all means of improvement are exhausted, the burner cannot be brought above the given percentage I was to complete a specific form in triplicate, date and sign it and turn it in.

I was to do two inspections per day, if possible, in any sequence I preferred.

I was given sufficient petty cash, which would be replenished at the end of each week, upon receipt of proof of purchases.

When the day arrived for me to start, I was handed a stack of work orders. Each one showing the location of each Post Office, the name of the Post Master there, and a record of recent services performed. There was a space at the bottom, for me to date and sign each form.

I was given identification, and a letter of authority, at the bottom of which was a 1-800 number. I was instructed to verify I was talking to the Post Master, and then use it if I was refused entry.

All went very well. In the following weeks, I serviced Post Offices far and wide. This was a good job. I did two a day, and spent evenings at a hotel or motel. Sometimes I would take in a movie, or watch a movie in my room. I would spend time at a bar, or drive around the town, just exploring. Start time was eight a.m.

Life was good.

I was able to achieve efficiency above the required percentage at all places. Some were not right up to standard, and I ran into some inferior workmanship, but nothing that was too serious.

185

The most efficient service work was encountered around the Orillia area. I recall that the furnace at the Rama was absolutely excellent. All services had been done in a very efficient manner, and the initial test was the same as the final one. Where Rama Casino is now located was an open field, at that time.

Then I arrived in Minden.

I walked into the post office and up to the counter. A lady came to the wicket and asked if she could help me. I asked to speak to the Post Master.

I had known the Post Master here before I moved away in 1969, but having been away from the area for more than ten years, I had changed some. I had gained a little weight and my hair was being cut differently.

She called to him, and in a minute he came to the wicket. He looked at me as though he should know me, but didn't.

"Can I help you," he said.

"I have been commissioned by the post office department to inspect the heating system here," I replied.

He looked rather puzzled, then his expression turned to disgust, then almost anger. "Oh no......this furnace has been cleaned and serviced regularly and is fine."

"I appreciate that sir, but I am checking the furnaces in all of the Post Offices in this area. I have a work order to work on this one." I laid the form on the counter." And here is my letter of authority sir." I laid that before him.

"I don't care if you have a letter from the Queen. I am in charge of this office, the furnace has been serviced by a reputable firm, and you are not touching it."

"According to this form, the Post Master here is XXX. Is that you sir?"

"Yes, that's me."

"And you are refusing to let me work."

"That's right too."

I went around the corner to a pay phone and called the 1-800, number. After answering all the questions asked by the person on the other end, I was told to go have a coffee, then return to the Post Office, I would be allowed in.

As I approached the counter the second time, the girl turned and said, "He's here again."

He yelled from behind a screen, "Okay, go around to the back door, I'll meet you there. Don't block the back entrance, the mail truck is due any minute."

He met me, still mumbling something about how foolish this was, and how it was a total waste of money, as the local people were very efficient, and the best and all that.

I could tell the minute I entered the furnace room that things were going to be different here. There was a thick accumulation of dust on top of the oil filter, even though it was reported to have been changed just weeks before. The smoke pipe hadn't been disturbed in years, and the draft regulator was seized partially open.

The initial efficiency test was much less than the required standard..

I removed the access panels, and viewed the clean out ports. The bolts holding them in place were rusted and corroded and hadn't been removed in years. I soaked them with rust remover.

I removed the oil filter bowl and found the filter cartridge totally covered with slimy oil residue. I installed a new one.

I removed, and cleaned the smoke pipes, and cleaned the base of the chimney. I freed the draft regulator.

I checked the firebox, removed the drawer assembly from the burner, and found the wrong nozzle had been installed for this furnace. I cleaned an amount of dust from the burner fan, and cleaned the assembly and the blast tube. I inspected the nose cone, replaced the nozzle and returned the assembly to the burner.

I removed the clean out ports, with a degree of difficulty, as the bolts were still partially seized. Some of the passageways through the heat exchanger were plugged entirely, and others were partially clogged. I vacuumed the whole thing, and replaced the gaskets around the ports. I vacuumed the exchanger inside the smoke pipe opening and replaced the pipes.

I fired the thing up, adjusted the choke, adjusted the air over the flame to a number one smoke, and set the draft regulator at the required .02.5 inches of water column.

The final test was well over the required percentage.

I had planned to do both Minden and Kinmount that day, but with all the work I had to do here, it was too late to start another one. I looked at the order for Kinmount and saw written in the comments box, it had been condemned by local technicians, and scheduled for replacement in the near future, but I was to do the inspection and report my findings.

The next morning I went to Kinmount. As I entered the front door, my eyes watered almost immediately from furnace fumes. The door was propped open, and any windows that would open were ajar also. I walked up to the counter. A lady approached dabbing at her eyes with a tissue.

"I am from the post office department and I'm here to inspect the furnace," I told her.

"They are supposed to change it any day now," she replied blowing her nose.

"I know that, but they have told me to inspect it anyway."

"Fine. By all means. Just go around to the back door, I'll meet you there."

The back door was also propped open, and fumes were even stronger there.

I followed her to the furnace room. There were the same signs of inefficient service work as Minden. I looked into the fire inspection door and could see that the flame was dark red with smoke curling off the tips of the flame. I knew that a test was useless, with combustion as incomplete as that, so I just turned the furnace off and went to work.

I inspected the fire box and found it to be okay.

The oil filter hadn't been changed in a long while and changed it.

The furnace was very dirty. A lot of debris clogged the passageways, as well as a coat of thick black oily soot. When I had cleaned the exchanger, I was surprised to find that there were no holes in it.

I then suspected the burner might be the problem. There I found the choke plate lying on the floor under the burner. This was allowing the choke to move around freely. I removed the drawer assembly. It was very dirty. The nozzle was not the proper one. I looked into the blast tube and could see that the missing choke plate had allowed the flame to impinge on the nose cone on one side. This would be what was causing poor combustion.

I replaced the nozzle, adjusted the ignition points, replaced the choke plate, and replaced the drawer assembly. I fired it up, got a nice blue flame, with just a hint of red on the tips, then set the choke, and draft regulator. I brought the air over the flame to a number one smoke, and ran a test. The efficiency percentage was well over the required amount.

I turned around and the woman was standing behind me. The building had aired out while I was working.

"It is running, and I am not rubbing my eyes," she said.

"No, and you won't have to either," I replied.

"What in the world did you do, this is marvellous."

"Just what I was trained to do lady ....just what I was trained to do."

I filled in the report.

I don't know if the furnace was changed or not. It sure did not need to be at that time, as far as I am concerned.

I attended an oil burner course that Shell Oil sponsored, when I worked for Dave Stamp, (now Sid Stamp Fuels), in 1965, when oil burner licensing became mandatory. The Ministry of Consumer and Commercial Relations for the Province of Ontario issued certificate number 003535 in my name on July 10th, 1965. This certified me as an Oil Burner Mechanic-Class 2. The last sticker on that document is dated May 25 1990. I have not renewed it since then.

While working for Certified Heating, under the direction of Mr Max Nuttle, in 1974, he encouraged me to take a course in natural gas fitting. On September 12th 1974, I was issued certificate number 024341 as a Gas Fitter-2. The last sticker on that document is dated 1978.

Because I have not kept these licenses current, I have not received any of the many amendments to the code, therefore, I am really out of touch now, but I am proud to display them in my office. They hang over my shoulder as I write.

The name of the governing department for these licenses has been changed, and oil burner mechanics are now called oil burner technicians. It doesn't really matter what they are called, if they don't do their job properly, they are just guys working on furnaces. A license just means that they know what they are supposed to do, it doesn't mean that they do it. I have seen some terribly shoddy work.

When I moved into the house in which I live, the first thing I checked was the furnace room. There I found three violations of the code.

The oil supply tube from the oil tank to the burner was suspended in mid air about a foot above the floor. The door struck it as it was opened. This could have separated the tube from the tank causing a spill.

There were far too many joins in the pipe between the tank and the shut off valve. Any of these could have leaked and caused uncontrolled leakage.

The tank vent pipe was terminated too close to windows, and too close to the ground.

The fume pipe from the furnace to the outside of the building was not secured, and the door was also striking it. Knocked from the furnace, this could have caused fumes to enter the living quarters.

I tweaked this furnace system and reduced our fuel bill by 40%. Our oil delivery people had to adjust the degree day* numbers for our account as delivery was required less often.

. I had Don Barker Heating and Cooling Service rectify the problems. A duly qualified burner technician arrived with license in hand. He corrected everything in a professional, tidy and reliable manner.

I have done burner work periodically, since my initial license was issued. I worked for J.O. Jackson Heating, Dave Stamp Fuels and for his son Sid when he took over the business. I formed my own company, Ray Miller Heating, then, after Lloyd Endicott moved me to Peterborough in 1970, I worked for him (Endicott Fuels) for a time, then Faulkner Fuels, Wayne Lucas Burner Service, Fitzgerald Fuels, and Kelly Fuels. There was a Service Manager at one who wanted me to do shoddy work and get more done. I would not do that, so I left. However, most of the time, it was my love for driving that took me away from oil burner and gas fitter work. Even though I enjoyed the challenge of service work, I was never truly happy to be called out of bed at three in the morning, and have to crawl under someone's house.

I have many stories of tradesmen neglect in the heating industry. At least one instance involved the fire department.

*Degree day is a very effective system oil delivery companies use to schedule automatic delivery to your home or office. It measures the amount of degrees of discomfort accumulated each twenty-four hours. Then based on the amount of the first delivery ever made to your account, from full tank to full tank, the company knows how many degrees of discomfort is in your tank. When that amount of discomfort is recorded, they will fill your tank.

When I operated Ray Miller Heating, in the early 1960s, I had to record the overnight low and the day time high every day. Then a formula used to arrive at the degrees for that day. This was very useful and reliable, but wind chill factors were not known then, and a lot of wind would change the system. To compensate for this, we delivered a little early each time, and even then, we occasionally had run outs.

High tech statistic gathering equipment is now used, and today's delivery is a lot more reliable. Delivery schedulers can now calculate exactly, what is remaining in your tank.

The system has to be reset, whenever there is a change in the residents of a house. Children leaving doors open, elderly folk require more heat, different lifestyle, illness, and many other elements will change the whole heat loss spectrum

A Day at Smith Transport

I was on city delivery with Smith Transport in 1981.

I drove a single axle tractor called a jackass. It was for shunting trailers around the yard, much as a jackass was used in earlier days, to shift wagons. It, much like the animal itself, was not an especially pretty thing, but it soon became my little buddy, as it was a very powerful and efficient little vehicle. It had power steering, which was a bit of a luxury, as Smith did not have this convenience on their over-the-road units. It was a nippy little outfit, that could snap your head back into the back of the cab, if you happened to jab the throttle a bit when bobtailing.

My job as city driver, was to take all incoming bonded trailers to the customs agency, in the industrial park in Peterborough, first thing every morning.

Then, I would spot trailers at various shippers' docks, as requested. By this time, the incoming mixed freight trailers would have been unloaded, the freight sorted and loaded onto smaller vehicles, for delivery to various routes throughout the area.

The city deliveries were usually on a short trailer, for the convenience of getting into small alleys and back yards.

I was a busy boy. Sometimes the inbound customs trailers had to be backed into the dock at customs, and completely unloaded for inspection. When this happened, I had to run the forklift, to pull off enough skids to let the inspectors see what they demanded to see. But most of the time, it was what was called a "walk through", where you just had to loop around the lot, and pull up to the door of the office, where an inspector would come out, break the seal, get up into the trailer, and just peer up over the freight. He would then stamp and sign the papers, and I would take the trailer back to the yard for another driver to take out of town, or I would spot it at the receiver's dock, if it was an in town consignment.

Every afternoon I would pick up loaded trailers from various shippers, bring them back to the terminal, where I would make up trains, when necessary, put highway tractors under them, fuel and check under the hoods for fluid levels, and have them ready for the over-the-road drivers to take out overnight.

Start time was six a.m. and I worked until all the vehicles were ready for the road that evening. Overtime was paid after five, and, if I were to happen to finish early, I was to sort of putter around cleaning up the yard until five. I guess the yard must have been a bit messy, as I cannot recall ever finishing with the outbound line up much before eight or nine. I really didn't mind the hours, as I was doing the work that I love.

As I drove in one morning, I viewed the usual line up of incoming vehicles. There were several of the standard Internationals, some with long trailers, others with two short trailers called trains, and a couple backed up against the dock for unloading.

Among all this boredom, stood an ugly looking, swept-back, front axle monstrosity called an Autocar Diesel. Behind all the lights and winches on the tractor, was a low bed trailer, with two chase cars sitting on its belly, looking very small in their present surroundings. I knew this had to be for an over-load or wide load. These chase vehicles are the small pickups, with flashing lights all over them, seen "chasing", ahead and behind, vehicles carrying specially licensed, wide, high, long, or slow loads on the highways. .

Arriving in the office, the dispatcher greeted me with a pleasant, "Good morning lad," as he laid my dispatch orders on the desk. "You have a busy one today. First I want you to shift that Autocar over to the ramp. I will have a dockhand unlash the cars and unload them, while you do the in-bond stuff at customs. There are only two in-bond trailers this morning, and they are both walk-throughs and both out of town consignments, so that won't take long. Then you are to take the flat bed to DeLaval, and spot it under the crane in their yard. On your sheet, you will see that there are two forty fivers to go to Ovaltine shipping, and one to Outboard Marine, and one to General Electric. Take one to Ovaltine, the others to Outboard and GE, then the other to Ovaltine, so they all have a trailer fairly early, as we need to get them out of there this afternoon because the goods are to be on the road tonight."

I grabbed my orders and was about to head for the door, when he gave me a list and said, "Pick this up at The Carousel, on your way back with the second in-bond trailer." The list read: Vic, Black coffee two sugars and toast; Carl, regular coffee two sugar toast and jam; and so on, covering all the people who were on duty at the time. As I left, he said, "Oh! Victor will do your town deliveries today, so that will help."

There were three ramps at the back of the yard, to assist in loading wheeled items onto the three standard vehicle heights. There was one for low beds, one for single axle trucks, and one for high bed trailers.

Smith's former company colours were dark blue with dark yellow fenders. The Autocar was still in old colours and, with that sweptback front end, it resembled a bear showing its teeth, with yellow lips.

The hood stuck out three or four feet in front of the fenders and front wheels. The grill was huge.

I climbed up into this damned thing and looked around. I must have looked like a small kid, the first time he sits in a fire truck.

I had never driven an Autocar before, so by the time I found my way around the dash, I could see two dockhands standing by the low ramp at the rear of the yard.

When I found the key, I spied a button that said "start", so I gingerly turned the key and hit the button. The engine sprung to life with a mighty roar, the entire cab shook and vibrated, and then it settled down into a low throbbing hum. Lights flashed and buzzers and beepers sounded all over the place. I touched the throttle. It barked out harshly, as if I had kicked a sleeping dog, and then settled back.

I was familiar with nine, ten, and thirteen speed transmissions, with one splitter button on the side of the gear shift lever, but this thing had a knob the size of the palm of my hand, with two splitter knobs, and a little red button. Now what the hell do I do with all of this?

I looked up at the headliner above the windshield, and there was the answer to it all.

There was a three-channel H pattern with the numbers, 1/7/13 up in the left corner. 15/9/3 in the middle channel, 17/11/5 over on the right corner. Down in the left bottom was 2/4/14, in the centre bottom was 4/10/16, and in the lower right was 6/12/and18. Leading off the centre of the pattern was a tiny spur to the right and down. On the end of that spur was printed R1/R2/R3. The damned truck had 18 forward gears and 3 reverse.

Beside the pattern was printed all I needed to know.

"Move right split button up/down between 6th and 7th gear.

Move left split button up/down between 12th and 13th gear.

Hold red button down to access reverse gears.

Both splitter buttons down =R/1

Left splitter button up, right splitter button down =R2

Both splitter buttons up =R3."

By now, the lights had gone off, and all the buzzers were quiet. All I could hear was a low throaty, throbbing roar. I can handle that. I touched the throttle again. It barked and settled back. The tachometer was sitting at a quiet 700 rpm.

I stepped on the clutch, and was delighted to feel the power clutch take over. I also felt the transmission brake come on, as the pedal reached the floor.

I looked into the mirrors, and seeing that the ramp was directly behind me, I pushed the shift lever to the right, then pushed and held the little red button down. I felt the lock release, and the lever went on over to the right. Both splitter buttons were down, and I brought the lever down toward the seat. It slipped in nicely. I released the clutch as I stepped on the throttle. The engine jumped to 1200 revs. It took several seconds for the slack in all the gears to gather up, only then did it move backward. I could have set the throttle at 2500 revs and rolled a cigarette, and it still wouldn't have moved the length of the running board. Even at full throttle, it would have taken a half an hour to reach the ramp. This won't do. I have work to do.

I clutched again, pulled both splitters up, shifted into neutral and back down against the seat. This time the truck was reversing naturally. This time I was in R/3.

I backed it against the ramp, then went back to the line up. I checked the trailer numbers, until I found one of the trailers and tractor my dispatch manifest said that I needed to take to customs. I drove over there, circled around, stopped in front of the office door. A person came out and took the papers from me. Checked the numbers against the tag numbers, cut the tag off, climbed up and looked over top of the load. He stamped the papers, signed the stamp, and handed them back to me. I returned to the yard and put it back into the line up for another driver to deliver to the consignee.

I found the other trailer and took it over. The same thing happened, and I was on my way back. I pulled into the parking lot at the Carousel Restaurant, parking beside a couple of other transports, and went into the restaurant to get the coffee and toast for the crew back at the terminal. I had been doing this for a couple of weeks now and the waitress knew me.

She said, "Smith, right."

"Yes," I replied.

"Your office called and said for me to add a couple of more coffees and toast. They said something about the chase drivers showing up?"

"Oh yeah, we have a heavy hauler in today."

When I got back to the office, the dispatcher said, "They are ready for the flatbed. Now, don't sign any papers for this load. They are to come here, after you pick it up, and we will look after that here. One of the chase cars will follow you and bring you back."

I said, "Okay where is my chase car driver?"

A woman sitting and talking to a dock worker in the corner, said, "Over here."

As we walked to where the Autocar and chase cars were, I said, "Now the clearance on this thing is pretty low, and the curb is quite high going into their yard, so when we get there ..." She interrupted, "I know what to do. I will block traffic for you, and... which way do we have to turn to get into the place?"

I said, "Left."

"Is it two lanes or four?"

"It's four there."

"Okay! I will go ahead of you. When we get close, turn on your left turn signal in lots of time, then your four ways, as we approach the driveway. You wait in the left turn lane, until I can block both oncoming lanes. Then turn and take whatever time you need."

She got into her car and I climbed up into the truck. She waited at the street, and then, with a wave, she started with me close behind.

The gears really weren't much of a problem, as I only had to remember the other split, and I was quite happy tooling along Lansdowne Street. We passed the lights at Clonsilla Avenue, where it turned to four lanes, down over the hill past K-Mart, along past Sears and across Monaghan. I pulled into the left lane there and she did the same. I turned on my left signal on and slowed down. When I turned on my four way flashers, on she went past the driveway, turned on all her flashing, revolving lights, waited for the light at Lansdowne and Park to change. This was exciting.

As soon as she had a break, she moved at an angle to block traffic, and I started my turn. The tractor went over the curb. All was fine, until the belly of the trailer started to drag. I backed up and moved over a little, and tried again. This time it cleared.

The chase car was sitting corner ways in the lane. It simply backed to the white line and drove in behind me.

DeLaval made cream separators, as well as other milk handling tools and tanks. They had a row of arches that extended out into the yard, seventy-five feet or more, and a crane ran along a beam in the middle of these arches.

There were workers out there, signalling for me to back under these arches.

As I did, I could see in the mirrors, that there was a large stainless steel tank lying on its side, just inside the building.

As I got into the car, the woman said, "You had a little trouble with the curb."

"Yes, but not as bad as I thought it might be."

"Do you think we should have the police, in case you have trouble getting out this afternoon?"

"We will be turning sharp right, so the trailer wheels will come down off the curb one wheel at a time. I think it will be alright."

We went back to the yard. I did the remainder of the spotting and the day went along well.

I came into the yard about three that afternoon, dragging a trailer loaded with Ovaltine, that I had picked up. I backed it into the out-going line up and unhitched. I went into the office and the dispatcher said, "The flatbed is ready. Now I cannot emphasize this enough. I know you are used to signing for loads, but this is different. This load is their responsibility, all we are providing are wheels and escorts. Don't sign anything. Just get it, and bring it here."

The two chase cars were up front and I climbed in with the woman.

She said, "How was your day?"

I said, "Okay, but you guys didn't get much sleep. Are you supposed to follow this thing into the night?"

"Oh, we were in early last night . We came by bus and we were here before supper. We had a good nights' sleep at the Holiday Inn. We will stop and sleep as we go. This thing doesn't have to be in Calgary until next week, sometime. There's lots of time."

The flatbed was sitting where I left it, but now it had a large tank on it. The tank was twelve feet across, so it was barely under the height limit of thirteen foot six, lying on its side on the truck. It was easily fifty-five feet long, tapered on one end, with legs to stand on. Large steel straps, about two inches across, fastened it to the trailer.

The shipper said, "I will follow you up to the yard, and we will get the paper work done there."

The chase cars went out into the street ahead of me. One stopped traffic coming from the east, the other pulled along to the west and sat there waiting.

I turned on the revolving lights, as I eased the tractor over the curb, going straight out to nearly the centre line. Turned, and watched in the curved mirrors, as the rear trailer wheels eased down over the sidewalk, to the travelled portion of the pavement.

It was exciting to have all this attention. I moved along, taking up most of both lanes, to where it narrowed to two at Clonsilla. There I slowed and placed the truck in the middle of the lane, taking up as little of the oncoming lane as possible.

I looped around to the right, in front of the office, and backed it down by the fuel pumps.

While I was fuelling it up, one of the older men who worked there, came in with a truck. He climbed out and came over. He looked at the load, then said, "I hope you didn't sign for this stupidity."

I said, "No, I was told not to."

"Good. Where is it going?"

"Calgary."

"It will never make it outside Ontario like that."

"Why?"

"It is not chocked," he said pointing under the side of the tank.

"What do you mean?" I asked.

"There should be chocks wedged in there, to keep it from sliding sideways," pointing again to where the tank meets the bed of the trailer.

"Well I don't know, DeLaval loaded it. There's a guy in the office from the company now talking to dispatch."

"I have to talk to him," he said, heading to the office.

Before I finished fuelling, the office door opened. It was plain to see the conversation was serious. He came out of the door with the DeLaval man right behind him. Our man was talking over his shoulder, pretty much saying the same thing to him as he had to me. There have to be chocks in there.

The DeLaval man said, "Those straps are torqued down to thousands of pounds pressure. They have that tank so tight to the platform, that the friction will hold thousands of pounds of skid before it can move. According to the book, you would have to have thousands of pounds of side thrust for it to move."

"Well, throw the damned book away. What would it take to cut four timbers the shape of the tank on one end, and long enough to wedge in between the tank and the straps. Then nail them to the wooden platform?"

"That system is so outdated," said the man, laughing.

The old man walked into the terminal.

Two weeks later when I went to work, there sat the Autocar with the tank on it. The tank was bound with chains now, and there were chocks under it.

It was all bent to hell.

I went into the office. The dispatcher looked at me and said, "Did you see the tank?"

I said, "Yes, what happened?"

He told me that the tank had shifted somewhere near the Ontario-Manitoba border. It came off and struck a rock cut. He said the police made them put chains on it, and had overseen the placing of chocks.

When the chase cars were ready, I took it back to DeLaval. They immediately unloaded it with the crane. They told me it would be cut up and they would salvage whatever they could.

Experience does make a difference, after all.

Life Was Not Good

On December 3rd, 1981 I hired on with City of Peterborough Transit. This was a job that I had applied for several times, during the preceding years. I was delighted. I thought I had it made. Finally a job with excellent pay, benefits and good hours. I thought I was set for the rest of my working days. I was doing something I love – driving.

Three years went by happily until 1984. We had visited Ferne's cousins, Don and Marlene Currie, at Stratford, Ontario for the weekend, and were returning to Peterborough late Sunday, January 29th, when I began to experience severe pains in my chest, down my arm and in the back of my throat. Having experienced other symptoms that reminded me of those suffered by my Dad, just months before his death, I was greatly concerned. The pain woke me several times through the night, and continued at a low-grade level at breakfast, Monday morning so I decided to call in sick and give Dr. Trusler's office a call. Nurse Linda Monroe told me that Dr. Trusler was out, but Dr. Hartere would see me and, given my symptoms, she thought I should come in right away.

I arrived just before office hours. Dr. Hartere noticed me in the waiting room, and took me in right away. He checked me out, then said, "I want you to go to St. Joseph's Hospital."

I said, "Okay, I'll go home and get some things and go up."

"No, I want you to go directly. Now! Linda will call, so they will know you are coming. I will be up, as soon as I can get away from here."

I called Ferne, and then went to emergency. They put me on a stretcher in the hall, checked my vital signs, hooked up a monitor, took some blood and started an I.V. drip.

Dr. Hartere came in just before noon, looked at my charts, and said, "I would like to have you in intensive care for a while. It is not that you are that critical, but we can monitor you much better there. I need to have you here for 72 hours, so we can check for enzymes in your blood."

There wasn't a bed available in ICU, so I remained in the emergency room for 72 hours then I was released with no diagnosis.

Several times during the next three weeks, I would wake in the early morning with severe pain. I would call the doctor and be admitted for another 72 hours, with no results. On most occasions, by the time I would arrive, the pain would have subsided enough, that a nitro glycerine tablet would suffice, but one Sunday afternoon it was still bad, and they gave me a small injection of morphine. That time they called Dr. McLean, a cardiologist, for advice. Once again, I was released in 72 hours. Each time I was sent home, I felt like it was a death sentence, as I was following the same pattern of symptoms as Dad had, only more often. Each time I thought, "The next one will kill me."

On February 21st, I had pain and called Dr Trusler. He said, "Go to the hospital Ray, I am going to have you admitted under both my and Dr. Hartere's care. We are not going to give up until we get you into ICU. We need to have you monitored properly."

Mabel, Hazel, and Floyd and Marg came to see me that evening. The homestead in Minden had burned to the ground the day before.

In the evening of February 23rd, Dr. Ross McLean gave orders for me to be released the next morning at eleven o'clock. His diagnosis was that I was a damned nuisance, or words to that effect.

I was asleep in ICU, at five o clock in the morning of February 24th, when I was woken by severe pain. I was reaching around trying to find the call button, when a gentle hand touched my shoulder.

"You're alright, Mr. Miller," a kind voice said. "We see it on your monitor; I have already injected nitro into your I.V. I think you will be going to Toronto this time." I looked up, and a nurse was standing at my head.

I thought, "Thank God, they have seen something. They will be able to help me now."

Dr. Trusler came in before breakfast and said, "Dr. McLean has signed the papers for you to be transferred to Toronto Western Hospital, as soon as we free up an ambulance. The girls here will get you ready. I will see you when you return." He touched my shoulder assuredly, "They will fix you up there."

The ambulance arrived around two thirty in the afternoon. There was a woman patient on board from Civic Hospital, to go to Wellesley Hospital, in Toronto on our way. I was loaded and was surprised to see a nurse board. She had a mobile defibrillator with her.

I had never been inside a rolling ambulance before, and it was interesting to hear how they use their radio.

"Peterborough dispatch this is unit 40-02, (fictitious number), leaving St. Josephs with two patients, one for Wellesley Hospital and one for Toronto Western."

"Ten-four 40-02 have a good trip."

"We have a nurse with a defib."

"You have a heart patient then?"

"Yes."

"Ten-four."

We travelled along 115 to 35 Highway, then they radioed again, "Oshawa dispatch this is unit 40-02."

"Go ahead 40-02."

"We are entering your area with two patients, one a transfer to Wellesley; one is a heart patient for Toronto Western. We have a defib nurse on board."

"Ten-four 40-02, let us know when you leave the area."

"That's a copy, Oshawa."

The same radio transfer happened each time we got close to a different hospital.

We entered the outskirts of Toronto, and the nurse said quietly, "Oh damn."

The attendant turned quickly in his seat and entered the back, "What is it." he asked anxiously.

"It's this defib, the battery is going down."

"We will soon be to Wellesley; we will attend to it there."

"They have landed a man on the moon, but they can't seem to come up with a defib that plugs into the vehicle's electrical system," the driver remarked.

"I hear that they have them, but we don't have one yet," said the nurse.

We unloaded the woman at Wellesley, and the nurse and the driver went into the building to tend to the defibrillator.

It was well into evening rush hour, when we left Wellesley. We immediately ran into traffic jams. The driver said jokingly, "If you could get your patient to develop a little pain, I could use the siren to get through this mess."

They talked about where they would eat on the way back, as we trucked through traffic in the early darkness.

Toronto Western was in a state of expansion and renovation. They put me into a step down part of the Cardiac Care Unit, with a writing desk beside my bed.

A little oriental nurse came up beside me. "Hello, Mr. Miller, how did you stand the trip?" She looked across my bed at the desk. "Oh look, you have a secretary. Well isn't that nice. That wasn't here on my last shift." She checked my I.V. then continued, "Oh dear, we will have to change that. it won't work here very well." She changed my I.V., got me settled in nicely, then said, "I will order some supper for you."

Just before midnight, Dr. Susan Lenkei appeared at the foot of my bed, flanked by two others. She introduced herself as the head over the Cardiac Care Unit, looked over my charts, and said, "You will have your angiogram on Tuesday," she touched my foot, "and your bypass surgery is scheduled for the next day. The surgeon will be in on Sunday to talk to you about it." She walked away.

My mind was running full tilt now. "Angiogram...Bypass surgery?" This was the first I had heard of that. I was somewhat relieved though, as this meant that they could do something for me.

Ferne caught up to me the next day and my niece Joy also arrived.

I wasn't allowed to do much more than blink my eyes for the next day or two. They put me on a pill called 'Adalat' : It made me feel like I was floating four feet above the bed for fifteen minutes after I took it.

I didn't see Dr. Lenkei again until Sunday, a little after noon. She appeared with two other doctors, and introduced them as Dr. Robert Burns, and Dr. William Uden.

"I am retiring soon, and Dr. Burns is to take my place as head of Cardiac Care, and Dr. Uden will supervise your angiogram on Tuesday," she explained. Just then, another doctor arrived. She introduced him as the surgeon who would conduct the bypass surgery, but I cannot remember his name.

He said "Okay, Mr. Miller, the fellow beside you is to have bypass surgery tomorrow morning, so we will push your beds together." He looked at the desk between our beds and said, "What the hell is that doing there?"

"They put it here until they finish an office somewhere," a nurse replied.

"Well, get housekeeping to move it," he said in disgust.

The nurse left the room. In a few minutes, two men came and moved it out into the hallway, and pushed me next to the other bed. In the meantime, a technician had brought an overhead projector and screen into the room and set it up.

When that was done, he continued, "Okay, I am going to go over the procedure we are going to follow and explain to you guys exactly what the advantages, and risks are." He did that, gathered up his paraphernalia and left.

On Tuesday afternoon, I was loaded onto a stretcher and two orderlies wheeled me out into the hall. Suddenly, the fire alarms sounded, and a lock down went into effect. Orders came over the PA system for all fire doors to be closed, and the use of elevators avoided until further instructions were received from the fire department.

It was soon announced, the fire was in the part of the building that was under construction and minimal, but it was still an hour or more before instructions came, for things to return to normal. By now, the stretcher had become very hard, and the sedatives that I had been given were beginning to wear off. They wheeled me into the lab, but couldn't proceed with the examination until I was administered more sedative, it was given time to take effect.

During the procedure, I heard Dr.Uden saying things like, "Look at all the Myocardial Bridges," and, "He has the heart of an athlete."

It was six o'clock, by the time I was returned to my room. I wasn't to move a muscle for six hours. A nurse was by my side, checking my vitals, paying strict attention to the pulse in my right foot and the incision in my right groin.

Have you ever tried lying absolutely still, on a stretcher, for six hours?

The part of me in contact with the stretcher got so damned hot. My nose itched, and the nurse scratched it. She did everything she could to make me as comfortable as possible, but she could do nothing about the heat that built up between the stretcher and me. Once I tightened a muscle in my arm, to try to relieve the pressure there. She got very excited and told me not to do that again.

Dr. Uden came by about eight o'clock and checked things out. I asked him what he found. He said that Dr. Lenkei, Dr. Burns and himself would be back at midnight to talk to me.

I said, "I heard you talking about a lot of Myocardial Bridges. Is that a bad thing?"

"No. That is actually a good thing. You also heard us speak of an athlete's heart. They are somewhat connected. You must be an athlete of some kind. Are you?"

I said, "No. By no means, I am a city bus driver."

"At sometime in the past few years you were very active, doing something that made you absolutely winded a lot of the time."

I remembered the times when I would run up and down stairs most of the day, with things as heavy as hundred pound sacks of rice and flour on my back, when I worked at Strano Foods. I rolled my head a little, as I told him about that.

He said, "No, No. Don't move your head, don't move anything... When you become absolutely winded, your body, and especially your heart, cries out for more oxygen, that is why you breathe so intensely. Some parts of the heart are better supplied than others, so nature creates little channels through the muscle between the arteries on your heart, to supply oxygen to parts of the heart muscle where oxygen is lacking. These are called Myocardial Bridges. When there are a lot of these, we refer to it as an athletes heart. You have a lot of bridges."

All three doctors returned around midnight. Dr. Lenkei looked over the results of the test, and then the conversation went like this.

Dr. Lenkei, "Well! There is absolutely no blockage. You have a very healthy heart. Your medication is to be discontinued immediately. You will be moved to level seven for two days and then your on you're way home." My hopes were dashed. They were going to send me home, and I knew that I would likely die the same as my dad.

Dr. Burns, "What! I don't believe it, with the elevated ST segment on the chart from Peterborough? Let me see that thing."

He took the papers from her and looked closely. "Who crossed out 'with provocation'? I ordered provocation with this patient. Who crossed it out?"

Dr. Lenkei, "I did. It's a waste of time. I have never seen it prove anything yet."

Dr. Burns, "I think that he displays the symptoms of spasm, and I want to try to provoke that."

Dr. Lenkei, "I have signed him out."

Dr. Burns, "I will sign him back in as my patient then, and reschedule another test, as soon as the lab is free. I will do it myself this time. I think he has Prinzmetal Angina, spasm of the coronary arteries."

He turned to me. "I hate to put you through another test, but I am not satisfied that we have done all we can for you. I want to do it again, and do it myself, if you agree." I was relieved that there was going to be another chance for treatment.

Dr. Lenkei and Dr. Uden left.

He checked my incision, the pulse on my right foot, and the pulse on my left foot. He turned to the nurse, and said, "Did you find the pulse less on the left foot than the right?"

She said, "Yes it is not as strong as it could be."

He turned to me, and said, "You can start to move around a little now." Wow, was I relieved.   To the nurse, "Get someone in here, to move him onto a proper bed, and get him some food."

He came in the next morning, just before noon, with Dr. Uden. "I have booked your next angiogram for tomorrow afternoon. Dr. Uden will assist me this time. We will have to use the same incision as before, since your other leg has less pulse than this one, even though it received some punishment yesterday. Using the same entry point will be a little more painful, but we will do everything we can to alleviate that. We need you to be as alert as possible for this one."

On Thursday, I was laying on the table in the lab with two doctors to my right, a nurse with defibrillators, a full syringe on a rack near the nurse at my I.V. to my left, a monitor above my feet, and a technician in a booth above and to my left. There was a gun shaped x-ray machine pointed at my heart. A catheter had been inserted into the large artery, in the groin of my right leg and pushed up into my heart once more. I could see it on the monitor.

Dr. Burns said, "Is everyone ready?"

The lights were all turned off, to allow full view of the monitors.

He inserted some dye into the tube, I could see it pass through the arteries and dissipate into the muscles of my heart.

"You are right, Bill," he said. "He has a very strong heart and look at all those bridges. Are you with us, Mr Miller?"

I said, "Yes, I'm okay."

"I am going to inject various chemicals into your heart, in an attempt to make your arteries go into spasm. If I can produce spasm, you will feel pain. Now, if this happens, I will need you to imagine the worst pain you have ever had in your chest as level ten. I will need you to let me raise that pain to a seven and a half level, and I will hold it there until it is recorded. Then we will relieve you. Don't be afraid, we are not going to lose you. We have all the equipment in place to revive you, if need be, but I don't anticipate any problem. Do you understand?"

"Go for it, Doc."

A constant flow of dye kept the arteries visible as he introduced various chemicals. A time or two there was sign of change but no pain and nothing significant. Then suddenly there was pain, and I could see the arteries narrow. I flinched and he said, "Okay, now on a scale of one to ten, how much pain are you in right now?"

I thought for an instant, and then said, "Five."

"Tell me when it is seven and a half." The arteries narrowed, and the pain increased.

I said, "Stop! It's there. That's seven and a half."

A female voice on the intercom said, "Got it."

The nurse on my left, injected fluid into my I.V. The arteries widened and the pain was gone.

He said, "It's all yours Bill," and left the room.

Dr. Uden removed the catheter from the fitting in my groin. Then with, personnel all around him, he said, "Okay now." Someone beside him removed the fitting. Blood squirted. He reached for the opening with a gauze swab, and applied a lot of pressure. I had been through this procedure before, but this time he had trouble. In a few minutes, he released the pressure to peek. Blood flew again, and he replaced the gauze, and pressure. This happened a couple more times. The wound wouldn't clot. He spoke to a man that had entered the room.

"Take over here, I have to rest. It is the second time in this opening, and it is too big to clot."

This was hurting very much, but I knew that it had to be. I trusted these people, and I believed that they were going to help me. A nurse was instructed to inject something into my I.V. And the pressure was applied for what seemed like a long time. Finally, they released it and the clot held.

Dr. Uden took me back to the room. There were two nurses there this time.

"Watch the pulse in his foot very closely," he told them. "We had a hell of a time closing, and I am afraid we might have narrowed the artery."

One nurse kept her stethoscope on my foot constantly for a few minutes, and then checked it often. They were very attentive to the wound in my groin. In an hour or so, Dr. Uden returned. He checked things out and seemed pleased.

When the six hours of stillness was over, Dr. Burns, Dr. Uden, and Dr. Lenkei came in. They studied the chart and talked in medical terms I didn't understand.

Then Dr. Burns said,. "You have a condition known as Prinzmetal Variant Angina. It is not unheard of, but it is not common either. What happens, a chemical that your body produces, causes all of the arteries in your heart to go into spasm and narrow. This is more painful than a clogged artery, or heart attack. One clogged artery puts a small area of the heart in distress. Prinzmetal Angina puts the whole heart in distress. This can cause instant death, but we are going to put you on medication immediately. You should live to be an old man. You will go up to level seven and will likely be released on Saturday."

Ferne picked me up on Saturday and took me to a room at a Howard Johnson's, that our friends Ruth and Bob Boyes had arranged, thinking I would benefit from a rest before going home. I really just wanted to go home, but it was done with good intentions, so I agreed to stay.

I knew that my groin area was sore, but I was amazed at what I saw when I could look in a mirror. My right thigh was bruised from my knee to my waist, from the pressure of the closing.

I feel that I would not be alive today, if that little red headed doctor hadn't persisted.

When my dad died, in 1959, the electrocardiogram was the only heart test available, especially in a town with no hospital.

I benefited greatly from the immense change in medical procedure in only 25 years.

I understand that modern medicine and constant invention has greatly changed this procedure, in just 20 years since, 1984. The six-hour "still period" is not necessary now, and closure is achieved without the great pressure that was needed then. Suspected heart patients are no longer required to remain in hospital for 72 hours, and with the invention of better batteries, mobile defibrillators are much more reliable.

But it was not over

I returned to work at Peterborough Transit on May 15th working days and afternoons, driving bus on a full shift. The medication seemed to be working fine while I was at home, and I had been free of pain for several weeks. As soon as I began to get up at five, to be at work by six in the morning, I began to tire and in a few days time, I would experience some pain by the end of a shift. The pain would appear earlier each day, and I would resort to nitro pills to finish each shift.

By June 14th., the pain was almost constant, so I booked off and went to the doctor. With rest and relaxation my health returned, and the doctor gave me permission to return to work on August 17th, only to have a repeat of the symptom progression, and I booked off again on September 25th.

I was very anxious to beat this damned thing. This was the best job I had ever had in my life, and I wanted to remain here until retirement. When I was feeling good, I would beg the doctor to let me return.

I returned on November 5th, and was able to tough it until February 6th 1985, when I had to go home because of pain. I implored the doctor to let me return on April 23rd.

Saturday June 8th was my weekend off. I woke that morning with a different pain. By noon, it was getting so bad that I had Ferne drive me to Civic Hospital Emergency, to have it checked. They took blood, checked my vitals, and held me until results of the blood tests came back. They were determined that I had appendicitis, but there was no fever or enzymes present in the blood. Surgeon, Dr. Jeresonek, checked me out and sent me home saying, "I still think it's your appendix, but the usual fever is not there. Go home, and if it is not better in the morning, go to St. Josephs as I will be there."

I spent one hell of a night. By morning, I knew that something had to be done, so I went to St. Josephs, as soon as I thought it was feasible. The nurses called Dr. Jeresonek, and he came right away.

He looked at my chart, and said, "You still don't have the proper symptoms, Ray but with your permission, I want to go in. The pain and tenderness yells appendix, but nothing else."

He turned to the nurse, and said, "Prepare him now. I'll call the O.R."

There was a flurry of razors, disinfectants, changes took place in a hurry, and I was on my way to the O.R.

I woke up in recovery and it wasn't long before the doctor arrived.

"Your appendix was red hot Ray," he said. "It appears that the little artery that feeds the organ, stopped working, and the darned thing simply rotted. There was no blood carrying enzymes back to the brain, so there was no fever or enzymes in the blood."

"Could this have been caused by the same spasm that affects the little arteries on my heart?" I questioned.

"I really don't know much about that I, just know that it wasn't working. Anyway, they will be sending you home in a day or so. Dr. Trusler assisted me in the O.R. He will be checking on you, from time to time."

On August 5th., I returned to work without a medical. I had been back and forth from work so much, that the inspector didn't ask for it when I said I was coming back, and I didn't mention it.

About a week after I returned, he asked, and I told him what I had done. He gave me trouble, and told me that was only half as much as I would get, if I ever tried that again!

I was on the morning shift one day in September, when I noticed quite a bit of eyestrain. The late morning sun, shining through some trees, caused little red dots to appear in both my eyes. This got worse, and I brought it to Dr. Trusler's attention. He sent me to an optometrist, who sent me to Ophthalmologist, Dr. Drysdale. After conducting various tests, he told me that degeneration of the macula was apparent in both eyes, and I could become legally blind within five years.

On October 9th., I couldn't stand the chest pain, and booked off again. October 20th, I returned to work, but now my troubles really began.

It was Saturday, December 14th,1985 I was working the Barnardo route. It was mid-morning. I had passed my outside terminal and was returning to the terminal downtown, when I realized that one of my migraines was about to start. The migraine became evident with what appeared to be a "flickering light" in the centre of my field of vision. It would quickly become a flickering ring of light, that continued to grow, until it disappeared. This time the light stayed in the middle.

I pulled into the stop at Reid and Parkhill streets, to pick up a fare there. When I looked into the mirror to check traffic before pulling out, I could only see the rim of the mirror, and nothing in the centre of it. I rubbed my eyes and looked again. The flickering light had become involved with the swollen areas of degeneration, and was creating a huge, red flickering distorted blind spot. When I looked ahead through the windshield, I could not see the traffic light. I could see the other two, but not the one I was looking for. This was scary. I had a busload of people sitting at the curb, and I couldn't see.

Everyone at work knew of my eye trouble, but no one, including myself, expected this. Art Sykes was acting inspector that morning, and Eldon Wildman was in the tower with him. I radioed dispatch.

"Barnardo to dispatch."

"Go ahead Barnardo"

"Art, I have a problem here at Reid and Parkhill"

"What is it Ray."

"I can't see. I'm at the stop, and I can't see my mirror or the light ahead of me."

"Stay where you are. We'll get someone to you. We just sent our spare driver from here, to cover an overload. Is there anyone at the garage? No, … not likely, its Saturday isn't it? We'll get to you Ray, if I have to come myself."

Highland Road heard the call. *"This is Highland Road. Art, if I miss one stop at the senior's residence on Park Street, I could cut across Parkhill and come in ahead of him. He could follow my bus."*

"Negative, Highland Road. Stay on your route. Is there anyone at the shop?" No response.

"Art, this flickering light usually becomes a ring, and then I will be able to drive." I said.

"Stay where you are Barnardo. Eldon is calling the next senior man on the overtime sheet now."

The light was beginning to spread, and I could see some of the centre of my vision. In a minute or so, I could tell if there was traffic coming up beside me, and I could tell which traffic light was on. I waited, until I was sure I wouldn't interfere with traffic, then eased through the intersection. My sight was returning, as I serviced the stop at Reid and McDonald. I was on the one way portion of Reid now, and there was only two stops to go. I gingerly pulled across the lanes to make a left onto Simcoe. The little dip across Rubidge gave me trouble, but my eyes were clearing quite a bit by then. There was no one waiting at either stop on Simcoe and no-one rang for a stop.

Dispatch called: *"We have a replacement coming, in Barnardo. Eldon will bring him to you as soon as he arrives, and you'll have to inform your transferees that they will not make their connections, as I have to send these other buses back out now."*

"Its Okay now, I'm right here at the terminal," I said, as I pulled into my bay.

My replacement took my bus out, but the strain in my eyes was still bad enough that I stayed in the drivers' room for a few minutes. Art came down and joined me. He asked me what I thought the problem was. I really didn't know, but we both thought it was a combination of migraine and degeneration of the macula. I went home as soon as I was sure I could drive.

The strain dissipated over the weekend, and I reported for work on Monday. The acting inspector told me that the chief inspector wanted to see me in his office. He handed me a memo that read,

> To: Ray Miller   From: Ralph McKay, Manager of Transportation, City of Peterborough.
> *Re: Medical Condition – Eyesight.*
>
> *In as much as you reported on Saturday, December 14, 1985 that your eyesight was such that you were unable to safely drive your bus, it is requested that you receive a full medical outlining your health problem.*
>
> *It is requested that your doctor advise Mr Murray Hynes, Director of Personnel for the City of Peterborough, under confidential cover, whether or not your condition can be successfully treated, allowing you to continue your employment as a Transit Operator.*
>
> *You will be placed on Short Term disability coverage, pending reply to this request from your doctor.*
>
> ### AUTHORITY TO RECEIVE INFORMATION
>
> *I, Ray Miller, authorize release of the necessary medical information requested above, under confidential cover, for the purpose requested.*

I signed this paper. The results effectively removed me from the job that I loved and had sought most of my life.

I returned to work on March 6th,1986, at a non-driving position, (washing buses), and at reduced hours, to try to remain on the work force.

On July 4th,1986, Mother died of stroke. She had been in Hyland Crest Home for the Aged since June 14th 1971.She died in the little hospital in Minden. Mabel and Hazel were by her side. She was laid to rest, beside Dad, in Minden Cemetery.

In April 1987, after a routine medical, the Ministry of Transportation and Communication for Ontario, asked for evidence from my doctor that I could still operate heavy vehicles safely. If this were not forthcoming by May 15th., my classification would be reduced to 'G' status. (I carried an 'AZ', which allowed me to drive everything but a motorcycle). My sight was deteriorating rapidly now, and after consulting with my doctors, it was decided to turn my license in entirely.

From this time onwards I would never drive again.

With the reduced hours, and booking a few days off, I was able to last until September 25th 1987, when I succumbed to chest discomfort again. After some difficulty proving that I couldn't be retrained, I went on long term disability.

During my work in the bus garage, Laurie-Lee had a serious operation on her back. As much as I desperately wanted to, I was unable to get to see her in hospital. Ferne and a friend went, while I was working, and I was unable to drive on my own. This added greatly to the mental stress that my poor health, the loss of work as well the loss of my privilege to drive, had already placed on me. My mental health was in jeopardy.

Lindsay's Grand Old Night Of Country Music

In 1987, Leroy Nesbitt and his sister Wendy, along with Jim Higgins, Danny McDonnell, and some others, had started a show at the Academy Theatre, in Lindsay. They called it "Lindsay's Grand Old Night of Country Music". Their goal was to bring local artists together one Sunday night a month, to play country music.

We saw an ad in the Peterborough Examiner, and planned to attend. Ferne called Doreen and Grenville, and Simon and Brenda and her sister Doreen in Kirkfield. I told some of the bus drivers, and we all got together and went to see what it was all about.

We ate at a restaurant in Lindsay, and attended what turned out to be a really good country show. The theatre was almost full to capacity, so we decided we should get tickets for the next month, and do this every month. A lot of other people had the same idea, as there was a long line up at the wicket after the show. We barely got ours, when it was announced that they were sold out.

Ferne purchased a VHS video camera at Kawartha TV and Stereo to record some things she was interested in. I looked this thing over and realized that it had possibilities. I called Jim Higgins, asked him if it would be alright if I were to tape the show and maybe sell a few copies. After talking with the others, he called back and said to give it a try. My eyesight was failing at the time, and swelling was causing too much distortion for me to use the tiny viewfinder, with one eye closed. I discovered I could wire the camera to a TV, and see what was going on the tape.

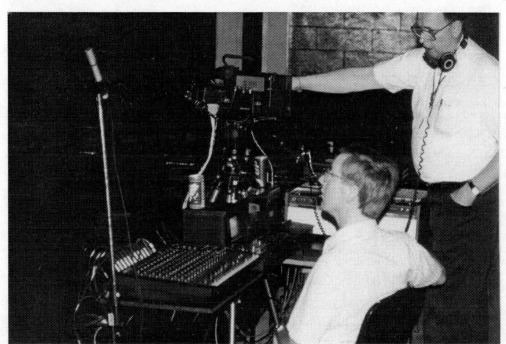

So I purchased a five inch black and white TV, and mounted it all on the tripod.

This worked okay for the first show, but the lens on that camera wasn't a good one, and the reproduction was not the best. I sold a few copies that night, and the customers weren't totally satisfied. I went to Kawartha TV and talked to a salesman there about it. He sold

Roy Craft of Custom Sound and I discuss acoustics at my portable video recording studio.

202

me a machine with a much better lens. It cost $3500.00, which was a lot of money.

I wanted to have remote control of the zoom, record, and focus, so I took the side off the camera and took a look. I saw there was a ribbon cable running from the controls to the main circuit. I looked really close, with a magnifying glass, and could see where the circuitry controlling these things was soldered to the cable. I could tell which strands of the cable were the controls I wanted to extend. I gingerly scraped away a tiny bit of the insulation and dropped a tiny bit of hot solder onto the very tiny wire inside. It stuck very well, so I now knew I could solder in an umbilical to each one I needed.

I carefully cut the tiny fibre-like circuits, bared them back, and soldered a fine wire to each end of the cut. I fastened a small box on the side of the body, and brought these wires through a small hole I had drilled into the box. I put a connector on the bottom of the box, and fastened the wires to it. I put the matching connecter on the end of a wire, and plugged the ends to the box. By bringing the ends of these wires together, I could make the camera work without touching it. I mounted another box on a small console I fastened to the tripod, and put the necessary switches on it. I moved the little TV to the same console. I could now run the whole thing by remote. I managed the pan and yaw with the handle of the tripod, and controlled the rest from the console. This produced a much better picture and my customers were satisfied.

I decided to start a video recording business, but my company needed a name, so I could purchase supplies wholesale. We were living on the corner of Stocker Road, and Crawford Avenue. I used part of each street name and called it 'Stockford Productions'.

Sound was the next problem. John Van Haltern, of Van Haltern Music, was mixing sound and doing an excellent job, but the tiny microphone on the camera was not getting good sound all the time. I asked John if he ever heard of a snake* that had the usual inputs, but outputted to another snake, as well as to a separate soundboard. He made some calls, and found that Rapco would build it. They built it to my specifications. All the microphone wires would plug into it, then a short lead went to John's snake, and a thirty foot one went to a mixer, that I had also purchased from John. This worked really well. I placed two color TV sets on stage, so the audience could see what I was filming, and I began to sell up to one hundred tapes per show.

I was paying the performers a royalty, so the price of the tapes went to twenty-five dollars. I put together a reproduction studio in my basement, and could duplicate five copies at once.

The show became very popular. Tickets were sold months in advance. Many came from Minden and Haliburton. So much so, local bus companies were considering running charters to the Academy. I built a custom trailer, to move my equipment from place to place, and Ferne pulled it behind her Chrysler Royal.

I filmed Nashville stars. Mac Wiseman, Bobby Helms, Jack Green, Stonewall Jackson, Kitty Wells, Wilf Carter, and others, as well as great locals like, Lorne Buck and The Flatland Mountaineers, Mountain Country, Cindy Thompson, and many, more. My tapes soon became thirty-seven dollars, due to larger royalties being paid. I started paying royalties to producers and writers around the world through SOCAN.

One performer to grace the stage was a trucker named Larry Kousack. Larry sang those trucking songs. 'Giddy-up Go', 'Phantom 309', 'Widow Maker', and did a great impression of Stomping Tom. Jim Higgins served as the Master of Ceremonies and would always wear a tuxedo that was donated to the show by Nesbitt Men's Wear. The first time he introduced Larry, Jim asked if he was nervous. Larry said, "Of course I'm nervous. Right now you couldn't drive a thermometer up my ass with a sledge hammer."

The favourite of the audience though, was a performer who grew up in Minden. He was a friend of mine from childhood. In the chapter, 'Minden Monarchs', you will have read that he went to hockey games with Audrey and I. It is rumoured that his first guitar had no strings.

Murray Gartshore could easily have been a Nashville star. When he and his band, 'Southern Comfort', stepped out on stage, they shone with professionalism. Dressed in snow-white jackets, black pants and ties, they took your breath away without ever playing a note.

With a shy glance toward his lead guitar player, he would belt out the favourites: 'Don't Come Home Drinking This Christmas Daddy'; 'The Writing on The Wall'; 'Don't You Ever Get Tired of Hurtin' Me'; would echo through the auditorium. You could close your eyes and imagine the Nashville stars who made the songs famous, then open them, and see perfection at its best. Murray could sing for five hours at a dance, then go to a house party and sing until daylight, without ever repeating a song. I asked him why he never pursued a career in Nashville. His answer was that of a true redneck. "That would interfere with my truck driving."

Word of my video business spread to the producers of Bluegrass Festivals. I taped the festival at Palmer Rapids, Tottemham, and Tony Deboer wanted me to go to his big show at River Valley, but I never made it there. I filmed step dance contests at Bobcaygeon, and Drayton, Ontario, and many singing contests, and charity variety shows.

Things went quite well for me. Ferne would drive me to the shows, and then sell copies. Ron and Shirley Cox, were always there to help in any way they could.

I spent hours reproducing videos and shipping them.

One afternoon I received a call from a disc jockey in England. He was planning to do a marathon broadcast, to see how long he could stay on the air without sleep, to raise money for charity. I sent him a set of audio tapes.

I received a phone call from a fellow in James Bay. He said that he operated a small community radio station there, CHMO. He had heard of me, from God knows where, but he was interested in the sound track from the Lindsay shows. His was a unique situation. He would put country music on the air, then go to the local community centre, and play it over the loudspeakers for people to dance to on Saturday night. I sent him a whole set, and he sent me a cap with a radio in it, with earplugs. It works really well for local stations. It is on a shelf in my office now.

My eyesight was slowly failing, but I was keeping busy.

I enjoyed five years of measured success, then came the little recession in 1991. This caught me just as I was upgrading my equipment. I had installed several office machines, to handle the load of packaging and posting videos all around the country. Videos are something that people can do without in lean times, so my sales dropped ninety percent. In desperation, I tried putting on shows in Stirling, Ontario. I called them 'The Great Pine Ridge Jamboree'. Small towns don't support out of town producers, and this effort failed.

I went into bankruptcy.

It was a sad day, when I watched my trailer, loaded with all my equipment as well as thousands of hours of master tapes, and my copyrights, go out the driveway behind the bailiff's truck. I had inventoried all the components, complete with purchase invoices, serial numbers, and manuals. I packed it into the trailer myself. I attended the sale of my goods at the bailiff's. I was there to demonstrate the equipment in order to achieve as much money as I could, for the people I owed. It sold for a tenth of its original cost.

Ferne had hired on with Rocklands Talent and Management, during that time, and began to travel coast to coast, with country music stars. She was away for months with Stompin' Tom during his come back tour, as well as Mac Wiseman, k d Lang, and Tommy Hunter.

I was alone a lot. Life was not good.

The Lindsay show carried on for several years after I left. Country music became much less popular and attendance began to fail.

Snake *This is a collection box that is put on stage into which the bands' instruments and stage microphones are connected. A large cable with multiple circuits then runs from there to a sound mixer.*

I Hit Bottom

When Ferne left on January 2nd, to work in the North-West Territories with the Tommy Hunter Show for a month, our thirty-six year relationship, that had disintegrated to a disastrous level, finally came apart.

By the time, Ferne returned that February 4th, I was a complete mess. I couldn't stop crying. She finally had enough and took me to Civic Hospital, where they sent me to the Nichols wing (a psychiatric unit), for counselling and treatment. It was Friday afternoon, February 10th 1995.

They took everything away that I might use to hurt myself, including my belt, and I found myself in a big room with people acting strangely all around me. I continued to cry so a nurse gave me an injection and I felt better. Laurie showed up almost immediately, and continued to do so every night I. Bless her heart! with all the troubles she had of her own, she still found time for her Dad. Being out of character, I was sometimes unreasonable with her, but she never faltered.

Grenville came that evening and found me in a small room, with no catch on the door. There was a closet and a bed. My dinner arrived, so I took it to the big room and ate it there. Then I tried to watch the O.J. Simpson trial on television, but I broke down and Grenville accompanied me back to my room.

He left around 9p.m. and a counsellor came to visit me.

She introduced herself as Jane, said she had been assigned my case, and asked some questions. She told me that someone would check on me every twenty minutes, night and day, as long as I was there. She asked me not to let any of the other patients talk to me about their problems, and not to be offended, if I wanted to talk to any of them, and they walked away. It was all right to talk about anything else, but not to discuss our problems.

She gave me some medication to make me sleep, but it didn't work well, and I was awake a lot through the night. People walked the halls all night long talking to themselves, and sometimes entering my room.

When my five a.m. check came, they couldn't find me. I was taking a shower.

I was asked if I wanted my meals in my room or prefer to go to the cafeteria. I chose the cafeteria. So come 8a.m. I entered the big room with several round tables.

Breakfast was good, as all the meals were.

Scott came from Toronto and joined me for lunch. He stayed the afternoon and dinner. then went to see his mother, and went back to the city.

My cousin, Yvonne Newell, phoned me that afternoon as did Hazel and Mabel. Laurie came right after dinner, and Grenville spent the evening with me. With all this support, I felt better, but the hurt in my stomach still felt like a large, heavy cannonball.

After breakfast on Monday, my counselling started in earnest. Jane told me that a Psychiatrist would visit me that morning. He took me into a room where we talked for twenty minutes.

Then he said, "Okay Ray," (nobody has a last name in there), I am going to remove your depression medication. Now if you want it back, just tell Jane, but I don't think you need it. The nurses are going to be observing you for the next day or so, and I will see you again on Thursday. Jane told you not to talk about your problem to any other patients, and not let them talk to you didn't she? Now it's good to talk, but just don't talk about what put you in here."

I followed him back out into the TV room, where I watched the O.J. trial for a while. Jane and a male counsellor came and took me into another room. We talked about my life and they asked me to name the events in my life that depressed me, in the last ten years. They had a list of questions to ask, and checked each thing off as the questions continued.

When we had finished, my list included: my Mother dying; an illness that seemed life threatening; failed eyesight; bankruptcy; loss of work; loss of my license to drive; son moving into his own apartment; daughters' marriage breakdown; loneliness; confinement; and marriage breakdown. They said that, with a list like that, they wouldn't have been surprised if I been brought in wearing a straightjacket.

Some flowers came from some neighbours, Simon and Brenda Kloostra visited one night, Laurie and Grenville were there every night, Yvonne phoned every day, and my sisters called frequently.

Jane had me attend some group therapy meetings and counselled me frequently. People wandered around aimlessly.

The physiatrist returned on Thursday morning. He asked me some very strange questions. They made no sense. This made me angry, which was apparently the reaction he was looking for. He then said, "The nurses have been watching you closely, and you are doing fine. You are in a bind here Ray. You don't belong in here, and I don't think you are ready to return to your life out there, do you?"

"I feel protected in here."

"That's what I'm afraid of. You have improved so much, without medication, but it's because of the care they are giving you here. I am going to keep you here for a week or so. You will have outpatient privileges. You can go out during the day, but be back by nine each night, or we will have the police looking for you. Your counselling will be less intense, and you can now talk to others about their problems, if they approach you. We don't want patients getting into discussions when they are deeply depressed, because it is like the 'blind leading the blind'. Poor advice can do a lot of harm. The nurses tell me you always look for company in the cafeteria, and don't like to eat alone. They say, if you have to take a table where there is no one, others will join you. These are signs of good communication, that they trust you and want to talk to you."

"Can I have my personal things back now?"

"Ask for them when you leave the building. You must turn them in immediately, upon returning. Keys and even large coins could be used as a weapon, in the wrong hands."

Late that night, after Grenville and Laurie had left, there was a lot of noise in the elevator. The door opened, and two police officers ushered in a young man kicking and screaming abuse and profanity. He broke partially free, and tossed a nurse against the wall, as if she was made of cardboard. There was a very large male nurse in the TV room. He joined the police officers in trying to overpower the patient. They pinned him down and I knelt on his legs. The nurse was able to get a needle into his hip. He calmed down and passed out immediately. They dressed him in a straightjacket, and carried him down the hall and placed him in the bubble room.

A nurse came down the hall, and said, "What was all the commotion?"

"Jimmy is back again," the first nurse replied, rubbing her arm from the throw.

"The poor guy. Is he really bad again?"

"He's in the bubble room."

"He seemed so good when he went out the last time."

"Yeah, well I guess life has kicked his ass again."

I was beginning to feel better generally, but the knot was still in my stomach and I cried sometimes. When I asked for my belongings, to go out for the first time, I was very surprised to find that my keys to the house were missing. The nurses told me that Ferne had taken them. It was a bit of a set back, to be locked out of my own house. I wouldn't have entered it anyway, but I felt like a fugitive.

I caught the bus downtown, but felt that everyone knew I was from the Nichol's wing. I was actually nervous and went back.

Life went along. Laurie and Grenville came each night. Yvonne and my sisters phoned. Scott visited again on Sunday, and had lunch and dinner and took me out for a while in the afternoon.

I attended group sessions and had regular counselling from Jane.

I talked to a truck driver. He told me that he had come home unexpectedly, to find a guy in his bed with his wife. He just went right back to work, got into a truck, and drove it without making his scheduled stop. He kept driving east, out of Peterborough, the police finally got him stopped the other side of Montreal.

I talked to a lady who had several bad relationships, and each time she would steal a motorcycle and ride it through town, naked.

I talked to a young lady in her upper teens, who had loved her father very dearly. Every since she was old enough to realize what was going on, she watched her mother's lover visit every day, while her father worked, and join her mother in bed. When she was barely a teenager, her beloved Father died a slow, agonizing death. Immediately after the funeral, her mother's lover moved in and began to abuse her verbally, physically and sexually. She reported it and was placed in foster care, only to be sexually abused by more then one foster father. She begged not to be released.

I became friendly with a young fellow who truly believed he owned a big company, with a lot of fibreglass pickup trucks. When he was on the streets, he would call local dealers and try to negotiate a deal. He would phone transport companies and try to set up contracts to move freight. He called stores to arrange deliveries and pick ups. The nurses would give him a dead phone and he would use it for a while. Then he would go into a state of manic depression for a few days.

I watched a man walk the halls, day and night. He talked to himself all the time and seldom slept. The counsellors had to keep pace with him, to talk to him.

One morning, they found a young lady at the back door, in a pool of blood. She had left her dog with a relative in northern Ontario, cut her wrists slightly, and driven her pickup all that way to the hospital, alone and bleeding. Her truck was in the parking lot, idling, with the door open. They took her over to Civic Hospital and patched her up. She was back before noon. Apparently, she had been in this facility before and, not being able to handle life on the outside, she just wanted to return.

I talked to a man whose only ambition in life is to kill his Father. Every time he had been released, he stole a car and tried to get to where his Father lived, to do just that. He may never be released.

I talked to a lady who led a normal life every day, and returned each night, just before nine to sleep. She had been attacked in her home, tied to a bed, and raped by several drunks repeatedly. She had become familiar with the environment in the facility and felt safe. With treatment, she would probably be able to return to her new home and family, but not yet.

I talked to a lady who was obsessed by demons within her.

Jimmy, (the fellow in the bubble room), was at the breakfast table one morning, looking rather ragged, but there none the less. He turned out to be a very nice fellow, but we had to watch our meals or he would steal from them.

I was getting quite a bit better. The knot in my stomach had shrunk to a walnut size. I cried only when I first woke in the morning.

On Wednesday, February 22nd, Jane told me the physiatrist had looked at my chart and signed the release.

She said, "I told him it was all well and good, but you have no place to go, do you."

"No, I don't."

"There is a local paper in that room, with a desk and a phone. You can look for places to rent and call them. When you find something that appears to be suitable, you can go out and look it over. Your personal effects are on the desk, at the nurse's station. Now, the Doctor said do not accept a basement apartment or anything gloomy."

I spent two days running around Peterborough, looking at apartments I could afford on my pension. Everything in that price range was not at all suitable. If I moved into any of them, I would have been back in the facility soon.

I came back on Friday afternoon without finding an apartment.

Jane said, "We have to find you something. I am going to phone upstairs to a fellow who is a social worker, and see if he can help."

I went up and we discussed my financial situation. Then he said, "I will call some of the government assisted places in town."

He made a call, and got me into a one-bedroom apartment at 211 Hunter Street East, number 301.

Grenville brought his pickup and helped me get some furniture from the house, on Saturday, February 25th. He left and I was alone. The knot grew to be the size of a baseball, and I cried.

God bless the people who work with the emotionally disturbed in those facilities. They have the patience of Job. They are so kind and gentle when the need is the greatest. Their work is not pleasant at the best of times, but imagine what it must be like, when they had to go into the bubble room and clean up patients who had been in a straightjacket for a few hours.

The bubble room was a solitary confinement cell, with bubble like lining, so the patients couldn't hurt themselves. It also had several windows, that were round and bubble into the room, allowing the nurses to peer into every possible corner without entering.

Although I had a rough road ahead of me, I came away with a different perspective and the courage to go on.

I met some people there who had lived a very tough life. In most cases, they were very intelligent. No one will ever show those poor unfortunate souls anything but respect around me ever again.

A Caribbean Cruise

Photo Courtesy of Michael W. Gilbert

I was listening to the radio one August afternoon in 1995, when I heard an announcement that Country 105 in Peterborough, was offering a Country Music Cruise to the Caribbean. Wondering how much this would cost, I made a call to the radio station. They put me in touch with a cruise company in Hamilton and cruise consultant Shirley Hullman. It was set to sail on January 13th, 1996, and would feature three country stars, Crystal Gayle, John Berry, and Neal McCoy. I am fond of all these performers, and finding that I could afford the outing, I booked it immediately.

When time came to go, Scott offered to pick me up at my apartment, on the Wednesday night prior to departure, and take me to his place in Toronto, for a few days. He was working until midnight, so it was late when we arrived at his place. I enjoyed the next two days as he and the other drivers who stayed with him, came and went to work. On Friday night, he and some of his buddies from work, had a bon voyage party for me, and then he took me to catch my plane early next morning, on his way to work. He was doing crew shuttles for Trentway Wagar at the airport at the time..

Saturday, January 13th 1996: The flight to Miami airport was uneventful. An escort met us when we landed and led us to a bus to transport us to the pier.

We crested an overpass, and there ahead and to the right was an amazing sight. Towering above the houses was our ship, the SS Norway. 1,035 feet long, 11 decks above the water, 188 feet from the waterline to her top deck, she stood like a majestic lady. We drove up to it as you would drive into the foothills of a mountain range.

The guide directed us into a building, where I was issued a purple, non-U.S. citizen boarding pass. I was told to guard it with my life, as I would need to show it to immigration several times during the cruise and would not be allowed to board the tenders each time I went ashore without it. I was advised to purchase a waterproof body belt, put my pass and passport into it and wear it at all times even swimming, or in the shower. I was told that these passes were very valuable. They could be sold on the black market, to citizens of the islands for a lot of money. I was also given a white ticket to use as admission to various events on board.

I went out to a large open-sided shelter on the pier, where passengers were having their picture taken with Neal McCoy. We were to wait here until called to board, according to the color of our pass.

Departure time was scheduled for four o'clock, but they announced that a plane from western Canada had been delayed due to weather, so departure would be late.

At 2:30, they called passengers with purple passes to board. As I went up the gangway, I looked up. I felt like an ant must as it looks up at an elephant. It towered above me like an eighteen story building. Many questions came to mind. How does this thing float? How in hell do they steer it?

Right inside the door, was a young fellow who took my pass and said, "Welcome aboard, sir. You're in cabin B192. It's right on this deck, straight ahead." It was laid out for two people, but I had paid extra for single occupancy. There was ample closet space on one side and a nice bathroom on the other. A bed stand, straight ahead, separated two single beds. There were lifejackets under each bed. A little mint lay on each pillow, and a copy of the daily 'Cruise News'.

My pass indicated I was to eat in the Leeward dining room. Dinner wasn't until 8:30. I hadn't slept much the night before, so I laid down on the bed and was soon asleep.

I woke up when the ships' paging system began to bark out a welcome announcement from the captain.

"Good evening ladies and gentlemen, this is the Captain Haakkon Gangdal speaking from the bridge. We are finally clear of Miami Harbour and steaming out to sea at a grand gallop of 25 knots. We don't usually travel at this speed on this lap of our cruise, but we were late departing so we will be making up a little time during the night. Don't forget to turn your timepieces ahead one hour, before you retire tonight.

We have 2543 passengers on board as well as 900 crew. Of those 2543 passengers, 35% are travelling with spouses or significant others. The other 65% is made up of 78% women, travelling alone. Have fun guys."

One of six stairways onboard-Photo Courtesy of Michael W. Gilbert

I was unattached, on a cruise with 1289 unattached women. I got a silly grin on my face, that lasted for three weeks after I returned home.

It was 6:30 I had missed cast off ceremonies.

Leeward Dining Room
Photo Courtesy Michael W. Gilbert

At 8:30, I went to the Leeward Dining room, found table 192, and sure enough, there were five ladies seated at my table. A young fellow came over and said, "Good evening folks, welcome to the Leeward Dining Room. I be Jacob. I be your waiter for the entire cruise. At the end of the cruise you will give me big, big tip, because I be excellent waiter." He was not kidding. He was excellent.

During dinner, we agreed that all six of us would tour the ship together. We looked out over the ocean from the Grande Promenade. It was now very dark, but we could see that we were travelling right along, from the reflection on the water. Two dance instructors were giving line dance lessons in the Windjammer Lounge. We came out onto a balcony overlooking the Saga Theatre, where 'Broadway Tonight' was starting its second presentation of the evening. We went to Club Internationale and had a drink, while the band, 'The Keys', were playing top 40s and oldies. There was a singles party going on in Dazzles Disco, but it was all young people so we passed on that. We learned there was going to be a Ladies Night, beginning at midnight, featuring two drinks none of us had heard of before, 'Sex on The Beach' and 'Fuzzy Navel'. The girls decided to return for that later. We met a couple on a stairway. Seeing me with five women the husband gave me a big smile and thumbs up. We went back to the Leeward Dining room, where a midnight buffet was laid out. It was called 'Flavours of the Pacific Rim'. It was wonderful. I ate my fill, then walked the ladies down to Dazzles, and said good night to them at the door. I returned to my room. It had been tidied up, another mint and the next day's copy of 'Cruise News" was on my pillow. I was soon asleep.

Every time I went out of the room, it was tidied up and a mint left on the pillow. One of the ladies said, she went to the bathroom in the night, and when she returned to her bed, it had been made and there was a fresh mint on her pillow. She thought maybe there was a little black fellow under her bed, so she looked, but no such luck. She was exaggerating of course, but not by much.
Sunday January 14 1996: A Day at Sea.

I looked at my watch. It was 9:30. I looked at the back cover of 'Cruise News' and discovered that there was continuous breakfast service, in both Windward and Leeward dining rooms, until 10:00 a.m. and late breakfast from 8:30 until 11:00 a.m. in the Great Outdoor Restaurant. Evening attire would be formal, tuxedo, or jacket and tie for the men, and formal gown or cocktail dress, for the ladies. The captain would join us for dinner. There would also be a Captains' Welcome Buffet, served at midnight, in the Windward Dining Room. Drink of the day will be Kalapana Colada. Today we would be hard at sea all day.

I went to the dining room, where it was general seating. I met an oriental couple from California, and they invited me to sit at their table.

After, I went to a port briefing, at the North Cape Lounge, took a walk through the casino, looked into the various shops at the mall, and enjoyed a drink while I watched some pool games on the pool deck.

I showed up early in my formal attire, for the Captains' welcome party, in Club Internationale. I was sitting on a sofa, waiting for activities to begin, when I was joined by a tall, black haired lady and a short, giddy redhead. We introduced each other, and they suddenly

disappeared. They soon returned with another lady and introduced her as their room mate. Her name was Delia. She was very nice, and turned out to be a lady that I would spend time with for the rest of the cruise, and for a while after. She also carried a white ticket for the entertainment, so this allowed us to attend things together.

We met the captain, had photos taken with him, then proceeded to The North Cape Lounge, for champagne.

After dinner, we went back to comedy show at The North Cape Lounge. We enjoyed a drink then went to the Windward dining room for the Captains' Midnight Welcome Buffet.

Windward Dining Room- Photo courtesy of Michael W Gilbert

The Author. Picture taken by Delia on the Promenade before going out on the forward deck.

We took a couple of drinks out to the forward deck around one in the morning, and found a nice little table near the railing. Other couples were there. Some joined us.

It was hard to understand how so much water could ever be as still as the ocean was that night. There was only enough of a ripple to make the reflection of the moon seem to dance on the water. Silence was broken by the low rumble of the engines and the lap of the water, as it flowed away from the ship at the bow. We looked down to a lower deck, where two large tenders were stowed and cranes hung over them.

We talked and got to know each other better, as the moon rose overhead and disappeared over the bridge.

On the bridge, we could see the crew steadily guiding us through the dark night.
After a while, a clean up crew came onto the scene, and I looked at my watch. It was 2:30 a.m.

The other couples had gone.

We planned to meet for the Crystal Gayle show the following night.

I walked her to her cabin and said good night. Life was good.

Monday, January 15 1996: A Day at Sea.

We were steadily steaming toward the island of St. Maarten. According to the 'Cruise News', evening attire would be Caribbean and the drink of the day would be Black Storm.

An item that caught my interest was a Navigational Bridge Tour. I was very interested in what made this enormous vessel run and how it was navigated, so I planned my afternoon to be outside the Windjammer Lounge at 2:00 p.m. to join the tour.

I was surprised to learn that the Norway used 24 satellites in its global positioning. This navigation system could pin-point the ship's location at sea within 15 feet, in every direction. This allowed the ship to travel at full speed in any weather and in darkness. It also allowed ships to meet or pass each other, much closer than ever before. The old compass was there, but only as an ornament and relic of the past. From the bridge, the horizon was ten miles off ,in every direction.

The Bridge – Photo courtesy of Michael W. Gilbert

I saw Delia several times during the day, as I checked out the photo shop and looked over the pictures that had been taken the day before with the captain. I walked through the casino, where one of the ladies at my table was in the middle of a winning streak, and then checked out the gift and jewellery shops.

The waiters were dressed in Caribbean attire at dinner. There were peg-legged pirates with daggers and glass eyes, roaming around, and one even had a live parrot on his shoulder.

Saga Theatre – Photo Courtesy of Michael W. Gilbert

I met Delia at 10:30, in front of the Saga Theatre. We attended the Crystal Gayle and Magnum Cloggers show. Then we rushed to the Caribbean Deck Party at Checkers Cabaret. A limbo contest was underway when we arrived, The crowd was dancing, then a conga line formed. It went out the door, along the promenade and in the other door. There were several hundred people in that line, as it was over four hundred feet long. We really enjoyed that, then moved on to the Caribbean Jerk cookout, at the Great Outdoor Restaurant, at midnight. Some other ladies joined us at our table for some drinks and laughs. I walked Delia to her cabin around 1:00 in the morning, made plans for the next day, and said goodnight.

Life was good.

Tuesday, January 16 1996: St. Maarten.

'Cruise News' said St. Maarten. Evening attire would be casual or 50s. Drink of the day was Rum Runner.

The SS Norway had a thirty-five foot draft. This meant it was unable to dock at these islands, so it had to anchor three miles offshore, and use tenders to transport passengers to shore. I was booked to go ashore on the first tender, but as I approached The North Cape Lounge, where we were to gather for instructions and tender numbers, I looked out from the promenade and noticed that we were not anchored, as we were supposed to be at this time. Instead, we were moving very slowly. As I entered the lounge, an announcement came over the public address system.

"Due to a very busy night at sea, we are sorry to inform you, there will be a slight delay in going ashore. We had several small ships pass us in the night. They are also lying at sea in front of us. There has been some legal activity in port, and several coast guard cutters are evident. We have been assured that we will not be delayed more than an hour. Also, please remember to take your boarding passes with you. You will not be allowed on the tenders to return without it."

Just then, another coast guard cutter went roaring past, with sirens howling, and turned toward shore.

It was only a few minutes before the ship came to a full stop, and another announcement was heard.

"We have been informed the port is now clear. The ships in front of us have begun to move to their piers. We have dropped anchor and are in the process of unloading the tenders. Please, please be sure you have your boarding passes with you. Immigration will not allow you back on board without it. All passengers on morning tour will now proceed to the gangway, on the Biscayne Deck. Just passengers on the morning tour, now. Those wishing to go ashore and are not on morning tour will wait for the announcement at ten-thirty. Then you may go ashore at your leisure. Tenders will depart continuously, every thirty minutes, from the Biscayne deck aft. Last tender back to the SS Norway will be at six thirty p.m. We cannot remind you enough. Be sure you have your boarding pass with you."

My cabin was on the Biscayne deck, so I had no trouble finding the gangway. I soon realized that the gangway to the tenders was from the same door I had boarded through in Miami.

The tenders were even larger than they looked from the deck. 87 feet long, they held 450 people, complete with washrooms, and a bar. Two-inch sisal ropes held it snugly against huge four-foot thick rubber fenders, between it and the ship.

It filled quickly, and we were soon steaming toward shore. There was a seat available beside a pretty, middle-aged lady, with short brown hair, so I sat down and introduced myself. As we talked about how unique it was that the island had two governments, Dutch, and French, and divided by an invisible boundary, with no formal border. We discovered that we had both booked time at the clothing optional beach on the French side. We decided to spend the day together.

Our tender docked at a pier, behind a cruise ship, and

View from the tender- Photo courtesy of Michael Gilbert

we went on shore. A bus was waiting for us, so we boarded immediately. When we reached the limits of the city of Philipsburg, it became evident that there had been much damage from recent hurricanes. Our tour guide announced that the city is the first area to be rebuilt after every storm, so the port will remain as attractive as possible to the tourist.

We bumped along a narrow, one-way road with the ocean on one side and a mountain on the other. The scenery was marvellous on both sides. To our right, with all its might and beauty, the ocean reached to the blue sky. The heavily forested mountain, on the left ,went up to that same sky. We stopped in front of a church, nestled between the road and the mountain. One of the double entrance doors was hanging on one hinge and the other was missing entirely. The roof was completely gone but some pews were inside. The guide said that church service was being held regularly.

He pointed out that many people on the island were poor and boarding passes brought a high price on the black market, as a valid pass was a ticket to financial freedom in another world. I felt a little guilty, when I realized that other world, was the world we live in, and don't appreciate as much as we should.

We bumped along uphill and down, until the bus stopped in front of a place resembling the ticket booth at a fair. We showed the beach passes we had purchased on board ship, and passed through the building to Cupecoy Beach. We walked to the far end, where my new friend handed me a bottle of sun block lotion and, as she quickly disrobed, she said, "If anything burns, it's your fault."

Life was good.

I enjoyed watching people paragliding. I enjoyed watching people water skiing and swimming. However, most of all, I enjoyed the scenery on the beach.

The trip to Philipsburg was a little longer, as roads were one way, and we had to go quite a distance to get back to the other side. We shopped a little in the city, then caught a tender back to the Norway.

I went to my cabin and slept, until it was time for dinner.

I met Delia at the North Cape Lounge at 10:30 for the John Berry Show. We enjoyed it very much. We had a couple of drinks, then went to The Great Outdoor Restaurant for the Viking Buffet, at midnight. She, and one of her roommates, walked me to my cabin. We planned to meet the next night, and said goodnight.

I sat my alarm for 5:30 a.m. and went to sleep.

<u>Wednesday, January 17 1996:</u> St John/St Thomas.

The alarm sounded and I sat on the side of my bed, wondering for a minute where the hell I was, and why. Then it came to me. It was Wednesday, January 17, 1996, and I was on a cruise in the Caribbean Sea.

I looked at the 'Cruise News'. At the top left corner of the front page I read, "St. John/St Thomas."

I looked on the back page, where it said, "Evening Attire: Country and Western or Casual, Drink of The Day: N.C.L. Cruiser.

Okay, this is fine but why am I up so damned early? I looked inside and the answer was written in large bold letters, on the top of the left hand page.

"6:15 a.m. Saga Theatre, pool deck, **IMMIGRATION INSPECTION. All Non-US Citizens, Resident Aliens, and Canadian Citizens must clear with the US Immigration Officials before proceeding ashore. Please bring your boarding pass with you. A staff member will be on hand to assist you and direct you to your tenders.**

Can you ever imagine 2000 people in a line, that zigzagged back and forth, for what seemed like miles, at six o'clock in the morning? Some were bright eyed and bushy-tailed, with a gleam of anticipation in their eyes, looking forward to a great day ashore. Others were scratching and yawning with that, 'Good Lord...Morning', look, wondering what the hell they were doing here. The line moved fast, and we were soon through the inspection.

The inspection was early because the tenders to St. John started leaving at 7 a.m. Passengers could go ashore and then at their leisure, they would catch a ferry from St. John to St. Thomas before 1:00p.p.m. The ship moved from St. John to St. Thomas as soon as the tenders returned. I thought this was causing too much stress, so I booked to depart at St. Thomas. I had booked a flight over the islands as well as a helicopter flight around the island.

The first tender to St. Thomas was not until 9:00 a.m. so I trundled back to my cabin for a while. Then I noticed just how much of an idiot I was. In the 'Cruise News', I found that there was another immigration inspection, for those going to St. Thomas, at 7:15. I scratched my head, and looked in the mirror. No! I didn't look like an idiot, but I knew I was.

Oh well, I just had to go back and do it again. At least there wouldn't be as many people this time, as some would have departed.

The people on the Norway knew they were dealing with people who didn't pay attention. There was a big sign at the entrance to the Saga Theatre this time, that read, "Those who cleared Immigration at 6:15 a.m. and had their passes stamped, do not have to do it again." I read the message and went to breakfast, relieved to know that they expected people like me.

When I boarded the tender, at 9:00 a.m., I spied a seat beside a blonde lady, and went over to her. "Is anyone sitting there?" I asked.

She looked up at me and smiling, she said, "You are if you want."

She was very pretty and my knees got a little weak. I felt like a schoolboy again.

"My name is Ray," I said, in a silly nervous voice.

She knew exactly how to break the ice.

"I'm Caroline. Get laid yet?"

She caught me by surprise. I said, "No. You."

"Not yet, but I have a hot date this evening. Tonight's the night" she absolutely beamed at the

thought. "Whatcha doing on shore."

"Plane ride, then helicopter."

"Me too. Let's do it together."

The thought of spending the day with this bubbly open-minded lady made me kind of weak all over.

Life was good.

When we arrived at the shore, they lowered the front ramp on the tender. The boat stopped with the ramp resting on the sand. The storm surge from a hurricane, earlier that year, had turned the pier upside-down. It was made of wooden pilasters driven six or eight feet into the ground. Then steel frames, filled with concrete. The pier was three hundred feet long. It weighed hundreds of tons, and had been folded over on top of the heliport, as if it was made of Styrofoam. A temporary dock had been built, big enough for one of the smaller ships to dock. There was one of them at the dock, and another standing out to sea, waiting.

Our tour guide came on board and told us about the storm damage. She said many small water craft sunk when they were carried far up the hill, and when they returned, filled with water. She said to look back when we went ashore, we would see them under water. Then she told us to look up the mountain. About four hundred feet from the shore, sat a very large sailboat. The area between where the boat rested and the shore had been "scrubbed clean" by the sea surge. She pointed out where buildings stood. They had joined the boats at the bottom of the harbour. As we walked down the ramp, I looked over the side. In the bright Caribbean sun, I could see a lot of rubble and several lovely boats sitting on the bottom. We were told that insurance companies were slow to reimburse hurricane damage. Many people could not afford the high cost of hurricane insurance in such a storm prone area, so some would never be recovered.

As she led us to a bus that would take us to a lodge, where the helicopter was landing temporarily, she said, "As you fly over the island, you will see most of the homes and buildings have a partly orange roof. These structures have lost all or part of the roof to the storms. The orange areas are tarps covering the building, until the roof can be replaced. Although it has been months since the storms came through, the insurance companies have not settled. They keep sending inspectors out to look at the damage, but no settlement has been made yet."

We approached a small bus with a young, pregnant woman driving it. The bus was full, so I wound up sitting in the jump seat beside her. Storm damage was evident all along the one-way, single lane paved road.

"Sure is a lot of storm damage" I commented.

"Yeah... It was especially bad last year," she answered. "One storm, right after another, for a while."

"You must get tired of things being torn apart like this"

"Oh... yes, I guess I do, sometimes. But this is life in the Caribbean. I have never been off the island, so I don't know anything else. This is where I want to raise my baby. I'm content here."

"How do you prepare each time a storm approaches?"

"We just put everything away, and wait it out. I guess a hurricane is something the same to us, as a summer storm is to the rest of the world. The weather is so nice the rest of the year, so storms are just a sort of trade off I guess. I am lucky to have this work. I love what I do and it pays better than most, so I can support my baby. You're from the Norway, aren't you?"

"Yes."

"You're also Canadian"

"How can you tell?"

"I don't know. A certain twang in your voice. I can just tell. You don't have hurricanes there do you?"

"No, just the tail end of some. They usually lose their strength, when they come inland."

"Gets cold there in winter doesn't it."

"Yes, that's why we're here."

"How cold does it get?"

"It can go to thirty below sometimes."

"I'll take the hurricanes."

We had been climbing all this time. Now we started down. This young lady twisted the bus through tight turns and narrow passages, like it was stuck to the road. We passed a large lodge, and then the road levelled out and the bus stopped in a large parking lot, that seemed to be stuck on the side of the hill. I got out and looked up the hill. There was a splendid looking building at the top of a stairway leading up from our location. Another stairway went down to the ocean, far below. A lady stood, leaning on the railing along the edge, with her back to the ocean.

Caroline went over to her and said, "Get laid yet?"

She told us that the helicopter had landed there just before we arrived, but it had to fuel up, so it would be back soon. A man came down the stairway from the lodge and joined her.

The helicopter returned a short while later and it was our turn. We boarded and it took off. We flew directly out to sea, then rose to where we could see the whole island. Most of the buildings had at least part of the roof covered with orange tarps. The pilot told us that the tarps had been loaned from the Home Owners Hurricane Relief Association. The Association was putting pressure on the insurance companies to pay the claims. He felt that settlements would be forthcoming.

He brought us back to the shore, then began to circle the island just above the water. He ducked into a big cove and hovered there, while he told us that this is where Black Beard, the pirate, would hide. Merchant ships, carrying spices and jewels from South America, would come around the point, and Black Beard would be waiting for them. He would simply emerge from hiding and pace his ship beside theirs and board it before much of the crew on the merchant ship even knew he was there. He would capture the crew , unload the merchandise, then tow the ship out to sea, and sink it, to destroy the evidence. The male prisoners he would convert to pirates, or kill them. Any females would be used for the pleasure of his men, until they grew tired of them, then he would have them beheaded. He also took several wives. If they disobeyed, or he grew bored with them, he would give them to his crew, then have them beheaded also.

The same bus met us at the parking lot and took us back to the pier.

The airplane was tied to a makeshift dock. We boarded it almost immediately. I don't know the make of the aircraft, but it had one seat on one side of the aisle, and two on the other. It had twin engines and held about twenty people.

A wind had risen during our helicopter ride, and was now blowing directly into the little bay. The plane floated out to the middle of the bay and turned into the wind. It rolled and bounced like a cork over each wave. I wasn't entirely happy with the situation, but I figured, these guys knew what they were doing, and would not fly if they thought it was dangerous. The pilot and co-pilot seemed unconcerned as we just sat there bouncing around. They both put a hand on the throttle, looked straight ahead, and I heard the pilot say, "This next one."

A huge wave rolled toward us and, just as it reached the front of our pontoons, he pulled the stick back and said, "Now!"

They jabbed that throttle ahead. The engines roared painfully. We rode up the wave and, as we reached the crest, we left the water. We were airborne.

We flew directly out to the Norway and circled it. It sat there like the regal lady it was. The pilot came on the PA.

"For those of you that are not from the Norway, that is it."

We could see the two anchor chains, one from each side of the bow, leading down into the water, and the one from the stern. They were taut holding that seventy-six thousand ton ship still, as the waves rolled around her. We could see the pool on the deck. People on board waved, as the pilot dipped our wings in salute.

We flew out to sea, and soon were over the Island of St. John. We saw the same orange on the roofs, and wind torn damage. We flew around the island and back to St. Thomas, where we flew over the island, high enough to see it all at once.

It was a wonderful ride, but I was a little concerned about how we were going to land in these choppy seas. I watched as they flew very low over our bay, upwind and away from the dock. Then we turned sharply, and kind of fell right on the forward slope of a big wave. The plane sort of glided along the edge of the wave, like a surfer, right into the bay. We had actually surfed in on a big wave.

Caroline and I went shopping, among the many bead and souvenir shops, on the dock. These, mostly makeshift shops, had been erected in order to profit from the cruise passengers. She purchased pail after pail full of loose beads of many sizes and all colours. She also bought balls of string. I asked her why she was buying so many. She told me that she operated a shop in the US and her helpers would thread, these making custom necklaces and bracelets. She does this once a year, and her profit more than covers her holiday expenses. This way, her holiday is also deductible.

I watched and talked to a large red-headed man who was having his moustache braided, while Caroline had her hair braided into little tiny braids with beads in them, and then we caught the last tender back to the Norway.

On my way to the dining room that evening, I found a couple on the stairway dressed in line dance outfits. It was obvious that not all was well. He was holding her tenderly, and when she looked up, I saw that her face was almost green. The Norway has a deep V hull and normally doesn't sway at all, but the seas were a bit rough, and I could feel a slight sideways shudder now and then. Apparently this, along with the constant forward motion, was enough to make this lady seasick. He explained that they were part of a line dance competition. She started to cry and nestled her head into his chest. A crewmember came along just then. He went to the doctor's station for medication. I went on to dinner.

Talk was lively at the table that night. The lady who gambles, had won even more that day, while the rest of us were ashore. She now had a good bundle and was high-spirited.

Delia came by our table, as we finished dessert, to go with me to the Will Rogers Follies at the Saga Theatre. She joined in the laughter, and then we left for the theatre. The show was wonderful. We then hurried to the Pool Deck, where the line dancing competition was underway. The costumes were beautiful and the dancing was precise. During a break, the couple I had seen earlier came over to our table. The medication had worked and the sea was calmer, so she was fine now and they were enjoying the evening. They had a drink with us and went back onto the floor. We danced to the music of DJ Roseann Richardson for a while. I saw Caroline across the room. She pointed to a handsome young man, about half her age, who was with her, and gave me the okay sign. I never saw her again the rest of the cruise.

At midnight, we went to the Great Outdoor Restaurant for the Country and Western buffet. You guessed it, hamburgers, and hot dogs were the main course, but there were other delicious entrees as well. Always a redneck I had several burgers with lots of onion and chips with gravy.

Life was good.

<u>Thursday, January 18 1996:</u> A Day at Sea.

Evening attire: Formal. Drink of the Day: Blue Coral. Please turn your timepieces back on hour before retiring tonight.

We are now heading north west toward the Norwegian Cruise Lines own Great Stirrup Cay. We had 863 nautical miles to cover, so we were travelling faster then we had so far this voyage. I looked out over the ocean. It was evident that we were moving fast. According to the paper, I got on my bridge tour, we were sailing along at 20.9 knots.

I spent most of the day shopping at the on board shops. I bought a nice Wittnauer watch at the duty free and some photos at the photo shop. Went to my cabin and added up my on-board credit account. Wow, that adds up fast. I got my receipts and papers ready for customs, saw Delia a couple of times, had a drink at Checkers Cabaret. With so many women around, I was never alone. I would sit at a bar and company would always show up on the barstool beside me.

I heard that the lady at my table had won big at the Norway Downs Horseracing game, at The North Cape Lounge, so I went there and had a congratulatory drink with her and some of her friends.

At 10:30, Delia and I met at the Saga Theatre for the show "Sea Legs Goes to Hollywood." Then we went to the Internationale Deck for the French Gala Buffet. The display of food was presented in a variety of Caribbean shapes and patterns. It was so beautiful that, between 11.30 and midnight, we were not allowed to touch it. The display was there to be admired and photographed. Then everyone dipped in and ate. It seemed a shame to ruin something that took so much skill to create.

<u>Friday, January 19 1996:</u> The Great Stirrup Cay.

Evening attire: Casual. Drink of the day: Red Snapper.

I knew that we were still moving fast when I climbed the stairs for breakfast. I went onto the promenade and looked out. It was partly sunny much as it had been for the whole week. We were indeed moving along at a good pace.

I went to breakfast and then back to my cabin for another look at the Cruise News. Early tender ticket distribution was scheduled for 8:00 to 9:00 at Club Internationale, and there was an important debarkation briefing in the North Cape Lounge at 9:00. The first tender to the island was not until noon, so I attended these things, then just browsed around the ship.

I was standing at the rail on the starboard side, when I noticed the forward thrust start to decrease. On the horizon, I could barely make out the land, some ten miles away. We moved towards it, until I could see two rock type formations sticking up out of the water, and beyond them land.

We came to a full stop and things began to happen fast. The sound of chain was evident, both fore and aft, and crew members started to lower the tenders. I went forward and watched the mighty cranes lift, swing, and lower the tenders over the side of the bow.

The engines of one of the tenders began to hum, and they pulled it around to the gangway on the starboard side. Gangways were set in place and trolleys of food and drink were loaded immediately.

The PA system came to life, calling out tender numbers. Mine wasn't called this time, so I watched as people came out of the side of the ship below, and filled the tender. The other tender was waiting nearby, and pulled into place as soon as the first one cleared. This time my number was called, so I made my way to the gangway.

As we approached the island, I could see that we were landing on a beach that curved gently around to our right. On the left was a point of land that protected the beach from any waves that could upset the tranquility of the bay. The sand was white, the water as clear as white wine. When we got closer, and the engine of the tender died down, I could hear the sound of a limbo band in the tiny band shell. A barbeque was sending smoke up into a still midday sky. To my left were three, very muscular young men, tossing a well-tanned young lady, with long black hair, over their shoulders into the water. She was as brown as a berry, wearing a fluorescent orange thong bikini. I could have covered everything that swimsuit covered with my left palm - and wanted to!

Life was good.

They lowered the front ramp of the tender, and gently drove it into the soft sand. Then, with a slow forward trust of the engine, they held it there, until we had all disembarked.

Great Stirrup Cay is a small Island in the Bahamas. Norwegian Cruise Lines own it. There is no potable water available, so it's only habitants are lizards, and seagulls. Beautiful coral reefs are evident just below the water, not far from the beach, and extend above the water in places. Palm trees sway in the gentle eighty degree breeze.

NCL built a few small buildings, to accommodate their passengers. The washrooms and another building were the only ones with walls. The remainder was just a roof supported with poles. A tender is left on the island. It brings natives from nearby islands, to sell their wares. They sell the ever present beads, T-Shirts, towels, and souvenirs.

Towels were provided at the gangway as we left the ship, to be returned when we came back. Beach chairs, a bar, and a barbeque were brought from the ship. When the last tender leaves everything is gone but the tender and the little buildings. The seagulls are alone again.

Not being a swimmer, I enjoyed the day eating hamburgers and hot dogs at the barbeque, chatting with people, looking over the wares for sale, watching native women braid beads into people's hair, and watching that young lady, as she went headfirst over those guys' shoulders, time and again. Hamburgers, hot dogs, beer, and well-built, nearly-naked women. This is redneck paradise.

There was a sign pointing to a pathway. It read, "Light house." I walked along this path for a distance. On both sides, the vegetation was very thick. You could not leave the path any more than ten feet. This wasn't very interesting so I went back to watching the young lady.

They began to dismantle the equipment and pile things unto the tender so I caught it, and returned to the ship at 4.30.

At some point during the cruise, Shirley Hullman, my cruise consultant, had informed me that the plane from Miami to Toronto was going to be one seat short. She had asked me if I would mind taking a later flight. I had said okay, but wondered what I would do to spend the time while waiting for my flight. I looked at the Cruise News and the answer was there, on the right hand page.

7:30-9:00: Shore excursion desk open for final transactions and the purchase of Miami Scenic Tours and airport transfers.

I got ready for dinner, went to the International Deck, and booked the tour.

During dinner, I learned that the lady who gambled all the time, had actually wound up with enough winnings to pay for her cruise, pay her on board credit and had some left over.

After dinner, I met Delia at North Cape lounge for the Neal McCoy show. He put on a wonderful performance and after came down and danced with various ladies. He is a very personable guy.

We went to the Latin American Farewell Buffet in the Leeward Dining Room, and then I walked her to her cabin, where we said good-bye, believing it would be for the last time.

Saturday, January 20 1996: Miami

My cabin was on the Biscayne (water level) deck to the stern. I had become accustomed to the sound of the engines, they didn't bother my sleep at all. I woke this morning around 4:30 to a different sound. This was not the usual steady hum, but a humming buzz, then silence, another buzz then a distant buzz. I thought for a moment, and then it came to me. I had been told during the bridge tour, the ship has side thrusters, 3 in the bow and 2 in the stern. There are also bridge wings. These are smaller versions of the bridge, that hang over the side, with some of the same instruments and controls. These are used, in combination with the thrusters, to turn the ship in port and hold it against the dock, until land lines are in place. I thought, "Wow, we are in port, and I can run up and watch them turn this thing." I went to the bathroom and noticed that there was no sound at all. I realized I was too late, so I went back to sleep.

We had been told to put our luggage outside our cabin door this morning so I did that and went to a disembarkation seminar, scheduled at the North Cape Lounge at 7:00. On my way, I looked out over the side. We were docked. I looked down at the pier. Cargo doors were open and trucks of all descriptions were coming and going from them. Fork lifts and loaders were buzzing around like ants.

I went on to the seminar. There were a lot of people there already, but it hadn't started yet. Dottie Kulasa, the cruise director, appeared on stage and stepped up to the microphone. She just started with her canned speech, "Good morning everyone, I hope you enjoyed your cruise," when a crewmember came from behind and interrupted her. She handed Dottie a small blue book, spoke to her briefly, then disappeared.

Dottie turned to us and said, "I have just been handed this little book. Apparently, it has been found somewhere on board. Does anyone recognize it?" She held it above her head.

"Nobody? Okay let's look inside and see if we can find an owner." She turned a few pages then said, "Oh. It's someone's diary." She turned another page. "A lady's diary."

"Let's see if something inside will remind someone." She turned a page and read.

"*Saturday: Boarded ship in Miami, got settled, watched the ship leave dock, had a delicious dinner, toured the ship, retired early.*" She turned a page and read on.

"*Sunday: At sea today. Attended the Captain's welcome party. He is a very handsome man. He seemed to take an interest in me. Attended some very nice shows. Had a wonderful day.*"

"*Monday: At sea all day, looked at some things in the shops, played some slots, went to a show, as I joined the conga line on the pool deck tonight, the captain joined immediately behind me. He asked me to join him in his cabin after for a drink. I refused politely, and retired. Had a nice day.*"

"*Tuesday: Went ashore at St. Maarten. Had a wonderful time there. I was sitting enjoying the music of DJ Roseann Richardson, on the pool deck this evening, when the captain appeared at my table. He bought me a drink and asked me to dance. He is good looking and dances divinely. He said he had some art in his cabin he wanted me to see. I refused and retired.*"

"*Wednesday: Went ashore at St. Thomas. Very interesting. Purchased some things ashore and returned. As I was enjoying some music and a drink at the Pool deck this evening, the Captain appeared again. He asked me to dance. He brushed my check with a kiss, and asked me to accompany him to his cabin to see the view from there. When I refused, he got quite frustrated and left. Retired. Had a good day.*"

"*Thursday: At sea again. Browsed around the ship. Lay by the pool. I was having a drink and listening to some country favourites at Checkers Cabaret late this evening when the captain appeared. He was very sincere when he asked me to join him. He is a very handsome man and I was lonely, so it was hard to refuse him, but I did. Hurt showed on his face. He said that he wanted me badly and if he couldn't have me he would scuttle the ship drowning all 2543 passenger and 920 crew.*" I felt guilty as he shuffled away with his head down. He is such a nice man and it must be lonely being the captain.

"*Friday: Went ashore at Great Stirrup Cay. What a beautiful island. Went to the Latin American Farewell buffet. Then I saved the lives of 3463 people. Having a wonderful time.*"

When the laughter died down Dottie continued her instructions.

"Your luggage will be piled in bunches, in a shelter, on the pier, sorted as much as possible, according to your cabin numbers. You are to locate your luggage and, if it is not all there, try to find any missing pieces and put it all together. If there are any pieces in your pile that don't belong to you separate it immediately, then stand beside it. There will be a dog arrive called 'Benjie'. He will have two of his friends with him. If Benjie shows any interest in your luggage you had better hope he pees on it, because if he doesn't, you will be in a lot of trouble with his friends. One of the officers will have a cane like stick in his hands. When Benjie is happy, the officer will tap your pile with his stick. Those of you who are US citizens, will then take your luggage to a desk marked 'customs'. Others will go to one marked 'buses'. Bus drivers will take your luggage from there and take you to the airport, where a guide will direct you to your airline registration desk. You will not see your luggage again, until you claim it at your home airport. Thank you for travelling with us and hope to see you on another cruise soon."

I went to my cabin and packed my carry-on, then disembarked by the same gangway I had used to board a week before. I went to the area of the pier where the luggage was to be. I joined some people already there behind a rope . Forklifts were buzzing in and out of a cargo door, carrying sided pallets full of luggage. They would drop a full one beside some workers unloading them, then take an empty one back into the bowels of the ship.

When this operation was finished, the rope was lowered and we went into the compound. I found my pile without much trouble. It was all there, so I leaned against a pole nearby and waited. Benjie, a good-sized, angry looking bulldog, entered the area with his friends. They were big and armed and, in comparison, Benjie looked the friendliest. He wandered around the rows of suitcases, came to mine, sniffed it for a minute, peed on the pole and left. They tapped my luggage, and I carried it to the desk marked 'buses'. The people ahead of me were putting their luggage on a low platform, behind the desk, and luggage handlers were putting it on various buses parked just beyond, according to the airline on which the owners were travelling. I told the woman that I was taking the Miami tour, and a handler said, "Follow me." We went to a bus parked at the back of the line. Neal McCoy's two buses were loading back there.

I was sitting there in the bus, looking back toward the pier. What I saw was amazing. On the pier, there were all kinds of trucks and transports, wheeling around and backing up to a ramp, leading into the side of the Norway. There were meat trucks, bread and pastry trucks, cooking oil, flour, egg, and fuel. You name it, there was a truck there carrying it. A loader was diving into the ship, returning with a bucketful of brown sand, and depositing it unto a tractor-trailer dump truck. This as what was left of the garbage and sewage incinerated during our trip.

The organization required to have this vessel restocked, ready for sailing again within hours, is beyond my imagination.

I went on the tour. I would not recommend that to anyone. It was a boring day, to say the least. We went around the city, had a lunch, and then the bus let me off at the airport.

Now, this is where my intelligence really shows. No one but me could ever get himself into such a mess as I did at the Miami airport that day. It is a good thing that this was before the terrorist attacks in 2001, because, if it were after, I am sure I would have been shot on the spot, my luggage taken out to the desert and blown up without any further investigation.

I arrived at the final boarding desk with all my luggage in hand. My luggage hadn't been scanned or checked. I hadn't passed through the metal detectors, and my ticket hadn't been processed. I had no boarding pass.

I had gone through a simple passageway door, above which was a small sign that read "Air Canada." The door was a small one, that appeared as though it should be locked, but it wasn't. I walked along the hallway, then I saw a small sign on a door that read, "Loading Lounge." I pressed the latch, went through the door with a great deal of flurry, and the door closed and locked behind me. There was no handle on the inside of the door, just a keyhole. I looked around, and there I was in the loading lounge. A planeload of people was looking at me, as if I had just arrived from Mars, and you cannot blame them. This idiot had just popped through the wall, with his luggage.

I started looking for the luggage check desk, but all I could see was the final boarding desk. The sign indicated that the next flight was indeed mine, but things weren't right. I sat down for a minute and tried to figure out how I came to be here like this.

A little later, a ground hostess came to the desk and started to prepare for loading. I went over to her. She looked at me, looked at my luggage, and said, "What are you doing here like that."

"I really don't know, lady; I just came through that door over there."

"I had better get security."

Oh yeah, people are really going to laugh, when they hear on the news that I have been jailed for trying to smuggle hot luggage on board an aircraft in Miami. Here I was in the middle of an airport, where attempts to smuggle drugs are detected regularly, with luggage that had not been processed at the loading desk. Well done!

Two security officers showed up immediately. They were not happy with the whole situation. When I showed them the door through which I had arrived, they took me over to it. One of them opened it with a key and went through. She returned, and said to the other officer, "He's right, it wasn't locked." She turned to me and said, "That first door you went through? It should have been locked. Someone left it unsecured." I was attracting a great deal of attention from everyone in the lounge.

My luggage and I returned to where we should have gone and started the whole process over. I was thoroughly scanned, my luggage was thoroughly scanned, and my ticket was processed, but the luggage compartments had been already closed for the flight, so mine couldn't be loaded in the regular way. The guards gave me a form to give the loading clerk, put some special tags on my things, and took me back to the lounge.

The call came, "Passengers needing assistance to load will board now." Then, another call. "The flight will be delayed, as a flight scheduled for Montreal is experiencing mechanical inspection difficulty, and the passengers may have to be transferred to this flight." I had a Trentway Wagar airport shuttle limousine meeting me in Toronto. I had already rescheduled it, when I found I was going on a later flight. Now I was going to be late.

In forty-five minutes, some workers came from the other flight, and we started to board. When I arrived at the boarding desk, the girl took the form and wrote out another. Giving me half, she said, "Give that to the flight attendant at the door of the plane."

When I arrived at the door, the attendant said, as she reached for the form, "So you're Mr. Miller. I have heard about you." I always thought it would be nice to be recognized, but not for being an idiot. "Put your things right there by the door." She stepped ahead and pointed to an area behind her.

"It won't get left behind or lost, will it," I asked.

"No, Mr. Miller. Your luggage will be as safe on this flight as it ever will be on any flight. Believe me."

"Where will I be able to claim it, in Toronto?"

"It will be right at the carousel." I thought, ' yes, with a big sign on it reading "IDIOT."'

The flight was very fast. We landed in Toronto just minutes behind schedule. I went to the carousel and she was right. Sitting right beside it was my luggage. The other luggage had not even begun to come down yet. I gathered it up, went through customs before anyone else, and found the Trentway limo was waiting for a lady to arrive from the Bahamas anyway. I arrived in Peterborough a little after midnight. What a trip. What a day. Anyway, my cat was glad to see me.

Statistics of the SS Norway

The keel was laid in 1957 in St. Nazaire France. She was launched on May 11th, 1960, as the SS France, a trans-Atlantic passenger vessel.

Due to the high operating and maintenance cost and increasing competition from airlines, she was taken out of commission and moored in Le-Havre, France, in 1974.

Norwegian Caribbean Line purchased her for $18 million, (scrap value), and invested another $130 million to refurbish her and convert her into a Caribbean cruise ship. She was launched in May of 1980 as the SS Norway.

She weighed 76,049 tons, was 1,035 feet long, and had a beam of 111 feet. She had 65,000 square feet of open deck space. (This would be equal to nine city building lots each 65x110 feet. If you were to lay all 14 decks out, end-to-end, you would have over 100 building lots, 65x110 feet. In other words, a subdivision could be built on board the Norway).

Five diesel generators, plus six steam turbines, generated 25,000 kilowatts of electricity. This would be enough to power a city of 30,000 people. (So you could also power up your subdivision on board).

It had three forward anchors, (one is auxiliary), and one aft. The forward anchors weighed 15 tons each, and the aft anchor weighed 7 ton. Each link of the anchor chains weighed 250 pounds.

The propellers were 18 feet wide and weighed 18 tons each. The shaft that drove each one was 2 feet in diameter and 540 feet long.

She converted 850 tons of seawater to fresh water each day and had a fresh water-holding tank of 2,400 tons.

Garbage was separated for incineration or taken ashore for recycling.

There were 7 firefighting teams on board, as well as 4,000 smoke detectors. Five professional firefighters trained the crew regularly.

She carried two, custom made, going-ashore tenders on her bow, "Little Norway I," and" Little Norway II",. Each weighed 72 tons, was 87 feet long, and held 450 passengers. The captains of these boats had to have a sea-going captain's license.

Her maximum passenger capacity was 2,560, and approximately 900 crew.

Deck Department	56
Engine Department	79
Purser Department	17
Doctors	2
Nurses	3
Dining Room Staff	152
Chefs and Cooks	168
Bar Department	60
Gift Shop Department	24
Hotel Department	197
Cruise staff/Entertainment	83
Spa/Saunas	21
Casino	34
Photo	7
Laundry	17 total 920.

We travelled 2189 nautical miles during the week at sea. The average depth of the water was 10,000 feet, with the deepest being The Puerto Rican trench at 26,200 feet.

We burned 200 tons of crude oil a day. This is 33 feet per gallon or 31 gallons to move the ship its own length. (Almost the same as my Dodge Ram!)

On May 25th 2003, she returned from a weeklong cruise and, after the usual tight squeeze turn, she settled against the pier in Miami at 5:00 a.m. Cargo doors opened and gangways were lowered into place. Two hours later, as the 2135 passengers aboard were beginning to wake and prepare to disembark, an explosion occurred in the boiler room. Crewmembers were blown through an open cargo door and into the water. Over twenty were injured. Four died immediately. Reports were that up to seven died. All passengers were evacuated safely. There was initial fear of terrorist action, but that was quickly ruled out.

On June 27th 2003, the magnificent vessel, that had provided such memorable vacations for thousands of people, left her home port of Miami under tow, with no destination announced. She had run up a dock fee of $284,000.00 and had to leave the dock. Eighty-five crewmembers were aboard, as she disappeared over the eastern horizon.

On July 21st ,after three weeks at sea, Norwegian Cruise Lines announced that she was laying up at Lloyd Werft in Bremerhaven, Germany for repairs.

On September 25th 2003, after many delays in repair schedules, and no indication of further service, it was rumoured that she would be used as a hotel in Amsterdam.

As of this writing March 5th 2004, I know of no further plans for her future.

I enjoyed my week on the Norway. It provided me with a 'time out' from a very troubled period in my life. Once again, as with my memories of Cutler, when I heard that the ship was no longer in active service, I felt that a piece of my life had been taken away.

I Have Reached the Top

The cruise was over, and although it provided a respite from my lonely life, I found myself falling into a rut. Every day was a carbon copy of the one before: Have breakfast; wait for the mail; watch the same talk and variety shows on television; cook dinner; watch more TV; and go to bed.

Delia came to visit me during the summer, which broke the monotony for a few days.

I went to everything in the way of entertainment , but not being able to drive, my choices were very limited. I went to the Peterborough Fair, and attended most of the 'Festival of Lights' shows in Crary park, but there was always the walk both ways. I had a bus pass, but I wonder if the people who operate the city bus system, realise just how difficult it really is to use the buses after six. Some of the top officials would be well advised to try a trip across town sometime.

I took a bus trip to Branson, Missouri, another to the Agawa Canyon, but I was always alone.

I still had some money left, from the sale of our house on Stocker Road. I started to put a sound system business together. I called it Surround Sound Services and began to collect music on CDs and tapes. This took some of my time but it was difficult to get anywhere when, I couldn't drive myself.

I wanted to be able to make a list of the music I had, so I purchased my first computer from a lady on the upper floor of my building. It was a Compaq. I spent a lot of time learning how to run this ignorant thing, but I finally got the hang of it, and eventually wrote a program that would list my song titles in alphabetical order, using DOS. When Scott saw what I had created he said, "You're good at this Dad. Why don't you take some of the money you have left and buy yourself a new computer? You could get on the 'net then. I think you would enjoy that."

I went to Radio Shack, in Peterborough Square, and purchased an IBM Aptiva, and a cheap computer desk. It was delivered that night. It only took me one evening to completely screw that up, but the guy who answered the 1-800- number at IBM, very patiently lead me along the path to recovery. I think I crashed that contraption only 16 times, before I learned how to run it in a manner that it would accept!

I found a program on it that would play music. I ripped a couple of CDs onto the hard drive, and found that was all the 2 GB drive would hold. I really wanted to have the computer play songs at any family DJ gig I might get, so I went to a store on Simcoe Street, opposite the bus terminal, called 'Phantom Leap', and ordered the biggest hard drive available at the time. It was 8 GB. When it arrived, I got up enough nerve to open the computer and install the additional drive. I spent three days trying to tell this piece of hi-tech machinery it had a second drive. It flatly refused to listen. Then it crashed, and I had to format the whole damned thing for the 17th time. When it came up again, it proudly announced that it now had a 'C' and a 'D' drive. I typed in, "I told you that three days ago."

Delia invited me to her place for Christmas and congratulated me on my great computer skills when I told her the story. I had a good holiday there and returned to my lonely existence.

I found a program that would assemble resumes and other documents, so I created some letterhead. That was fine but, it didn't look too good when I printed it on the old dot matrix printer that I bought with the Compaq. I went to Radio Shack and purchased a new printer. I got that all connected and printed a letterhead. I was thrilled to be able to do this as I had always wanted to have my own letterhead ever since the 'Ray Miller Heating' days.

I heard there was a committee formed to raise $1.9 million, to build a heart catheter lab in Peterborough. Having had this procedure, and feeling it saved my life, I got very interested, and wanted to help. I got the bright idea to play music, for some fundraising dances, with my new equipment. I made up a proposal and printed it out. I looked in the newspaper and found that there was an office on George Street North, so I went there with my proposal. The receptionist looked it over, took me to an office in the back and introduced me to a girl named Lisa. She got quite excited, and encouraged me.

I went back home, and gave my project the name, 'Here's to Your Heart Dances', and started to call community centres and dance halls, all through Peterborough, Victoria, and Haliburton Counties. Some places gave me the hall for a reduced rate, but others had set a price, and that was it. Some offered to help me with a lunch and bar, and others wouldn't. I wound up hosting a dance at Cambray Community Centre, where I received good support, Minden, where I had to call on my friends Ron, and Shirley Cox to help me, and Stanhope, where I received the most help of all. David and Darlene Johnson were wonderful.

For transportation to Cambray, I had to hire a cartage company. Grenville Harrison took me to Minden, and Mervin Cowan trucked me to Stanhope. I wound up making a small amount for the cause, but nothing substantial. During all this stress, I had an emotional relapse, and fell out with Delia.

1999 is not a year that I like to recall. I put my sound equipment up for sale at Wayne's Music World on George Street.

I was terribly lonely and turned to the internet for entertainment and companionship. I put my personal profile on every match-making site I could find, no matter what it represented. This led to contacts that led to dishonesty and betrayal. I corresponded with a few decent people, but most were not good. I entered into a relationship with a woman in Orangeville. She was English and had three sons. That only lasted six weeks. Then I moved in with my sister Hazel in Minden. I was an emotional mess. I was bordering on a breakdown again. Hazel helped a lot. We both tried our best to get along, but there was too much difference in our ages and lifestyle.

I took counselling again. I knew I needed someone who could cope with my relapses, and would understand and love me enough to see me through them. I knew I didn't have a hope in hell of finding such a person.

My application for rental accommodation at Staanworth Seniors Apartments in Minden, was accepted, and I moved there after only ten weeks at Hazel's. Hazel, Murray and Mabel, helped me get my possessions from storage in Carnarvon,. I tried to settle in.

The same routine started again. I watched TV constantly. Late in December Tom Prentice began to flood the racetrack for 'Car Racing on Ice' at the fairgrounds next door, and I would watch the truck on the track and wish I could drive tractor-trailer again, but I knew I would never even drive a car. This depressed me and I would turn back to TV.

I placed a personal ad on the internet noting that I had been born in Minden, but had been away from the area, and had returned recently.

After Christmas, I started to go to Minden United Church every Sunday. They were planning to upgrade the sound system, and I offered to help. The church's sound person and I looked the existing equipment over and decided what was needed. On February 29th 2000, I caught a bus to Peterborough, and purchased the necessary components from Wayne's Music World. I returned that night, to find an email from a lady saying she had seen my ad "everywhere" on the internet. She had recently been widowed and wondered if I knew 'the Kelletts'. She was curious as I sounded like someone she knew.

I answered, "Do I know the Kelletts? Lady I was born with them all around me like bad weather."

She answered, "Do you know Glen and Craig?"

"Yes, I do, I know Glen and Craig, and Doug and Sonny, and about a million more. I was best friends with Gareth when we were young."

Emails flew back and forth until midnight. I learned that her name was Caryl, she had three sons, two here, and one in England. We decided to phone each other. She told me her husband had passed away, just a year before, and she lived near Eagle Lake. She wanted to meet me as much as I wanted to meet her, so we set up a meeting for next day at my place. I told her that I was going to install the new sound equipment at the church and she offered to drive me there.

She rang doorbell the next morning and I answered. I unlocked the security door and headed down the hall. As I turned the corner, she was coming toward me. She tossed her head back and said, "I think I do know you. Are you sure you are not a Kellett, you look like them?" She laughed. I was a little flattered, as I have always considered the Kelletts to be good looking guys, but I replied, "No, but I was around them so much, when I was young, some looks may have rubbed off."

We loaded the sound equipment into her car and went to the church, where she helped me with the installation and testing. Then she took me to her place, where I met her two dogs, Purdy, and Lucy, and six cats, Maggie, Buffy, Ginny, Ernie, Harry, and WYSIWYG, (What You See Is What You Get). We had dinner, chatted for a while and she took me home.

I phoned Mabel and told her that I had met a really nice lady, she is from England, and has three sons. Mabel said, remembering my relationship in Orangeville, Turn around, and run like hell,".

Caryl and I were together, most of the time, from then on. We went to the ice car races where we stood on the frozen snow bank, in a very cold north wind, and watched her two sons race. Then I met them both. Andy was from Toronto, and Daniel from Gelert

When I told her of my emotional instability, she said, "We will overcome that in time love." She had a little trouble understanding the first relapse, then said, "This is what you are talking about when you say you have a problem, isn't it?" I sobbed and nodded. She held me tightly in her arms, and said, "Never mind poppet, I understand now. This is not you. We are going to be okay." I knew I had found that one in a million. I loved her deeply, and have ever since. I had a few more problems, but instead of condemnation and lack of understanding, I received love and praise. I no longer have relapses.

At this point, I met a man who is the epitome of life's 'other side'. He lives across the road from us enjoying a lifestyle many would not believe still exists in the modern world. Bob Johnson manages to survive, and is content with, a life very few could even begin to envision. With no sanitation or indoor plumbing, he carries water from a spring below a hill, and uses an outhouse. He cooks and heats his home with wood, he has a limited number of hydro outlets. Deafened by years of operating an air hammer drilling rock, and knocked about by life, relationships, and social inequality, he has chosen to let the world pass him by. One would expect a depressed and self-pitying attitude from a man such as this, but Bob never complains. He is honest as the sun. I have loaned him money, back when he found it difficult to stretch a meagre pension to the end of the month, and he always paid me back on the very day he received his next cheque. Unsupervised he would give you an hours' work for an hours' pay, and finish with a smile. He recently had open-heart surgery and is fighting back admirably. I am proud to point him out as one of my friends.

Caryl and I flew to Barbados in March 2000. This was a wonderful adventure. We walked on the beach where we held hands in the moonlight and watched the sand crabs walk sideways into the surf. We shopped, and explored the island by taxi. We went to a private beach, where I went to sleep in the sun and received horrendous sunburn. We took a helicopter ride and waved to the people on the ship, 'Jolly Roger." They were having a wonderful time. It is rumoured that they take on a supply of rum, and stay at sea until it is all gone. It appeared they were working on an early return.

I gave my apartment up in June of 2000 and moved in with Caryl.

Caryl's late husband had purchased a trailer at a yard sale. It had a solid iron frame and the wheels were in good working order, but it needed re-wooding badly. One day I bought some plywood and began the job. Our little dog, Lucy, was barking her head off. I said to Caryl, "What in hell is that dog barking at?"

"Well, you see, Lucy is on tiger patrol, and she is doing a fine job. There hasn't been a tiger on the property since she started. However, Lucy has never seen a tiger, so she barks at everything. That way if there ever is a tiger, she has it covered."

Later that afternoon, while Caryl was in town, I stood the plywood sides of the trailer on edge and cut two inch round openings in the sides to attach tie-down straps. When she returned, she said that it looked like something to keep animals in.

"It's a box to keep Lucy's tigers in, if she ever catches any," I said. We called the trailer 'the tiger box', after that.

Caryl's son Daniel, and his fiancée Tammy, were to be married in our garden in August 2001. We were looking for a disc jockey for their wedding. This required a kind of sound system that no local DJ offered. We were in Radio Shack in Bracebridge when I saw a mixer for sale. I had experience with that particular model and knew it was a good one. We decided to buy it, some speakers, and do the wedding ourselves. We went to Wayne's Music World in Peterborough, and discovered that two of the speakers I had owned were still in the store. We bought them, an amplifier, some wire, and a microphone from Wayne.

We were to fly to England in July 2001, to attend Caryl's nephew's wedding, when I received an invitation from Scott. He and Kaoru would be getting married while we were away. It was a welcome letter, but we had already booked everything for our flight to England. Scott and Kaoru understood, and met us at the hotel in Toronto, the night before our flight. We had dinner and a great evening. I was thrilled to meet his delightful fiancée for the first time.

Our flight to England was exciting for me. I would be going to where the soldiers had been during the war, but my trip over the Atlantic would last only six hours, theirs took days.

We flew from Toronto to Montreal, where they changed flight crews. A very large blonde flight attendant came on board there. She was really well proportioned.. I shrunk down in my seat by the window. Caryl noticed me and said, "What is the matter?"

"That blonde could hurt me," I said.

"Don't worry poppet, I am here, and I won't let her hurt you.. Actually, I think she is pregnant," she continued.

"Only because she wants to be," I said.

We flew through the night. It seemed strange to fly into the next day. I changed my watch to the other zone. I raised the blind on the aircraft window as the sun came up. I witnessed a sight I had never seen before. The sun was on the horizon where it was clear. We were above the clouds, so the sun shone up through the clouds.

The engines cut back, and the plane changed attitude. I knew we were approaching Gatwick Airport.

As we came in low over the shoreline and I got my first look at Europe. I thought, "My God, the whole of England needs a paint job." I was to learn, as I spent the next two weeks in the land of "lorry, loo, tip, bloke, and poppet," that the sun never shines long enough in England to dry paint. When a ray of sun breaks through the clouds, everyone rushes outside to enjoy it.

We landed, and I escaped without any harm from the big blonde. We retrieved our luggage and went to our rented car. When we got to the car, the steering wheel was on the wrong side! We got in and pulled out on the street. Not only were we driving on the wrong side of the road, but also we were trotting along at a jolly good pace. We came to a four-lane highway, and I was relieved to see that they too were driving on the wrong side of the road. There was no cloverleaf, or approach lane, just cars whizzing past at about ninety miles an hour. Finally, there was a break in traffic and Caryl floored it.

After I retrieved my head from the back seat, I grabbed the panic strap, and looked around. A hedge was flying past the mirror, on my side at about one hundred miles an hour. It was so close, there was actually a slot along the hedge, right where the mirror travelled. I looked past Caryl and there was the safety rail of a lorry, right against the window. Mere feet in front of us was another car, and a lorry loomed in the rear window. I wanted to go home. I wanted my Mommy!

Next, we came upon a 'roundabout'. People simply drive into these things at great speed, and go around and around, until they are dizzy and fall off. When we fell off, Caryl claimed that she was "exactly where she wanted to be", but then, she always says that when she tries to back up a trailer, so who knows. In all fairness, these things do actually work well, if everyone knows what they are doing. They handle traffic through intersections, without stopping or even slowing down very much

Then suddenly the hedge disappeared, and for a brief moment, I could see across the countryside. Rolling green fields stretched out for miles, with hedges dividing them. I was just beginning to enjoy that when the hedge returned, so suddenly it scared me.

Realizing I would never see my kids again, I laid my head back, and waited for the end.

We left the throughway and drove into the town of Dorking, where Caryl had rented a 'quaint little medieval cottage', on the internet. This was a prime example of a town that had grown too fast. The streets, although busy, were very narrow.

We found the cottage and parked in a small, short-term, parking lot. We unloaded the luggage. We walked to the cottage and she unlocked the door. I walked right into the top of the door frame. A lump appeared on the top of my head, reminiscent of the ones on the back, from the flail years before. She brought the car from the parking lot and she parked that thing, with the mirror no more than three inches from the cottage wall. The wheels on the other side were on the sidewalk. The street was only nine feet wide, for two-way traffic. Safe at last, I found a sofa and went to sleep.

Caryl woke me at suppertime. We walked around the corner and ate at a nice restaurant. Then we went shopping for groceries. We went through another doorway at which I received yet another lump, then up very narrow stairs, to the bedroom. I slept like a log.

I awoke to the smell of toast and coffee. While I was enjoying the meal, I reached up and found I could touch the ceiling, while I was sitting. It was at this point I realized I was sitting in a cottage that was older then Canada itself. The walls of this little house were originally built in Roman times. The town was also many hundreds of years old.

During the week, we went to London, and rode the double-decker buses. I got a glimpse of the Queen Mother and her little entourage of motorcycle outriders. We went to Littlehampton, and I met Caryl's son Rick and Francesca, and her triplet girls, Lucy, Bella, and Nina. What a pleasant time that was. We also visited Caryl's house in Carshalton.

We left the little cottage, after a wonderful week. Although I was bent and bruised, I am glad I had the experience.

The drive north to Sutton Coldfield, where Caryl's sister Lindy, and her husband Mike live, was not nearly as frightening as before. I was beginning to get used to high speeds, and narrow roads. I was also beginning to accept driving on the other side of the road.

There we got involved with the preparations for the wedding. Weddings are different in England. The bride's parents lived in a beautiful Elizabethan home. This home is registered as a heritage or 'listed' building. That means that the owner cannot renovate in any way that would change the appearance or structure of the original building. If they must change a brick, or anything else, it has to be aged to appear to be original, and the work must be done under the scrutiny of inspectors.

Behind their home was a very large white tent. It was lined with lace, draped across the ceiling, and down the walls. It was stunning.

It was not far from the bride's parent's home to the church, so the bride, all the bridesmaids, together with the guests, walked along the village street. Cars stopped to let us pass, nodded, and honked their horns in approval. We stopped at a pub, where other guests were waiting. That is where I enjoyed my first lager and lime, which I affectionately refer to as a 'limey beer'.

When we left the pub, the procession was a large crowd. We walked to a very old church. In the grounds was a tree, believed to be hundreds of years old. The huge limbs were tied together with chains and cables, and propped with rails to hold it from splitting. Robin Hood is reported to have married Maid Marion under that very tree.

Caryl and I on our way to the wedding.

I sat in the church during the ceremony, and looked at the structure. The walls were two feet thick, of solid stone, finished inside and out. They say the construction stretched over several generations. Workers died, and their sons took over, before it was completed.

A lovely meal was served, in the tent, after the wedding, and the evening was a lot of fun for all.

We boarded a train for Wales. We had hoped to meet Caryl's grandchildren, but to no avail. Owing to a lack of communication, we missed them, but their mother called that night and said she would bring them to the airport the next day, so they could have a visit. She did, and we spent an enjoyable time with Colin and Donna.

I looked back, as the plane roared down the runway. I had enjoyed two weeks of adventure. I felt the lumps on my head from the low cottage doors and ceilings. They were almost bearable to touch. I looked the crew over. There was no sign of the big blonde. I laid my head back, and relaxed.

I have no specific desire to return to England, but I will go wherever life takes me, as long as it is with Caryl.

We returned to a withered and brown lawn. The area had experienced a severe drought. The creek had dried up completely, rendering the sprinklers useless. Caryl loves her garden and was quite upset. Daniel's wedding was in a few days. It was very depressing. The grass was so dry it rattled under foot, like dry hay. I was afraid someone would drop a cigarette at the wedding, and the whole place would go up in smoke, but it went without a hitch.

There were eighty people here. The music and speaker system was good, both here, and at the reception at the Legion Hall. We were approached by some organisers of upcoming events to supply music. We did, and that resulted in more requests. We had fun doing this so we decided to get more equipment and start a DJ business.

At first, we moved our equipment in the trailer I had rebuilt, and we called the tiger box. When we needed a name for our business, we decided on Tiger Box DJ Service. I built a state of the art console. Music was played digitally through a computer. The business grew. After a year, we found we were booked far in advance. We purchased a large truck. This was very recognisable with its huge tiger logo on the side. We wore smart uniforms of black pants and shirts with the tiger logo. We were working weddings, re-unions, openings, races, Anniversaries, Birthdays, Easter parties, Christmas parties, and all kinds of events. This was almost a seven-day a week job. By the middle of January 2003, we were booked until September 15th. We had back-to-back gigs on Friday and Saturday nights. We knew we couldn't handle this alone, so we advertised, in the papers from here to, and including, Toronto for help. Any responses we received, were not at all suitable. We had established a solid reputation and would not sacrifice it. Applicants didn't want to dress in tuxedos when necessary, or play what the customer wanted. Some of them didn't want to work week-ends! We decided to work the booked events and close down as it was becoming far too stressful for just the two of us. We worked a wedding in Harcourt in the middle of September 2003, our last event, and then began to sell off equipment.

In the meantime, Dave Sovereign approached us. A committee had been formed to start a community radio station in Haliburton. They had arranged with the township to use the old hospital for a station. He asked at Radio Shack if there was anyone in the area who built technical equipment from parts, and they had referred him to me. Caryl and I got very excited, and joined the committee immediately. She began to set up ways to raise money.

Dave and I drove to Loyalist College in Belleville, so I could look at the station. I came back and began to design a console to fit the studio at the station. I donated the time and spent three weeks gathering components, wire, a computer, and building the first studio. I built speakers for the hall, and for the studio itself. I installed a two-way switch so the operator wouldn't cause feedback, by having the microphone and the console speakers on at the same time. When it was finished, I loaded it all into my trailer, and set it up. I understand the station has been upgraded several times since. I have no idea whether the same equipment is still used, but I have the satisfaction of knowing I built the first console for 'Canoe FM'.

We went to Kingston, to visit Laurie-Lee and her family, and took the boys, Kevin and Erik to a toy store to shop. Erik picked out a talking toy called 'Furby'. I played with it and found it to be very amusing. Caryl bought one for me. When we would wake this thing up, it would say, "Me Toto, Toto sleep more."

We purchased a motor home, a car dolly, and a small car and headed down east. I had no license to drive, of course, so Caryl drove all the way. I was so proud of her, piloting a forty-foot rig through the traffic of Montreal in a heavy rainstorm.

We took Toto, (the Furby), with us. The bumps in the road would wake him, and he would "talk" through his whole vocabulary, over and over. He would get into his, "Me hungry," routine and keep it up until he got attention. We often wished he would shut up. I am not one to be quiet for any length of time, and often tell people how to build a watch, when they only asked the time. One day, as we were travelling through the state of Maine, on our way home, I was yapping away about something, and then said, "I bet you often wish I would shut the hell up?" Caryl answered, "You're as yappy as Toto." That has been her nickname for me ever since.

In the spring of 2002, when I was attending my optometrist for my yearly inspection, he told me that the degeneration of the macula had stopped entirely, and, as there was no further damage, the swelling had subsided. There are still blind areas, but they are far off to the side. The only thing that we can think of that would cause this miracle, was change in tension caused by a change in lifestyle, and medication. I asked if there would be a chance I could get my license to drive. He tested my eyes again, and said I could drive a tractor-trailer, without glasses, as far as sight was concerned. He filled out the forms, and I went to the local licensing office, and got a 'G1' license. This allowed me to drive for 365 days, with a licensed driver with me, and with other restrictions.

I pulled out from the curb and headed toward home. The restrictions that I had endured for more then sixteen years, were replaced by a great feeling of freedom. I drove to Peterborough that afternoon, and a deer crossed the road in front of me. Thirty-three years of commercial driving took over, without a second thought, as I refrained from braking hard, and steered to avoid it. I drove through the city, and the fond memories of my transit driving days were a joy beyond compare.

On May 26th, Caryl and my niece, Joy Mann, hosted a 65th birthday celebration for me at the Minden Community Centre. Caryl gave me a certificate, "Good for One Backhoe". It arrived the following Thursday.

WOW!

Laurie-Lee's first marriage, in September 1983, produced my three grandchildren, Kayla, Kevin, and Erik. On January 5th 2003, she married Steven Steels, in their home in Kingston. Laurie and her children, and Steven and his two boys, James, and Jason, all vowed to join in an extended family of seven. This brought my count of grandchildren to five.

We flew to Cancun, Mexico in late February, 2003. On March 4th, Caryl and I were married on the beach, on the Mayan Riviera, as the warm wind blew in from the ocean. The wedding organizer had special cake served at our dinner that evening, and a bottle of champagne in our room. The maid made a heart on the bed from rose petals, and folded the towels into swans everywhere. We didn't tell the kids until we got home.

Andy said, "I wondered if you guys were up to something like that."

Rick said, "Can I borrow the truck, Dad."

Daniel said, "Hey, my Mom eloped. Cool."

Laurie-Lee said, "Dad... That's so sweet."

And Scott said, "I can deal with that."

In May of 2003, I tried out for my 'G2' driver's license. As I left the parking space I was in, the examiner said, "You have driven large vehicles, haven't you?"

"Yes...I drove transports, buses, and large trucks for thirty three years before I lost my license. Why do you ask?"

"Because you went straight to your mirrors, before you pulled out. Why did you lose your license?"

"Health reasons... eyesight and chest pain."

He only marked me for one thing, stopping too close to the vehicle ahead of me at the red light. I explained, the instructor at Peterborough Transit trained us to do that, so more traffic can get through the light when it changes. As many as thirteen buses were dispatched there at once. If every bus stopped as far from the one ahead, as is recommended, at the first light, it would back up traffic for city blocks. He accepted my explanation. After the test was over, he asked me if I would be interested in becoming an examiner in a year after I had received my 'G' permit. I could now drive without supervision. I brought Caryl home and dropped her off in the driveway! I drove onto the highway, and headed out on my own for the first time in seventeen years. I called home from my cell phone from the parking lot of the Canadian Tire store in Lindsay.

In August 2003, Andrew and Heather were married, in a pretty medieval wedding in the valley in Gelert, where they were building a new home. They held the reception at Daniel and Tammy's place next door. Andy's Dad and Hilda, his stepbrother, Peter and his wife Marriam, and his brother Rick, Francesca and the girls, all attended from England. Caryl, with the help of the girls, produced an amazing setting, with castles, turrets and the works. When it was all lit up at night, it was utterly stunning. I produced the music, and Rick was master of ceremonies.

In September 2003, we went north to the Agawa Canyon, with the motor home pulling the car, but this time I could drive. Here is a picture of the two Totos going north.

"There may be deer riding bicycles here Dad"... "I see the sign, Son."

The catch that holds the door open on the motor home broke while we were camping at the KOA campgrounds in Sault Ste. Marie. We went to Christie's RV Sales to get a new one. Instead, we traded our rig on a fifth wheel trailer. When we got into it, we couldn't find the steering wheel! We had to go to Maple Leaf Motors, to buy a truck to pull it!

On June 17th 2004, I drove to Lindsay and took my driving test to achieve my 'G' license.

I passed!

I was once again, a full-fledged driver.

When I was alone, I would often dream of climbing a hill so steep, I was afraid I would fall off backwards. Then I would arrive at the top, and there were flowers, green grass, and friendly people.

I don't dream that any more, but I often look at my life now and think how it is reflected in the last ten years. Keeping my sanity was an uphill effort, and then I arrived here. Caryl deals with my short comings with such care, love, and tenderness. There are flowers all around and green grass every summer. I have many near and very dear friends, as well as an extended family.

I have a dog, a truck, a backhoe, a chainsaw, an axe, and a round mouth shovel.

My wife buys my beer, cigars, and Playboy magazines.

What more can a redneck ask?

I have reached the top.

Life is good.

ISBN 1-41204894-X

9 781412 048941